The Third Department

Published by the Syndics of the Cambridge University Press
Bentley House, 200 Euston Road, London, N.W. 1
American Branch: 32 East 57th Street, New York, N.Y. 10022

Library of Congress Catalogue Card Number: 69–10198
Standard Book Number: 521 07148 8

Printed in Great Britain
at the University Printing House, Cambridge
(Brooke Crutchley, University Printer)

The Third Department

The establishment and practices of the political police in the Russia of Nicholas I

P.S.SQUIRE

Lecturer in Russian in the
University of Cambridge and
Fellow of Churchill College

CAMBRIDGE
AT THE UNIVERSITY PRESS
1968

Foreword

Complete consistency in the vexed question of transliteration is difficult to achieve in view of the minor discrepancies that exist between the various systems in current use in the English-speaking world. No one of these systems is wholly satisfactory.

Two special cases in the system adopted throughout the present work require a brief explanation. First, as regards the transliteration of the letter 'e', a 'y' is inserted before the 'e' in certain stressed syllables or in instances where it has seemed essential to indicate the correct pronunciation. Secondly, the ending i-diphthong-i in adjectives and proper names is transliterated as '-ii'. Where this ending occurs in surnames, the transliteration '-y' is used to conform to the endings normally encountered in western literature, e.g. 'Speransky'.

The spelling of surnames has been chosen to approximate as nearly as possible in English to the pronunciation of the Russian, e.g. 'Kiselyov' in place of the closer transliteration 'Kiselev'. It will be seen that in some instances the spelling of surnames in the text differs from that used in the notes and bibliography. In such cases the former spelling is that which conforms to the normal English pronunciation, e.g. 'Dolgorukov', or to the customary western form of the surname, e.g. 'Herzen'; the latter is that which corresponds to the spelling used in the work quoted, e.g. 'Dolgoroukow', or to the exact transliteration of the surname as spelt in Russian, e.g. 'Gertsen'.

Except as stated above, all words and names are transliterated letter for letter in accordance with the versions most generally favoured in this country. An apostrophe is used to indicate the presence of a soft sign.

Dates are given according to the old or Julian calendar instead of to the new or Gregorian calendar adopted in 1918. This so-called 'Old Style' system is used in order to avoid possible confusion in identifying the dates of the many ukazes referred to in the work. (The dates of Foreign Office dispatches are given in both styles wherever possible). The Julian calendar is eleven days behind the Gregorian in the eighteenth century, twelve days behind in the nineteenth and thirteen days behind in the twentieth.

Acknowledgements

Valuable help in locating books, articles and documents has been given by the staffs of the Cambridge University Library, the Reading Room and State Papers Room of the British Museum, the London Library, and the Public Record Office; the Ecole Nationale des Langues Orientales Vivantes, the Institut des Etudes Slaves, and the Bibliothèque Nationale; the K. und K. Haus, Hof- u. Staats-Archiv, Vienna.

Acknowledgement is gratefully made to the following for permission to reproduce photographs: the Trustees of the British Museum for plates 2 and 8, J. Colomb-Gérard for plate 4, and the University Library, Cambridge for plates 5, 6 and 7.

I am indebted to various scholars whose encouragement has greatly assisted me: Dr N. E. Andreyev and Professor Elizabeth M. Hill of Cambridge, Professor L. B. Schapiro and Dr R. Bolsover of London, and the historian Constantin de Grunwald. I must also acknowledge the helpful replies received to my queries from Mr Sulo Haltsonen of the Yliopiston Kirjaston, Helsinki, the late Professor S. P. Mel'gunov of Paris, the late Professor B. I. Nikolayevsky of New York, Professor B. Unbegaun of Oxford, and the late Count Benckendorff of Claydon, Suffolk.

I owe a special debt of gratitude to my wife for assistance in collating the bibliography and, in particular, for her help in preparing the maps.

Introduction

It is the aim of the present study to examine the system of political investigation and surveillance in Russia which was created by Nicholas I in the second quarter of the last century. Its institution marked an important stage in the development of Russia's national administration, representing as it did one of the most characteristic features of that epoch.

This system was not without its precedents, for by the end of the eighteenth century Russia already possessed a long and dismal tradition of arbitrary cruelty practised by successive 'Chancelleries' and 'Offices' to which was entrusted the task of conducting secret internal surveillance. The objectives pursued were those of preventing the outbreak of rebellion, conspiracy and subversive activities in general, and the methods employed to achieve them were so universally loathed and feared that the abolition of the secret police on the accession of the young Emperor Alexander in 1801 was widely acclaimed. However, no political régime in Russia having yet succeeded in dispensing for long with the services of a secret police, only a few years elapsed before its reappearance—as was customary—in a somewhat altered guise. Its official, though concealed, reintroduction in 1805 was partly due to immediate political developments outside Russia, but also, in a wider context, to the general climate of international opinion resulting from recent profound changes in European history. As a writer on this period has correctly stated, 'The first decades of the 19th century were an era which witnessed the blossoming in Europe of the secret political police...echoes of the French Revolution had not yet died away, and here and there the muffled upheaval of social forces frightened European governments.'[1] Thus, although Alexander theoretically distrusted and disapproved of secret polices with the abuses they inevitably engendered and although his use of their methods was relatively restrained, secret political surveillance continued intermittently throughout his reign. It enjoyed no great authority, however, and was given no opportunity to forestall the abortive conspiracy known as the Decembrist Revolt.

[1] A. Vasyutinsky, 'Tainaya Politsiya vo Frantsii i Avstrii v epokhu restavratsii', *Golos Minuv-shago* (1913), Kn. III, p. 245.

   (Even in England, the troubled years after the overthrow of Napoleon led to the temporary adoption of 'secret police' methods by the Home Secretary, Viscount Sidmouth, who relied on them to frustrate the activities of the 'machine-wreckers', see R. J. White, *Waterloo to Peterloo* (London, 1957), pp. 106–7 and ch. XIII, 'Spies and Informers', pp. 152 ff.)

Responsibility for the failure of Russia's security organs in December 1825 was largely the result of Alexander's refusal to take resolute action when confronted by unwelcome facts, but this failure was also inherent in the system, or lack of system, of secret police organizations existing between the abolition of the Ministry of Police in 1819 and the end of the reign six years later. Alexander's successor, Nicholas, realized that the defects of this vital branch of state administration required speedy rectification. Shortly after his accession to the throne he inaugurated a new type of political police on a semi-militarized and highly centralized basis, establishing it as one of the Departments of his own Chancellery and placing at its head one of his most trusted aides-de-camp, General Benckendorff. He created Benckendorff 'Chief of Gendarmes' and entrusted him with the formation of a special Corps to act as the executive arm of the new 'Higher Police'.

This organization, known as 'The Third Department', quickly became the most powerful force in the country. It deeply affected not only every branch of the administration both during and after Nicholas' reign, but also the development of all aspects of the national life—political, social and cultural, influencing directly or indirectly the fate of countless Russians and, to some extent, of foreigners as well, if they had any connexions with Russia. Its effect on the country as a whole was immense. For this reason an examination of its establishment and practices may be said to constitute a suitable subject for historical research.

It is not altogether surprising that a body wielding so much authority should have received relatively scant attention at the hands of historians. Russians who have had perforce to refer to its existence have readily acknowledged its importance and consequences but, owing to the political atmosphere in which many of them wrote and, particularly until recent years, the difficulty of obtaining access to the relevant state archives, almost none have attempted to present any specific study of its organization and methods. It may be surmised that pre-Revolutionary writers were frequently reluctant to delve into a subject, the investigation of which might be expected to incur official doubts; yet without official sanction no writer could hope to provide himself with sufficient material for his researches.

The first official History of the Ministry of Internal Affairs (by Varadinov) appeared in 1858–63. It evaded the need to present a detailed account of the Third Department by claiming, quite correctly, that after a certain date, 1826, the latter no longer formed any part of that Ministry's responsibilities.[1]

[1] N. Varadinov, *Istoriya Ministerstva Vnutrennikh Dyel* (SPB, 1858–63), pt III, p. 10. (It is noteworthy that even when the activities of the secret police did fall within the competence of this Ministry, Varadinov was careful to give only the barest details of its work and did not mention a single name of those who directed it.)

The second History (by Adrianov), written in 1902 to commemorate the first centenary of Ministries in Russia, was more informative. It describes the composition of the Third Department and gives some particulars of its organization and terms of reference; but the scope of this material may be judged from the fact that it is concentrated into a mere five-page summary and mentions only Generals Benckendorff and Orlov as leading figures in the Department's history.[1]

Even so, Adrianov is quoted as one of the main sources of knowledge concerning the Department by M. K. Lemke, who was the first to investigate its work and consequences in any detail. Lemke obtained temporary access to archive material at the end of 1904 ('taking advantage of the short-lived "epoch of trust" ')[2] for the purpose of investigating the effect of the censorship on the development of Russian literature. In the eighteen months that he spent working on the archives he discovered that in order to appreciate the full effect of this censorship he must first examine the nature of the political police. 'When I was studying material for the *Sketches*, I realized that the real struggle—and the one in which, furthermore, Nicholas I himself, who so well knew how to lay his imprint on everything done by his government, took a direct part—was conducted, properly speaking, not in the Ministry of Public Education, but in the interrogation-cells ['zastenke'] of the Third Department. It is quite natural that I should have wanted to undertake research into this aspect of a subject on which our literature has thrown very little light, after which I could consider my preliminary work already completed and proceed directly to the '60s.'[3] The 'unusually valuable and hitherto almost inaccessible archives' provided Lemke with a rich source of material, and his book entitled *Nicholas' Gendarmes and Literature 1826–1855* must be accounted the most authoritative study that exists on the stultifying influence of the Third Department in the field of literature and education.

Lemke devoted the first four chapters of this book[4] to an examination of the Third Department. His chief sources, apart from Adrianov, were

---

[1] S. A. Adrianov, *Ministerstvo Vnutrennikh Dyel. Istoricheskii Ocherk* (SPB, 1902), pp. 97–101.

[2] *Ocherki po Istorii Russkoi Tsenzury i Zhurnalistiki xix stolyetiya* (SPB, 1904).

[3] *Nikolayevskie Zhandarmy i Literatura 1826–1855 gg. Po podlinnym dyelam Tret'ego Otdeleniya Sobstv. Ye.I.V. Kantselyarii* (SPB, 1908), pp. xii–xiii. (In Dec. 1906 Lemke was refused permission to continue working on the Third Department archives, see p. xiv.)

Some details of Lemke's biography are relevant to an understanding of his approach to his subject. He lived from 1872 to 1923 and edited various journals between 1898 and 1906. He studied in particular the epoch of Nicholas and that of the 1860s, with special regard to the history of the censorship. From 1915 to 1916 he was a military censor, and from 1920 to 1921 was one of the editors of *Knigi i Revolyutsii*. Just before his death he entered the Workers' and Peasants' Party (Bolsheviks). See *Literaturnaya Entsiklopediya* (1931). He was temporarily arrested in Petrograd in 1919, see R. V. Ivanov-Razumnik, *The Russian Review* (1951), Apr., p. 151.   [4] *Op. cit.* pp. 1–29.

Shil'der's histories of the reigns of Alexander I and Nicholas I[1] and a wide variety of articles printed in current historical journals, in particular *Russkaya Starina*, *Russkii Arkhiv* and *Istoricheskii Vyestnik*, all of which have been consulted by the present writer. Lemke includes a short summary of secret police activities before the accession of Nicholas and discusses the measures which immediately preceded the Department's creation. In chapter 4 he gives a useful account of Benckendorff's career and character together with a brief mention of von Vock. The remainder of his work relates not to the organization and expansion of the Higher Police but to the latter's increasing interference in the literary and cultural life of Russia. In the course of this examination, however, it includes valuable information on the operation of the Department and (in chapters 20 and 24) on the personalities of Generals Dubbelt and Orlov. No other work has yet appeared which gives so informative a sketch of Nicholas' Higher Police, and it has proved of great assistance to the present study.

Only one other important source appeared before the October Revolution. This was an article in *Vyestnik Yevropy* entitled 'The Third Department of His Imperial Majesty's Own Chancellery. A self-appraisal. (An unpublished document)', containing the full text of 'A Review of the Activities of the Third Department of Your Imperial Majesty's Own Chancellery for the last 50 years, 1826–1876'.[2] The 'Review' was written to commemorate the Department's fiftieth anniversary and destined for the private information of the reigning Emperor Alexander II. Not until 1917 did this so-called 'Jubilee Report' reach a wider public when, 'thanks to a quite exclusively fortunate accident', it came into the hands of its contributor, V. Bogucharsky. In his introduction to it he, like Lemke, commented on the absence of any 'biography' of the Third Department, drawing attention to its 'undesirability' from the point of view of the authorities and paying a reluctant tribute to 'the sky-blue ministry' for its painstaking skill in preserving its secrets.[3] Bogucharsky correctly stated that the Third Department's 'self-appraisal' required critical reading in view of its obvious bias, claiming that 'the real and doubtless voluminous "report" on this organization, a report in which it is hard to say which pages will be the most numerous—those that are dramatic or those that are humorous—will surely

---

[1] N. K. Shil'der, *Imperator Aleksandr Pervyi. Yego Zhizn' i Tsarstvovanie*, 4 vols. (SPB, 1897–8); *Imperator Nikolai Pervyi. Ego Zhizn' i Tsarstvovanie*, 2 vols. (SPB, 1903).

Both histories are standard works on these reigns, although the latter only covers the reign of Nicholas up to the year 1831. It is, however, especially valuable for the present study in that it discusses the formation of the 3rd Dept. and also contains some of Benckendorff's memoirs not published elsewhere, see chapter Four, p. 118, note 1.

[2] See Bibliography under *Bogucharsky*.

[3] Bogucharsky, pp. 85, 86.

be the concern of the future historian of this tragi-comic institution.'[1] But whether or not the 'Jubilee Report' contained an accurate account of the Third Department's activities, its value for the historian is incontestable. It undoubtedly provided the basis for the larger part of the account given by Adrianov, although he nowhere acknowledged its existence. (Lemke too did not refer to it.)

The Revolution naturally brought about a radical change in the official attitude to historical records. Research into their contents was encouraged, albeit less in the interests of academic study than in those of exposing the abuses practised in Russia's recent history. Published excerpts from Tsarist archives tended to be strongly biased in favour of a class interpretation of the historical phenomena of the past and hence usually dealt with the less attractive aspects of the old régime—the injustices perpetrated by the Tsars and the upper classes generally on the one hand, and the trials and tribulations endured by the lower classes on the other. In 1922 the publication was begun of an historico-political journal entitled *Red Archives (Krasnyi Arkhiv)*, and its third number included an article by A. Sergeyev drawing attention to the 'rich material' provided by the annual reports submitted by the Third Department to the Tsar. Subsequent numbers carried further extracts from these reports, although it was not until 1929 that this journal printed the full text of the earliest reports in existence and hitherto unpublished.[2] Sergeyev states in his introduction to these articles: 'Unfortunately this institution is wrapped in the darkness of secrecy as much for those who in their day directly suffered at its hands as for historical research also. Up to the present day we have no special work on the genesis, functions and activities of the Third Department...

The publication of the first four important reports of the Third Department...is an attempt to attract the attention of research workers to a study of this institution.'[3] (This attention was indeed attracted as early as the following year.)

The material presented in *Krasnyi Arkhiv* has proved of the greatest assistance in establishing the aims and methods of the Third Department and its officials, and it is only to be regretted that the publication of its annual reports (with their informative supplements covering the activities of the Corps of Gendarmes) was discontinued after 1931. As late as 1938, however,

---

[1] *Ibid.* p. 122. He goes on: 'And this historian, in drawing up a history of the Third Department, will in all probability be guided not solely by the cases preserved in the Department's archives, for it is unlikely that they have also retained what is left of many 'cases', interpreting this word not in the official sense but in that of humanity as a whole, since these cases crystallized the sufferings, blood and tears of ordinary people', *ibid.*

[2] See Bibliography under *Sergeyev* and chapter Six, p. 200, note 3.

[3] Sergeyev, *Kr. Arkh.* (1929), no. 37, p. 139.

articles continued to appear in this periodical based on the Department's archive records, although this material was printed to illustrate not the methods or organization of the former Higher Police but individual aspects of Russia's past history which had once been the object of official investigation.

These records have provided an outstandingly useful source of information for historians. To quote three specific instances, in 1932 and 1933 the German scholar Stählin made use of material drawn from the Department's unpublished annual reports for an examination of certain historical questions relating to Nicholas' reign,[1] Nifontov in 1949 produced a work on the year 1848 based almost entirely on this source and more recently Gernet has consulted it for his researches into the history of Tsarist prisons.[2] These works do not, however, investigate the Department itself.

The only Soviet study exclusively devoted to this subject (and possibly inspired by Sergeyev's articles) appeared in 1930, when the All-Union Society of Political Convicts and Exile-Settlers issued a booklet entitled *The Third Department in the reign of Nicholas I*.[3] In his introduction the author, I. M. Trotsky, refers, again like Lemke, to the lack of any history of the Russian political police, pointing out that such research workers as had had access to the Department's archives had consulted them only for the purpose of studying the history of the revolutionary movement. He states that his work cannot claim to provide 'an exhaustive character portrait' and that the object of the booklet is 'in individual sketches to present a cursory summary of the now known material on the Third Department, and, where possible, to trace the general outlines of this institution. For the time being the subject is not capable of any other presentation in view of the relevant material in our historical literature.'[4]

Within these limits (the booklet contains only some 140 short pages), Trotsky achieves his aim, although the absence of exact references detracts from its value and he makes almost no use of foreign sources. He prints a brief bibliography, from which it may be seen that his chief authorities were Varadinov, Adrianov, Shil'der, Lemke, the 'Jubilee Report' and a limited

---

[1] Karl Stählin, 'Aus den Berichten der III. Abteilung S. M. höchsteigener Kanzlei an Kaiser Nikolaus I', *Zeitschrift für Osteuropäische Geschichte*, vol. 6 (1932), pp. 477–512; vol. 7 (1933), pp. 357–86.

(Stählin spent 5 weeks in Moscow studying the archives and the above two articles discuss individual events of historical and literary interest occurring in 1831–2, 1836–42 and 1850–4—Decembrist exiles in Siberia, Sectants, Peasant questions etc. He appears to have been the last foreigner to examine these archives, see Obituary Notice on Karl Stählin (1865–1939) by Leo Loewenson publ. in *The Slavonic and East European Review* (1949), vol. 28, no. 70, p. 160.)

[2] See Bibliography under *Nifontov* and *Gernet*.

[3] See Bibliography under *Trotsky*.

[4] Trotsky, pp. 3–4. He adds: 'In certain cases I have, however, included some unpublished material.'

number of articles from nineteenth-century historical journals. His sketch of political police organizations in the reign of Alexander contains some useful quotations from the archives. He assumes, somewhat surprisingly, that Russia's first and only Minister of Police, Balashov, was the man chiefly responsible for the formation of Russia's secret police system,[1] although Balashov was closely connected with this work only from 1810 to 1812 and the system underwent complete reorganization in 1826. As regards the following reign, he does not investigate in detail the regulations which laid down the status of the Corps of Gendarmes and, again like Lemke, he merely reproduces the bare facts recorded by Adrianov. His descriptions of Benckendorff, Orlov, von Vock and Dubbelt add little to the information given elsewhere, but his views on the influence each exerted on the Department's development are of interest. In general, Trotsky's researches have undoubtedly contributed to a better understanding of the Department's aims and methods, in particular with regard to the petty nature of many of its pursuits, and his estimate tends to confirm Bogucharsky's view of its character as 'tragi-comic'. In many respects, however, his treatment of the subject is superficial, and a closer examination of the available material is essential for a proper understanding of Nicholas' Higher Police.

No work specifically dealing with the Third Department appears to have been published in the Soviet Union since Trotsky's survey. No relevant articles are contained in the regular periodicals *Istoricheskii Zhurnal* (1942–45), continued since 1945 under the title of *Voprosy Istorii*, or *Istoricheskie Zapiski*, published from 1940; or in the sporadic issues of *Istoricheskii Arkhiv* issued by the Academy of Sciences since 1940. (An examination of similar periodicals in the Western world, notably *The Slavonic and East European Review*, *The American Slavic and East European Review* and the *Revue des Etudes Slaves*, has proved equally unproductive.)

A lengthy Soviet work has recently been published containing sketches of 'intelligence activities' over the past five centuries in a wide variety of countries, but the reader will search in vain for any section in it relating to the aims and methods of Nicholas I's Third Department. In his introduction the author merely states: 'I have had almost no occasion to touch upon the exceedingly interesting past of Russia's intelligence services. This is a subject for another book which, unfortunately, has not so far been properly written—indeed, for a series of books'.[2] For a number of reasons it will probably be many years before any such book—or series of books—can be expected to appear.

The 'relevant material' which Trotsky claimed was required for a proper

---

[1] *Ibid.* p. 18.
[2] Ye. Chernyak, *Pyat' Stoletii Tainoi Voiny. Iz istorii razvyedki* (Moscow, 1966), p. 4.

study of the Third Department may well be relatively scanty. At the same time more exists than has been recorded by either him or Lemke. The latter was not primarily interested in presenting a detailed account of its formation and development, and Trotsky limited himself to tracing its outlines only. For this reason much of the material consulted by both these writers merits further examination in a number of instances. (Two such examples are von Vock's letters to Benckendorff in the summer of 1826 and Dubbelt's private *Notes*.[1]) It can also be claimed that the present study incorporates evidence left by a variety of nineteenth-century Russians of which there is no mention by either Lemke or Trotsky. In many cases this evidence, chiefly culled from the issues of *Russkaya Starina* and similar journals, provides little more than incidental information, but its relevance is beyond dispute.

To sum up, Lemke and Trotsky must be considered the best Russian sources that exist on the history of the Higher Police in the reign of Nicholas, although neither writer can be said to have exhausted all the available material on some of its aspects. (Their main source on its organization, for example, is the brief summary provided by Adrianov.)

As regards the West, however, an American scholar who had been working for some years on this subject published in 1961 an entertaining book which for the first time presented the English-speaking reader with an account of this little-known institution.[2] Like the present writer, Dr Monas had no access to archives in the Soviet Union; and his work is based entirely on published sources which, as he correctly states, 'though fragmentary, are nevertheless voluminous'.[3] He has succeeded in making a worthwhile contribution to the history of the period, and the conclusions he draws from his study of the Third Department are wholly acceptable: 'The political police had been entrusted with two irreconcilable tasks: on the one hand, to create a broader basis for the regime in public opinion; on the other, to maintain all initiative in political action in the hands of the autocrat. Only a totalitarian regime could resolve and reconcile these terms successfully, and the conditions for totalitarianism not only did not exist but were very remote from nineteenth-century Russia...Far from connecting the sovereign with the public, as Nicholas I had envisaged, the political police guaranteed his isolation and ineffectiveness.'[4] Dr Monas has adopted the approach of a social historian, setting himself a wider task than that of tracing the development of a typical phenomenon of a past age. He has concentrated on placing the Third Department in its contemporary environment and conveying the atmosphere of Nicholas I's Russia, discussing in particular its effect on cer-

---

[1] These are examined in chapters Two and Five respectively.
[2] S. Monas, *The Third Section. Police and Society in Russia under Nicholas I* (Harvard U.P. ,1961).
[3] *Ibid.* p. 297.   [4] *Ibid.* pp. 286, 293.

tain prominent writers and on the evolution of literature and journalism.
From this standpoint his book must be accounted successful; and it has the
merit of appealing to the general reader with limited knowledge of the
period.

Nevertheless, the Third Department's pervasive control over literature
has been investigated so thoroughly by Lemke that a modern Western
writer can hardly hope to do more than reproduce in translation a selection
of his findings, which is what Dr Monas has done. Individual biographies of
Russian men of letters in the first half of the last century, including those
which have appeared in English, have incorporated the evidence set out by
Lemke and other scholars; and little of extra value is now likely to emerge.
For this reason the present study attempts no further examination of this
aspect of the Department's activities.

Many other questions still remain, however, which specialist historians
may justly ask and to which they will find no detailed and substantiated
answers in either Dr Monas' book or any other specific works relating to the
reign: by what stages did the Third Department come into being, what was
its organization, who headed it and why, how was the Corps of Gendarmes
recruited, allocated and distributed, how large was Russia's political police
force, what were its exact aims and how far were they achieved? Dr Monas'
book supplies only some of the answers such questions demand; and his
study of the Third Department cannot be regarded as definitive. It contains
too few particulars to help the specialist.

The present writer has therefore thought it appropriate to narrow his field
and produce a work of 'administrative history' intended to supplement the
more general account given by Dr Monas. This task has necessitated the
inclusion of a plethora of detail, but all too often scholars are confronted
with unsubstantiated statements from unrevealed sources (especially but not
solely those found in Russian historical works); and the writing of administrative history surely requires that precise evidence be quoted wherever
possible. The only criteria should be its relevance and importance to the
subject.

An attempt has accordingly been made in the present study to analyse the
evidence available in the work of Lemke and Trotsky, basing this analysis
on a careful investigation of the various ukazes which created the Third
Department and Corps of Gendarmes and laid down the regulations which
governed their subsequent development. The *Complete Collection of Laws*,
compiled by the Second Department of His Imperial Majesty's Own
Chancellery under the direction of Speransky, is the most authoritative
source in this connexion.[1] It has been consulted with a view to tracing the

---

[1] See Bibliography under *Polnoe Sobranie Zakonov*.

9

growth of political police offices from the eighteenth century up to the accession of Nicholas[1] and thereafter quoted extensively to illustrate the stages by which the Third Department attained its immense importance in the history of his reign. As far as is known, these ukazes represent the only source from which these details can be taken. No other work, for instance, appears to contain the exact particulars of the development of the Corps of Gendarmes—the information given by Adrianov (who does not quote ukaz references), albeit generally accepted, was not invariably accurate[2]—and it is possible to establish from ukazes such relevant details as the precise location of Gendarme Districts, the distribution throughout these Districts of Gendarme officers and troopers, and the numerical strength of the Corps. These details, indispensable to any close research into Nicholas' Higher Police organization, have not been recorded in any history of his reign.[3] The area-boundaries of the Districts into which Russia was divided for Higher Police purposes from 1827 onwards are not marked on any known maps, but they are recorded in ukazes and two maps have been specially drawn for inclusion in the present work.[4] The particulars extracted from the contents of Imperial and Senate ukazes are claimed to represent material not previously quoted on this subject. The sections in which this source has been of exceptional value are those dealing with the composition of the Third Department headquarters (described in chapters two and six) and with the organization of the Corps of Gendarmes (described in chapter three).

Much of the present study is devoted to an examination of the careers and influence of leading Higher Police officials. No specific biographies of any of these men having appeared, an attempt has been made to collate all available sources of information; and chapters Four and Five contain more biographical material on each of these officials than has been recorded elsewhere. (Benckendorff's memoirs and Dubbelt's *Notes* have been examined in detail.[5]) In some cases the search for information on this subject has proved disappointing, in others it has been possible to estimate with some accuracy the rôles of those who directed political police policy. In view of the secrecy of Third Department activities, details of the personalities of most of the junior officials who served in its headquarters have naturally proved difficult to obtain. As regards the Corps of Gendarmes, however, much of the work

[1] This growth is traced in chapter One.
[2] See chapter Three, p. 89, note 3.
[3] There is only one reference to the Corps of Gendarmes in the chapter entitled 'The Structure of the Military Establishment' in a recent work on the Russian army of the day ('The Corps of Gendarmes, which served as a special police force throughout the Empire, was also nominally part of the army'), J. S. Curtiss, *The Russian Army under Nicholas I, 1825–1855* (Durham, N.C., 1965), p. 109; and the Corps is not mentioned elsewhere in this book.
[4] These maps reproduce the details contained in the relevant ukazes, see Appendix D, pp. 245–9.
[5] See Bibliography under *Benkendorf* and *Dubel't*.

entrusted to its members was conducted openly, and this has greatly facilitated the investigation of individual officers of the Corps. The memoirs of
Colonel Stogov and Major Lomachevsky[1] and official reports on the
activities of the Corps[2] have proved particularly valuable sources for the
study of its methods and personalities. Chapters Three and Six contain
original material based on information obtained from these sources with the
assistance of various historical memoirs and books of reference.[3]

In the hope of discovering hitherto unknown material on Nicholas'
secret police an examination has been made of Foreign Office archives in the
Public Record Office,[4] but this examination has not proved rewarding.
Regrettably little information relating to the Third Department is available
at this source. No dispatch from London to St Petersburg appears to have
requested such information, and relatively few dispatches from St Petersburg
so much as deal with the internal condition of Russia as a whole, let alone
with that of one of her administrative branches. Official diplomacy relates to
the proper conduct of foreign affairs between states, and the Foreign Office
of the day was primarily concerned with Russian foreign policy, the Eastern
Question, Anglo-Russian trade relations, the normal functioning of the con-
sular system, and so on. No evidence has been found to show that the Third
Department was ever made the subject of a special inquiry, and it seems
probable that none was thought necessary at that period. The archives contain few references to its existence and none to its organization or activities.
No contemporary dispatches to London from British envoys or even from
local consuls to these envoys throw any light on this subject. Only in very
few instances is it evident that British diplomats had any official contact with
the Higher Police and none whatever occurred before 1840. Details of what
little contact there was are included in chapters Four and Six.[5]

The State Archives in Vienna have similarly been investigated.[6] Diplo-

---

[1] See Bibliography under *Stogov* and *Lomachevsky*.
[2] The first of these is reproduced as Appendix E, pp. 250–5.
[3] In this connexion special mention should be made of the *Russkii Biograficheskii Slovar'*,
published between 1896 and 1918, which is the best available source on Russian nineteenth-
century personalities. It consists of 25 volumes, not issued in alphabetical order. Regrettably
it does not cover the whole alphabet—no volumes were published for the letters V, E, M, U,
and those for the letters G, N, P, T were not completed; see Charles Morley, *A Guide to Research
in Russian History* (Syracuse University Press, 1951), p. 48—and hence it has not been possible
to trace the careers of some senior Corps of Gendarme officers. This Dictionary (abbrev. *RBS*)
has, however, provided valuable information on certain officers, particularly in cases where
these men subsequently reached high positions in the administration (see chapter Six). A search
has been made in it for the name of every Third Department official encountered in the present
study and the findings recorded in the text and footnotes.
[4] Public Record Office, series F.O. 65, 181.
[5] See chapters Four, p. 127, note 2; Six, p. 193, note 1, p. 217, notes 1, 2.
[6] K. und K. Haus-, Hof- und Staatsarchiv, Vienna, Series 'Russland'.

matic links between the Russian and Austrian governments were strengthened after the meeting between Nicholas and Francis at Münchengrätz in 1833; and Benckendorff and Metternich, who had first become acquainted in Paris in 1807–8,[1] thereafter corresponded more or less regularly for some years.[2] Their letters, however, throw relatively little light on the workings of the Higher Police.

A more informative source—one almost entirely overlooked by both Lemke and Trotsky and not fully exploited by Monas—must be considered: the memoirs published by numerous foreigners resident in Russia during the first half of the last century. A number of contemporary British, French and German travellers wrote accounts of their experiences, and not infrequently referred to the conduct of the secret police. A wide variety of such accounts has been consulted, although only those which have proved of definite value to the present study are carried in its bibliography. The relevant information obtained from this source, most of which has not previously been quoted, is included in chapter Six.

A close examination has also been made of the books published abroad by Russia's earliest political émigrés.[3] Despite the understandably biased outlook of such writers, their evidence is of particular value because it was not subject to any censorship. In contrast to present-day conditions, no official who served in the Higher Police during Nicholas' reign is known to have left its employment, thereafter revealing its secrets to Western Europe. Consequently the disclosures of these few émigrés represent a source of special interest.

The evidence provided by these and other sources both Russian and foreign is set out in the Notes and in the Appendices to the present study. All the conclusions drawn from it, unless otherwise stated, are those of the writer.

In addition to the two maps, the book also contains eight plates included with the aim of presenting under one cover portraits and drawings relevant to the subject.

[1] See chapter Four, p. 110.   [2] See chapter Six, p. 212.
[3] See Bibliography under *Gertsen*, *Dolgoroukow* and *Golovine*.

I

The Preliminary Phase: 1801–25

Intriguers in the state are just as useful as honest men; and sometimes the former are more useful than the latter.

Emperor Alexander to de Sanglen in 1811[1]

Brief survey of precedents

The organization of a political police in Russia, accorded extensive powers and enjoying nation-wide authority, dates from the summer of 1826, when it was inaugurated on a centralized basis by Nicholas I as an indispensable part of his Chancellery. Before this date it had existed in a variety of guises, but had never been openly recognized as one of the accepted bastions of the state's administration.

A study of the various forms it assumed from the sixteenth century onwards is not, however, strictly relevant to an examination of Nicholas' 1826 creation except in so far as it shows that the practice of secret political surveillance in Russia had its roots in the relatively distant past. For this reason its development may be surveyed briefly and without precise documentation.

As one of the institutions of an autocratic government, the political police probably had its origins in the personal bodyguard of the ruling Prince and thereafter grew into a separate office entrusted with the task of protecting the state against its internal enemies. These origins may possibly be traced back to the reign of Ivan IV when that monarch, terrified by the power and personalities of the boyars, created his system of Oprichnina, or Oprichina as it is sometimes called, in 1565. The Oprichnina was instituted primarily not as an investigatory but as a punitive organ. Its members—the Oprichniki—formed a *corps d'élite* representing the will of Ivan, however cruel and arbitrary, and this distinction was further emphasized by the introduction of an Oprichnik uniform consisting of 'black robes of coarse cloth, lined with fur, with rich clothing worn beneath them, and black pointed caps; a dog's head attached to their horses' necks and their quivers bearing a kind of tassel or brush as a sign that the Oprichniki were required to "gnaw traitors to the state" like dogs and sweep away "treason" from the State of Muscovy'. It is interesting that this practice of distinguishing by their dress the members of Russia's 'political inquisition' recurred later in her history, notably with the

---

[1] 'Zapiski Ya. I. de Sanglena', *Russkaya Starina* (1883), vol. 37, p. 44; see also N. K. Shil'der, *Imperator Aleksandr Pervyi*, vol. 3, p. 367, note 62.

uniform chosen for the Corps of Gendarmes, and has also been perpetuated in more recent times. A further characteristic peculiar to these bodies may be seen in the rapid rise to immense power of comparatively insignificant men. The Oprichnina included in its ranks, in addition to many titled members of the aristocracy, others of far humbler origin. Of these the most notorious was a certain Malyuta Skuratov (died 1572), who came of a minor provincial family yet rose to become a member of the Oprichnina Boyars' Duma and Commander of the Detachment of Tsar's Bodyguards. In this capacity Skuratov became Ivan's favourite companion and executioner-in-chief—he personally murdered Mitropolitan Philip in 1569—and his cruelties were so infamous that his name was preserved in folk songs as the descriptive epithet of a villain. Despite its success in crushing the potential opposition to Ivan of the old boyar aristocracy, however, the Oprichnina was abolished seven years after its creation.

No further attempt to establish a political police operating as a government department is known to have occurred before the reign of Aleksei Mikhailovich, whose Prikaz for Secret Affairs (Tainyi Prikaz) was instituted about 1656. Details of its methods may be found in the work of Grigory Kotoshikhin, a well-informed if biased political refugee whose evidence has generally been accepted as accurate. In Kotoshikhin's words, 'this Prikaz was instituted under the present Tsar so that his intentions and requirements should all be treated according to his will, and that the boyars and high officials should know nothing of them'. Its functions were the normal ones of investigating all persons and events capable of disturbing the security of the régime; and its aims were, like those of the Oprichnina, to counter any possible subversion by powerful officials. Its existence did not extend beyond Aleksei's reign, being abolished at the beginning of that of his successor Fyodor Alekseyevich in 1676, but a precedent had nevertheless been established for an institution which was shortly to become a recurrent phenomenon of Russia's historical development.

The office which replaced the abolished Secret Prikaz was known as the Preobrazhenskii Prikaz, the name being taken from the village of Preobrazhenskoe outside Moscow where the young Peter established his court. It was probably created in the 1690s and is in any case known to have been in existence by 1697. When the second Strel'tsy rising occurred in 1698, Peter turned to one of his closest associates, Prince Fyodor Yur'evich Romodanovsky (died 1717) to suppress it and thereafter to head this new Prikaz. From 1702, and for many years to come, the practice known as 'the Tsar's Word and Deed' ('Gosudarevo Slovo i Dyelo')—the formula used by informers to denounce persons suspected of treasonous or even disrespectful conduct towards the Tsar and his State—was to provide Romodanovsky and his successors with thousands of victims. Inevitably this practice laid itself open to abuse. In 1713 Peter made it illegal for anyone to pronounce his 'Word and Deed' except in cases where persons were alleged to have offended 'against the first two points' covered in his 1702 ukaz and comprising (i) knowledge of conspiracy against the Tsar's person and (ii) information relating to revolt and treason; but this new ukaz did little to mitigate the atmosphere of widespread suspicion and fear engendered by a system of private and public denunciations.

In 1718 Prince Ivan Fyodorovich Romodanovsky (167?–1730) succeeded his father as head of the Preobrazhenskii Prikaz, and although evidence exists that his methods were milder—inclining less to the torture—his sphere of competence was greater because the same year witnessed the creation of the Secret Chancellery (Kantselyariya Tainykh Rozysknykh Dyel), an office which continued the work of Peter's private 'cabinet' conducted by a minor functionary named Makarov. Romodanovsky controlled both institutions, although the latter was abolished by Catherine I after Peter's death. Its cases were transferred to the Preobrazhenskii Prikaz, which was thenceforward called the Preobrazhenskaya Chancellery. By the reign of Peter II Romodanovsky had largely retired from the scene owing to ill-health; and the Chancellery ceased to exist in 1729, at least in its current guise.

It is unlikely, however, that there was any break in the now established pattern. The next ruler, Anna Ioannovna, recreated the Chancellery for Secret Investigatory Affairs in 1731; and it was administered by Andrei Ivanovich Ushakov (1672–1747), who had worked under Romodanovsky the Younger in the closing years of the preceding decade. Ushakov retained this post until 1746 in spite of the fact that he had been a supporter of Biron and had refused to participate in the *coup d'état* which brought the Empress Elizabeth to the throne in 1741. While others were dismissed or exiled, he gained a seat in the newly formed Senate and was made a Count in 1744. During his fifteen years of office Ushakov did nothing to mitigate the sinister reputation of his department, and the reign of Anne was particularly notorious for its cruelties.

There is little evidence that these decreased during that of Elizabeth. The positions of highest favour naturally fell to the men who had played leading rôles in gaining her the throne, among whom was Count Aleksandr Ivanovich Shuvalov (1710–71). He had worked under Ushakov since 1742 and as the new head of the Chancellery acquired great wealth and high honours. The young Princess Catherine was later to describe him as 'the terror of all the Court, the city and the entire empire' and as 'both intelligent and cruel'. He inspired in her a feeling of revulsion for the Secret Chancellery, although she herself, as Empress, was to sanction an analogous body with all its attendant cruelty. A nineteenth-century writer summed up the position accurately when he wrote: 'Cruelty engendered cruelty and the Secret Chancellery for Investigatory Affairs greatly contributed to the maintenance and growth in the Russian people of coarse and inhuman instincts'.

The brief reign of Peter III that followed the death of Elizabeth introduced another short-lived respite in the continuous existence of the political police. By abolishing it in February 1762 'for ever' in an ukaz which also put an end to the hated expression, namely: 'Word and Deed', Peter rightly considered that this decision would earn him a wide measure of approval.

The lesson was not lost on Catherine II who, after her assumption of power, confirmed this abolition in October 1762, repeating almost word for word the provisions of the ukaz issued by 'the previous Emperor'. Apart from motives of popularity-seeking, she probably still retained her former feeling of repugnance for the Secret Chancellery. At all events she prudently omitted to promulgate any ukaz authorizing its reinstitution; and the exact date of this resurrection remains uncertain. Notwithstanding both ukazes it probably continued its work under cover from the earliest years of the new reign without interruption if with less notoriety, and its leading functionary soon earned himself a reputation no more savoury than that of his predecessors. This man, Stepan Ivanovich Sheshkovsky (1719–94), is known to have been engaged as early as 1740 on cases in the Secret Chancellery, in which he held various appointments, earning the commendation of Shuvalov himself who transferred him to his personal staff. By 1757 Elizabeth had appointed him Secretary of the Secret Chancellery, a post he presumably still held in 1763 when he is known to have conducted at least one interrogation. Catherine made him 'Chief Secretary' ('Ober-Sekretar') in 1767; and from then until his death he was entrusted with all important cases including that of Pugachov. He made free use of the knout to assist him in these tasks, so that by the end of the 1780s he had become universally loathed and dreaded.

No account exists of Sheshkovsky's organization of the Secret Chancellery during his tenure of office, although it must have been relatively extensive, at any rate in St Petersburg. It was widely believed at the time that a network of informers enabled Sheshkovsky to learn 'everything that went on in the capital'. There is no reference in extant memoirs to his control over provincial 'malefactors'; and it was probably only after these had acquired sufficient local notoriety that their cases were brought to his attention.

Sheshkovsky seems to have been a typical product of the seamier side of Catherine's Russia. Although he reached the rank of Privy Councillor in 1791, this honour was merely in the nature of a bone flung to the 'faithful hound'—to use his own words—that he was. He paid lip-service to the tenets of religion, flogging his victims 'to the accompaniment of prayers', and, on the existing evidence, was a cruel, cowardly and hypocritical official elevated to a position of power by an Empress who dared not dispense with his abilities. Certain of his personal immunity, he did not hesitate to abuse his functions in the already time-honoured fashion of his kind.

The personality, achievements and even reputation of his successor are a good deal more obscure. Aleksandr Semyonovich Makarov (1750–1810) began his career in the Secret Chancellery under Sheshkovsky and replaced his superior when the latter died. As far as can be stated with any certainty, he remained in this appointment even after Catherine's death in November 1796, when her son Paul succeeded to the throne. Paul was normally anxious to undo as much as possible of his mother's work, but it is noteworthy that he did not, like his father Peter III, decide to abolish the Secret Chancellery. It continued to exist under that name, or its equivalent the Secret Office (Tainaya Ekspeditsiya), throughout his reign. The part played in the Secret Office by Makarov, however, was evidently a covert one. Possibly he considered it prudent to remain as far as possible in the background after Catherine's death, having attained his position in the final years of her reign. For this reason alone it is unlikely that he gained the confidence of her successor whom he failed—or perhaps was not permitted—to protect. Yet had he himself been implicated in the plot to remove Paul from the throne, his reappointment to high office would scarcely have been authorized a few years later by Alexander. The probability is that Makarov's rôle was overshadowed by that of Paul's Procurator-General, Prince Kurakin, who was given control over the Secret Office and all its officials in December 1796. Even so Makarov must have been regarded as a figure of some importance, for he was raised to the rank of Senator in October 1800.

Little can be said of the methods and development of the political police departments which existed in the eighteenth century. The scant information available indicates that their activities were organized on a strictly *ad hoc* basis dependent on the individual whims of each successive chief official, who retained all executive power in his own hands. Except in special instances his sphere of competence was mainly restricted to operations in the capital; and these were probably conducted not so much by a large junior staff of permanent officials as by numbers of private informers who reported to him direct. The latter, however, were extensively employed and as a matter of course all persons of any prominence, whether Russians or foreigners, were regarded with suspicion and kept under the closest possible surveillance.

Abolition of the Secret Office

By the end of the eighteenth century the Tainaya Ekspeditsiya had inevitably acquired the kind of distasteful reputation inseparable from the worst practices of a secret inquisition conducted on a purely arbitrary basis; and its temporary removal from the political scene was widely acclaimed. Paul's reign was notorious for its atmosphere of cruelty and spy-mania. Madame Vigée-Lebrun, who lived in Russia throughout it, commented that 'everybody's words and actions were watched to such an extent that I heard it said there was no social circle without a spy'.[1] With the abolition of the Secret Office it was hoped to embark on a new era.

However, just as previous similar abolitions had led only to new reincarnations, so too in Alexander's reign there reappeared new forms of secret political investigation. These constitute what may fairly be called the background to the formation of the so-called Third Department, for much of the legacy earned by these institutions during the first quarter of the last century was inherited by their successor in the following reign. Both as regards persons and events the 'preliminary phase' thus merits close attention.

The accession of the young Emperor Alexander in the spring of 1801 came as a relief to his countrymen. His father's nightmare reign was forgotten in an atmosphere of optimism hitherto unknown to Russian society and the often quoted 'excellent beginning of Alexander's days'[2] may be judged from the new Tsar's earliest decrees. The sixth[3] ukaz[4] of his reign, issued to the Senate only four days after Paul's death, admirably illustrates his desire to introduce a fresh era in Russian history:

Having careful regard for all conditions of the people entrusted to Us by God, and desiring above all to lighten the onerous lot of persons detained on cases that have arisen in the Secret Office, We forward four lists[5] . . . graciously pardoning all those named in these lists without exception, restoring those deprived of rank and nobility to their original dignities, and ordering Our Senate to liberate them instantly from their present places of confinement and to permit them to return wherever they desire, annulling the surveillance over them.[6]

This ukaz was merely an interim measure—a prelude to the more important decision it preceded, for although Alexander preferred no charges

---

[1] *The Memoirs of Madame Vigée-Lebrun*, trans. Lionel Strachey (London, 1904), p. 120.
[2] 'Dnyei Aleksandrovykh prekrasnoe nachalo', from Pushkin's *Poslanie Tsenzoru* (1822). *Poln. Sobr. Soch.* (ed. Acad. 1935), vol. 2, p. 82.
[3] The first four dealt with the arrangements for Paul's obsequies; the fifth authorized the export of goods previously forbidden.
[4] Ukaz of 15 Mar. 1801. *Poln. Sobr. Zak.* [1-oe Sobr.] (SPB, 1830), vol. 26, no. 19784.
[5] It is noteworthy that these lists contain the names of only 156 persons.
[6] *Loc. cit.* pp. 584–5.

against the officials responsible for the work of the Secret Office, he was not prepared to allow the continued existence of so unpopular an institution. A fortnight later he issued a Manifesto[1] as famous as that[2] of his grandfather and with remarkably similar contents. Its text[3] is particularly interesting for its vague justification of Catherine's Secret Office and for its explanation of the reasons for its final abolition:

The morals of the century and the particular circumstances of bygone days induced Our Sovereign Ancestors among other temporary statutes to create the Secret Chancellery of Investigatory Affairs, which existed under various names and on various bases even until the times of Our All-Gracious Grandmother the Sovereign Empress Catherine II. Recognizing this court of judgement unnatural to the form of government established in Russia and merely running counter to its own principles, she solemnly abolished and overthrew it by the Manifesto[4] of 1762. Thus the name of this Chancellery was in that year effaced from the statutes of the law; meanwhile, however, in deference to circumstances, it was considered necessary to continue its existence under the name of the Secret Office, with all possible toleration thanks to Her Majesty's own wisdom and personal examination of all cases.

Thus briefly Alexander paid his late grandmother the compliment of attributing to her the initiative that properly belonged to her husband, and carefully refrained from unfavourable comment on her reintroduction of the old Secret Chancellery. Omitting any reference to the deeds of its Head, the notorious Sheshkovsky, his ukaz maintained that the Secret Office's shortcomings had become manifest only in its latter years:

But since on the one hand it has recently been discovered that personal rulings, which by their very nature are subject to emendation, have been unable to provide a reliable defence against abuses and the force of law has been necessary to lend these rulings the required degree of stability; and on the other hand considering that in a well ordered State all crimes should be embraced, tried and punished by common law: We have considered it expedient to abolish and destroy forever not only the name but also the actual operation of the Secret Office, ordering that all its cases should be entrusted to the State Archives to eternal oblivion, and that in future such cases should be dealt with by the 1st and 5th Departments of the Senate[5] and by all official bodies concerned with criminal affairs.

---

[1] Manifest of 2 Apr. 1801. *Poln. Sobr. Zak.* vol. 26, no. 19813.
[2] Peter III's Manifest which abolished the Secret Chancellery was dated 21 February 1762, see *Poln. Sobr. Zak.* vol. 15, no. 11445.
[3] *Poln. Sobr. Zak.* vol. 26, pp. 603–4.
[4] This is historically inaccurate. Catherine merely repeated the provisions of Peter III's Manifest in an ukaz dated 19 October 1762, see *Poln. Sobr. Zak.* vol. 16, no. 11687.
[5] A year and a half later the responsibility for reviewing cases previously awaiting decision in the Secret Office was transferred to the Third and Fourth Departments of the Senate. See Ukaz of 28 Sept. 1802. *Poln. Sobr. Zak.* vol. 27, no. 20434.

The Manifesto ended with a benevolent expression of the Tsar's confidence in the loyalty of his subjects and his solicitude for their welfare 'which alone will always constitute the whole substance of Our thoughts and will', as a reflection of Alexander's obvious desire to please all sections of the community. It should be noted, however, that he did not renounce the established principle of secret police control in Russia. His Manifesto merely announced that the eighteenth-century form of this control with its supra-legal status was no longer admissible.

The 'personal rulings' of the Secret Office had resulted in administrative as well as political inefficiency. The archives examined on its closure showed that in many cases it was impossible to discover the exact reason why its victims had been sentenced—no records existed either at their place of confinement or at the Office itself.[1] One unfortunate man in this category was found to have been incarcerated since 1757 and, being by 1801 both old and feeble-minded, was himself unable to give any explanation of his long detention. The majority of prisoners, however, had been sentenced during the reign of Paul, especially in 1800, when that monarch's mind had become increasingly unhinged. The numbers involved were relatively few. The Schlüsselburg Fortress contained 49 inmates—of whom 23 had been imprisoned only a year; the Alekseyevsky Ravyelin and St Petersburg Fortress contained not more than 19.[2] The total of those detained up to 12 March 1801 amounted to 691 persons,[3] but it was later discovered that this was not a complete list and later additions had to be included. In all something over 700 cases, previously the concern of the Secret Office, were recorded,[4] but the extent of their guilt, if it existed at all, was not immediately evident and remained to be established some months later.

The 'Commission for the Review of Formerly Criminal Cases' was, in fact, created[5] on Alexander's Coronation Day. 'Amidst the general celebration of the true sons of the fatherland extending the gaze of compassion also to its fallen children...' it was given the task of examining whether among those who had suffered imprisonment and exile were any 'whose offences were unintentional and related more to the opinions and trend of thought of a former day than to acts of dishonesty liable to harm the state... These

[1] M. N. Gernet, *Istoriya Tsarskoi Tyur'my*, 4 vols. (Moscow, 1951–4), vol. I, pp. 158–9.
[2] *Ibid.* p. 159.
[3] From 'Secret Office Lists relating to all arrested persons in general in various places of confinement and all those living under surveillance in towns and villages'; quoted by Gernet, p. 162. He gives details of the number of persons held at each place, explaining in a footnote on p. 167 that his information has been taken from the Tsentral'nyi Gosudarstvennyi Arkhiv Dryevnikh Aktov in Moscow (*TsGADA*), vol. VII, no. 3640.
[4] Gernet, p. 167.
[5] Ukaz of 15 Sept. 1801 with additional instructions dated 23 September. *Poln. Sobr. Zak.* vol. 26, no. 20012.

victims I should like to discover and alleviate their lot. To bring them to my attention in the places of their incarceration and exile will be the object of the Commission.'[1] Its sphere of competence was later extended to include the investigation of persons accused of military offences.[2] This Commission, composed of Senators chosen by the Senate itself, consisted of Prince Kurakin and Senators Novosil'tsev, Kozodavlev, and Makarov;[3] and is noteworthy for the re-emergence of the last-named in a high official post. There appears to be no record of Makarov's activities after the death of Paul, but as he is known to have been present at Senate meetings during July[4] it may be assumed that he personally was unaffected by the abolition of the Secret Office. Possibly his services were retained as being those of the one man capable of using his past experience and knowledge to the advantage of the new régime. The official history of the Senate states[5] that the Commission undertook a thorough investigation into cases of persons who had innocently suffered, and on its initiative Civil Governors were instructed[6] by the Senate to submit monthly reports on 'mental cases previously dealt with by the Secret Chancellery [sic]'. According to the same source, the work of the Commission continued until 1809, although it was not officially closed until seven years later[7] when its members included only Kozodavlev and Senator Lt.-Gen. Salagov. Of the many cases it reviewed only 46 remained unsolved and in these there was some doubt as to whether the criminals in question were still alive. But however conscientiously the Commission's work was conducted[8] with the beneficent aim of amending or cancelling the unjust 'personal rulings' of the past, only a short period was due to elapse before the secret creation of a new 'Office' with its own discretionary powers to imprison and exile—and with Makarov again at its head.

The year 1801 was also remarkable for a further demonstration of Alexander's resolve to alleviate the burdens of his subjects. His Manifesto abolishing the Secret Office had not included any reference to the practice of torture by investigating authorities, but in September the case arose of a man at Kazan' who was suspected of arson, tortured to obtain a confession and

---

[1] *Loc. cit.* pp. 789–90.

[2] Ukaz of 31 Mar. 1802. *Poln. Sobr. Zak.* vol. 27, no. 20206.

[3] Kurakin's connexion with this Committee must have been nominal, for on 4 Feb. 1802 he was appointed Governor-General of Little Russia, see *RBS*. Novosil'tsev was Alexander's Personal Private Secretary. Both Kurakin and Kozodavlev subsequently held the post of Minister of Internal Affairs.

[4] *Istoriya Pravitel'stvuyushchago Senata za dvyesti lyet* (SPB, 1911), vol. 3, pp. 37–8.

[5] *Ibid.* pp. 383–4.

[6] Ukaz of 7 Feb. 1802. *Poln. Sobr. Zak.* vol. 27, no. 20137.

[7] Ukaz of 5 Feb. 1816. *Poln. Sobr. Zak.* vol. 33, no. 26168. *N.B.* The practice of allowing Commissions or Committees to remain nominally in force long after their original purpose had been achieved was by no means unusual.

[8] *Ist. Prav. Sen., loc. cit.* p. 383.

subsequently proved to be innocent. Alexander sent one of his aides-de-camp to investigate the circumstances and issued an ukaz[1] containing a résumé of the incident and the steps taken to punish the officials responsible; and ordering the Governing Senate 'to ensure with all strictness throughout the whole Empire that nowhere in any shape or form...should anyone dare to permit or perform any torture, under pain of inevitable and severe punishment...that accused persons should personally declare before the Court that they had not been subjected to any unjust interrogation...that finally the very name of torture, bringing shame and reproach on mankind, should be forever erased from the public memory.'[2] Copies of this instruction were circulated to local authorities on 18 November.[3] It is interesting to note that the officials guilty of this malpractice were evidently not prosecuted to the Tsar's satisfaction, for over three years later in an ukaz[4] dealing with this same case he reprimanded the Fourth Department of the Senate (which was by then responsible for investigating such incidents), declaring that 'Its Senators... to Our astonishment have failed to pay due attention to so outstanding a case and We therefore reiterate the need for this Department to show more circumspection in dealing with cases of this kind in future'.[5] It may be presumed that the officials of this Department had long been inured to the established practice of torture not only by the Secret Office and its predecessors but also by local police headquarters, and it therefore distressed them considerably less than the youthful Alexander. The Secret Office had been abolished with a stroke of the pen; the use of one of its accepted methods proved more difficult to eradicate, and even the former institution had not disappeared for good.

A state secret police was not, however, reinstituted during the first few years of the new reign. Nor was the subject raised in any of the sessions of the so-called 'Nyeglasnyi' or 'Intimnyi' Komitet of this period.[6] Alexander

---

[1] Ukaz of 27 Sept. 1801. *Poln. Sobr. Zak.* vol. 26, no. 20022. [2] *Loc. cit.* pp. 797–98.
[3] *Ibid.* (footnote).
[4] Ukaz of 13 Nov. 1804. *Poln. Sobr. Zak.* vol. 28, no. 21516. [5] *Loc. cit.* p. 705.
[6] See Le Grand-Duc Nicolas Mikhaïlovitch de Russie, *Le Comte Paul Stroganov*, trad. française de F. Billecocq. 3 vols. (Paris, 1905). (The Russian text was published under the title of *Graf Pavel Aleksandrovich Stroganov (1774–1817). Istoricheskoe issledovanie epokhi Aleksandra I* 3 vols. (SPB, 1903).)

This work contains Stroganov's account of the 40 sessions of this Committee which took place between 24 June 1801 and 19 Nov. 1803. Vol. 1, Introduction, p. xxvi, footnote (1). In footnote (3), *ibid.* the Grand Duke records that among the questions examined by the Committee occurred that of the secret police. (vol. 1, no. 133); but it is clear from Stroganov's transcript that this discussion concerned only the undesirable practices of a local secret police acting under the orders of the Military Governor-General of St Petersburg, see p. 101, Session of 27 Jan. 1802. There is a further reference to this body (not recorded in the Introduction) which states that 'Colonel Féodor Féodorovich Aegerström' (Egershtrom) was in charge of it, *ibid.* no. 115 Session of 17 March 1802. Apart from these two references there is no mention of any discussion relating to the theory or practice of a state political police in Russia at this time.

evidently preferred to rely on a system of internal security which did not provide for the existence of an 'independent' branch of this kind. The creation of Ministries[1] in September 1802 was intended to place the organization of the country on a sound administrative basis subject to the law. Count Kochubei, to whose influence this delegation of executive responsibility was largely due, was appointed Minister of Internal Affairs and, according to the text of the Manifesto, was 'to be responsible for the universal welfare of the people, the tranquillity...and well-being of the whole Empire...all civil and military service units to be subordinated to this Minister...'[2] The ministry itself was subdivided into four Sections ('Ekspeditsii'), of which the Second was responsible for 'matters of public law and order') ('dyela blagochiniya') and controlled two, and later three, Departments ('Otdeleniya') dealing with rural and urban police forces.[3] It is clear, however, that 'police affairs' of every kind, including criminal investigation, censorship, secret surveillance of societies and individuals, were also the concern of this Second Section.[4] That is to say, no 'Special Branch' existed to deal with cases that would normally be considered the concern of a Higher Police.[5] The Second Section of the Ministry of Internal Affairs made no administrative distinction between criminal and political offences, and—possibly owing to its many other commitments—it may have been unable to accord the latter sufficient attention. At least it never gained the reputation of the old 'Tainaya Ekspeditsiya', and was not granted any extraordinary powers.

In October 1802, however, Kochubei was sufficiently interested in the secret police question to make inquiries of the Military Governor-General of St Petersburg.[6] He was informed that a secret police[7] existed in the capital[8] 'on strictly conspiratorial principles' and he was furnished with a list of its agents and a copy of its regulations. One of these stated that this office 'endeavours to have accurate and continual information on the thoughts and opinions of the people concerning the Emperor and his

---

[1] Manifest of 2 Sept. 1802. *Poln. Sobr. Zak.* vol. 27, no. 20406.

[2] *Loc. cit.* pp. 244–5.

[3] Varadinov, pt. 1. (1802–9), pp. 14–16, 75.

[4] *Ibid.* It was known as the 'Section for Law and Order' ('Ekspeditsiya o Spokoistvii i Blagochinii') until 1806 when its name was changed to the 'Section for State Control and Welfare' ('Ekspeditsiya Gosudarstvennago Blagoustroistva'), pp. 16, 40.

[5] The Secret or Political Police was normally referred to in contemporary and later documents as the 'Vysshaya Politsiya' or 'La Haute Police'.

[6] Trotsky, pp. 8–10. The details of this inquiry and the answer received were extracted by Trotsky from State Archives which have not yet been published. He quotes as reference 'Arkhiv 3-go Otdeleniya, Dyelo 1802 g., no. 2.'

[7] It was referred to as 'The Secret Police Office' ('Ekspeditsiya Tainoi Politsii').

[8] As Kochubei was a permanent member of the 'Nyeglasnyi Komitet' he must have known this already (see p. 22, note 6) although Trotsky does not say so. It may therefore be assumed that the newly-appointed Minister of Internal Affairs was merely seeking official and detailed confirmation.

government...' that is to say, it claimed the normal sphere of competence of a local Secret Police; and another regulation laid down that 'it should be informed of all arrivals of foreigners, where they reside, their connexions, business, contacts, way of life, and should pay close attention to their conduct'.[1] The interest taken in foreigners was due to fears especially prevalent since the French Revolution that this infection might penetrate into Russia, and these fears increased with the menace of Napoleon. Trotsky contends that the existence of this Ekspeditsiya proves that the Secret Office was not abolished at all;[2] but it is in fact more likely that the Governor-General in the capital permanently controlled his own network of agents to conduct local investigations. (This is confirmed by later evidence towards the end of Alexander's reign.[3]) If this Ekspeditsiya had represented the State Secret Police, it would not have been necessary to create it shortly afterwards. Kochubei is not reported to have raised any objection to the force controlled by the Governor-General, and it may be assumed that the retention of secret investigatory organizations by local high officials had long been an established custom.

The resurrection of the former Secret Office, however, with its control extended over the whole Empire, was merely a question of time.

The committee of 5 September 1805

In 1805, when Alexander was about to leave Russia to join his army abroad, the need for some form of additional political control was recognized in an 'imperial command'[4] addressed to 'The Committee of Higher Police.' It ordered that the Ministers of Land Forces (Vyazmitinov), Justice (Lopukhin) and Internal Affairs (Kochubei) should form a Committee for general consultation on matters of internal security. Shil'der states that the abolished Secret Office was thus to some extent 're-born out of its own ashes' and that this 'radically undermined all the Emperor's endeavours to introduce legality into his empire';[5] at the same time it appears probable that the initiative for recreating this discredited branch belonged to Alexander himself. He is reported to have said: 'I wish that a Higher Police, which is not yet at our disposal, should be created; it is necessary in the present circum-

---

[1] Trotsky comments that 'the only recurring expense item of the Ekspeditsiya was the payment of pensions to the concierges ["shveitsaram"] of foreign embassies', p. 9.

[2] Trotsky, p. 10.

[3] See p. 45.

[4] See N. K. Shil'der, *Imperator Aleksandr Pervyi*, vol. 2. He describes this order as a 'vysochaishee povelenie' (p. 162), later referring to it in his Appendix as 'Secret Instructions ["sekretnoe nastavlenie"] to the Committee of Higher Police dated 5 Sept. 1805' (p. 362). No imperial ukaz was issued creating this Committee.

[5] Shil'der, *loc. cit.* p. 162.

stances.'[1] It is impossible to contend that the Committee of 5 September 1805 existed merely to assume responsibility for controlling Russia during the Emperor's absence. The Instructions[2] issued to it comprised eleven points dealing with 'the preservation of public tranquillity and order' and 'the prevention of want and high food prices in the capital', but in addition they provided for the collation of information from all sources including that of the Directorate of Postal Services. Emphasis was also laid on the necessity for 'preserving everything in complete secrecy', even to the extent of ordering that any measure decided on by the Committee should only be made public in the name of the Minister specifically concerned. It existed only as a consultative body, created no new organization for the purposes of political investigation and, apart from the above Instructions, nothing is known of its activities.[3] These may be regarded, however, as having been undertaken primarily as a wartime expedient and it is permissible to doubt whether at the time Alexander envisaged them as more than temporarily necessary.

The committee of 13 January 1807

The same motive may be ascribed to the creation in 1807 of the Committee for Public Safety. In November 1806 an ukaz was issued containing precautionary measures to be adopted against French subjects resident in Russia,[4] but these were evidently judged insufficient for the preservation of national security. An 'imperial command' dated 2 January 1807 ordered the secret formation of a Special Committee, the provisions of which were laid down in a Memorandum drafted by Novosil'tsev and confirmed by the Emperor.[5] This Memorandum proposed as Committee members the Minister of Justice, Prince Lopukhin, and the Privy Councillors and Senators Makarov and Novosil'tsev, to be assisted when required by the Ministers of Internal Affairs and Land Forces. Novosil'tsev's draft contains several points of interest. In seven articles it set out the Committee's terms of reference in

---

[1] Ye. F. Komarovsky, *Zapiski* ed. by P. Ye. Shchegolev (SPB, 1914), p. 138. (These memoirs were first published in *Russkii Arkhiv*, 1867 and 1877.)

   General-in-Waiting Count Komarovsky (1769–1843), to whom these words were addressed, was Deputy to two Governors-General of St Petersburg, Kamensky and Vyazmitinov; and from 1802 to 1806 held the post of Chief of the St Petersburg Police. For many years he was one of Alexander's closest confidants and was later entrusted with the organization of Internal Security Troops (see p. 31, notes 1, 5). See his *Zapiski, ed. cit.* pp. 124, 142; Shil'der, *loc. cit.*; *RBS* under Kamarovsky.

[2] These instructions were signed by Alexander ('byt' po syemu'), with a note of the place and date by Novosil'tsev, and subsequently filed in the Arkhiv Gosudarstvennago Sovyeta. They are quoted in full by Shil'der, *loc. cit.* pp. 362–4.

[3] Shil'der *loc. cit.* p. 364 (footnote).

[4] Ukaz of 28 November 1806. *Poln. Sobr. Zak.* vol. 29, no. 22371.

[5] The full text of this Memorandum is printed by Shil'der, *loc cit.* pp. 364–6.

much greater detail than had appeared in the official ukaz which created this Committee a few days later. He proposed the institution of a nation-wide investigatory system empowered, like the 1805 Committee, to obtain information from all sources including the inspection of suspect correspondence. Clause 6 reads: 'In general, all cases relating to treason to the state and secret conspiracies against the public security, which should be preserved in the greatest secrecy, are to go before this Committee at their very outset; and will be followed up by it.' The Committee's sphere of competence was hence extensive and included specifically:

(a) Persons suspected of correspondence with the enemy and divulgation of secrets;

(b) Rumours concerning the restoration of Poland;

(c) Incitement of the people by rumours of the liberation of the peasants;

(d) Suspected conspiracy against the Tsar;

(e) Insults to the Tsar and member of the Imperial Household;

(f) Treason to the state;

(g) Persons spreading false and dangerous rumours on military matters;

(h) The preparation and propagation of mutinous appeals, harmful publications, etc.;

(i) Secret societies and proscribed meetings;

(j) The investigation of projects for victory over the enemy submitted to the government...the detection of ill-disposed persons;

(k) Persons claiming or mistakenly thought to be personages of the Imperial family;

(l) Misbehaviour on the part of officials;

(m) Harmful books;

(n) Suspected forgery of coinage;

(o) Individual acts constituting a threat to public morals.[1]

The official ukaz[2] creating this Committee made limited use of Novosil'tsev's draft, although it incorporated much of its phraseology. Both documents referred to 'the wily government of France' and her employment of secret agents as the chief motive for the Committee's formation; both stressed the need for efficient investigations 'because any errors of omission or commission may lead either to the persecution of innocent persons or to the failure to discover criminal practices'; and in both the same Committee members were nominated. The ukaz, however, mentioned the original 'precautionary measures' ukaz of November 1806 and explained that the new Committee was now considered necessary 'because it is impossible to be certain of everything...and the vigilance of the police should continue its unsleeping surveillance...' It defined the Committee's powers in four

---

[1] Shil'der, *loc. cit.* p. 367.   [2] Ukaz of 13 Jan. 1807. *Poln. Sobr. Zak.* vol. 29, no. 22425.

Articles only,[1] making no mention of postal censorship. Article I enacted that 'All important criminal cases, in which there is any suspicion of potentially dangerous persons or of treason to the detriment of the general tranquillity and safety of the state, as soon as they are discovered, are instantly to be reported through the St Petersburg Police and Military Governor to this Committee, which, according to the circumstances, will determine the course of investigation and conduct the whole case to its final conclusion'. Articles II and III ensured that the Committee be informed of cases of expulsion from Russia proposed by other departments of state; and that local authorities should act solely under the Committee's jurisdiction. Finally, complete control over security affairs was guaranteed by Article IV: 'All offices and persons, on the demand of this Committee, must provide it with satisfactory information with all speed and fulfil its orders and instructions ...' It may thus be seen that this second Committee enjoyed absolute executive power, and there can be no doubt that it replaced the Secret Office abolished in 1801.[2] Its importance lay first in the subordination to it of the Governor-General's police force with its secret office and the widening of the latter's scope to include political investigation outside the capital; and secondly in the appointment of Makarov.

The 1807 Committee was composed of well-known figures, statesmen and generals, but 'its most active member was Aleksandr Semyonovich Makarov ...the successor of Sheshkovsky'.[3] He evidently found much to occupy his attention, for the Committee's activity was such that it felt itself obliged to report in a memorandum, dated 19 February and submitted to the Tsar, that the number of cases entrusted to it was increasing daily, 'for these are being sent in from all areas' and 'the Committee has therefore recognized the need to create its own Special Chancellery'.[4] These cases consisted mostly of attempts to stir up the people with rumours to the effect that the peasants were to be liberated and that Bonaparte would achieve this aim by destroying the landowners.[5] Alexander recognized the potential menace of such rumours and hence, it must be assumed, decided to entrust their investigation to the one man whose career, as far as is known, had lain exclusively in the field of secret police work. Three years later Makarov died and it is not known whether he was replaced; however, the Committee was still in existence in 1817 with twenty-three persons employed on its staff.[6] As rumours of peasant liberation continued to persist throughout the reign, it can be concluded that the

[1] Loc. cit. pp. 983–4.
[2] See M. K. Lemke, Nikolayevskie Zhandarmy, p. 8; and Trotsky, p. 10.
[3] Shil'der, loc. cit. p. 162.   [4] Ibid.   [5] Ibid.
[6] Ist. Prav. Sen., loc. cit. p. 394. This History records the appointment of Makarov but this is the only reference to his connexion with the 1807 Committee. His dates are given in vol. 5, p. 135.

Committee was kept fully occupied and it was officially closed down only on 17 January 1829.[1]

The Committee's records contain the first printed Secret Police Instructions known to us. They directed that employment should be given 'to persons of varying classes and different nations but of as reliable a character as possible, obliging them... to submit unbiased reports containing nothing but the truth and to preserve secrecy in the highest degree, even if subsequently the employee relinquished this branch of service...' and that such persons should circulate everywhere and should 'observe, listen, inquire, and do their utmost to penetrate into people's minds'.[2] The authorship of this directive is not established. No evidence has been published to show either that Makarov was responsible for it[3] or that, as might be expected, he used his predominant influence in the 1807 Committee to expand the work of the Governor-General's 'Ekspeditsiya' into a nation-wide system of secret political control. It can only be stated that no other high official at that time is known to have had the necessary knowledge and experience to have been able to plan such an undertaking.

As far as can be discovered, Makarov never possessed Alexander's confidence.[4] He was a much older man, he had worked with the detested Sheshkovsky, he belonged to the old régime; and therefore he was permitted only to serve on Committees, not to control them. It is easy to understand the young Tsar's attitude on his accession. His early ukazes show a probably genuine abhorrence of all that secret police work entailed. Nevertheless, by 1807 this attitude had clearly undergone a significant change. At home, he had made the painful discovery that internal reforms were more easily planned than realized; abroad, the successes of Napoleon and the defeat at Austerlitz had increased his awareness of national and personal insecurity. In addition, the complex 'duality' of his character admitted by all historians further contributed to the inner struggle perpetually waged in his mind between conscience and duty. Events outside his control necessitated the partial resumption of methods which he had earlier discarded. But while obliged to countenance the secret reintroduction of a political police, he continued to regard it with repugnance, and this possibly explains why he never fully trusted those who controlled its destinies—either at this or later periods of his reign. His decision to create the 1807 Committee, however, must be attributed less to a vague distrust of his own countrymen than to a

---

[1] Shil'der, *loc. cit.* note 276, p. 289.

[2] Trotsky, p. 10, quoting unpublished Archives—'Arkhiv 3-go Otdeleniya, Dyelo 1807g., No. 8.'

[3] Trotsky's summary of the 'Political Police in the Beginning of the 19th century' includes no mention whatever of Makarov.

[4] It is worth noting that his name was never mentioned in any of the deliberations of the 'Nyeglasnyi Komitet' recorded by Count Stroganov. (See p. 22, note 6.)

definite fear of foreign agents. And it was not until the reorganization of the Ministries that the country became aware of the existence of a regenerated 'Secret Office' in their midst.

Foreigners, on the other hand, soon realized that their previous freedom of action in Russia was to be more strictly controlled. In the uneasy peace that succeeded the Treaty of Tilsit it was decided in October 1809 that the interests of security would better be served by the creation in St Petersburg (and later in Moscow) of a 'department of the police in which persons of both sexes and every class engaged in any work in private houses are obliged to register'.[1] The task of establishing this so-called 'Address Office' was to be entrusted by the Senate to the Minister of Internal Affairs and the Acting Military Governor-General of St Petersburg. Foreigners were obliged to exchange their passports for a residence permit obtainable only after the completion of a form. These measures were embodied in an ukaz[2] addressed to Balashov, the Acting Governor-General in question, to whose Chancellery this 'Special Department of Addresses'[3] was attached. The Address (or Passport) Office continued in operation for many years and was, as will be seen, a constant source of vexation to foreign residents and travellers. As its work was conducted openly, it cannot properly be regarded as part of the current Secret Police organization; at the same time it undoubtedly provided the latter with a reliable source of useful information, and foreigners in Russia continued to attract the particular attention of the authorities years after the disappearance of the temporary state of emergency. But although foreigners were especially suspect from 1807 onwards, it soon became evident that the Government had equally little confidence in its own compatriots.

The Ministry of Police, 1811

Alexander's apparent friendliness towards Napoleon after Tilsit caused serious misgivings in the minds of many of his subjects and he in his turn became increasingly apprehensive of the dangers inherent in their passive opposition to his foreign policy. He had no intention of sharing the fate of his father and grandfather,[4] and finally decided that the whole question of

---

[1] 'Polozhenie dlya Kontory Adresov v Stolitsakh' of 15 Oct. 1809. *Poln. Sobr. Zak.* vol. 30, p. 1215, no. 23911.

[2] Ukaz of 22 Oct. 1809. *Poln. Sobr. Zak.* vol. 30, no. 23928.

[3] The original name of 'Address Office' was retained. See Ukaz No. 24043 of 21 Dec. 1809 which increased its establishment by a further interpreter. Details of the ukazes relating to this Office may be found in *Poln. Sobr. Zak.* vol. 42 (pt I), p. 18 under 'Adres-Kontory'.

[4] Despite these fears and 'in accordance with the inner contradiction of his nature, he could not abide coming across any of the police agents whose job it was to guard him'. Trotsky, p. 11. No source is quoted for this statement.

police organization required reconsideration. His decision was also influenced by two other factors: the recommendations of Speransky on the one hand and the success of Napoleon's domestic policy on the other. Speransky complained in his 1809 Plan of State Reorganization that the sphere of competence of the Ministries created in 1802 had only been outlined and that their functioning had frequently been inefficient. Among his proposals he submitted that 'a Ministry of Police must of necessity constitute an independent unit. The internal security of the state is as valid and many-sided an object as those relating to all other sections of the administration'[1] and suggested that this Ministry should have complete control over all security measures including that of 'the higher police'.[2] Speransky was known to be in favour of the 'Code Napoléon' which itself relied upon the existence of such a ministry; and the effective results achieved in France by its famous Minister Fouché[3] evidently interested not only Speransky but also Alexander. The Archives of the year 1810 contain a letter sent by the Minister of Police, Balashov, to the Russian envoy in Prussia, Lieven, in which he refers to Alexander's active interest in the regulations governing the Secret Higher Police in France.[4] And it is clear that at this period the Tsar had become convinced of the need for a stricter control over this branch of the national administration. Speransky's proposal for a Ministry of Police consisting of two Departments was incorporated in a Manifesto 'On the Division of State Affairs into Special Directorates'[5] which speaks of the Ministry as though it were already established. (The Manifesto in fact appointed only its Minister,[6] who was then entrusted by Speransky with the task of drawing up the necessary regulations.[7]) It was intended to ensure better and more centralized control over the country by the transfer to itself of all police organ-

[1] See Shil'der, pp. 388–9.

[2] *Ibid*. Speransky proposed that the Ministry should consist of the 'Politsiya Uchrezhdennaya' (to anticipate infringements of security and act as a Higher Police) and the 'Politsiya Ispolnitel'-naya' (to organize internal security troops and perform normal police duties).

[3] Joseph Fouché, Duc d'Otranto (1759–1820). He was Napoleon's Minister of Police from 1799 to 1802 and again from 1804 to 1810. A valuable study of his methods may be found in Nils Forssel, *Fouché, the Man Napoleon Feared*, tr. from the Swedish by Anna Barwell (London, 1928).

[4] Trotsky, p. 14, quoting unpublished Archives—'Arkhiv 3-go Otdeleniya, Dyelo I-i Ekspeditsii. 1810, no. 7.'

[5] Manifest of 25 July 1810. *Poln. Sobr. Zak.* vol. 31, p. 279, no. 24307. It refers briefly to the two departments of this projected Ministry as the Preventive ('Predokhranitel'naya') and Executive ('Ispolnitel'naya') Polices. Pt 2, clause 12.

[6] 'for the general co-ordination... of all matters proper to the state police, hitherto dealt with in the Ministry of Internal Affairs, the previously existing title of General-Policemaster is reinstituted under the name of Minister of Police'. Pt 1, clause 5. (The title of General-Policemaster, first created in 1718, fell into disuse after 1766. See *Poln. Sobr. Zak.* vol. 42 (pt 1), p. 304.) This office was held by Gen. Balashov from 25 Jul. 1810. See Adrianov, p. 21.

[7] 'Zapiski Ya. I. de Sanglena', p. 17.

izations including that of the Internal Security Troops[1] which in later years were to form part of the lower ranks of the Corps of Gendarmes. And when the reorganization of Ministries was announced in the summer of the following year, this control was effected by the creation of a new Ministry of Police[2] based on Speransky's recommendation. It was formed from the Second and Third Sections of the Ministry of Internal Affairs,[3] and its Minister was accorded wide powers to ensure the efficient execution of normal police duties. He could insist on receiving information and general co-operation from the Heads of other Ministries and was further authorized to demand it directly, if necessary, from their subordinates.[4] He was permitted to make use of Internal Security Troops[5] and in special circumstances to demand their reinforcement by regular units without consultation.[6]

Although, however, both Speransky's Plan and the 1810 Manifesto envisaged a Ministry of Police empowered to deal with 'measures incumbent upon the higher police', neither had proposed the establishment within its framework of any special branch for political investigation and control. Nevertheless, the new Ministry was found to contain just such a branch in the shape of a 'Special Chancellery'[7] ('Osobennaya Kantselyariya' Ministerstva Politsii), and this 'small addition' brought it extraordinary power 'just as sometimes a postscript in a letter describes the main importance of the letter's aim'.[8] This office, with an establishment of thirteen persons, was

[1] These garrison troops were known collectively as 'Vnutrennyaya Strazha' and had previously been controlled by local authorities acting on the instructions of the Ministry of Internal Affairs. The 1810 Manifesto now proposed their subordination to the Executive Police of the new Ministry. Pt 2, clause 12. See also Varadinov, pt 2, p. 5.

[2] 'Creation of the Ministry of Police', 25 June 1811. *Poln. Sobr. Zak.* vol. 31, no. 24687.

[3] *Loc. cit.* p. 719, 'Manifest'. These Sections were reorganized into 3 departments: Administrative, Executive and Medical. *Ibid.* clause 2.

[4] *Loc. cit.* p. 725, clauses 65, 66.

[5] *Ibid.* clause 68. All units of 'Vnutrennyaya Strazha' had been reclassified as part of the Armed Forces and subordinated for purposes of training and recruitment to the Minister of War (Ukazes of 16 Jan. and 3 Jul. 1811, nos. 24486, 24704), but the Minister of Police was responsible for their tactical deployment. See Adrianov, *op. cit.* p. 98.

On 7 July 1811 Gen. Komarovsky was appointed Inspector of 'Vnutrennyaya Strazha' in its reconstituted form. See his *Zapiski*, p. 182; *RBS.*

[6] *Loc. cit.* p. 725, clause 101.

[7] A 'General' ('Obshchaya') Chancellery was also created to control the routine work of the Ministry. *Loc. cit.* p. 723, clauses 50–2. And both Chancelleries were allotted a quota of officials for performing special duties of inspection or investigation at the Minister's discretion, pp. 723–4, clause 55.

[8] F. F. Vigel', *Zapiski*, ed. by S. Ya. Shtraikh. 2 vols. (Moscow, 1928), vol. 1, p. 316.

(Filipp Filippovich Vigel' (1786–1856) had a long career in the civil service during the first half of the nineteenth century. Though he never occupied any high post, he came into contact with many important personages of his day and his memoirs 'provide rich material for the history of Russia's internal life... up to the year 1830'. They were originally published as articles in *Russkii Vyestnik* (1864–5) and first appeared in book form in 1866. See V. Ye. Rudakov's article on him, *Br. Efr. Enc.* vol. 6, p. 226.)

organized in three sections controlling Foreigners in Russia and Russians travelling abroad, Censorship, and 'Cases which the Minister shall consider necessary to have submitted for his own information and decision'.[1] No reference was made in these or other clauses of this ukaz to the very similar duties previously allotted to the 1807 Committee—possibly because of the essentially secret nature of its activities. But the police organization whose task it was to provide this Committee with information had been controlled by the office of the Governor-General of St Petersburg; and for over two years this office had been under the orders of the same man who, while retaining (until 1812) the post of Governor-General, now headed the new Ministry of which the Special Chancellery formed a vital part. It therefore seems permissible to conclude that the functions of the 1807 Committee were in practice superseded by this new office in which 'many saw the renascence of the Secret Chancellery, the shame and terror of Russia's past. . .'[2]

Balashov and de Sanglen

Two officials shared the responsibility for reintroducing this unpopular branch into the national administration.

Of these General Balashov,[3] the new Minister, has been regarded somewhat inaccurately as the 'initiator' of the secret police system[4] which later in the century was destined to play a larger rôle in Russian history. It is at least true that in its opening stages he was the highest official concerned. After early service in the army he had been appointed 'Ober-Politseimeister' of Moscow in 1804 and St Petersburg in 1808, and in this post rose quickly in the Emperor's favour. In 1809 he was promoted General-in-Waiting and the same year was appointed Acting Governor-General of the capital in the rank of Lieutenant-General. In 1810 he was made a member of the newly created State Council and, in view of his past experience in police matters and his outstanding organizational ability, was the natural choice for the appointment of Minister of Police. Although nominally he retained this rank until the abolition of the Ministry nine years later, his personal direction of its affairs lasted only until 1812,[5] after which, as a member of Alexander's private staff, he was entrusted with a variety of special missions, military

---

[1] *Poln. Sobr. Zak.*, *loc. cit.* p. 723, clauses 53, 54; Adrianov, p. 21. Particulars of the ranks held by these 13 officials and also a description of their sphere of competence are given by Varadinov, pt 2, p. 604. [2] Vigel', *ibid.*

[3] Aleksandr Dmitrievich Balashev (1770–1837), see *RBS*. (His surname was alternatively spelled Balashov; and, in the interests of correct pronunciation, I have adhered to the latter spelling.)

[4] Trotsky, p. 18.

[5] The Ministry of Police was in practice directed from 1812 to 1819 by the C. in C. and Military Governor-General of St Petersburg, Count Sergei Koz'mich Vyazmitinov (1749–1819), Adrianov, p. 21.

and diplomatic.[1] Despite an early lack of education, he possessed unusual talents equalled only by an ability to inspire in others feelings of strong distaste for his character and methods. 'He was endowed by nature with all gifts save that of a handsome appearance; this she denied him, but had allowed him everything else necessary for success: the cunning of a Greek, the resourcefulness and boldness of a Russian, the patience and discretion of a German. . . Had one spark of nobility been implanted in that unusual mind, had set it aflame, the country would have been proud of him. . . Balashov's words were as clear as his powers of reasoning and as cold as his heart.'[2] The shrewdness of Russia's first and only Minister of Police enabled him to retain this high position, but 'his ambitions and an innate love of intrigue cut short his prosperous career'[3] and prevented his permanently enjoying the favour accorded later, for instance, by Nicholas to Benckendorff. There is even reason to believe that both Alexander and Speransky came to realize that their choice of Balashov as Minister had been unfortunate, and Balashov himself was compelled to indulge in further intrigues in order to prevent his dismissal. Baron Korff states that 'by character and outlook, the *means* never troubled him provided he could attain his *purpose*' and calls him 'one of the most unattractive figures of Alexander's reign.'[4] Balashov, however, was not chiefly responsible either for the reintroduction of a state secret police or for its subsequent development. The creation of the Special Chancellery nominally under his direction must properly be ascribed to a more erudite official, Ya. I. de Sanglen.[5]

This man, the son of a French émigré, St Glin, after early education in Moscow and Revel', began his career in 1793 as an interpreter and had first become acquainted with Balashov as early as 1800.[6] After a period abroad when he attended courses at Leipzig and Berlin, he was appointed in 1804 Lecturer in German Literature at Moscow University, where he later special-

---

[1] *RBS.*

[2] Vigel', pp. 316–17. It is noteworthy that Vigel''s opinion of Balashov was fully supported by M. I. Bogdanovich and was quoted verbatim in his *Istoriya Tsarstvovaniya Imperatora Aleksandra I i Rossii v yego vremya*, 6 vols. (SPB, 1869–71), vol. 3, pp. 8–9.

[3] Trotsky, p. 21. (It is noteworthy, however, that even after the abolition of the Ministry of Police, Balashov held an important post as Governor-General until 1828, see *RBS*.) In this appointment too he was generally disliked and his tenure of office was marked by widespread abuses in the administrative system. See A. V. Nikitenko, *Zapiski i Dnevnik*, 2 vols. (SPB, 1904, 1905), vol. 1, pp. 67–8; vol. 2, p. 380.

[4] M. A. Korff: 'Dyeyateli i Uchastniki Padeniya Speranskago' (1847), an unpublished chapter of his *Life of Count Speransky*, contrib. by N. A. Bychkov to *R. Star.* (1902), vol. 109, pp. 484–5. Korff states that Balashov left a ms. autobiography, but apparently it was not published and Korff refers to it merely as 'a trivial panegyric'.

[5] Yakov Ivanovich de Sanglen (1776–1864), see *RBS*; also 'Zapiski de Sanglena', pp. 17–18.

[6] In this year Balashov was sent to Revel' as Military Governor and Garrison Commander to defend the Baltic coast against the British, see *RBS*. De Sanglen does not specify in his memoirs the exact nature of his employment at Balashov's Revel' headquarters.

ized in Military Science and Tactics as a Reader. In 1807 he renounced an academic career in favour of a post on the staff of General-in-Waiting Prince P. M. Volkonsky,[1] who was then engaged on a study of army organization. Two years later Balashov, who was by that time Acting Military Governor of St Petersburg, entrusted to his care the Foreign Department of his Chancellery; and when the Address Office was created de Sanglen was appointed Head of its Foreign Section. He was decorated for his part in the organization of this office and, according to his memoirs, was made personally responsible by Balashov for compiling the code of regulations for the new Ministry of Police.[2] The regulations were approved by the Emperor, Balashov was confirmed as Minister and de Sanglen was then[3] made Director of the Ministry's Special Chancellery. In this capacity he was generally known as 'The Head of the Secret Police' and was frequently consulted by Alexander over the head of his superior.

De Sanglen's character is less easy to assess[4] than that of Balashov, a far more prominent figure. While undoubtedly the most scholarly of all Russia's secret police chiefs,[5] he occupied a position which could hardly fail to gain him enemies. Vigel', who was working at the time in the Ministry of Internal Affairs under Kozodavlev, attributes to him 'a reputation for effrontery, baseness and cleverness' but comments that society did not greatly fear him: 'I do not know whether it was because Russians were at that time spoiled by Alexander or whether it was because they felt that their unanimity of heart and thought put them in a strong position, but not one desired to conceal his profound contempt for persons of this sort. No matter how dangerous or formidable this de Sanglen was for each of them, no one wished to talk to him or pay him respect.'[6] Later writers have not seen fit to qualify this appreciation.

It is difficult not to sympathize with the attitude of contemporary Russian society to the appointment of de Sanglen. Any official chosen to occupy such a post would have been subjected to similar criticism. Ten years' relative freedom from secret police surveillance had encouraged the growth of

---

[1] De Sanglen states that Volkonsky took a great dislike to him and that this was the reason for his preferring employment elsewhere. 'Zapiski', p. 15.

[2] 'Zapiski', p. 17. He was taken on to the establishment of the Ministry of Police on 21 July 1811, (from the files of the Ministry of Internal Affairs, quoted by Korff, p. 503).

[3] 7 August 1811. (*Ibid.*) On 3 Aug. 1811 he was appointed to the rank of 'Kollyezhskii Sovyetnik' ('Collegiate Councillor')—equivalent to that of Colonel. (*Ibid.*)

[4] See Korff's article, *op. cit.* He lists a number of hostile opinions on de Sanglen but adds that 'all agree that he was a very clever man' (p. 504). He also stresses the importance of the Special Chancellery as 'the key to the whole Ministry' and the high reputation in it of de Sanglen, quoting the evidence ('pokazaniya') of one G. V. Lerkhe who was employed there (*ibid.*). I have been unable to trace this evidence—it does not appear to have been published.

[5] A full list of his printed works is given in the *RBS* article; they deal with military, historical and literary subjects and include two novels.   [6] Vigel', p. 318.

political freethinking and the Tsar's apparently friendly policy towards Napoleon was not generally understood. There was also a feeling of strong resentment against Speransky, to whose influence was correctly ascribed Alexander's obvious liking for the methods of French governmental administration. It was bad enough that a Ministry of Police should have been thought necessary at all; it was worse that it should contain a secret and ominously powerful branch controlled by a minor official of foreign extraction. At the same time de Sanglen does not appear to have been a careerist of the calibre of Balashov, and this may well account for Alexander's readiness to accord him, if only temporarily, a measure of that confidence which by this date he normally extended to Arakcheyev alone.

Historians of Alexander's reign owe a debt to de Sanglen. At the age of over 80 this once powerful official devoted himself to the preparation of memoirs which with 'their detailed knowledge of events from behind the scenes, the author's sincere tones...and their wealth of factual material'[1] represent a unique source of information on an important phase of Russian history. His *Notes* on this period deal almost exclusively with the part played by their author in the events which culminated in the fall of Speransky and do not contain more than passing references to the Special Chancellery. Their interest for the present study lies, however, in their disclosure of the involved relationships and unhappy intrigues which developed between the Tsar and his entourage; they reveal the astonishing lack of mutual confidence that was bound to ensue from this state of affairs and provide an explanation of Alexander's subsequent attitude to the question of secret political investigation. The general instability of his autocratic rule is admirably illustrated by these personal reminiscences of an old police chief.

In the early days of the Ministry of Police Alexander was disposed to trust Balashov completely, telling him that his Special Chancellery was superior to all other departments, but by December 1811 he was already complaining to de Sanglen of his Minister's increasing greed for power and requesting that de Sanglen should spy on Speransky in place of his chief.[2] There seems no reason to doubt the likelihood of this request. Speransky himself in conversation with Balashov is reported to have said: 'You know the mistrustful character of the Emperor...he does everything by halves...he is too feeble to rule and too strong to be ruled...' and this mistrustfulness even led to his asking de Sanglen to spy on Balashov as well, overriding the former's protests with an assurance that he would be responsible for any

---

[1] A. Cherkas, article on de Sanglen, *RBS*. These memoirs were entitled 'Zapiski—Nye dlya Sovremennikov' ('Notes—Not for Contemporaries') and were published in *Russkaya Starina* (1882 and 1883). Those dealing specifically with events that occurred during the reign of Alexander I (pt 3) may be found in vol. 37, pp. 1–46; 375–94; 539–58.

[2] 'Zapiski de Sanglena', pp. 18, 22, 23.

consequences.[1] The Tsar's contradictory nature emerges clearly from the opinions he expressed to the Head of the Special Chancellery. On the one hand he would declare: 'I trust absolutely no one' or 'You do not know people; you do not know how black, how ungrateful they are'.[2] On the other, he would insist on a surveillance of his own Ministers resulting inevitably in an atmosphere of intrigue and secrecy in which no official could feel secure, witness the following conversation between Balashov and his chief asisstant during their preparations for the exile of Speransky.

DE SANGLEN: A funny thought occurs to me, and one that is at the same time not very consoling. What if he [Speransky] is exonerated, and in his place Your Excellency and I, your faithful servant, are exiled?

BALASHOV: I must confess that when alone I too have been disturbed by that idea. Heaven knows—one can be sure of nothing.[3]

The anxiety of both men was justified shortly afterwards. Each proceeded to quarrel with the other and Alexander's distress on 'losing' Speransky, which a stronger man might have avoided, turned to dissatisfaction with his own agents.

Balashov thereupon ceased to direct the everyday affairs of the Ministry of Police. De Sanglen was relieved of his office and in March 1812 was sent to Vilno to report to the War Minister, Barclay de Tolly.[4] Neither man ever regained more than a part of the Emperor's confidence, although Balashov continued to hold his ministerial rank.

Alexander's words and actions on the eve of the War for the Fatherland show the extent to which he was prepared to use intrigue as a means of controlling his subordinates. This tendency was constantly deplored by de Sanglen who admitted to not having understood Alexander,[5] but the latter's policy of playing off one official against another meant that each was too concerned in protecting himself to become potentially dangerous to his master. And this perhaps explains the Tsar's readiness to encourage a sense of personal rivalry between one colleague and another. Shil'der comments that 'evidently the lessons of Napoleon, who put up with Talleyrand and Fouché among his collaborators and advisers, had not passed unnoticed and bore excellent fruit...'[6] By 1812 Alexander's sense of disillusionment had deepened still further and, with the removal of Speransky, he possibly felt

---

[1] 'Zapiski de Sanglena', pp. 24, 25. (No such consequences appear to have occurred because, according to one source, Balashov did not suspect that de Sanglen reported to the Emperor over his head. See M. A. Dmitriev, *Myelochi iz Zapasa moei Pamyati* (Moscow, 1869), p. 142.)

[2] *Ibid.* pp. 25, 34.   [3] *Ibid.* p. 384.

[4] *Ibid.* p. 394.

[5] *Ibid.* p. 394. It seems probable, however, that de Sanglen had formed an accurate estimate of some of Alexander's methods. Cf. 'It hurt me to think that Aleksandr Pavlovich preferred intrigue...', *ibid.* p. 46.   [6] Shil'der, vol. 3, p. 367 (note 62).

less inclined to place reliance on an institution that had come into being as a result of that statesman's influence. In any case the country was soon engaged in a major war in which both Balashov and de Sanglen could be and were employed in other capacities.[1]

Vyazmitinov and von Vock

The Ministry of Police now passed under the immediate control of the Military Governor-General of St Petersburg, Count Vyazmitinov.[2] The work of its Special Chancellery has never been studied,[3] and it is not certain that the post previously held by de Sanglen was thereupon entrusted to his chief assistant, M. Ya. von Vock,[4] who was to be in charge of secret police work for the remainder of the reign. It is however established that this able official began his important career in the early years of the Ministry of Police, in which he quickly attained a responsible position.

Von Vock had been appointed to the Special Chancellery by de Sanglen himself, who required a suitable deputy to report routine business to Balashov at hours when private consultations with Alexander necessitated his absence from the office. He first held 'the unimportant position of Duty Officer registering the reception and dispatch of the Minister's letters',[5] but

---

[1] Both men remained members of Alexander's personal suite. Balashov was sent as special envoy to Napoleon after the beginning of hostilities and thereafter was given various military and diplomatic missions. De Sanglen was appointed Director of the Military Police of the 1st Army and worked under the orders of the War Minister. Alexander made him responsible for the organization of counter-espionage and he subsequently became Army Provost-General, continuing in this rank until his retirement from active affairs in 1816, see *RBS* and his 'Zapiski', pp. 539 ff. (According to N. I. Grech, he was not trusted in this appointment and Kutuzov got rid of him. *Zapiski o moei Zhizni* (ed. Moscow–Leningrad, 1930), pp. 562–3.)
   Apparently neither man had any further direct contact with the Special Chancellery.

[2] See p. 32, note 5.

[3] Both Varadinov and Adrianov in their Histories of the Ministry of Internal Affairs (which include accounts of the Ministry of Police) limit their mention of the Special Chancellery to the fact of its existence and terms of reference, omitting any description of its work, methods or officials. Historians of the reign in its wider aspects merely quote one or the other of these authorities.

[4] Maksim Yakovlevich Fon-Fok (1777–1831). He is not recorded in the relevant volume of the *RBS* despite his importance in the Third Department from 1826 until his death. (His dates are given in the Notes of *Pushkin. Pis'ma*, ed. by B. L. Modzalyevsky, 3 vols. (Moscow–Leningrad, 1928), vol. 2 (1826–30), p. 426.)
   He was married to the daughter of one Doctor Frez of Moscow who had been doctor to de Sanglen's mother and had thus become acquainted with de Sanglen (Zapiski de Sanglena', p. 43). The Editor of *Russkaya Starina* refers to him as 'an extremely cultivated, subtle and exceedingly cunning man who spoke foreign languages excellently' (*ibid.* footnote).
   Lemke refers to the general testimony of his having been 'a man of undoubted education and good breeding', *op. cit.* p. 27. (His German surname was transcribed as Fok or, more usually, Fon-Fok by Russian writers.) Von Vock's later career in the Third Department is discussed in chapter Four.   [5] 'Zapiski de Sanglena', p. 43.

later de Sanglen felt obliged to confide in him and found this confidence was not misplaced. Von Vock did not inform Balashov that de Sanglen was spying on his superior, whether by order or not, thus proving loyal to his sponsor; at the same time he impressed Balashov with his capabilities. The latter even praised him to Alexander who, seeking de Sanglen's opinion, received the reply: 'He is a decent enough man,[1] Sire; but he has not betrayed me, his benefactor, because he is probably attracted by the idea of important gains in the future.' To which the Tsar rejoined: 'That is no recommendation, but indicates a man of capability. Intriguers are just as useful in a state as honest men; and sometimes the former are more useful than the latter.'[2] This equivocal viewpoint so typical of Alexander set the seal of approval on von Vock's appointment to the Special Chancellery and his work there evidently gave general satisfaction. Balashov eventually sent for de Sanglen only when von Vock was not available and de Sanglen entrusted his assistant with all routine business, reserving for himself only those reports specifically prepared for the Emperor.[3] In March 1812 a Ministry of Police order dealing with the confinement and treatment of special prisoners in the Alekseyevsky Ravyelin of the Petropavlovsky Fortress was countersigned by von Vock as 'Director'.[4] From the transfer in that month of his two immediate superiors to other spheres of activity, von Vock seems to have been the only official of the Special Chancellery to whom the conduct of its business could safely be entrusted; and the Acting Minister of Police Vyazmitinov evidently allowed his appointment to stand. From what is known of von Vock's views and personality some years later, it may be assumed that he did not consider it necessary or perhaps even possible to subject Russia to any very strict secret police control during and immediately after the life of the Ministry of Police. De Sanglen reports the following conversation between himself and Balashov in the early days of its existence.

DE SANGLEN: I may be mistaken, but it really seems to me that it is not worth keeping watch on Russians; they will gossip, criticize and perhaps do a bit of grumbling; but when it comes to the point, they will be completely subservient.

BALASHOV: Then you suggest that we need no spies?

DE SANGLEN: For foreigners, I agree; but not for Russians.[5]

Whether or not von Vock shared this point of view is unknown; at all events the secret police under his direction bore relatively little resemblance to its eighteenth-century predecessors and was not greatly feared.

---

[1] *Chelovyek nye durnoi.*   [2] *Ibid.* p. 44.   [3] *Ibid.* p. 377.
[4] N. I. Sidorov, 'Iz Zapisnoi Knizhki Arkhivista', *Krasnyi Arkhiv* (1925), no. 10, p. 323.
[5] 'Zapiski de Sanglena', p. 36.

Trotsky contends, nevertheless, that the work of the Special Chancellery was based on 'a subtle organization' of espionage and provocation 'as used by Fouché';[1] and although he quotes no evidence to support this assertion there seems no reason to doubt that such methods persisted, albeit on a comparatively modest scale, according to the established tradition of all Russia's secret chancelleries. It may be assumed that von Vock kept himself informed on current events from reports submitted by various sources ranging from petty sneak-thieves—whether recruited or voluntary[2]—to his own secret 'agents provocateurs'. One such man, Fogel', is known to have been introduced into the Schlüssel'burgsky Fortress in 1812 in the guise of a prisoner.[3] Other methods included the obtaining of information through postal interception[4] and the provisions of the censorship regulations. The stringency of the latter gradually increased until by 1815 the Ministry of Public Education could allow nothing to be printed without the consent of the Ministry of Police.[5] Von Vock personally, however, remained always in the background, drawing little attention to either himself or the Special Chancellery.[6] Indeed it is questionable whether von Vock, from the point of view of his superiors, may not have been guilty of a somewhat negligent attitude to his duties. He undoubtedly countenanced the activities of groups and individuals who might have been thought to represent a potential danger to the government,[7] as later events strongly disproved de Sanglen's

[1] Trotsky, p. 19.   [2] *Ibid.*

[3] Gernet, vol. I, pp. 206–7. In later years Fogel' became Head of a Secret Police office organized by the Governor-General of St Petersburg. See p. 45.

[4] See article ('Iz Zapisnoi Knizhki Arkhivista') 'O Perlyustratsii Pisem v nachale XIX vyeka' publ. in *Krasnyi Arkhiv* (1927), no. 25, pp. 201–4.

   The article discusses the long-established prevalence of this practice with particular reference to the provisions for the interception of correspondence included in the instructions issued to the 1805 and 1807 Committees; and quotes a series of unpublished letters on this subject that passed between O. P. Kozodavlev (Minister of Internal Affairs) and D. P. Runich (Moscow Postmaster-General) during the years 1813–17. The letters merely prove that franking did exist—in circumstances of extreme secrecy—but the article does not refer to the specific responsibility for this of the Ministry of Police. Despite the probability of interdepartmental rivalry, it may be assumed that some link existed between Kozodavlev's department and von Vock's. The latter was responsible both for Censorship and for the administration of the Address Office. But as the Postal Department was controlled by the Ministry of Internal Affairs (Ukazes of 9 June 1806, no. 22168 and 25 July 1810, no. 24307), it is probable that the information obtained from that source by Kozodavlev was passed to the Special Chancellery for its attention.

[5] A. Kornilov, *Kurs Istorii Rossii XIX vyeka*, 2-oe izd. (Moscow, 1918), pt 1, p. 234.

[6] Even Lemke mentions only the existence of an espionage organization in the Ministry of Police (p. 9) and includes no details of its Special Chancellery; and Trotsky's more recent information would seem to indicate that little available material on it is to be found in the Archives.

[7] 'Its [the Special Chancellery's] activities were inconspicuous, especially after the taking of Paris. Everyone talked boldly, even indiscreetly, according to his desire: the time was most suitable for the propagation of free-thinking' (Vigel', vol. 2, p. 273). It may be recalled that the years 1815–20 witnessed the creation of numerous semi-secret societies whose members later formed the nucleus of the Decembrist Movement.

contention that it was not worth keeping watch on Russians. The explanation probably lies in the fact that, as an educated man, von Vock himself sympathized with the spirit of the age and may well have underestimated its inherent menace to the autocratic system.

Outside the direct sphere of the Special Chancellery but closely related to the internal security of the country, the immediate post-Napoleonic era witnessed various changes in the structure of Russia's security regulations.[1] These changes were merely of an organizational character, representing a natural stage in the development of the forces controlling public law and order; but they are of interest to the present study in so far as they led to the creation of trained cadres subsequently available for reallocation to the more centralized police network of the Nicholas régime.

Military Police

Military Police were introduced for the first time in 1815, when the independent gendarme 'commands' of General Barclay de Tolly created in that year were replaced by the 'Gendarme Regiment' formed from the Borisoglebsky Dragoon Regiment.[2] As regards the civil police, Internal Security Troops were re-formed into an Independent Corps in 1816 and their 'Inspector', General Komarovsky, was appointed to command it.[3] Although theoretically the Minister of Police was authorized[4] to issue instructions to and request information from all civil and military headquarters dealing with security, it appears unlikely that this was in fact the practice. The Corps of Internal Security Troops and the Army Gendarme Regiment were basically military bodies, whereas the Special Chancellery was merely a Ministerial department headed by a civilian of apparently retiring character. The absence of references in published official documents to von Vock's position would seem to indicate that neither he nor the Acting Minister of Police, Vyazmitinov, exercised their authority in security matters primarily concerning military units.[5]

---

[1] See Adrianov, pp. 97–8.

[2] Ukaz of 27 Aug. 1815. *Poln. Sobr. Zak.* vol. 33, pp. 267–8, no. 25929. This 'Army Gendarme Regiment' was later placed in a privileged position by the allotment to it of double pay. See Ukaz of 26 Oct. 1816. *Poln. Sobr. Zak.* vol. 33, p. 1056, no. 26467.

[3] Ukaz of 30 March 1816. *Poln. Sobr. Zak.* vol. 33, p. 589, no. 26216. Details of its new status were published in a further Ukaz of 1 Feb. 1817, no. 26650; and subsequent recruitment to the Corps from the lower ranks of Army Cavalry Regiments was authorized by an Ukaz of 29 Apr. 1822, no. 29019.

[4] See p. 31, note 5.

[5] Even General Komarovsky, through whose personal recommendation Balashov was first appointed to Police rank (see his *Zapiski*, p. 142) and who, in his official capacity, must have been aware of the responsibilities of the Special Chancellery, makes no reference to it or to von Vock in his memoirs.

It may hence be concluded that the office originally intended to act as a powerful political police with centralized authority was largely in abeyance[1] after the removal from its control of Balashov and de Sanglen.

The Ministry of Police, 1819

On 15 October 1819 Vyazmitinov died, whereupon Balashov temporarily reassumed the duties he had relinquished seven years before. Nineteen days later, however, his post was abolished and the majority of the departments which had hitherto formed part of the Ministry of Police were incorporated 'for the improved distribution of business' into the Ministry of Internal Affairs.[2]

The Ministry of Police was never reconstituted as such in succeeding periods of Russian history. It had existed eight years, after which it was seen to be not so much unpopular[3] as inefficient. Varadinov, although he paid a measure of tribute to Vyazmitinov's work as 'director', went on to state that 'all sections...did not succeed in attaining that degree of governmental maturity which would have enabled it to achieve radical reforms', even adding that 'Count Sergei Koz'mich did not organize in its final form one single branch of the Ministry entrusted to him'.[4] Few historians have sought to assess the reasons for its abolition,[5] which indeed reflected little if any change in Russian internal policy. The most probable explanation may be traced to a divergence of views on the application of the wide powers originally delegated to this Ministry, powers which were 'so loosely defined that quarrels and disputes as to its competence constantly occurred'.[6] But in addition to the administrative disorder thus caused, high state officials were also irritated by the inevitable misuse of police authority when entrusted to ignorant and venal agents. Kochubei, who was again Minister of Internal Affairs in 1819 and therefore once more responsible for all police bodies, wrote to the Emperor: 'Entrusted to M. Balashov, the Ministry of Police soon fell short of its purpose, that of general surveillance... M. Balashov thought himself obliged to turn it into a Ministry of Espionage. The city is peopled with spies of every kind; there have been foreign ones, paid Russian ones and voluntary ones; police officers have been constantly engaged in

[1] This view is confirmed by the comment of the nineteenth-century émigré Dolgorukov, who states that throughout its life the Ministry of Police 'operated with great moderation'. P. Dolgoroukow [sic], *La Vérité sur la Russie* (Paris, 1860), p. 294.

[2] Ukaz of 4 November 1819. *Poln. Sobr. Zak.* vol. 36, p. 367, no. 27964.

[3] Vigel', for instance, does not mention its disappearance.

[4] Varadinov, pt 2 (1810–19), p. 625.

[5] Adrianov gives no explanation for its abolition (see pp. 39–45). Shil'der is equally reticent (*op. cit.* vol. 4, p. 174).

[6] Theodor Schiemann, *Geschichte Russlands unter Kaiser Nikolaus I* (Berlin, 1908), vol. 2, p. 96.

changing their costumes; it is even alleged that the Minister himself has resorted to disguise. These agents have not been confining themselves to gathering news and making it possible for the government to anticipate crimes; they have been seeking to incite crimes and suspicions...'[1] Baron Korff confirms this view, referring to this Ministry as 'a police office half of which spent its time robbing and the other half in engaging in espionage, investigations and slander. From its early formation it was universally discredited and lost all public confidence...'[2] The evil reputation of the Ministry of Police may be considered the main factor affecting Nicholas' decision that the direction of Russia's secret police in his reign should be entrusted to men of a different calibre. The Ministry's Special Chancellery had proved itself ineffective, despite the fact that its authority was theoretically strong enough to guarantee the country's security in every aspect. An English traveller who left Russia in 1819 bears witness[3] to the meticulous regulations of the Address Office, but his strictures on the venality and rapacity of police officials clearly indicate the rottenness of the existing system. Von Vock, however, by all accounts an intelligent and honourable servant of the state, cannot be held primarily responsible for its deficiencies, which were chiefly due to the absence of education and the low state of morality of most if not all of his subordinates.

The Special Chancellery

Von Vock continued to direct Russia's official secret police after the reallocation of the Special Chancellery to the Ministry of Internal Affairs. Its organization remained unchanged except for the inclusion of a 'Censorship Committee' to control printed matter,[4] but for various reasons proved no more effective than before.[5] Alexander, disillusioned by his past experience of

---

[1] Korff, p. 487 (taken from the French text of the Kochubei family papers—'Arkhiv Knyazya Kochubeya'). See also Trotsky, p. 20.

[2] Korff, p. 485.

[3] Robert Lyall, M.D., *The Character of the Russians and a Detailed History of Moscow* (London, 1823), pp. 108, cxlvi.

[4] See Varadinov, pt 2, p. 604.

[5] Dolgorukov goes so far as to state that for practical purposes the political police was non-existent from 1819 to 1825 (*op. cit.* p. 294). Another source states: '...l'espionnage dans l'intérieur de l'Empire était à peine connu de son [l'Empereur Alexandre] temps. Il y avait bien une direction de la haute police; mais les fonctions du chef de cette direction se bornaient presque à présenter de temps en temps au gouvernement des rapports sur l'état de l'opinion publique; et comme ce chef était un homme probe et éclairé (M. Fock...), les avertissements qu'il donnait au pouvoir ne pourraient qu'être utiles et salutaires. En effet, souvent il ne parlait, dans les rapports, que du juste mécontentement que le public éprouvait de telle ou telle mesure adoptée par le gouvernement, de telle ou telle oppression exercée par les autorités envers des populations sans défense' (N. Tourguéneff, *La Russie et les Russes*, 3 vols. (Paris, 1847), vol. 2, p. 517, note).

men like Balashov and de Sanglen, was even less inclined to place any confidence in this branch,[1] and Arakcheyev, whose influence over the Emperor now made him the most powerful man in Russia, was a dangerous enemy to every other Minister. Count Kochubei abhorred the work of a secret police, and the aged Lanskoi, who replaced him in 1823, took little interest in it.[2] The truth is that all highly placed officials felt insecure during the last five years of Alexander's reign. N. I. Grech stated in his memoirs:

Kochubei left good memories behind him, although he was not what he might have been had circumstances been different—both from above and from below and especially from sideways. No Minister could act honourably and usefully in the vicinity of Count Arakcheyev...Count Kochubei was so high-minded in all respects that it was impossible to injure him: and so attempts were made to deal with the functionaries of his department, to be exact, the most noble of them, M. Ya. Fon-Fok [sic], and he would certainly have been destroyed had Alexander not died. It is difficult to hold a pen in one's hand when describing this blindness of emperors, this vile behaviour of rascals, this impotence of honest men. Poor Russia!...[3]

No secret police organization could possibly function efficiently in the face of such obstacles.

The attitude of Alexander

The Tsar's disillusionment at the failure of the Ministry of Police was far from being the only factor which governed his future attitude to national problems. Other events inside Russia and far beyond her borders combined to increase his misgivings. At home, the revolt of the Semyonovsky Regiment in 1820 engendered in him fears that the spirit of revolution had penetrated from Europe into his Empire. Abroad, established authority was being undermined in Germany, Spain, Naples and finally Greece. In the interests of the Holy Alliance Prince Metternich was quick to seize every opportunity of influencing the Tsar and aggravating his fears of 'liberalism' by forwarding from Vienna a constant supply of police reports. One source states, albeit doubtless with some exaggeration, that Alexander maintained an almost daily correspondence with Metternich and relied on his information in preference to that of his own subordinates.[4]

---

[1] It is worth noting that von Vock at this period was a mere 'Statskii Sovyetnik' (Vigel', vol. 2, p. 258), thus ranking between a Colonel and a Major-General. Unlike de Sanglen, he does not appear to have had direct access to the Tsar.

[2] Vigel', ibid.

[3] Grech, pp. 533–4. The author was acquainted with both men at this period (pp. 411–12) and tells how von Vock himself hourly expected imprisonment in 1821 as a result of the intrigues of Magnitsky (p. 421). One of his Assistant Censors, the Lerkhe already referred to (see p. 34, note 4), was in fact imprisoned in August 1825 (ibid.).

[4] Comtesse de Boigne, Memoirs, 4 vols. (ed. London, 1908), vol. 3, ch. 13, p. 140.

Certain of the latter, however, presented him with circumstantial evidence of domestic conspiracies. The prevalence of secret societies in Russia and more particularly their popularity in military circles impelled one of his Generals-in-Waiting, Prince Vasil'chikov, the G.O.C. of the Corps of Guards, to forward to his Emperor,[1] then abroad attending a conference at Laibach, a project advocating the creation of a special military police and urging that it should operate 'in impenetrable secrecy'.[2] And no sooner had Alexander returned from Laibach than Vasil'chikov further submitted a detailed report on political conspiracies drawn up before the Semyonovsky Regiment mutiny and containing a list of implicated persons. 'The Tsar, after hearing these exposures which were evidently no surprise to him, remained pensive and silent for a long while, buried in profound and reflective thought; he then uttered the following words in French—words of important historic significance—'Mon cher Wassiltschikoff! Vous qui êtes à mon service depuis le commencement de mon règne, vous savez que j'ai partagé et encouragé ces illusions et ces erreurs', continuing after a long silence: 'Ce n'est pas à moi à sévir.'[3] This reaction, typical of Alexander's outlook in the final years of his reign, goes far to explain the inevitable powerlessness of any police organization, civil or military, which might have undertaken effective counter-measures.

Vasil'chikov was not the only high official who attempted to bring home to the Tsar the need for action. In 1821 another General-in-Waiting, Benckendorff, then Chief of Staff of the Corps of Guards, submitted a detailed Memorandum on Secret Societies, mentioning by name the very men who four years later headed the Decembrist Revolt (the Muravyovs, Trubetskoi, Pestel', Fon-Vizin and others).[4] Benckendorff stressed that 'a vigilant surveillance and the adoption of moderate but unremitting measures could gradually avert the danger',[5] but Alexander stubbornly refused to take any action whatsoever and this Memorandum evidently brought its author into some disfavour.[6] The Tsar, then more concerned with his mood of

---

[1] December 1820.

[2] Lemke, pp. 8–9. The text, entitled 'Proyekt o Ustroistve Voyennoi Politsii pri Gvardyeiskom Korpuse', is printed in *R. Star.* (1882), vol. 33, pp. 217–19. Vasil'chikov's project was approved on 4 Jan. 1821 and a certain Gribovsky was appointed its Director. A similar body was also instituted in the 2nd Army on the request of its Chief of Staff, Kiselyov. (*Ibid.*) Little is known of Gribovsky's activities (see note 4) and he seems to have played no part in the reorganization of the Secret Police in 1826. (*N.B.* The relevant vol. of the *RBS*—Gog to Dab—did not appear.)   [3] Shil'der, vol. 4, pp. 203–4.

[4] Shil'der, *ibid.* p. 204. The text of this Memorandum entitled 'Zapiska Benkendorfa o Tainykh Obshchestvakh v Rossii' may be found in Lemke, *Prilozhenie I*, pp. 575–81. Okun' states that this document was based on a denunciation of the 'Soyuz Blagodyenstviya' submitted by Gribovsky, a former member. S. B. Okun', *Istoriya SSSR 1796–1825* (Leningrad, 1948), p. 396.   [5] Lemke, p. 581.

[6] Shil'der, *ibid.* pp. 215, 472 (note 257). See chapter Four, p. 112.

religious mysticism than with the unhappy condition of his country, had become increasingly reluctant to adopt repressive measures, no matter how urgent the need, and Benckendorff's practical foresight was not to be rewarded until after his worst fears had been realized and a new Sovereign was impelled to introduce a different policy for ensuring internal security.

All sources agree that after the abolition of the Ministry of Police Alexander never sanctioned the direction of secret police affairs by one central authority. Instead, he tacitly permitted the existence of several secret police forces, each operating independently to the inevitable detriment of the national interest. Secret investigations were conducted individually by Arakcheyev, then virtually the ruler of Russia, by Miloradovich, the Military Governor-General of St Petersburg, by the Special Chancellery of the Ministry of Internal Affairs and, in the Army, by the Gendarme Regiment and Gribovsky's organization.[1] Von Vock succeeded in retaining his office as Head of the Special Chancellery, but his functions were in practice usurped by Arakcheyev and Miloradovich.[2] Although secret societies were banned in 1822, no real attempt was made to curb their activities and it is noteworthy that none of the above authorities succeeded in penetrating the Decembrist conspiracies.[3] This was primarily due to the absence of a centralized secret police organization, a state of affairs aggravated by the fact that all offices conducting political investigations invariably engaged in spying upon one another.[4] Furthermore, revolutionary upheavals abroad encouraged police agents in their belief that foreigners were more worthy of suspicion than Russians, and the Head of Miloradovich's organization, Fogel', subsequently admitted that 'in spying on every foreign hairdresser he failed to notice the Decembrist Conspiracy'.[5] As must have been evident to even partially informed observers, 'it would have been easy for the government, once it discovered the truth, to remove the guilty from the positions they occupied; and because they were so few in number, mere threats and strict supervision would have been sufficient to restrain them...'[6] What was lacking was any

[1] See Trotsky, p. 22.

[2] Grech, p. 711. Vigel' comments: 'That gallant knight Miloradovich turned himself into a voluntary spy-leader and tormented the Tsar every evening with whole note-books of denunciations, mostly false ones...' (*op. cit.* vol. 2, p. 258).

[3] Trotsky, pp. 22–3. Only Count I. O. Vitt, Chief of the Southern Settlements, discovered their activities through his local organization. (*Ibid.*)

[4] Miloradovich, for instance, constantly spied upon Arakcheyev (*ibid.*). Details of this 'mutual investigation' may be found in S. B. Okun', *Ocherki Istorii SSSR. Konyets XVIII–Pervaya Chetvert' XIX vyeka* (Leningrad, 1956), p. 300.

[5] Trotsky, p. 27.

[6] Vigel', p. 274. He attributes the failure of the government to take action to the private sympathies of von Vock; but, as has been shown, von Vock at this period held infinitely less responsibility than Arakcheyev or Miloradovich and is not known to have exerted any influence on the Tsar.

firm directive to ensure the political security and stability of the country. Only Alexander could have issued this, and administrative chaos was the inevitable consequence of his failure to do so.

The preliminary phase. Conclusions

The development of the Secret Police in the first quarter of the nineteenth century was marked by two constant factors: the absence of continuity in the government's attitude to the work of its political police and, with very few exceptions, the ignorant and venal officials who formed its staff.

After his accession the young Alexander undoubtedly hoped that it would prove possible to dispense with this cankerous institution altogether, and although the Committees of 1805 and 1807 to some extent embodied powers previously incorporated in the Secret Chancelleries of his father and grandmother, essentially they may be regarded as wartime expedients. Their existence was not known to the general public and neither contemporary accounts nor historians have commented on them adversely. The Special Chancellery of the 1811 Ministry of Police appears to have been considered a retrograde step in administrative policy, but never became the kind of Secret Inquisition associated with its eighteenth-century predecessors. The appointments of Balashov and de Sanglen earned little approval, but their tenure of responsibility for secret police affairs was short and neither appears to have inspired either respect or dread. Their successor, von Vock, was never more than a minor official of the Ministry of Police and later of that of Internal Affairs. Indeed, he might never have been known to history but for the part he played in the secret police of the following reign. Alexander's gradual disillusionment with men and events after the end of the Napoleonic Wars resulted in an increasingly apathetic attitude to questions of internal administration, and his deputy Arakcheyev was universally hated and distrusted. Thus it may be contended that Alexander was personally to blame for allowing a situation to arise in which no 'security organization' could feel secure from its rivals and therefore be itself in a position to safeguard public welfare. Nor is there any evidence that the officials and agents who worked in the various secret polices of the last five years of the reign were sufficiently honest, intelligent or competent to prove adequate guardians of the state's interests.[1] Bribery was universal[2] and the low-grade agents used

---

[1] Grech comments: 'In the latter years of Alexander's reign the old policy of the torture-chamber ["staraya zastyenochnaya politika"] again began to make itself felt' (*op. cit.* p. 104).

A Frenchman who witnessed the conduct of secret agents on the eve of the Decembrist Revolt commented on the need for foreigners to carry bribes with them to avert possible unpleasantness (J. B. May, *Saint Pétersbourg et la Russie en 1829*, 2 vols. (Paris, 1830), vol. 1, ch. 8, p. 107).

for investigating suspects submitted reports containing mere nonsense. The general standard of education was so poor that frequently agents had no idea of the meaning of such words as Carbonari, Liberals and similar appellations, and did not understand the conversation of higher class persons.[1] Even had some form of secret police training been envisaged, it is unlikely that suitable candidates for it were available in Alexander's Russia. Nor can it be assumed that the Tsar ever became fully reconciled to the necessity of an effective political police. He certainly did not lack advice on the subject. On the other hand, he knew from personal experience that few men were to be trusted and the Ministry of Police had been, after all, a remarkably unsuccessful venture. As regards Alexander's attitude to the secret police question during the final years of his reign, it is not clear whether he was personally aware of all the various offices engaged in the work of political investigation, nor whether he continued to maintain his earlier expressed view that intriguers were sometimes more useful to the state than honest men. Historians have thrown no light on this problem. Possibly he was aware of the existence of individual secret polices and preferred to allow them to dissipate their strength against each other, knowing that anyway in the prevailing circumstances little good would come from them. Possibly he remained intentionally ignorant of their petty ramifications and indifferent to them, never having overcome his early feelings of repugnance for work of this nature. (This conjecture seems credible in view of his reluctance to pay due heed to Benckendorff's Memorandum.) Or possibly he was simply resigned to events taking their natural course. Whatever reasons underlay his refusal to combine all secret police organizations into one central headquarters, their general inefficiency led to the outbreak of open conspiracy after the news of his death, and his successor was then forced to adopt a more realistic policy resulting in the formation of the Third Department.

[1] Trotsky, p. 26.

2

The History of the Creation of the Third Department

The rod, that symbol of justice, should never be allowed to remain inactive—it should thrive like the rod of Moses.

Von Vock to Benckendorff in a letter dated 22 September 1826[1]

The accession of Nicholas

It will be recalled that one of the first acts of Alexander on his accession in 1801 was the abolition of the hated 'Secret Office' in order to pave the way for what he hoped was to prove a new era in Russian history. A quarter of a century later came conclusive proof that these hopes were illusory. The social and political scene confronting his younger brother Nicholas in 1825 was of a radically different order. The very foundations of autocratic rule were menaced by the changes in social thought brought about by the growth of revolutionary successes abroad and their influence on internal politics at home; and the dismal episode of the Decembrist Revolt profoundly affected the attitude of the new Emperor towards his subjects. The uncertainty surrounding the events of his succession, the evidence of widespread if ill-organized political conspiracy, the fact of his personal unpopularity—all combined to convince Nicholas that if the autocracy he represented was to survive in its current guise he must embark on a policy embodying not less authority but more.

The character of Nicholas is too well known to require extensive additional comment in these pages except in so far as it was reflected in the development of the political police during his reign. In 1825 he was a man of twenty-nine who had not hitherto played any outstanding rôle in the life of the nation. Temperamentally he differed greatly from his elder brother in never having displayed the smallest inclination towards liberalism and having, on the contrary, already earned in army circles the reputation of a martinet. 'The predilection for things military displayed by Nikolai Pavlovich from his early years remained the basic feature of his character and never left him even after his accession.'[2] Regulations of one kind and another were the ruling passion of a somewhat narrow mind and till the day of his death he tried to insist on the enforced acceptance by his subjects of the two principles

[1] *Russkaya Starina* (1881), vol. 32, p. 554.   [2] Shil'der, *Imperator Nikolai Pervyi*, vol. 1, p. 15.

of Order and Obedience. Those writers who have dealt in detail with the effect of Nicholas' personality on his internal administration have, in the main, tended to show that the nickname of Nikolai-Palkin (Nicholas the Flogger) bestowed upon him by his innumerable enemies was more often than not justifiable.[1] At the same time it is difficult to see how Nicholas could have acted differently in the specific circumstances of his upbringing and the events accompanying his accession. As he himself was aware on 14 December, his own life and that of autocratic rule in Russia were placed in considerable jeopardy; and once the danger that threatened both had been at least temporarily surmounted, Nicholas could hardly be blamed for taking what seemed to him the best possible measures to avert any recurrence of so potentially grave a menace. It was patently obvious that no reliance could be placed on the security organs of his brother's régime. Even assuming that Alexander had personally paid insufficient heed to the problem of the state's internal security, the various individual systems of political surveillance that had been active during recent years had manifestly failed to achieve positive results. Now that the Decembrist Revolt was over, the new Tsar could review the situation in the light of such blatant inefficiency in matters of security.

Arakcheyev had voluntarily retired from any further participation in national affairs and was, in any case, no favourite of Nicholas. Miloradovich had been killed by an insurgent's bullet on Senate Square. There remained the Special Chancellery of the Ministry of Internal Affairs, whose efforts had been largely invalidated by the machinations of politicians on the one hand and rival police networks on the other. Clearly some new system of political surveillance conducted along very different lines was imperative in a situation aggravated by fears that the recent revolt might be the precursor of Revolution.

Benckendorff's project

General-in-Waiting Benckendorff, a man thirteen years his senior and of undoubted courage and distinction, had enjoyed the favour of Nicholas when the latter was Grand Duke, and on 14 December he earned the deep gratitude of the new Tsar by the prominent part he played in the suppression of the mutiny[2] as the Commander of all troops quartered on Vasilevsky Ostrov. It is thus not surprising that he should have been appointed on 17 December one of the members of the Secret Committee empowered to investigate the

---

[1] See evidence summarized by Lemke, *Nikolayevskie Zhandarmy*, pp. 1–4.

[2] 'Il [Nicolas] avait vu à l'œuvre, ce jour-là, l'aide-de-camp général Benckendorff, ayant l'œil à tout, se multipliant, se portant avec un prodigieux entrain sur tous les points de l'insurrection, donnant à tous l'exemple du sang-froid, de la fermeté et du courage.' Paul Lacroix, *Histoire de la Vie et du Règne de Nicolas I-er, Empereur de Russie*, 7 vols. (Paris, 1864–73), vol. 2, p. 231.

Decembrist Conspiracy.[1] Benckendorff's proved bravery and loyalty at Nicholas' accession were not, however, the only reasons which prompted the Tsar to promote him six months later to a position of unrivalled authority in Russia's internal administration.

After the death of Alexander, Benckendorff's 1821 Memorandum on Secret Societies was found in the Tsar's study at Tsarskoe Selo—without any notes on it.[2] This document had contained, besides its exposure of political conspiracies in the country, positive proposals for the safeguarding of the national interest by the creation of a 'gendarmerie' on the French model. In the words of Prince Volkonsky, the Decembrist: 'He submitted that the introduction of this branch of spies, if based on honourable principles and on the recruitment of honest and intelligent persons, might well be of use to the Tsar and the fatherland, and he prepared a project for the institution of this office; he invited us, many of his comrades, to enter this cohort, as he called it, of right-thinking men, and me among them. The project was submitted but not approved.'[3] But now that the political scene had changed and Benckendorff's own standing had improved, he lost no time in effecting certain alterations to his proposals and presenting the new Tsar in the first days of January 1826 with 'A Project for the Organization of a Higher Police'.[4] In it Benckendorff modestly made no reference to his earlier proposals, contenting himself with the observation that recent events had shown the uselessness of the existing police and the 'indispensable necessity' of organizing this branch along different lines. He envisaged the creation of a Minister of Police and Inspector of Gendarmes, stressing the importance of the moral qualities required by the holder of this post and the effect that would be produced on public opinion by the appointment of a man possessing the necessary character. This emphasis on what may be termed 'a moral approach' to the problem of political surveillance represents one of the most interesting aspects of Benckendorff's Project, showing that he was fully conscious of the highly undesirable features of earlier 'Secret Chancelleries'. 'A secret police is almost impossible; honest folk are terrified

---

[1] Shil'der, vol. I, p. 329. The appointment was announced in the press on 5 Jan. 1826, *ibid.* p. 332.
[2] Shil'der, *Imperator Aleksandr Pervyi*, vol. 4, p. 204. Note 254 on p. 471 states: 'On the envelope in which the Memorandum is preserved is a pencilled note in Benckendorff's handwriting: 'Le papier en question retrouvé l'année 25 dans le cabinet de l'Empereur Alexandre à Zarskoe Selo. Donné l'année 21.' On the Memorandum Benckendorff noted: 'Remis à l'Empereur l'année 21 — 4 ans avant l'évènement du 14 Décembre 1825.' Shil'der comments in this Note that Benckendorff's Memorandum constituted the main reason why the Emperor Nicholas subsequently appointed its author Head of the Corps of Gendarmes and the Third Department.
[3] *Zapiski Sergiya Grigor'evicha Volkonskago*, izd. Kn. M. S. Volkonskago (SPB, 1901), p. 135. Lemke believes, on the basis of Volkonsky's evidence, that Benckendorff submitted two memoranda to Alexander, one on Secret Societies and the other a project for a Gendarmerie, pp. 11, 20. Shil'der does not confirm this.
[4] The complete text of this Project in its original French is given as Appendix A, pp. 239–40.

of it, rogues sense its presence.' Therefore, he reasoned, this branch must acquire and deserve a wholly novel reputation, to be earned primarily by those destined to become its servants. In this way all civil and military authorities would come to look upon it as an aid and ally, for surely this approach would greatly contribute to the interests of the state. 'Every respectable person recognizes and desires the necessity of a vigilant police to preserve public order and to anticipate crimes and disturbances. But every man is apprehensive of a police based on denunciations and intrigues. The former gives honest folk the feeling of security, the latter terrifies them and alienates them from the throne.' While the appeal of these admirable truths may readily be appreciated, it is difficult not to feel that Benckendorff's proposals revealed a surprising naïveté of outlook and that such idealism was too far removed from the harsh realities of Russia's political administration in the mid-1820s. He sounded a note of caution in the final paragraph—'When this question is decided in principle, a plan must be formulated which, from the nature of its importance, cannot be done in haste but should be the result of mature consideration and even that of actual experience'—but he never afterwards renounced the high principles set out in his Project, and these may be considered to have provided the theoretical basis for the policy of the new Secret Police.

It is interesting to note here that his advocacy of a department served by 'honest' officials accurately reflects the identical sentiments of an earlier 'project-writer', Pososhkov, who had expressed this notion some hundred years before.[1] And a more contemporary reformer, in the person of the leading Decembrist, Colonel Pestel', included this provision in his *Russkaya Pravda*.

Though in the domain of economics Pestel' was a staunch believer in a *laissez faire* policy, in politics he evidently had less faith in the citizen, who, he insisted, must be watched by a special secret political police in order to prevent any possible subversive activity. Alongside the civil liberties which Pestel' was willing to grant, the prospect of a civil police spying upon the free individual seems a little illogical. But Pestel' assures the citizen that for such a task the state would have to select only wise and honest men, men of irreproachable character. However...Pestel' overlooked the fact that people of such admirable quality are not usually inclined to engage in such an occupation.[2]

[1] '...it would be fitting that a Special Chancellery ["Osoblivaya Kantselyariya"] should be created in which the director ["pravityel'"] should be a man most close and loyal to the Tsar. That he should be the Tsar's eye, a faithful eye, and that he should be supreme above all judges and officials and should maintain an all-powerful surveillance over all authorities, fearing none but God and his Imperial Majesty. And to this Chancellery there should be the freest access, and this director himself should be easy of approach and to all persons should be kind and not severe...' I. T. Pososhkov, *Kniga o Skudosti i Bogatstve* (ed. Moscow, 1951), pp. 85–6.
[2] A. G. Mazour, *The First Russian Revolution 1825* (California, 1937), ch. 4, p. 108.

Like Pestel', Benckendorff also showed himself insufficiently aware of this obvious incongruity. An efficient and respected secret police force requires, it is true, to be served by men not only of the highest integrity but of intelligence, and therefore education, to match it. In the Russia of Alexander and Nicholas these qualities were possessed by relatively few men; and the ideal secret police outlined in Benckendorff's Project suffered accordingly.

A further contradiction deserves mention here. In his anxiety that this new body should act as a centralized agency for receiving information and in general for lending a helping hand where required, Benckendorff was apparently prepared to sacrifice that degree of secrecy which is usually inseparable from all forms of political surveillance. 'Rogues, intriguers or dupes who repent of their mistakes or who endeavour to atone for their guilt by means of denunciations would know where to apply.' And, despite a proviso that the future Minister should be on his guard 'not to place positive confidence in anyone in particular' and 'that even the Head of his Chancellery should not know all his employees and agents', presumably in order to safeguard the preservation of secrecy, his proposal that the officials of this Ministry should 'wear a uniform as servants of the government' was nothing less than absurd. Admittedly this suggestion was submitted in the belief that thus the natural repugnance of honest men for the work of secret espionage might be overcome, but it seemingly escaped Benckendorff's notice that political investigation is, by its very nature, a clandestine proceeding and that to reduce its secrecy is to deny it its strongest weapon.

Despite these contradictions Benckendorff's Project was seriously considered and, with few alterations, was accepted by Nicholas as the blueprint for one of the most important administrative innovations of his reign.[1]

Nicholas' Chancellery

It seems probable, however, that what mainly influenced the new Tsar in this matter was the lack of control exercised by his predecessor over the officials entrusted with the direction of secret police affairs. He was hence unwilling to favour Benckendorff's proposal that this direction should be confided to a Minister of Police.[2] Shil'der suggests that he was discouraged from doing so by memories of the Napoleonic era, linked with the names of Fouché and

[1] 'Apart from this general Project, Benckendorff later presented Nicholas with several more private ones relating to individual aspects of the organization of gendarmes, but unfortunately it has so far been impossible to find them', Lemke, p. 13.

[2] It is possible that the views of General Diebich and Count P. A. Tolstoi, to whom Benckendorff's Project was sent for perusal in April (see Appendix A, note, p. 240), may have induced Nicholas to renounce the idea of a reinstituted Ministry of Police; but their reactions to Benckendorff's proposals are not known, see Lemke, p. 14.

Savary.[1] In addition he was unfavourably impressed by the lack of success achieved by Alexander's Ministry of Police under Balashov and Vyazmitinov.[2] For all these reasons Nicholas decided to divide its functions into two distinct halves, with the Ministry of Internal Affairs responsible only for the administration of the normal overt police force, the so-called 'Lower Police'. The 'Higher' or political Police would in future become his personal concern and be controlled by officials immediately subordinated to his own Chancellery.

The office known as 'His Imperial Majesty's Own Chancellery' was not itself a new creation. Throughout the nineteenth century the Sovereign's private office had been known as his or her 'kabinet' or 'kantselyariya' and had slowly grown in importance until by the reign of Paul it became the nerve-centre of the whole administrative machine. It temporarily lost this influence in 1802 with the establishment of Ministries, but was reinstituted[3] in 1812 to deal with all reports and questions subject to Imperial review. From 1812 to 1825 it was controlled by Arakcheyev. Under Nicholas its sphere of competence was extended until it included a number of independent Departments equal in importance to Ministries.[4] The advantage of this expansion of H.I.M. Own Chancellery from the point of view of the Tsar was clear. In future he could much more effectively exert his personal influence on the direction of such branches of the country's internal administration as he considered of primary importance to its safety and welfare; and it is typical of Nicholas that his attitude towards his Chancellery should so closely have resembled that of a Colonel to his staff. The officials of his Chancellery Headquarters were put into uniforms conforming to the Civil Service rank of the wearer.[5] And just as Headquarters must expand with the additional duties they assume, so His Majesty's Chancellery gradually extended its control over a number of administrative branches.[6] Its First Department performed the former functions of Arakcheyev's office and dealt with affairs of state awaiting the Imperial decision. The duties of the Second Department[7]

[1] Shil'der, *Imperator Nikolai Pervyi*, vol. 1, p. 464. (Future references to Shil'der apply to this work only.)
[2] A. Kornilov, *Kurs Istorii Rossii xix-go vyeka*, 2-oe izd. (Moscow, 1918), pt 2, Lecture xv, p. 32.
[3] No ukaz authorizing its reinstitution is included in the *Poln. Sobr. Zak.*
[4] V. Rudakov: article entitled 'Sobstvennaya Yego Imperatorskago Velichestva kantselyariya', *Br. Efr. Enc.* vol. 30, p. 653.
[5] Ukaz of 14 Jan. 1826. *Poln. Sobr. Zak.* 2-oe Sobr. (SPB, 1830), vol. 1, no. 57.
[6] H.I.M. Own Chancellery ultimately included 6 Departments. The First, Second, and Third were formed in 1826; the Fourth (which continued the work of the Dowager-Empress Mariya Fyodorovna and administered charitable and educational institutions) in 1828; the Fifth (which dealt with questions relating to the administration of State Peasants) in 1836; and the Sixth (which dealt with civil affairs in the Trans-Caucasian Region) in 1842. The last two existed on a temporary basis only, until 1856 and 1845 respectively.
[7] Created on 24 Apr. 1826. Shil'der *loc. cit.* p. 460. In his 'rescript' addressed to the President of the Council of State Prince Lopukhin, Nicholas stated that he considered it necessary to take

—the first to be introduced by the new Tsar—were concerned with the complex and long overdue necessity of codifying Russian laws. In which connexion it is of interest to record the words addressed by Nicholas to his former tutor Balug'yansky on 13 December 1825. 'I desire', he said, 'that all the strength and severity of the laws should form the basis of our governmental system.'[1] No law Codex had been issued since 1649 and little had come of attempts to deal with this problem in the reigns of Catherine and Alexander. The positive steps now taken by Nicholas to rectify this omission thus represented a considerable achievement which provided at least a theoretical foundation for better government. It now remained for him to establish a centralized control over the national administration capable of ensuring that the 'strength and severity of the laws' was also observed in practice.

This aim, in Nicholas' view, could only be achieved by the reorganization of the police.

During the first few months of the new reign, Benckendorff, in the capacity of General-in-Waiting and member of the Commission for the investigation of the Decembrist Conspiracy, continued to enjoy the Tsar's special favour. In a letter to his life-long friend Prince M. S. Vorontsov on 16 January 1826 he wrote of the Emperor: 'Il daigne me traiter avec une bonté toute particulière; ce que je puis lui offrir, c'est un zèle pur et infatigable.'[2] This devotion of Benckendorff to his Sovereign was amply rewarded, and he was selected to act as Nicholas' private emissary on occasions when the Emperor required some important but delicate information. Prince S. P. Trubetskoi, awaiting sentence as a Decembrist conspirator in the Petropavlovsky Fortress, recounts in his memoirs how on 28 March 1826 Benckendorff visited him in his cell with the words: 'Je suis venu chez vous de la part de sa Majesté l'Empereur. Vous devez considérer comme si vous parliez avec l'Empereur lui-même',[3] when it transpired that his master's object was to discover the political reliability of Speransky! Benckendorff's past career[4] had scarcely been such as to qualify him for that of a statesman,[5] but Nicholas

this branch under his own direct control 'desiring to ensure as far as possible its successful performance'. Lemke quotes this statement to support his opinion that this motive likewise influenced Nicholas in the creation of the Third Department, p. 14.

[1] P. Baranov, *Mikhail Andreyevich Balug'yansky, Stats-Sekretar', Senator, Tainyi Sovyetnik, (1769–1847). Biograficheskii Ocherk* (SPB, 1882), p. 23. Balug'yansky was appointed the first Head of the Second Department in the rank of Actual State Councillor (Shil'der, *ibid.*), but in practice this post was titular only and the real work of Law Codification was undertaken by Speransky.

[2] *Arkhiv Knyazya Vorontsova*, edited by P. Barty'enev (Moscow, 1870–95), vol. xxxv (1889), p. 265. Letter no. 110.

[3] *Zapiski Knyazya S. P. Trubetskago* (SPB, 1906), p. 55.   [4] See chapter Four.

[5] Benckendorff himself stated: 'Never having thought to prepare myself for this kind of service, I possessed only the most superficial understanding of it; but the noble and beneficent motives

regarded him as an eminently reliable staff-officer who, furthermore, had shown by his previous memorandum on security matters that he possessed both initiative and discretion. Besides, Nicholas found his personality congenial. On 25 June, the Tsar's birthday, Benckendorff relinquished the post of General Officer Commanding the 1st Cuirassier Division and was appointed Chief of Gendarmes and Commandant of the Imperial Headquarters.[1]

A similar but more important appointment followed on 3 July with the creation of the Third Department of His Imperial Majesty's Own Chancellery under Benckendorff's command.[2]

It was this ukaz, destined to affect the public and private lives of countless thousands, which marked the introduction of a new phase in the development of Russia's secret police.

Ukaz of 3 July 1826

Except in so far as it provided the legal authority for the transfer of certain officials from the now abolished Special Chancellery of the Ministry of Internal Affairs—to be selected by Benckendorff—headed by their senior representative, Actual State Councillor von Vock, the text of the ukaz[3] did not deal with the organization of the Third Department. It merely announced the creation of a new state institution and established the lines along which it was to operate. But what emerged most clearly from this announcement was the subordination of the responsibility for Higher Police matters previously vested in the Ministry of Internal Affairs to this new Department of the Emperor's Chancellery. According to the current hierarchical system with its exact balance of civil and military equivalent ranks, Benckendorff was now automatically senior to the Head of the Second Department, Balug'yansky, who held the same rank as von Vock. And it was not only this higher rank which raised the Head of the Third Department to an unrivalled position. Benckendorff, although nominally only a General-in-Waiting (one of many), in practice outranked all the other high officials of Nicholas' régime at this period by virtue of the authority he now enjoyed over the work of its Ministers and the fact that, unlike the First and Second Departments of His Majesty's Chancellery, the Third Department was accorded wide executive powers. The ukaz of 3 July made it the most influential

which gave rise to this institution and the desire of being of use to our new emperor did not permit me to evade taking on a post created by him, to which his high confidence had called me.' Shil'der, *loc. cit.* p. 466.

[1] Shil'der, p. 464. The appointment was made by 'an imperial order'. No ukaz officially inaugurating the Corps of Gendarmes is included in the *Poln. Sobr. Zak.* Its regulations were published in an ukaz dated 28 April 1827 and are dealt with in chapter Three, pp. 87–8.

[2] Ukaz of 3 July 1826. *Poln. Sobr. Zak.* vol. I, no. 449.

[3] The full text is given as Appendix B, pp. 241–2.

office in all Russia, charged with the express task of implementing the Emperor's views on every aspect of national security and welfare.

Actual State Councillor[1] Maksim Yakovlevich[2] von Vock, in his new capacity of Director of Chancellery of the Third Department, was presumably retained by Nicholas as Benckendorff's senior assistant for the same reason that had induced the young Alexander to retain the services of Makarov in the early years of the previous reign. He was the only highly-placed official with extensive practical experience in this field and, being 'a man of undoubted intelligence, wide education and good breeding',[3] was considered to possess the personal qualities required for this post. Furthermore, Nicholas was probably aware that von Vock could not be held to blame for a situation in which the powerful intrigues of Arakcheyev, Miloradovich, Magnitsky and others had rendered the efforts of the Special Chancellery so ineffective a safeguard against the Decembrist conspiracies.[4] At all events, von Vock was frequently summoned to the Committee of Investigation, where he naturally became closely acquainted with his future Chief, Benckendorff.[5] Alone among the few writers who have discussed the question of the responsibility for the creation of the Third Department, Vigel' attributes to von Vock the initiative for this decision, basing his argument on Benckendorff's lack of ability.

This was just what von Vock required. He had seen the senility, powerlessness and approaching fall of his superior, Lanskoi, and conceived the notion of aiming far higher and attaining a more stable and vastly more responsible post. He probably represented to Benckendorff how advantageous it would be for him to hold great power in his hands without much trouble and without any responsibility and at the same time to remain in this way in daily and uninterrupted contact with the Emperor. He suggested to him a Ministry of Police, but this time in a new guise and under a different name, and drew up a project for it. How was this done, was anyone summoned to a Committee on it? This apparently remained a secret to all, for shortly after the coronation this new institution was for everyone an unexpected item of news...[6]

---

[1] The military equivalent of this rank was Major-General. Schiemann, in stating that the 'real burden of the work of the gendarmerie' devolved upon him, refers to him as 'General von Fock' (*op. cit.* vol. 2, p. 98). In fact, he remained a civilian throughout his career in the Higher Police and is referred to as such by all Russian writers.

[2] Shil'der calls him incorrectly Mikhail Maksimovich, p. 464. This error is amended by later writers.　　　　　　　　　　　　　　　　[3] Shil'der, *ibid*.

[4] The writer and censor N. I. Grech, always a loyal supporter of the autocracy, states in his memoirs: 'The next day after the St Petersburg outbreak I wrote a memorandum on the reasons for this incident and said *inter alia* that it had been assisted by the removal of many capable persons including Maksim Yakovlevich von Vock (*op. cit.* pp. 711–12). The fate of this memorandum is not known, but it seems permissible to assume that this or similar evidence of von Vock's good character was reported to Nicholas.

[5] Vigel', vol. 2, p. 274.　　　　　　　　　　　　[6] *Ibid.* p. 275.

Vigel''s evidence cannot in this instance be regarded as biased, because although he shared with the majority of his countrymen a feeling of revulsion for the methods of the Third Department, he was not animated by any personal unfriendliness towards von Vock and explains that it was the latter's 'wish and intention that an enlightened, as he saw it, trend of thought should not wholly perish in Russia and that persons possessing it should be protected from persecution'.[1] No historian, however, has discovered the existence of any project on Higher Police matters submitted by von Vock; and Vigel' does not state that he was aware of Benckendorff's 1821 Project or its revised version of January 1826 which von Vock, he assumes, so strongly influenced. It can only be conjectured with some certainty that between the accession of Nicholas and the creation of the Third Department these two men had ample opportunity for appreciating each other's outlook and that Benckendorff reported favourably to the Tsar on von Vock's intelligence and ability.

Benckendorff himself explained the circumstances of the Third Department's creation in the following terms:

The Emperor Nicholas was striving to eradicate the abuses that had crept into many governmental offices, and was convinced by the sudden exposure of the conspiracy which steeped in blood the first moments of the new reign of the necessity for a universal and more vigilant system of surveillance of an essentially centralized character; the Emperor selected me to form a Higher Police whose aim it would be to afford protection to the oppressed and to keep a watchful eye on abuses and persons thereto inclined. The latter had increased to a frightening degree ever since French adventure-seekers in large numbers who had taken over the education of our youth introduced into Russia the revolutionary principles of their country, and even more since the last war as the result of the contacts established between our young officers and the liberals of those European countries where our victories had led us...It was decided to establish under my command a Corps of Gendarmes... the subsequent development and organization of this new body was left to a later date and the lessons of experience. The Third Department of His Imperial Majesty's Own Chancellery created at the same time represented under my command the focal point at once of this new directorate and a Higher Secret Police which, in the person of secret agents, was required to assist and contribute to the activities of the gendarmes. In order to make this post more agreeable in my sight, the Emperor deigned to appoint me to the additional rank of Commandant of his Headquarters.[2] I set about my task without delay and God helped me to fulfil my new duties to

---

[1] *Ibid.* p. 277.

[2] Lemke comments: 'The reader may observe the care with which Benckendorff conceals from the public his own initiative in creating the new "oprichina". He should also understand that the rank of Commandant of the Imperial Headquarters was given to Benckendorff not at all in order to assuage his personal feelings but rather to add greater weight and confidence in the eyes of a public which even then was already aware of the value of its native police', p. 17.

the satisfaction of the emperor without arraying public opinion against me. I succeeded in doing good, in being of service to many, in exposing many abuses and, in particular, in anticipating and averting much evil.[1]

Disregarding, for the moment, the self-righteous and even sentimental tone of Benckendorff's assessment of Nicholas' aims and their successful realization, it at least rightly attributes the Emperor's decision to create a new form of Higher Police to the changed political climate of Russia, characterized by the outbreak of the Decembrist Rising.

The particular circumstances of this Rising had drawn attention, above all else, to the complete estrangement of governmental spheres from society. Once the immediate dangers it represented had been overcome, the new régime in the person of Nicholas was primarily concerned with the task of removing any possibility of a similar state of affairs recurring in the future. This aim, it was felt, could only be achieved by paying closer regard to the influence exerted on events by public opinion and, in order to achieve it, an effort must be made to penetrate the trends of thought current in the various classes of contemporary Russian society. At the time no political press existed in Russia, and even the possibility of discussing in print questions of a social and political nature was then regarded as the equivalent of anti-governmental heresy. The conviction reigned that only those governing the country were capable of deciding exactly what was needful and useful for the governed. On the other hand, the Decembrist Revolt acted as a warning to the government of the dangers to itself inherent in a negligent attitude towards the inner aspirations of the country's thinking classes. The idea of establishing an improved system of secret surveillance thus came into being as a direct consequence of this realization, for all that this system in fact pursued the same ends as those prosecuted by similar institutions which had existed at different times and under different names during the eighteenth century. If, however, the necessity of a political police was acknowledged in principle with no less conviction than in the past, its requirements were now somewhat different—a difference duly reflected in its altered character. 'The system was inaugurated in its new guise with incomparably milder terms of reference and was entrusted to persons who were to some extent well-educated and who possessed in addition a certain society veneer. It was the Emperor's intention that the best families and persons in close contact with the throne should stand at the head of this institution and take an active part in eradicating abuses. In this form it could only be hoped that this phoenix, reborn of its ashes, disposing of means to discover everything, would enable the government to put an end to the countless abuses suffered by Russia. . .'[2]

[1] Shil'der, pp. 465–6.　　　　　[2] *Ibid.* p. 467.

The Emperor's decision to concentrate the direction of the political police in a Department of his own Chancellery thus represented a notable change of attitude towards this branch. Administrative malpractices had increased to such a degree that strong counter-measures were considered unavoidable, but at the same time public opinion was to be canvassed in order to enlist general sympathy for this new approach. Nicholas desired, in fact, to alter the character of Higher Police work by endowing it with what Trotsky has termed 'a certain appearance of nobility'.[1]

Undoubtedly Nicholas looked upon his Third Department as a beneficial addition to his future administration. It is recorded that when Benckendorff, in entering upon his new duties, asked the Emperor for a directive to guide him in his control of Third Department activities, the Emperor, who was at that moment holding a handkerchief in his hand, held it out to the surprised General with the words: 'Here is all your directive. The more tears you wipe away with this handkerchief, the more faithfully will you serve my aims...'[2] The authenticity of this story is not finally established,[3] but the 'Handkerchief Legend' has found its way into history partly because in the general view it accurately reflected the Tsar's mood of sentimental benevolence at the time, and partly because the numerous critics of the Third Department were struck—in the light of its later development—by a certain obvious irony in Nicholas' words, whether true or false, and maintained with some justice that precisely the opposite result was achieved. Nevertheless, Nicholas certainly intended that his new police force 'should redress the wrongs which are unknown to the public, punish such crimes as the law cannot reach'.[4]

The changed character of this force was noticeably reflected in its com-

[1] 'Nyekotoroe blagoobrazie', Trotsky, p. 33.

[2] Ye. Dubel't, 'Leontii Vasil'evich Dubel't. Biograficheskii Ocherk i yego pis'ma', *R. Star.* (1888), vol. 60, p. 495. (The author writes: 'This handkerchief is preserved even to the present day under a glass cover ["kolpakom"] in the Archives of the former Third Department', *ibid.*) See also P. P. Karatygin: article entitled 'Benkendorf i Dubel't' published in *Istoricheskii Vyestnik*, vol. xxx (1887), October, p. 166.

[3] Both Shil'der (p. 467) and Lemke (p. 17) refer to it as a 'legenda', and this view is repeated by de Grunwald who adds, however, 'Il est fort probable que Nicolas ait effectivement fait ce geste dans lequel entre beaucoup plus de naïveté que d'hypocrisie. Le colonel Sgotov [*sic*] raconte dans ses Mémoires que Benckendorff lui répéta la même formule en l'expédiant comme officier de gendarmerie à Simbirsk: "Votre tâche consiste à sécher les larmes des malheureux." Constantin de Grunwald, *La Vie de Nicolas Ier* (Paris, 1946), p. 184.

The officer's correct name was Colonel Stogov, and Benckendorff's actual words to him on the above occasion were—'Utirai slyozy nyeschastnykh i otvrashchai zloupotrebleniya vlasti, i togda ty vsyo ispolnish' ('Wipe away the tears of the unfortunate and avert the abuses of the authorities, and then you will accomplish everything'), see 'Zapiski E. I. Stogova', *R. Star.* (1903), vol. 114, p. 313.

[4] A. Leroy-Beaulieu, *The Empire of the Tsars and the Russians* (London, 1894), Book II, ch. 5 p. 141.

position. Whereas, during the previous reign, the official political police was left in the hands of relatively junior and primarily civilian functionaries (Makarov, de Sanglen, von Vock) and was not authorized by the Tsar to take precedence over rival networks, Nicholas combined under one Head the now centralized direction of all Higher Police affairs both civil and military. And his decision to do so marked a most significant advance in the development of Russia's successive secret police forces.

From July 1826 Benckendorff was responsible for both the Third Department (civil) and the Corps of Gendarmes (military), which together constituted the Tsar's 'private oprichnina' and represented 'the central nerve of his entire governmental system'.[1] Accordingly it enjoyed the authority and prestige of a particularly favoured branch, and Nicholas intended that it should be generally considered as his 'corps d'élite'. It is noteworthy that from the beginning of its existence the executive branch of this new organization was destined to play an entirely overt rôle in the Higher Police. (Evidently secrecy was not always observed even in the preliminary planning phase, for over a month before the 3 July ukaz an English resident noted in his diary that its creation was imminent.[2]) It is therefore permissible to assume that Nicholas, having resolved to effect certain radical changes in the basic character of political surveillance as conducted by his predecessors, decided that these changes necessitated the creation of a patently non-secret organization accessible—as Benckendorff had advised—to the general public; and the Corps of Gendarmes, with its distinctive sky-blue uniform, was inaugurated for this purpose.

Organization of the Third Department

The Third Department itself, however, to which this Corps was subordinated, was staffed by civilians under von Vock and operated covertly with the collaboration of secret agents. The relative absence of information available[3]

[1] Trotsky, p. 30.
[2] '29th (O.S. [= Old Style]) May 1826...Dr Paterson, who, as a missionary, had traversed the Crimea and Caucasus as far as Tiflis...told me that the Emperor had organized a secret police for the purpose of collecting information respecting...abuses and ...everything that is said respecting himself and the government, an account of which is to be presented to him without the names of the individuals whose opinions are related. A very excellent man is said to be at the head of this new species of police or inquisition'. Robert Lee, M.D., F.R.S., *The Last Days of Alexander and the First Days of Nicholas* (London, 1854), p. 137. (Dr Lee was the private physician of Count Vorontsov.)
[3] Varadinov merely reports that the Special Chancellery of the Ministry of Internal Affairs was transferred on 3 July 1826 to 'the newly-created Third Department of His Imperial Majesty's Own Chancellery', pt 3, Book 1, p. 10, and gives no details of the latter's organization. Shil'der is equally reticent. Even the 'Jubilee Report' (see p. 62, note 2) omits these particulars, and Lemke was not, of course, concerned with this aspect of the Third Department's existence. Such

on its early composition and organization (in marked contrast to the details of the Corps of Gendarmes published in ukazes) must hence be attributed to the clandestine nature of its activities. According to the only authoritative source in existence, the Third Department in 1826 consisted of a mere sixteen officials and was originally composed of four Sections ('Ekspeditsii'). Of these the first dealt with matters brought to the attention of the Higher Police and collated information on persons under police surveillance; the second dealt with sects and dissenters, cases involving forged currency and documents, and questions concerned with the administration of all places of confinement for State criminals; the third dealt with all matters concerning foreigners resident in Russia; the fourth dealt with correspondence on all events in general inside the country.[1] It would appear from later research, however, that there existed no strict division of business between these Sections and for a long time there was no established office procedure. The most secret cases, which included the work of agents, came under the immediate control of the 'Director' of the Third Department—first under that of M. Ya. von Vock and later under that of A. N. Mordvinov and L. V. Dubbelt. The Director, together with two or three of his most responsible assistants, was in fact the central operative of the whole system. He was in direct contact with the secret agents, the huge number of denunciations and complaints were sent to him and his was the responsibility of deciding a case one way or the other, of choosing the form in which a report submitted to the Emperor should be drawn up and so on.[2] The conclusion is unavoidable that the personalities of the few men at the top of the Third Department were bound to exert an immense influence on its development as a political factor in the national life. These men were answerable only to the Tsar, and their influence tended to increase with the growth of Nicholas' reactionary policies. Their importance was extreme because, as will be seen from later pages, the Department which was originally intended to ensure a due observance of the 'strength and severity of the laws' assumed by virtue of its unique position a supra-legal status.

This unrivalled state was achieved, of course, as a direct consequence of the provisions of the 3 July ukaz. The spheres of interest of the Third Department were defined in nine brief but comprehensive clauses[3] which in

authoritative writers as have sought this information (e.g. Schiemann and, much later, Trotsky) have relied *in toto* on the details given by Adrianov, see following note.

It is pertinent to record that the only ukaz referring to the Third Department in 1826 was that which created it on 3 Jul. (no. 449); and details of its official ranks did not appear in ukaz form until 29 Dec. 1829 (no. 3389), when the total of officials employed on work in its Headquarters was fixed at 20, see chapter Six, p. 182.　　　　[1] Adrianov, p. 98.

[2] Trotsky, p. 49. For details of these officials see chapters Four and Five.
[3] 'How few points and how great their content!', Lemke, p. 15. See Appendix B, p. 241.

practice authorized the new Higher Police to assume control over a wide variety of affairs previously the sole concern of individual Ministries.[1] In particular, Clause 8—which stated that one such sphere of interest was 'information and reports on all events without exception'—sanctioned the unlimited interference of the Third Department in any aspect of Russian life that attracted its attention. The fact that the powers conferred by these nine clauses 'remained in force for fifty years with almost no alteration'[2] provides sufficient proof of the profound influence exerted by this Department and of its lasting popularity with the Tsar. And this in itself represented an inevitable development of autocratic rule in Russia.

An efficient autocratic régime cannot continue to survive without a force capable of ensuring obedience; and everyone knew that Russia's administration was deplorably inefficient. By the 3 July ukaz Nicholas—for the first time in Russian history—laid the foundations of a multifarious supervisory network under his own immediate control. He endowed it with unprecedented authority, allotted it its own Staff-Officers and Troops in the shape of a Corps of Gendarmes and placed at its head the most devoted of his Generals-in-Waiting. The Third Department was to be ubiquitous and omnipotent; and was to possess moral as well as physical authority. Above all, Nicholas saw in it the essential link between himself and his people—observing all that went on, righting wrongs and averting evils.

Such were the principles that may be said to have led to its creation. It is nevertheless hard to disagree with Lemke's assertion that 'in the guise of the Third Department there entered Russian life of the first half of the 19th century the old "Secret Chancellery", cleaned, curled and dolled-up'.[3] For although Nicholas intended that his new Department should earn for itself a more honourable place in his country's history, in fact its contemporary and subsequent reputation differed little from that of its predecessors.

The police archives of the period immediately following the establishment of the Third Department record feverish activity on the part of all

---

[1] It is interesting that the ukaz contains no reference to the control of Censorship by the Third Department. New Censorship Regulations were issued in an ukaz (no. 403) dated 10 June 1826, which subordinated this branch to the Director of Chancellery of the Minister of Public Education (see *Poln. Sobr. Zak.* vol. 1, p. 551). Gradually, however, the Third Department assumed more and more control over Censorship questions. (This subject is dealt with in detail by Lemke.)

[2] 'Obzor Dyeyatel'nosti III otdeleniya sobstvennoi vashego imperatorskago velichestva Kantselyarii za 50 lyet. 1826–76gg.' contained in article entitled 'Tret'ye Otdeleniye Sobstvennoi Ye.I.V. Kantselyarii o Sebye Samom. (Nyeizdannyi dokument)' by V. Bogucharsky, *Vyestnik Yevropy* (1917), Mar., p. 91. This 'Obzor' is the so-called 'Jubilee Report'. Future references to it in these Notes are recorded under Bogucharsky.

[3] Lemke, p. 19.

spies,[1] both amateur and professional. Officially instigated inquiries, however, indicated a change of emphasis brought about by the revelations of the Decembrist Commission. If previously investigations undertaken by political police organs had been concerned mainly with foreigners and noblemen of some standing, these two groups were now accorded second place;[2] and the new Higher Police's attention was chiefly concentrated on the ranks of the Military and the Intelligentsia. This explains why the Third Department at once began paying close heed to the state of public opinion in the country in general and to the influence exerted on it by these two classes in particular, as being the most implicated in the events of 14 December. The official history of the Ministry of Internal Affairs states that 'in addition to their earlier police duties, the task of political surveillance[3] became from 1826 onwards the most important function of all ranks serving in the gendarmes';[4] and although in the summer of that year the Corps of Gendarmes existed only in an embryo form, little time was lost in issuing the appropriate instructions to all gendarme units.[5]

After the execution of the Decembrist leaders on 13 July, Nicholas accompanied by Benckendorff left for Moscow to be crowned there on 22 August.

The von Vock–Benckendorff letters

During Benckendorff's absence from the capital the affairs of the Third Department remained in the charge of von Vock, who corresponded with his chief from St Petersburg with great assiduity, writing on an average every other day from 17 July to 25 September. Fortunately for posterity these letters have been preserved[6] and represent a unique source for the study of the Third Department's aims and interests immediately after its creation. They deal, as might be expected, with any and every subject likely to concern the new Grand Inquisitor; and, being of a confidential nature, are frequently revealing. For instance, when von Vock, in recommending Mr

---

[1] 'Police cases of this period tell of hundreds of persons expelled from the capital...merely because they were not engaged on any official job and looked suspicious in the eyes of police detectives.' Trotsky, p. 32.

[2] *Ibid.* p. 33.   [3] 'Nablyudatel'naya dyeyatel'nost'.'

[4] Adrianov, p. 99. It will be recalled that gendarme units already existed within the framework of the Army Gendarme Regt. and the Corps of Internal Security Troops.

[5] See chapter Three, p. 81.

[6] 'Pis'ma M. M. [*sic*] Foka k A. Kh. Benkendorfu (perevod s frantsuzskago)' published in *Russkaya Starina* (1881), vol. 32, pp. 168–94; 303–36; 519–60. 'The style of these letters, originally written in French, is purely intimate; their tone bears the stamp of the respectful friendship that might be expected between a highly-placed superior and a talented subordinate', Editor's Introd. *ibid.* p. 166. *N.B.* Lemke's use of the material contained in these Letters is strictly relevant to his theme, and is therefore confined to such topics as the impact of the Third Department on society and von Vock's views on public opinion, pp. 35–6.

Nefyedev and Count Lyev Sollogub as potential agents in Moscow, describes the former as 'a walking dictionary on Muscovite Society' and refers to the value of the latter's family connexions in that capital,[1] he is in fact—and in accordance with the new principles put forward by Benckendorff—advocating the employment of persons of some position in society; and it is clear from his mention of Collegiate Councillor Blandov, an employee of the Ministry of Finance, that even in these early days of the Third Department's existence its Director already possessed useful sources of information in well placed officials.[2] As these letters are not couched in official language, they are somewhat formless in style; but fully compensate for this by the extensive scope of their contents, reporting now the writer's views on current trends in public opinion,[3] now some individual detail relating to life in the capital,[4] together with long excerpts quoted from casual conversations. Occasionally the letters reveal a sense of humour.[5] That a state of complete mutual confidence existed between von Vock and his Chief may be seen from the former's readiness to mention names of prominent persons whose loyalty was temporarily suspect.[6] In general, von Vock has much to say on the subject of

[1] *R. Star.*, *loc. cit.* p. 168. Letter dated 17 July.

[2] *Ibid.* p. 171. Letter dated 19 Jul. Blandov had inquired of von Vock 'whether he would be protected from persecution at the hands of the Minister about whose administration he could provide a mass of most interesting information'; and von Vock sought Benckendorff's authority to give this agent encouragement and reassurance.

[3] E.g. the effect on public opinion of the Decembrist Revolt, discussed in Letter dated 20 Jul., *ibid.* pp. 172–3.

[4] 'The abolition of the Address Office is greatly desired by all, especially by the middle and lower classes of society, who are hopeful that this favour will be accorded them at the Emperor's coronation.' Letter dated 26 Jul., *ibid.* p. 179. Von Vock returns to this theme in Letter dated 30 Jul. (p. 184), saying that to abolish this institution 'which has made so many people groan' would create an enormous impression to the advantage of the government. It is noteworthy, however, that the authorities did not accede to this general desire—see Letter dated 1 Sept. in which von Vock comments on the public disappointment caused by the lack of reference to this subject in the Coronation Manifesto of 22 Aug., *ibid.* p. 334—and the Address Office, which clearly proved a useful source of information (see chapter One, p. 29) was not abolished until 1888.

[5] 'To amuse Your Excellency, I must report that at a small gathering at the house of Princess Konovnitsyna it was said that you, Your Excellency, and I are the most dangerous spies', *ibid.* p. 175, Letter dated 21 Jul. It is evident that von Vock was not disposed to underrate the influence exerted by society ladies, as is shown by an excerpt from Letter dated 9 Aug.: 'Among the ladies the two most irreconcilable ones, who are always ready to tear the government to pieces, are Princess Volkonskaya and Madame General Konovnitsyna', *ibid.* p. 191. In contrast, however, it may be noted that von Vock also acknowledged the assistance of other ladies in obtaining information: 'The sister of Mademoiselle Puchkova, Natal'ya, has left for Moscow with Madame Vereshchagina. Both these ladies serve the police under the protection of Prince Aleks. Golitsyn', *ibid.* p. 312, Letter dated 14 Aug.

[6] E.g. Mordvinov on whom von Vock reported that he was keeping close watch, *ibid.* p. 189, Letter dated 5 August. Count N. S. Mordvinov (1754–1845), although he was made one of the Judges of the Decembrist Commission, was himself suspected of Decembrist sympathies and was later exiled from the capital. *Ibid.* p. 322, Letter dated 24 August.

'the well-intentioned' and 'the discontented' in Russian society—views which he subsequently incorporated in the first of the Third Department's Annual Reports on the State of Public Opinion and which are dealt with in a later chapter[1]—and his assessment of the general atmosphere in St Petersburg (described by his translator as 'nastroyenie umov') is carefully and clearly presented. Of more relevance to the present chapter, however, is the evidence contained in his letters of the impact on society of the Third Department itself and of the circumstances attending its début. In the absence of any other equally important sources providing this information, these letters must be examined in some detail.

The circular [sic] of the Minister of Internal Affairs on the creation of the Third Department of His Imperial Majesty's Chancellery [writes von Vock on 29 July] also serves as conversational matter. Some say: 'Now the urban and rural police forces will be subject to proper control. It would be a good thing if this control were also extended over the actions, behaviour and morals of all those charged with executive authority in the administration because it is precisely there that the real evil is to be found. The project has been well planned and will produce an effect if only the Higher Police's instruments, that is, the "aces", are chosen from a very limited circle of respectable persons; otherwise the remedy will prove worse than the disease because, instead of one bad police, there will be two, and this will inevitably occur the instant Higher Police organs cease to constitute an individual category whose members are in a position to act as a corrective body and play an instructional rôle. But since a good example is the very best means of education, it is vital that their behaviour should be above reproach and that all persons serving in the Higher Police should never exceed their established duties.' All those who belong to the party of the 'discontented' hold different views. 'Experience has shown us', they say, 'that almost all measures of reform have hitherto merely produced the impression of a fine gesture. They want to embark on corrective measures! But have they thought what it means to cleanse Augean stables; that they should approach the task from the other end—they should first establish a reliable civil service and a simplified legal procedure. But as the government has at its disposal neither the financial nor the moral resources necessary for achieving this dual result, any corrective measures will be if not absolutely impossible at least exceedingly difficult to ensure...Besides it should not be forgotten that first and foremost relations will be strained between the new guardians of law and order and the old, and later on between the old guardians and persons subject to their surveillance. How will the government act, especially in the present circumstances, to anticipate and avert an inevitable reaction? This is a question of extreme importance.'[2] I must

---

[1] See chapter Six, pp. 201 ff.

[2] Lemke, who paraphrases part of this appraisal, comments: 'The "discontented" showed their complete sagacity on this point. Indeed up to 1880 the Ministry of Internal Affairs was perpetually and sharply at variance with the Third Department', p. 35.

(Proof of this rivalry may be found in the contents of the Third Department's Annual Reports, see preceding note. The Third Department was abolished in 1880.)

add that it seems as though reasonable people are agreed in their approach to the salutary trend of the government which, generally speaking, is evoking considerable confidence. The best proof of this may be seen in the fury of the malcontents.[1]

It will be observed that von Vock refrained from passing comment on the description of Russia's civil service as 'Augean stables', being doubtless no less aware than Benckendorff of its accuracy and of the imperative need for a stronger form of control over the national administration. The estimate of the Third Department and its tasks formed by friend and foe alike probably combined to convince both men of its importance and potential value. Above all it should be remembered that the summer of 1826 was a time of some uneasiness for the high officials of the new régime. The Decembrist leaders had been hanged, but the liberal notions they had fostered were still fresh in everyone's memory, at least in the society of the capital. It is thus easy to imagine Benckendorff's reaction on reading von Vock's reports. Such sentences as 'Our infected youth requires vigilant and perpetual surveillance'[2] could not have failed to strengthen his conviction that the proper steps had been taken to ensure it.

It is clear from the reactions to the institution of the Third Department reported by von Vock that society was generally aware of the important rôle that this organization was destined to play in Russia's future, even if the 'discontented' naturally regarded it with pessimism and disfavour.

The new Higher Police had been created, however, by a stroke of the pen and evidently did not enjoy, in its initial stages, that supreme power which it was to acquire with the passage of time. The prevalence of individual espionage networks during the final years of the previous reign could not be dispelled so quickly; and von Vock's early difficulties in his new post are well illustrated by his letter of 10 August:[3]

I am obliged to speak to Your Excellency on a subject as ridiculous as it is unpleasant. The police has given orders to keep under observation the activities of myself and agents of the Third Department.[4] Police officials, dressed in civilian clothes, patrol around the small house I occupy and observe the persons that visit me. Let us allow that my activities do not fear the light of day, but this kind of thing leads to a very harmful consequence: the Supervisory Police, in becoming itself an object of suspicion, contrary to all sense and justice,[5] is positively bound thereby

[1] *R. Star., loc. cit.* pp. 183–4. [2] *Ibid.* p. 185. Letter dated 30 July.
[3] *Ibid.* pp. 192–4.
[4] The translator of von Vock's letters uses the word 'nadzor'—'surveillance'—in this sense. It is translated in the present version as either 'The Third Department' or 'The Supervisory Police'.
[5] The words 'the Supervisory Police...justice' were underlined in pencil in the original letter and there is a note in Benckendorff's handwriting in the margin: 'It must be established whether it is Fogel' who has done this or whether he has had orders to do so.' *Ibid.*, footnote, p. 193.

to lose the respect that should be paid to it in the interests of the success of its activities. The agents used by the police make no secret of what they are doing and are not forbidden to do it. I have warned Mr. Dershau[1] about this, but he pretends to know nothing of it. It is permissible to control my actions—I have nothing against this, I would even be ready to approve of it—but to send such blockheads to keep watch over me and persons visiting me, blockheads pointed out by all the street urchins—this is really too inconsistent, to say the least of it. Furthermore I should add that Fogel' and his fellow-champions draw up and daily present the Military Governor with little reports on what several of my agents do and say. This, let us suppose, is in the order of things; but I venture to hope that no reliance will be placed on such impromptu evidence before there are some preliminary grounds for believing that they are justified. Painful experience[2] has made me, perhaps, over-cautious—but I am bound to be cautious for the sake of the cause I serve. Here are a few further observations culled from various circles which may serve as justification for my misgivings. 'The Emperor has declared himself particularly opposed to all equivocal and tortuous courses of action; this is a well-known fact; nevertheless one meets persons who attempt to resist the development of useful measures intended to contribute to the improvement of the governmental system and to its organization on stable foundations. The greatest evil confronting the government is the egoism of officials and their craving to take precedence in every branch. They could not, of course, achieve this aim without the assistance of their adherents who try to make themselves a career, to the detriment of the public interest. Higher officials do not dare to offend them openly because they have no wish to weaken their own party and therefore, albeit aware of the existence of an evil, they nevertheless put up with it out of personal considerations...'

There is no published evidence that Benckendorff took steps to put an end to the ludicrous situation created by the agents of one secret organization spying on another; but it is permissible to assume that the gradual increase of power entrusted to the Third Department resulted in a proportionate eclipse of potential rivals.[3] It is perhaps also worth recording that between von Vock and Fogel', who has been mentioned before[4] as the Head of Miloradovich's Secret Police, a state of rivalry may well have existed for many years. During the final months of Alexander's Ministry of Police,

[1] K. F. Dershau (1784–1862) was appointed Politseimeister in St Petersburg as Lt.-Col. in 1822, promoted Col. in this appointment in 1826 and became Ober-Politseimeister there in 1829, see *RBS*.

[2] This was clearly a reference to the persecution to which von Vock was subjected in the last years of the preceding reign, see chapter One, p. 43.

[3] This may be deduced from the fact that none of the published 'Annual Reports' submitted by the Third Department contains any further complaints of the kind of behaviour recorded by von Vock; and as these Reports are in general highly critical of the activities of other Ministries, it may be assumed that such complaints would have been included had there been grounds for them.

[4] See chapter One, p. 45.

when von Vock was Head of its Special Chancellery, a report[1] emanating from 'the Higher Police' contained in its section on Miloradovich's office unfavourable references to certain of its employees: 'The secret police of the capital has for the most part been entrusted to Fogel' who... has utterly disorganized this body. The reputation of Fogel', his depravity, are turning this police into a pernicious body of petty sneaks, a burdensome source of irritation to the public, especially to foreigners, and have a damaging effect on the police institutions of the entire government...A police of this sort obscures the fame of the man commanding it, the more so if its despicable instruments are defended by his personal protection.'[2] Whether or not von Vock himself wrote these words, the tone of his letter to Benckendorff indicates that the intervening six or seven years and even the death of his erstwhile patron Miloradovich had not materially affected Fogel''s status. That even such relatively highly placed servants of the state as von Vock were inured to a situation of this kind may be seen from his admission that Fogel''s reports on his activities were 'in the order of things'. But naturally such rivalry was harmful to the state and dangerous to its official guardians; and it is impossible not to feel that von Vock was fully justified in seeking increased powers with a view to eradicating from the bureaucratic system such elements as clearly contributed to its general inefficiency.[3] Certainly nothing could have seemed more ludicrous than that the Third Department, with Imperial orders to keep under official surveillance every branch of the national administration, should itself be kept under observation by spies acting at the behest of now considerably less influential offices.

At the beginning of its official life, however, the Third Department had to contend with some inevitable rivalry, a situation aggravated by the facilities already possessed by long-established police organs but not yet enjoyed by their new superior.

Von Vock was obliged to inform Benckendorff that 'the financial resources at the disposal of the police are countless; whereas those of the Department, on the contrary, are very limited...the latter's sphere of competence is insufficiently extensive because its resources are also restricted;[4]

---

[1] 'Tolki i Nastroyenie Umov v Rossii po donesyeniyam vysshei politsii v S. Peterburge s avgusta 1818 po 1-e maya 1819 g.' *R. Star.* (1881), vol. 32, pp. 667–76.

 These unsigned and individually undated reports represent one of a miscellaneous collection of articles on 'Imperator Aleksandr Pavlovich i Ego Vremya'. The Editor does not explain how they came into his possession.

[2] *Ibid.* p. 671.

[3] Von Vock continually reverted in his letters to the need for action in this respect, e.g. 'Everyone awaits if not a complete reorganization at least a reform of administrative practices'. *Loc. cit.* p. 303, Letter dated 11 Aug.

[4] It is of interest to note that the *Poln. Sobr. Zak.* contains no ukaz giving details of the financial resources allotted to the Third Department in 1826. Its financial position was not regulated

its activities could be far wider were it not for the obstacles placed in its way by the police...'[1] Subsequent letters develop this objection in greater detail. 'The hostility of the police to the controlling work of the Department is daily growing more and more acute. Control is necessary in any good administration. The Department, acting on principles hallowed by the approval of the Sovereign Emperor, does not fear inquiries; on the contrary —it is readily attentive to anything likely to contribute to the clarification of its actions. For this reason it would do no harm if the police limited itself to observation alone and did not play the part of teacher...I am far from thinking of making complaints against the police; on the contrary, I should like, as far as it depends on me, to maintain that excellent accord which ought to exist between these two institutions created in order to help each other; but I recognize my obligations and I do not wish to miss the opportunity of openly exposing the actions of "word and deed".'[2] Despite these protestations it is evident that von Vock was in fact preferring charges of interference against the police of the capital and that the desirable state of 'excellent accord' represented merely a pious hope on the part of the writer.

Notwithstanding the difficulties of his position von Vock found himself fully occupied. 'The activities of the Department are increasing every day and I hardly have sufficient time to deal with all the reports that I receive...'[3] —a state of affairs which may be readily appreciated in the light of the views reported in his following letter,[4] providing adequate justification for the Department's industry: 'Many people say that radical measures must be taken to put an end to the large number of abuses and the practice of official bribery; the latter is now too deep-rooted for us to limit ourselves to roundabout methods.' 'The punishment deserved by criminal action must not be postponed; half-measures must be avoided—there is nothing more harmful than this. The history of all countries and all times leaves no doubt of the obvious truism that in order to avoid greater evils it is imperative that punishment should be carried out in good time and without any pity. Consequently, the blow must be dealt now or never.'

until later (see page 182, note 3). In any case von Vock's complaint indicates that this omission was leading to administrative difficulties inside the Department.

[1] *Ibid*. pp. 305–6, Letter dated 12 Aug. The same letter contains the proposal of an agent (von Vock does not name him) for the allocation of 50,000 roubles for the purpose of establishing 'observation circles' outside the control of the ordinary police. A note pencilled on the margin by Benckendorff reads: 'An excellent idea; prepare this question by my return', p. 307.

[2] *Ibid*. pp. 309–10. Letter dated 13 Aug. It also contains specific details of the poor character of certain police agents and the absurdity of their denunciations. The final words of the letter's last sentence—'otkrovyenno vystavit' *dyeistviya slova i dyela*'—are printed in italics and are a reference to the dreaded 'Slovo i Dyelo' practices of the eighteenth century (see chapter One, pp. 14, 15, 16). Von Vock evidently considered a comparison between the old 'Slovo i Dyelo' and the malpractices complained of in his letter likely to impress his superior.

[3] *Ibid*. p. 312, Letter dated 14 Aug.   [4] *Ibid*. pp. 312–14, Letter dated 15 Aug.

Von Vock's informants were clearly aware, however, of the problems presented by the moral state of the nation's officials. 'A difficult task confronts the Higher Police, that eye of the government. It should establish a system of surveillance capable of embracing all branches of public administration; it ought to draw attention to malpractices and at the same time to the quickest and most effective counter-methods—methods which it should itself adopt speedily and knowledgeably. How many heavy duties and what a vast responsibility! But, in contrast, what a glorious harvest!'[1]

Von Vock does not state that these views are also his own, but this may be assumed from the constant emphasis that he places throughout his letters on the general need to eradicate the venal conduct of national affairs by unscrupulous officials[2] and from his firm insistence on the adoption of radical measures to achieve this end.

Time and again, in referring to the investigatory methods for which he was responsible, he returns to his theme of the state of public morals.[3] 'The policy adopted by the government of giving heed to denunciations exposing abuses, a policy so far conducted with firmness and discrimination, has had unusually good results. Informers know that if they submit false denunciations they will receive no mercy and therefore nobody does so. Some of them give information out of a desire to assist the public welfare, others for the sake of their own interests; but in any event horrors of one kind and another are brought to light and the government discovers things which would never be brought to its attention had it not set itself the task of seeing and hearing everything in order to act subsequently at all times and places with all conscientiousness. There is no doubt that it is a great advantage to have a clear straight road in front of one because, in following it, one sees how smooth it becomes. In this way much dishonesty is disclosed; the authorities

---

[1] It is interesting that von Vock adds: 'These are the kind of observations one often hears, especially among Russified foreigners.' *Loc. cit.* p. 314.

[2] The following quotation is typical of von Vock's views: 'The best touchstone of the honesty and disinterestedness of Ministers is a comparison of their financial status before they take over a ministry and when they leave it. Dmitriev, on leaving his ministry, had not sufficient means to travel from here to Moscow, whereas Gur'yev and others made themselves colossal fortunes.' *Ibid.* p. 190, Letter dated 6 Aug.

[3] 'The present condition of men and affairs is a very special one: the latter are clearly in decline, there is a complete absence of morality; men are possessed with egoism and give as much thought to the public cause as they do to the acquisitions of Austria. The education of youth is wrongly directed: young men spend time *arguing* when they could use it far more profitably. Trade and industry in the country suffer when men are careless about their status. What immense trouble is needed to carry out reforms as necessary as, from the point of view of the bureaucracy, they are unpleasant and irksome. The bureaucracy is a real hydra which can be destroyed only by prolonged efforts, by penetrating tirelessly to the very root of the evil. Therefore let there be no attempt to prove to us that it is almost totally impossible to be everywhere, to see everything and deal with everything...' *Ibid.* pp. 316–17, Letter dated 18 Aug.

too, one after the other, will be subjected to secret surveillance.[1] One now hears on all sides: "Honest men will be protected from injustices; only evil-doers will be afraid because they fear the light of day. It is time to put an end to dishonesty in public affairs and to punish those who deal in bribery.[2] The confidence aroused by a government which seeks to obtain the good will of those it governs is a powerful means of facilitating the success of its undertakings"...'[3] Although von Vock's appreciation of the situation should primarily be regarded as a justification of his Department's activities, it is fair to state that his analysis of Russia's internal difficulties also represented the average viewpoint of a sincere and intelligent patriot.

The majority of von Vock's succeeding letters deal with such topics as public reactions to the events of the coronation and its manifestos, current rumours and opinions in the capital and so on; but throw little additional light on the workings of the Third Department.

His views on 'The Police', however, given in a letter consisting of 'sketches', are worth recording. 'The Police maintains law and order; its first duty consists of showing each man his place. To do this it must itself know its place and must not forget that example is the best teacher. The police is the most difficult, the least resplendent but the most excellent branch of urban administration. It should anticipate crimes but, when they are committed, it should see that guilty persons do not evade the penalty of the laws. In order to anticipate crimes the Police should know what engenders them, just as it should also know the signs which precede them, so that in the latter case caution and skill are more needful than all the appurtenances of criminal legislation. The Police should be shrewd enough to observe the signs that threaten public tranquillity. Thus for every evil that occurs in the state one should almost always blame the authorities who have not been able to anticipate it. The authorities should not forget, however, that the Police does not represent a system of repellent espionage but simply an instrument for seeing that the laws are carried out. Hence those responsible for urban administration should know the laws and be as unprejudiced as they are. But, it will be said, this is the plan of an idealist. That may well be, but that is no reason for refraining from the task of perfecting police administration.'[4] Although von Vock was referring here not to the Third Department but to the ordinary

---

[1] It is evident from the contents of a letter dated 25 Aug. that von Vock was already conducting a private investigation into the prison system with the help of 'one of the most influential members of the Prison Committee who...wishes for the time being to remain unknown'. His letter contains details of the many abuses and deviations from the law which characterized this branch of the administration. *Ibid.* pp. 324–5.

[2] Von Vock commented in a letter dated 21 Aug.: 'For twenty-five years the bureaucracy has lived on extortion applied shamelessly and with impunity.' *Ibid.* p. 320.

[3] *Ibid.* p. 318, Letter dated 19 Aug.

[4] *Ibid.* p. 544, Letter dated 17 Sept.

overt Police,[1] and in particular to that of the capital, the above principles clearly accorded with his views on the proper conduct of Higher Police affairs and may be regarded as the credo of the man then chiefly responsible for the control of Russia's secret police. The high-minded character of von Vock's theories, however, was not known to the general public who, unfortunately if inevitably, soon came to recognize in the new Higher Police the very 'system of repellent espionage' which von Vock had hoped to avoid.

The views of the general public on this and other matters constituted a subject of the greatest importance to von Vock, for which he gives the following reasons: 'Talleyrand has acutely observed, "I know someone cleverer than Napoleon, Voltaire and his like, cleverer than all present and future ministers, and that someone is public opinion". Public opinion does not intrude; it must be followed because it never stops. The light of its illuminating flame can be lessened, can be weakened, but to extinguish it is not within the power of the government. Napoleon himself said that if it were possible to engage public opinion in battle he would not fear it; but that, not possessing artillery shells capable of hitting it, he was obliged to overcome it by justice and fair dealings which it would not resist; to act against it by other means, he said, meant wasting money and honours to no avail; one must submit to this necessity; public opinion cannot be imprisoned and by constricting it one merely embitters it.'[2]

It is a fair conclusion that von Vock sought by similar methods to dispose public opinion in the government's favour and avoid wherever possible all restrictive measures likely to have the opposite effect. Nevertheless he implied in a later letter that a careful watch must be kept to see that the general atmosphere was not influenced by too much freedom of thought. 'The force of public opinion constitutes not an absolute but a relative blessing. It can be called a blessing when it is enlightened and at the same time stable and moderate. But it constitutes an evil when it loses its sense of direction in choosing its purpose and the means of achieving it, thus becoming a force opposed to the government.'[3] In short, while he was careful to explain the power of public opinion and the need to study it with sympathy, he showed that he was fully aware of the danger of allowing it excessive scope.

Public opinion on the methods of the Third Department may be judged from a report submitted by one of von Vock's agents: 'The adherents of bureaucracy are beginning to be seriously disturbed. What has happened?

[1] The translator of von Vock's letters uses the words 'Nadzor' and 'Politsiya' respectively to distinguish the Higher Police from the Lower.
[2] *Loc. cit.* pp. 550–1, Letter dated 21 Sept.   [3] *Ibid.* p. 558, Letter dated 25 Sept.

Z . . . v [the agent] asks them. "Do you not know how General Benckendorff treats people and what measures he adopts to unearth family secrets?
Of course he possesses all the means of doing so, he has the force and the
authority, perhaps his intentions are kindly—but after all how easy it is to
make a mistake in sorting shadows! Some people seem guilty without themselves suspecting it; they behave in the usual established way. If persons are
regarded in this manner, not one just man will be found. Clearly in the eyes
of God this may be true, but in those of mankind—that is another question.'
Von Vock also quotes this agent to the effect that 'speeches of this kind are
daily becoming more and more vehement and serious . . . good sense requires
that attention be redoubled . . . not in order to take action against those who
are so incautious in their talk but, on the contrary, to allow them complete
freedom to express their views—so as to extract various items of information
from it'.[1]

With his long experience of secret police work, von Vock was doubtless
accustomed to adverse public criticism, which he recorded simply as a topical
item of conversation. He clearly had no real qualms about the current state of
internal security, as may be seen from one of his last letters from this series,
which incidentally also provides a vivid description of the writer's own attitude to the aims of the Higher Police.

My habit of conversing with Your Excellency has become a necessity for me, and
although I have nothing especially outstanding to report to you, since the most
perfect calm reigns in the capital, I nevertheless feel that I must write you a few lines.
Female critics are making a great fuss about the system adopted by the government
of seeing everything for itself. 'A fine occupation for a government', they say,
'sticking their nose into every detail! One cannot sneeze in one's own home, make
a gesture or say a word without the Emperor instantly discovering it![2] Should he
bother with such trifles, how has he sufficient time to study them? But let them take
care: surveillance of this kind is oppressive and will end by causing disturbances,
that is, it is equally harmful both to those it investigates and those who do the
investigating!' As you will, ladies! In your opinion the government should not
itself enter into all details with a view to studying the reasons underlying evil and
discontent. But in that case how is it to discover what it should do and how is it
to justify its decrees? This surveillance, so inconvenient of course for evil-inten-
tioned persons, is, on the contrary, very useful and beneficial for those who cannot
reproach themselves with anything. In order not to judge too precipitately—one
must know everything and then one is not influenced by the first denunciation that
is made nor deflected by the second. Persons to whom the government has entrusted this surveillance are bound, it stands to reason, to arouse the hatred and

---

[1] *Ibid.* pp. 554–5, Letter dated 22 Sept.
[2] These two sentences were marked by Benckendorff with the pencilled comment: 'C'est
beaucoup de gagné, si on le croit.' *Ibid.*, footnote, p. 556.

malice of those who try to conceal their activities—this is the inevitable lot of all true and zealous servants. For this reason the government, in its own interest, should openly support them, that they may fear neither the strength nor the cunning of those who would like to destroy them.—What do these Jeremiahs in skirts desire?...In their apprehension lest private interests be infringed, they probably desire that only palliatives be adopted, that is, that instead of healing the wounds themselves only the sufferings they cause should be eased. No, such a course of action does not enter into the government's calculations: it sleeps warily, like a lion, without closing its eyes, so as not to neglect the smallest circumstance capable of disturbing the existing order. Its system is based on the principle that punishments and awards are the two driving forces of good government, and that it is better to make do without the latter than forego the former...To be stern with those persons who derive profit for themselves out of the evil they do to others means to be kind to everyone; there is no greater mistake in the matter of government than clemency shown to those who infringe the interests of the public.[1]

These views may be regarded as the official expression of what may be termed the ideology of the Third Department.

The Department's aims and reputation

Its methods, however, were bound to earn the cordial dislike of society in general, and its unpopularity naturally tended to increase as its activities expanded. By the autumn of 1826 it had already begun to acquire its future dubious reputation as a Political Inquisition. Vigel', in a reference to the Third Department in his memoirs, commented: 'It was in September that this black cloud rose over Russia, and it lay on her horizon for many years. Time, of course, has weakened its activities and the horror it engendered, but it did not permit the complete state of happiness that we might have enjoyed without it during the first years of the reign of the most just of emperors. Its arrival on the scene saddened even those in its immediate vicinity and I can state on oath that I have not met a single person who could approve of this institution or speak of it without the greatest distaste.'[2] There can be little doubt that, in the general view of contemporary opinion, the benefits which the creators of the Third Department hoped to confer on society did not justify the existence of a political police empowered to interfere in any aspect of public or private life that might attract its attention.

It would, however, be incorrect to assume that the Third Department possessed no more constructive policy than that of controlling and restricting developments in the national administration. It was intended to act as a centralized intelligence bureau for collecting all information likely to assist

[1] *Loc. cit.* pp. 555–7, Letter dated 24 Sept.   [2] Vigel', vol. 2, p. 277.

the government. This policy, and the need for it, clearly emerges from the contents of von Vock's letters to Benckendorff; and the official history of the Ministry of Internal Affairs describes it in the following terms: 'From the very first months of its existence the Third Department undertook the study of Russia's condition and the discovery of those aspects of Russian life which, because they did not correspond to contemporary requirements, were now regarded in a negative light by the best and shrewdest minds, and which in the future, albeit distant, might lead to mass discontent and consequently to the disturbance of public tranquillity.'[1] A less vague definition of this objective states that the Third Department was primarily interested in waging a serious struggle against the bureaucratic methods which through long years had become deeply entrenched in the national life. The prevalence of abuses, the absence of a reliable judicial system, the very low salaries of officials and the extent of venality and embezzlement that characterized government administration—all contributed to the necessity of introducing some new form of strict control.[2] Only by obtaining a constant supply of accurate information on every aspect of Russia's life could this state of affairs be altered, and the Third Department was given the positive task of providing it.

The committee of 6 December 1826

No authority is known to have raised any objections to the creation or operation of the new Higher Police in its initial phases. But some six months after the publication of the ukaz of 3 July a special committee was set up, certain of whose members were evidently not prepared to give their un-reserved support to the Tsar's security policy. This committee was created by an imperial rescript of 6 December 1826 to deal with outstanding memo-randa from the previous reign relating to the reform of state institutions and in this connexion to review existing institutions.[3] At its thirteenth meeting on 19 January 1827, in a discussion of the duties of the Ministry of Internal Affairs, the committee expressed fears that the existence of the Higher Police as 'an entirely separate branch' would undermine the position of other branches of the administration, particularly those in the provinces. There would be 'a constant danger of unsubstantiated evidence' and the government 'would have difficulty in finding men worthy of occupying the

---

[1] Adrianov, p. 100.   [2] See Trotsky, pp. 38 ff.

[3] *Sbornik imperatorskago russkago istoricheskago obshchestva*, 148 vols. (St Petersburg, 1867–1916), vol. 74 (1891), p. xi. Its members, who did not include Benckendorff, were V. P. Kochubei (president), P. A. Tolstoi, I. V. Vasil'chikov, A. N. Golitsyn, I. I. Diebich and M. M. Speransky. The committee was never formally closed down but stopped meeting after 1832. Its papers were transferred to the first department of H.I.M.'s Own Chancellery in 1834, *ibid.* pp. xi–xii.

post of governor. . .' It therefore proposed that 'for preserving unity in the steps taken for the safety and welfare of the state and for checking information received it would be beneficial to attach the Chief Commander of Gendarmes controlling the Higher Police to the Ministry of Internal Affairs in the appointment of Vice-Minister or in some other suitable capacity'.[1]

Nicholas I was quick to react to this potential infringement of his prerogative. At the committee's fifteenth meeting on 26 January he commented that the Higher Police, combined as it was with his own headquarters, 'would not be suited to its functions' if it were attached to the Ministry of Internal Affairs. He pointed out that he intended 'not that any permanently defined obligations should be laid upon it, but that it should fulfil such commissions as. . . might be necessary in matters concerning the Higher Police'; and it would be authorized to act only on his own immediate instructions. This principle had guided gendarme policy up to the present, and in his view it was beneficial to maintain it. The staff-officers employed were to be 'most reliable persons of proven honesty', and they 'could in no case hinder the activities of local provincial authorities' as their duties were confined to the task of procuring information. For these reasons 'the Chief of Gendarmes could not be attached to the Ministry of Internal Affairs in the appointment of Vice-Minister or in any other capacity in view of the fact that this Chief might not infrequently be attached to the Supreme Person of His Majesty during the Sovereign Emperor's periods of absence from the capital'.[2]

An impartial critic might be excused for regarding this as a rather feeble excuse for retaining Benckendorff in his original appointment. The truth was of course that Nicholas had no intention at this or any other time of revising a policy which so admirably answered his own requirements; and after such a very definite refusal to accept its proposals the committee evidently felt that no useful purpose could be served by reverting to the topic. It was never mentioned again.

Nicholas' attitude

An account has now been given of the circumstances that led to the creation of this new branch of governmental apparatus. The scope of its aims and objects, the composition of its staff and details of its early interests and development have been provided from the relatively few available sources. The information they contain makes it possible to summarize the reasons that induced Nicholas to authorize a new era of political control in Russia.

The Decembrist Revolt need never have occurred if an efficient secret police had existed to prevent it. This lesson was not lost on the new Emperor

---

[1] *Sbornik, loc. cit.* pp. 44–5.   [2] *Ibid.* pp. 47–8.

who, by creating such a body under his personal supervision only six months after his accession, determined to make himself omniscient as well as omnipotent. It was a bold and unpopular decision, but Nicholas was no weakling and powerful autocrats can afford to disregard unpopularity. Besides, the declared aims of the new Higher Police were beneficial; and the men entrusted to control it were honourable and well respected. There was no intention that such a force should ever deteriorate into an eighteenth-century Secret Chancellery; and positive steps were taken to avoid the mistakes committed in the first quarter of the nineteenth century due to Alexander's weak direction of political surveillance. The new Tsar adhered to the opinion that the work of the Third Department could not but be of service to the country as well as to its ruler, for it would ensure a state of general security—provided, of course, that the subjects of that ruler agreed to fulfil his wishes. If they should prove recalcitrant, on the other hand, measures could at once be taken to guarantee obedience in future.

It is permissible to assume from what is known of Nicholas' temperament that such were the arguments he found convincing.

His decision to rely on a semi-secret police, whether or not of a different variety from that of his predecessors, was one of fundamental importance. 'From his time onwards...[it] remained the chief arm of tsarism in its efforts to stamp out, curb, or canalize anything that was regarded as politically dangerous, and one of the chief means of supplying the Tsar with information as to the state of opinion in the country and in addition...as to the malpractices of his own servants.'[1] Nicholas' possession and use of this arm thus not only profoundly affected the course of his reign, but also left its imprint on the whole subsequent development of autocratic rule in Russia.

[1] B. H. Sumner, *Survey of Russian History* (London, 1947), ch. 2, p. 112.

3

The History of the Creation of
the Corps of Gendarmes

Every man will see in you an official who through my agency can bring the voice of
suffering mankind to the throne of the Tsars, who can instantly place the defenceless
and voiceless citizen under the protection of the Sovereign Emperor.

from Benckendorff's Instructions to his Staff-Officers. January 1827[1]

Background and formation

The spirit of the age manifest in the new régime of Nicholas I could hardly
have found better expression than in the formation of the Corps of Gendarmes. The Emperor Paul's mania for things military was to a greater or
lesser degree inherited by all his sons; and the events of the 1812 War and
the subsequent period of 'Arakcheyevshchina' in the reign of his elder
brother strongly influenced Nicholas' attitude to his responsibilities as Tsar.
Before his accession he had played no part in affairs of state apart from
assuming the command of the Guards Division and fulfilling the functions
of General-Inspector of Engineer Troops. As Emperor he rarely appeared in
civilian attire; and the fact of his having worn uniform throughout his forma-
tive years accustomed him to approaching all problems from a military
rather than a political standpoint. His character as well as his background
contributed to this reaction. 'The society of military circles, of all kinds of
semi-literate generals and aides-de-camp was the one he liked the most
because it permitted him to remain himself, it did not cause the excessively
egoistic autocrat any qualms, it did not compel him to search for conversational themes.'[2]

What then could have been more natural than that as Tsar Nicholas
should have chosen to exert his autocratic power through the medium of his
own personally created Chancellery, corresponding as it did to a Staff
Headquarters? 'Nicholas was not only "the gendarme of Europe" but much
more the gendarme of his own empire. He ruled it as a colonel his regiment
and a paternalistic landowner his estates, yet toiling at mountains of reports,
with the same kind of assiduity as Philip II of Spain, whether they dealt with
great questions of state or individual personal details.'[3] Furthermore, he

---

[1] Shil'der, *Imperator Nikolai Pervyi*, vol. 1, pp. 468–9; see also para. 4, Appendix C, pp. 243–4.
[2] Lemke, *Nikolayevskie Zhandarmy*, p. 3. [3] Sumner, ch. 2, p. 112.

considered this approach entirely right and proper. Order and Obedience, Discipline and Regulations represented what he understood and appreciated, and the continued presence of Benckendorff in his immediate entourage undoubtedly lent additional support to his view that soldiers were more reliable instruments than politicians, for had not Benckendorff foreseen the dangers threatening the throne long before 1825 and was it not he who had once again submitted practical proposals to prevent their recurrence? It is impossible to over-emphasize the significance attached by Nicholas to the potential benefit to the state which, he fancied, would derive from the proper employment of staff-officers as the guardians of political stability. His devotion to his troops and their officers persisted as long as he lived and his interest in them 'on his own admission constituted "his only real delight" '.[1]

Confronted, therefore, with the problem of reorganizing the forces responsible for the preservation of security, Nicholas decided upon a novel solution. He would combine under one headquarters, subordinated to his most trusted General-in-Waiting, all responsibility for questions of security and intelligence; he would organize this headquarters into a department of his own Chancellery and this department would then operate both as a civilian and a military staff under his personal surveillance. As has been shown, the Third Department with the exception of Benckendorff himself was initially composed only of civilians whose Director, von Vock, had long been in charge of a section of political police. After the summer of 1826 it was to control a para-military organization to be known as the Corps of Gendarmes. It is probable that Nicholas adopted this original method of co-ordinating civilian and military branches with a view to eradicating the abuses which in the past had disfigured the work and development of Russia's successive political police organs. In future no semi-independent 'secret police', be it civilian or military, would be in a position to exert any influence on the national life except within the framework of a centralized organization immediately answerable to the Tsar. And this organization would in future be staffed by men of proven character, most of whom had already distinguished themselves in a military sphere.

The formation of the Third Department had been a simple matter, since it merely involved the transfer of a few officials from the Ministry of Internal

[1] See 'Zapiski Grafa A. Kh. Benkendorfa', izd. M. A. Korfa, *Russkii Arkhiv* (1865), 2, pp. 130–9.
'The Emperor', says the Count in his description of the Guards' manœuvres of 1836, 'was tireless; he spent the whole day on horseback in pouring rain, the evening found him beside the bivouac fire talking to young officers serving in his suite or in the ranks of the troops surrounding his small tent; then he would spend most of the night dealing with affairs of state which nevertheless were not in the slightest held up by the Emperor's interest in his troops...', quoted by Shil'der, vol. i, p. 15.
Details of all Benckendorff's published memoirs are given in chapter Four, p. 118, note i.

Affairs to Nicholas' own Chancellery, in which they exercised precisely the same functions as before. The Corps of Gendarmes, however, had to be created from other administrative organizations, and the regulations governing its status did not appear until April 1827. Thus, as in the case of Balashov who was made Minister of Police in 1810 before the creation of that Ministry the following year, Benckendorff was appointed Chief of the Independent Corps of Gendarmes nearly eight months before the form of its establishment was finally determined.

At the time of Nicholas' accession there already existed two security organizations with cadres potentially available for recruitment into the new Corps.[1] The first consisted of the Gendarme (ex-Borisoglebsky Dragoon) Regiment which had been in existence since 1815, was entirely military in character and carried out the normal functions of a military police. The second consisted of the Independent Corps of Internal Security, first inaugurated in 1810, whose members were under military discipline for training and recruitment but under police discipline for collaboration with the civil authorities in such duties as the capture of thieves and criminals, the collection of taxes, the apprehension of tax-defaulters and so on. From 1817 this Corps contained certain 'gendarme units'[2] who represented the forces primarily responsible for the preservation of local security and were thus ideally suited for transfer into the new Corps of Gendarmes. After the appointment of Benckendorff as Chief of Gendarmes on 25 June 1826 all gendarmes military and para-military were nominally put under his orders, although until as late as 1842 he controlled the Army Gendarme Regiment only in an inspectorial capacity. The Corps of Internal Security continued to exist[3] on the same basis as before,[4] dealing with the administration of garrison troops who worked in conjunction with the normal (or Lower) police.

[1] See Adrianov, pp. 97–8. Details of these two security organizations are given in chapter One.
[2] Adrianov describes them in the following terms: 'A police dragoon detachment ["komanda"], on the establishment of the Corps of Internal Security but subordinated to the civil authorities, was placed at the immediate disposal of every Governor; this arrangement was recognized to be inconvenient and led to reorganization in 1817: police dragoon detachments were abolished and gendarme units ["chasti"] allocated to capital, provincial and important coastal cities were formed within the framework of the Corps of Internal Security; it was then decided that gendarme squadrons ["diviziony"] in a capital should be subordinated to the Ober-Politsei-meisters of the capital concerned, whereas provincial and coastal city gendarme detachments should come under the orders of local garrison battalions. The duties of the gendarmes were the same as those of other ranks in the Corps of Internal Security, but they were not selected for tax-collecting duties nor were they used as sentries at official buildings or prison institutions' (p. 98).
[3] This Corps was abolished in 1864 and replaced by 'Local Troops' ('Myestnyye Voiska'), see article on 'Vnutrennyaya Strazha' in Br. Efr. Enc. vol. 6, p. 689.
[4] In practice certain gendarme detachments continued to be subordinated to it for a further ten years, after which they were finally absorbed by the Corps of Gendarmes. See p. 90; also Adrianov, p. 99.

ИМПЕРАТОРЪ НИКОЛАЙ I, великій князь МИХАИЛЪ ПАВЛОВИЧЪ, цесаревичъ АЛЕКСАНДРЪ НИКОЛАЕВИЧЪ,
князь П. М. ВОЛКОНСКІЙ и графъ А. Х. БЕНКЕНДОРФЪ.

Съ портрета писаннаго Крюгеромъ и находящагося въ Николаевской залѣ Зимняго дворца.

1. The Emperor Nicholas I and his suite. Portrait by Franz Krüger (1797–1857)

(Shil'der, *Imperator Nikolai Pervyi*, frontispiece to vol. 2)

facing page 80

2. General Count A. Kh. Benckendorff, First Head of the Third Department
and Chief of Gendarmes, 1826–1844

(Adrianov, *Ministerstvo Vnutrennikh Dyel. Istoricheskii Ocherk*, opposite p. 56)

It should be noted that for some years the only evident link between the Corps of Gendarmes and the Third Department was provided by Benckendorff himself who commanded both.[1] The intention clearly was, however, that members of the former should represent as it were the executive and local instruments of the latter's will, and that the discoveries and opinions of both should be channelled back to the Tsar through Benckendorff. This process has been accurately described by a writer of the early Soviet period in the following terms: 'The ideal requirements of the Third Department were that it, and through it its Head, the Emperor, should be informed of everything of the slightest importance from the police point of view which took place in all corners of the Empire. A regular supply of information was provided by a constant flow of reports by the gendarme officials who commanded the gendarme districts. All this varied material was reported to Nicholas and evoked on his part considerable interest and often energetic interference. "Resolutions" constantly appeared, demands for supplementary information about an incident in which he took an interest; gendarme officers (Nicholas knew them well and would often indicate who was to be given the task) were sent to investigate individual cases or to take special measures "on imperial orders".'[2] This quotation adequately illustrates the Tsar's intention that his political police organization should henceforth operate on a strictly centralized basis and be empowered to execute the will of the Sovereign in any direction he chose.

No specific instructions to the units of his new command appear to have been issued by Benckendorff until four months after his appointment as Chief of Gendarmes. During this period, for much of which he was absent from St Petersburg in attendance on the Emperor at his coronation in Moscow, he seems to have relied on von Vock's reports of events in the capital. After his return, however,

in an order dated 31 October 1826 General-in-Waiting Benckenorff proposed that all independent heads of gendarme units and detachments should report to him by the first post on all events which might take place not only in the units they commanded but also in the areas in which they were stationed; they should also submit reports on all facts worthy of attention which might come to their knowledge— with a rider that information deserving special note should be forwarded in envelopes marked 'for personal attention' ['v sobstvennyye ruki'].[3]

This all-embracing directive appears to have been the only order issued.

[1] Trotsky, p. 48.
[2] A. Ye. Presnyakov, 'Samoderzhavie Nikolaya I', *Russkoe Proshloe* (Petrograd–Moscow, 1923), no. 2, p. 16.
[3] Adrianov, p. 99. The 'Jubilee Report' (see chapter Two, p. 62, note 2) quotes this excerpt without including any additional information, Bogucharsky, *loc. cit.* p. 89.

It is permissible to assume, however, that the months from June 1826 to April 1827 were devoted to the organization of the Corps of Gendarme Districts[1] ('Zhandarmskiye Okrugi') and the recruitment of its staff-officers.[2]

With regard to the latter, it is regrettable that General Komarovsky,[3] who had been G.O.C. the Independent Corps of Internal Security since 1816, should have refrained from passing any comment in his memoirs on the formation of the Corps of Gendarmes. His complete reticence about the effect this innovation must have had on his own Corps and officers suggest that it led to a certain rivalry between the two organizations, which perhaps explains his vague mention of the 'unpleasantnesses'[4] culminating in his seeking retirement in 1828. It is interesting, however, that his memoirs include references to two officers serving in his Corps at the end of 1824— 'Major Kel'chevsky, attached to me for special assignments' and 'Duty Staff-Officer Repeshko, who administered my chancellery'[5]—both of whom evidently transferred to the Corps of Gendarmes.[6] It is not clear whether the transfer of such officers was effected voluntarily or compulsorily, although it is likely that the more competent or ambitious among them would have thought it advantageous to enrol in a body possessing increased authority and privileges. Their work in it would have been similar to that of their previous duties and their responsibility potentially greater owing to the favour accorded by the Emperor to his new creation.

Officers of the regular forces, on the other hand, may well have felt less inclined to transfer to such a unit, as may be judged from the memoirs of one of them, P. M. Tolstoi.

[1] Certain of these were in all probability instituted several months before the publication in April 1827 of the Corps' Statutes. For instance, Maj.-Gen. P. I. Balabin (1776–1855) was appointed Head of the 1st District (St Petersburg) on 16 Nov. 1826, see *RBS* article on Balabin.

[2] According to Vigel', 'the whole of this observation corps was formed by the end of the year' [i.e. 1826], *op. cit.* vol. 2, p. 276.

[3] See chapter One, p. 25, note 1; p. 40.

[4] Komarovsky, p. 258. In his foreword to this (P. Ye. Shchegolev's) edition of these memoirs, E. A. Lyatsky comments: 'Evidently this well-mannered and humane man himself felt that he did not fully suit the demands of the new régime; as one who had witnessed "the excellent beginning of Alexander's days", he could hardly also be in sympathy with this régime', p. vii.

Komarovsky was succeeded as G.O.C. the Corps of Internal Security by Gen. P. M. Kaptsyevich (1772–1840) who had been Governor-General of Western Siberia since 1822, see *Br. Efr. Enc.* article on Kaptsyevich.   [5] Komarovsky, p. 228.

[6] Kel'chevsky and Repeshko are both mentioned as Gendarme Lt.-Cols. in the 'Report on the Activities of the Corps of Gendarmes since its institution up to 1 Jan. 1829', published as a Supplement to the Third Department's 'Annual Report for 1828', *Krasnyi Arkhiv* (1929), no. 37, p. 173. (See Appendix E, p. 254.)

It is noteworthy that Lt.-Col. Repeshko is commended (*ibid.*) for successfully performing the functions of 'Duty Staff officer of the Corps', i.e. the same duties that he had fulfilled in the Corps of Internal Security. Lt.-Col. Kel'chevsky—promoted full Colonel in 1831—is mentioned in all four of the published 'Reports on the Activities of the Corps of Gendarmes'.

In 1825 [he wrote] I was an Aide-de-Camp attached to General-in-Waiting Benckendorff, the G.O.C. the 1st Guards Cuirassier Division. Shortly after the drama of 14 December I was reporting to him as the senior A.D.C. of this division. His first words were: 'Good morning, Mr Gendarme officer!' I could only regard this as a joke, because I was not yet aware of his appointment as Chief of Gendarmes, and when, surprised, I told him that my uniform was that of the Cavalier-Guards and not of the Gendarmes, which was always to be seen at the dispersal of crowds after public ceremonies, he said: 'That is the uniform I shall wear myself, and I want you to wear it too.' I replied: 'Your service is already known to all Russia, and you can restore and ennoble that uniform in the eyes of the nation; but it is impossible for me at my age (I was twenty-five) in my rank to begin a military career as a gendarme.' 'So we part company', said Benckendorff. The very next day I brought him my application for release from my duties as his A.D.C. and for attachment to a regiment. But Benckendorff told me that I could keep my application and that I should remain with him in my former post. Later I discovered that Benckendorff's words: 'Good morning, Mr Gendarme officer' were an expression of the wish of the Emperor himself. From this talk with Benckendorff I came to realize the intention of the Emperor Nikolai Pavlovich. In creating the gendarme police, he desired primarily to show society how important and noble was the purpose of this institution; the best families and members of the emperor's personal entourage were to head this establishment. I will refer to several such persons who were appointed as deputies to Benckendorff: Generals Balabin, Count Apraksin, Volkov and others.[1]

This memoir admirably depicts the recruiting methods favoured by Benckendorff at this period and Nicholas' desire to break with the past and encourage a new attitude to 'gendarme work' on the part of his loyal subjects.

[1] 'Iz pamyatnykh zamyetok P. M. Golenishcheva-Kutuzova-Tolstago', R. Arkh. (1883), 1, pp. 221–2.

Maj.-Gen. P. I. Balabin was G.O.C. the 1st Gendarme District (St Petersburg) from 1826 to 1832; Lt.-Gen. A. A. Volkov was G.O.C. the 2nd Gendarme District (Moscow) from 1826 to 1830, when he was temporarily replaced by Maj.-Gen. Count V. S. Apraksin, see supplements to Annual Reports and RBS; also chapter Six, p. 193, note 2.

P. M. Tolstoi's opinion of the reasons that led to the institution of the Corps of Gendarmes is also worth recording: 'Whatever the circumstances, the creation of the Corps of Gendarmes police [sic] was caused by the necessity of protecting the state after an event such as that of 14 Dec. Although indeed it was said that this institution was simply a repetition of the policy of Napoleon I and his creature Fouché, the general conviction was that it was caused by necessity', ibid. p. 221.

The latter explanation is the more likely—Shil'der comments that Nicholas was probably discouraged from reinstituting a Ministry of Police by memories of the Napoleonic era linked with the names of Fouché and Savary, op. cit. vol. 1, p. 464.

Benckendorff's 'Instructions'

This change of attitude, showing the 'philanthropic aims' of the new Emperor, can best be illustrated by quoting Benckendorff's 'Instructions' to his agents and staff-officers issued at the beginning of 1827.[1] It is interesting that the contents of these Instructions[2] became known to the general public very shortly after their composition;[3] but this may well have been intentional as perhaps it was hoped that the principles they enunciated would appeal to potential future recruits. There can be no doubt that these principles were inspired by the noblest intentions on the part of Nicolas and his closest

[1] 'The best characterization of the aims and methods of the newly created Third Department may be adequately provided by the quotation of a certain document: it contains the instructions given by the Chief of Gendarmes on 13 Jan. 1827 to Shervud-Vernyi, Lieut. of the Life Guards Dragoon Regt.; it will suffice to acquaint the reader with the spirit of the new institution and with the methods it devised to realize its intended beneficial aims and the protection of suffering mankind', Shil'der, vol. 1, pp. 467–8.

(I. V. Shervud-Vernyi (1798–1867), as an N.C.O. of the 3rd Ukrainian Uhlan Regt., had earned his title of 'Vernyi' ('the Loyal') by discovering and reporting on the existence of the Decembrist conspiracy early in 1825. He continued his undercover activities in the new reign, although he remained in the army (reaching the rank of Captain in 1831) and was not transferred to the Corps of Gendarmes. In Jan. 1827 he was sent to conduct an investigation into the state of political morale in the Southern Provinces as an *ad hoc* agent of the Third Department. After this date he does not appear to have been given any further official mission, although he is reported as having tried to organize a 'private' police force in Kiev in 1829, when he attempted to spy on the relatives of certain Decembrists. His intrigues were noted by Gendarme Lt.-Col. Rutkovsky (see chapter Six, p. 192, note 2; p. 194, note 2) who, fearing that these would affect his own career, succeeded in putting a stop to them. All further attempts by Shervud to ingratiate himself with the government proved unavailing, and he subsequently served a prison sentence for his activities. See *RBS* article on Shervud; and Trotsky, pp. 83–6.)

[2] The complete text is translated as Appendix C, pp. 243–4.

After the abolition of the Third Department it was first reproduced in *Russkii Arkhiv* (1889), 7, pp. 396–7 entitled 'Instruktsiya Grafa Benkendorfa chinovniku 3-go Otdeleniya'. The Editor, P. Bartyenev, stated in an accompanying note: 'The late Count D. S. Tolstoi on more than one occasion opened the archives of this [the Third] Department for the purpose of historical research. The Instructions quoted above were at the time printed for only a few persons and are now a rarity ["prinadlezhat k chislu ryedkostei"]. Evidently they were written by Count A. Kh. Benckendorff himself', *ibid.* p. 398.

[3] The same issue of *R. Arkh.* contains (pp. 522–4) an article referring to these Instructions entitled 'Po povodu Instruktsii Grafa Benkendorfa', quoting a local police report in the Province of Penza dated 6 Feb. 1827 which deals with rumours of the Instructions' existence. According to these rumours, these Instructions had been issued to 'Col. Bibikov of the Gendarme Regt. [*sic*]', and the correspondence recorded in this article deals only with the question of the improper copying of the Instructions by minor officials and does not deny or discuss their authenticity. The Archives in fact contained a copy of the Instructions which were issued to Col. Bibikov. See Shil'der, vol. 3, pp. 781–2.

It is interesting that none of the published 'Reports on the Activities of the Corps of Gendarmes' mentioned Col. Bibikov, nor is he recorded by the *RBS*. He is referred to, however, as one of 'Benckendorff's assistants' ('Col. Ivan Petrovich Bibikov in Moscow') by B. L. Modzalyevsky, *Pushkin pod Tainym Nadzorom* (Petrograd, 1922), p. 5. Possibly his service in the Gendarmes was of very short duration.

confidant. 'Taking into consideration the vast complexity of the laws, their lack of consistency and mutual contradictions—laws which at the time [1826] had not even been collated—it was necessary to offer the people an opportunity of obtaining speedy decisions of cases affecting them and to facilitate the means of communication with the supreme power. The noble-minded Sovereign, immediately following his accession, desired direct contact with his subjects through his own chancellery...'[1] Nicholas was doubtless fully aware of the truth of the old proverb, 'God is high and the Tsar far distant',[2] and that in so huge a realm as Russia a large proportion of his subjects were at the mercy of local bureaucrats who were frequently apt to misuse their authority. Irrespective, therefore, of whether the Corps of Gendarmes was created for motives other than those of enhancing the popularity of the new régime, it is clear that Benckendorff's Instructions represented 'an attempt to resurrect the ancient ideology of Tsarist power as the source of highest justice.'[3] The 'highminded patriots' to whom they were issued were intended to appear as Nicholas' personal representatives; and consequently the Corps of Gendarmes 'as an institution possessing particular trust had as it were to destroy the bureaucratic wall which shut off the autocracy from the mass of the population and to permit each to confront the other. This institution was in every way exhibited as "beneficial" to the "well-disposed" members of the population and it relied on their support.'[4]

But noble as may have been the intentions of Nicholas and Benckendorff, the Instructions themselves represented little more than a general directive of a vague and even sentimental character. The mere expression of pious hopes combined with wishful thinking could hardly contribute much to the practical task of cleansing those 'Augean stables' of the national administration so deplored by von Vock. Official misdemeanours of the worst order were widely practised throughout the country. The use of torture, for instance, had been strictly abolished in 1801;[5] but in February 1827 the case of a man tortured to death—'...a terrible occurrence and one which shows complete failure on the part of local authorities to avert cruelties...'—was quoted in a similar ukaz[6] abolishing this abuse once again. It was issued a mere fort-

---

[1] Bartyenev, *R. Arkh.*, *loc. cit.* p. 398.

  Discussing the creation of the Third Department and the well-known 'Handkerchief Legend', Bartyenev states: 'Apart from this, the original purpose of this institution was to keep watch on the doings of civil servants and to punish them suddenly and speedily, by-passing official procrastination', *ibid.*

[2] 'Do Boga vysoko, do Tsarya dalyoko'.   [3] Presnyakov, *loc. cit.* p. 17.

[4] *Ibid.* (see also Sumner, pp. 112–13).   [5] See chapter One, pp. 21–2.

[6] Ukaz of 9 Feb. 1827. *Poln. Sobr. Zak.* vol. 2, p. 169, no. 894. The text continues: '...By reason of this We order our Governing Senate most strictly and universally to ensure: that no one should in any place dare...to invent or make use of any methods of punishment or imprisonment other than those prescribed by law'.

night after Benckendorff's Instructions to his staff-officers and serves as a good example of the sort of conditions with which his representatives were required to contend. But although Benckendorff indeed drew attention to the need for 'anticipating and extirpating every kind of wrongdoing', he was apparently naïve enough[1] to imagine that such beneficent aims as 'the protection of the law and the establishment of complete and universal justice' could be achieved by openly disposing throughout the empire a small nucleus of trusted and trust-inspiring officials.

At the same time it must be recognized that there could have been no easy solution to the problem of Russia's internal difficulties. The idea of creating an efficient, powerful and genuinely secret police was evidently rejected as being repugnant in principle; but since some form of political control was acknowledged to be inevitable, the Corps of Gendarmes—an honourable and respected cohort—was theoretically encouraged to avoid the use of specifically clandestine methods[2] and its members were instructed to follow the dictates of their own 'disinterested and noble inclinations'.

In defiance of the obvious paradox created by the need for an overt organization to engage in activities many of which could not by their very nature be other than covert, the status of the Corps of Gendarmes remained unchanged throughout the reign and Benckendorff's orders to his staff-officers were not modified in succeeding years. A regular officer, A. I. Lomachevsky, who transferred to the Corps at the beginning of 1838 as a Major, thus described his first interview with the Chief of Gendarmes: 'After explaining to me in general terms the duties of a provincial staff-officer, he added that this post ["zvanie"] required not only an honest, noble and wholly irreproachable type of conduct ["obraza dyeistvii"] but also the caution of a diplomat because, as he expressed it, our Sovereign, in appointing a Gendarme staff-officer to every province, desires to see in him the same kind of emissary, the same kind of honest and useful government representative as he has in London, Vienna, Berlin and Paris.' Lomachevsky himself added the following comment: 'At that time there did not exist any directive dealing with the order of procedure ["o poryadke dyeistvii"] to be adopted by the ranks of the Corps of Gendarmes...there was only one briefing ["instruk-tsiya"]; some understood it in too broad a sense, and others, relying on their briefing, acted arbitrarily and almost without being answerable to any control.'[3] It is clear from this evidence that staff-officers were thus allowed

[1] There is a further instance of Benckendorff's naïveté in the actual wording of the Instructions. Clause 5 presupposes an impossibility—that officials 'suffering from extreme poverty' and 'unable to subsist on their salary alone' could 'serve disinterestedly the cause of truth and religion', that is, could live honestly.

[2] Hence the introduction of the conspicuous sky-blue uniform worn by the Corps of Gendarmes.

[3] A. I. Lomachevsky, 'Zapiski Zhandarma', Vyestnik Yevropy (1872), Mar. p. 245.

considerable freedom to act as they thought fit in any given circumstances—and it is equally clear from Benckendorff's Instructions of 1827 and their oral repetition in 1838 that this was the Tsar's fixed intention.

Organization of Gendarme Districts, 1827–1837

Plans for the practical organization and distribution of the Corps of Gendarmes were completed by the spring of 1827 with the issue of a short ukaz[1] addressed to the Chief of the General Staff. Its preamble contained an announcement of the decision to divide the country into five areas to be known as 'Gendarme Districts' each of which was to be staffed by members of the Corps. The only clause relating to the recruitment of its officers stated: 'To fill the posts appointed according to this order, the necessary complement of Generals and Staff-Officers is to be chosen from serving or retired officials ["chinovnikov"] known for their excellent service, efficiency, enthusiasm and especially their good moral qualities.' Otherwise the ukaz dealt exclusively with all regulations concerning the allocation of officers to these Districts according to the 'Imperially Ratified Statute' it contained. By these regulations Benckendorff was allotted the authority of an Independent Corps Commander responsible for all Gendarme units except those already incorporated in the Army Gendarme Regiment who were to retain their military status. The 'Gendarme Districts' were to be commanded by Generals with the authority of Divisional Commanders, and each District was to be subdivided into Sections commanded by Staff-officers with the authority of Regimental Commanders. The latter were empowered to report direct to 'Mr Chief' (i.e. Benckendorff) if they were stationed in Districts to which a General had not yet been appointed. The five Districts contained in all twenty-six Sections centred on the larger towns in each District; the responsibility of each Section extended over one, two or three provinces.

[1] *Ukaz of 28 Apr. 1827. Poln. Sobr. Zak.* vol. 2, pp. 396–7, no. 1062. (Ukazes in italics (see also p. 89, notes 1, 2, 4) denote those which established the organization of the Corps of Gendarmes *by Districts.*)

This was the first ukaz referring to the Corps since the appointment of Benckendorff as its Head in June 1826. It appears to have been overlooked by Nicholas' biographer Polievktov, who states that 'The Special Corps of Gendarmes was formed considerably later—in 1836'. M. A. Polievktov, *Nikolai I. Biografiya i Obzor Tsarstvovaniya* (Moscow, 1918), p. 80. (See p. 89, notes 2, 3.) This incorrect date is also given by Hugh Seton-Watson, *The Russian Empire, 1801–1917* (Oxford, 1967), p. 206.

According to Monas, the five districts formed on 27 Apr. 1827 were 'supplemented by two more in July of that year', *op. cit.* p. 63; but he quotes no evidence for this statement, which is quite inaccurate.

(Particulars of all regulations relating to the maintenance and administration of the Corps of Gendarmes and announced in the form of ukazes may be found in the 'Ukazatel' k 2-omu Sobraniyu' (*Poln. Sobr. Zak.*), vol. A–Zh, pp. 231–3 under the heading 'Voyennaya Politsiya'.)

The pay and maintenance of the Corps was, like the supply of clerks and watchmen, to be the responsibility of the Army. Particulars of the regulations governing the exact location of Gendarme Districts and the Headquarters establishment figures of the ranks serving in them were given in an Appendix[1] to this ukaz. As regards the latter, it is interesting to note that Benckendorff's Headquarters staff of 25 persons including clerks and watchmen relied upon only 4 staff-officers (three 'for special commissions' and one as Duty Staff-Officer), 4 A.D.C and 2 Secretaries (8th class, 'for Russian and foreign correspondence') to administer the whole Corps. Each District General was allotted only one staff-officer and an A.D.C. to deal with cases in his particular area. Each Section staff-officer was allotted one junior officer who also acted as his A.D.C. It is thus evident that the officer strength of the Corps was limited to a relatively small total.[2]

The areas to which these officers were appointed, however, were disproportionately vast and included almost the whole of European Russia.[3] Each Gendarme District consisted of approximately ten provinces ('gubernii') or their equivalent (e.g. 'oblasti'), and the size of each District was relative to the density of population it contained. Thus the 1st was responsible for the whole of North Russia including Finland—an area much of which was underpopulated—and covered over twice the geographical area occupied by the 2nd, which was responsible for the eleven provinces in the Moscow region. The eastern border of the 5th District extended from the northernmost point of the Province of Perm to the southernmost frontier of Georgia, a distance of some 1700 miles. The 1827 plan for the location of Gendarme Districts also contained such anomalies as the inclusion in the 1st District of the Province of Smolyensk, geographically situated between the 2nd and 3rd Districts; and the failure to include in any District the Kingdom of Poland.[4] After the Polish Revolt, however, a new 3rd District was created

---

[1] *Poln. Sobr. Zak.*, *loc. cit.*, 'Prilozhenie k ukazu 1062', pp. 130–2.

[2] Details of the total number of the Lower Ranks of the Corps organized as Gendarme 'Diviziony' and 'Komandy' were not recorded in either the text of this ukaz or the Appendix to it. Hence it is impossible to estimate the total strength of the Corps at this date.

[3] The distribution of Gendarme Districts from 1827 to 1836 is given as Appendix D 1, pp. 245–6. From this it will be seen that until the Corps' main expansion in 1836 and 1837, European Russia was roughly divided thus: North, 1st; Central, 2nd; Western, 3rd; South-Western, 4th; North-Eastern, Eastern and South-Eastern, 5th.

The exact location of these Districts is not recorded in any work mentioning the Corps of Gendarmes. Such works merely refer to their total number without giving geographical details.

N.B. Gendarme Districts must not be confused either with Military Districts (first created in 1862, see V. D. Kuzmin-Karavayev's article in *Br. Efr. Enc.* vol. 21, p. 832) or with the Districts of the Independent Corps of Internal Security. The latter were organized in 1829 into 9 Districts with a system of boundaries entirely different from those of the Gendarme Districts (see Ukaz of 27 Sept. 1829, *Poln. Sobr. Zak.* vol. 4, no. 3199).

[4] According to the 1876 'Jubilee Report', this unaccountable failure had serious consequences: 'The Polish Revolt which flared up on 17 Nov. 1830 led to a fresh expansion of Third Depart-

in 1832 to include it, and this led to the system of re-numbering which was to recur in succeeding years.[1] The six Gendarme Districts then in existence remained unchanged until four years later when on 1 July 1836 the Corps was reorganized and expanded into seven Districts with in many cases a revised allocation of provinces.[2] The newly created 7th District extended the operational area of the Corps to include Western Siberia and territories east as far as Irkutsk, so that in practice the General commanding this District was responsible for all the vast expanse of Asiatic Russia beyond the Urals. The final re-allocation of Gendarme Districts took place the following year in 1837[3] with the creation of a new 6th District to administer Russian territory newly annexed in the mountainous areas of the Caucasus.[4] The

ment activities. Surveillance did not extend to the Kingdom of Poland before 1831 and for this reason the scheming of the Poles could not be known to the Department. The events of 1831 showed the need to emend the existing order and extend surveillance activities to a part of the empire which particularly required them' (Bogucharsky, p. 92). It is noteworthy that this Report did not specifically refer to the Corps of Gendarmes, although the decision to form a new District in Poland clearly represented the Third Department's solution to the problem of Polish intransigeance. See Chapter Six, p. 208, note 2.

N.B. At the same time a 10th District comprising Poland was added to the 9 Districts of Internal Security (see Ukaz of 15 Nov. 1833, *Poln. Sobr. Zak.* vol. 8, no. 6573, Art. 39).

[1] *Ukaz of 27 Feb. 1832. Poln. Sobr. Zak.* vol. 7, no. 5192, p. 109. This ukaz gave no details of the distribution of Sections throughout the new District. See Appendix D 1, p. 246.

Benckendorff referred to the creation of this District in the following terms: 'The number of troops in the Kingdom [of Poland] was limited to a single Corps. In addition to this, orders were given to form a Corps of Gendarmes [*sic*] there, on the basis of the one created in Russia, consisting of Poles and Russians...Staff-officers of our service were appointed to command this Corps.' ('Imperator Nikolai I v 1832 godu. (Iz zapisok grafa A. Kh. Benkendorfa)'. Soobshchil N. K. Shil'der, *R. Star.* (1898), vol. 93, p. 283.) See also p. 95, note 3.

[2] *Ukaz of 1 Jul. 1836. Poln. Sobr. Zak.* vol. 11, pt 1, no. 9355, pp. 772–82.

By this ukaz the following provinces (or equivalent) were transferred:

From 1st to 2nd G.D.	Smolyenskaya
From 2nd to 6th G.D.	Tambovskaya, Voronezhskaya
From 5th to 4th G.D.	Kievskaya
From 5th to 6th G.D. [7th 1837]	Khar'kovskaya, Kurskaya
From 6th back to 5th G.D. [new 6th 1837]	Astrakhanskaya, Obl. Kavkazskaya, Zakavkazskii Krai
From 6th to 7th G.D. [new 8th 1837]	Permskaya, Orenburgskaya

Details of the 3rd G.D. in Poland were again not published. The ukaz merely stated: 'The Gendarme District in Poland is organized under special statute', *ibid.* p. 773.

[3] Adrianov states that 'the number...rose to eight in 1843', (p. 99). This is incorrect, as the 8th District was undoubtedly created in 1837. Possibly this error was due to the wrong assumption that the ukaz which set out the organization of the 3rd Gendarme District—it was indeed published in 1843 (see p. 95, note 3)—in fact marked the final stage in the expansion of Gendarme Districts. Adrianov's error is repeated by Polievktov, p. 80, and by Seton-Watson, p. 207.

[4] *Ukaz of 7 Dec. 1837. Poln. Sobr. Zak.* vol. 12, pt 2, no. 10779, pp. 974–5.

The final clause of this ukaz is interesting: 'Hereupon the Secret Military Police in the Trans-Caucasian Region existing according to the statute Imperially ratified on 7 Jul. 1831 is abolished.'

boundaries of the 1836 6th and 7th Districts remained the same but the Districts were renumbered 7th and 8th.[1] This geographical distribution of the Corps of Gendarmes was maintained with slight modifications[2] for the duration of the Corps' existence.

Ukaz of 1 July 1836

The ukaz of 1 July 1836 marked a turning-point in the administrative development of the Corps and, compared with that of 28 April 1827, it represented a complex variety of regulations set out in nine detailed chapters. Its compilation was the work of Major-General Dubbelt,[3] who played an outstandingly important rôle in the deployment of Russia's political police. Since 1835 he had been Chief of Staff of the Corps and was 'the creator of the gendarme system in the form it adopted during and after his tenure of office'.[4] The ukaz or 'Imperially Ratified Statute' for which he was responsible was an important step for several reasons. It recreated the Districts which formed the basis of Gendarme staff-work for years ahead, it established the final organization of this work and it put an end to an earlier anomaly by absorbing into the Corps' ranks all gendarme detachments that had remained under the orders of the Corps of Internal Security.[5]

The territorial expansion of Gendarme Districts and the increased authority of the Corps led to the introduction of certain fundamental altera-

No ukaz was issued inaugurating this body and it seems permissible to assume that it was a local and possibly *ad hoc* organization operating under the direct orders of the G.O.C. the Caucasus with the approval of the Emperor. (This is confirmed by a mention of the activities of Colonel Kil'chevsky [*sic*] in the Supplement to the 'Annual Report for 1831'.) There is also evidence that its primary aim was to frustrate Polish efforts to subvert this area, see chapter Six, p. 209, note 3.

Details of the numerical establishment of this newly-formed 6th District were printed in the 'Prilozhenie' to the above ukaz, *loc. cit.* p. 255.

Interpreters were attached to this District in 1838 (see *Poln. Sobr. Zak.* vol. 13, pt 2, no. 11894) and in 1840 (*ibid.* vol. 15, pt 1, no. 13195).

[1] The redistribution of Gendarme Districts in 1836 and 1837 is given as Appendix D 2, pp. 247–9.

[2] The allocation of provinces to Districts in 1836 contained some further anomalies. The Provinces of Kursk and Khar'kov, for instance, were included in the 6th G.D. (re-numbered 7th in 1837) with District HQ at distant Kazan', although geographically these provinces were closest to the HQ of the 5th G.D. at Poltava. Extreme delay in the conduct of business thus resulted, and these provinces were transferred to the 5th G.D. in 1841. At the same time, and for the same reason, the Province of Orenburg was transferred from the 8th to the 7th G.D. In the Caucasus, on the reorganization of the local civil authorities, the HQ of one Gendarme 'Komanda' were transferred from Shusha to Staraya Shemakha. See Ukaz of 4 Mar. 1841. *Poln. Sobr. Zak.* vol. 16, no. 14316. (See also Ukaz of 28 Aug. 1847. *Poln. Sobr. Zak.* vol. 22, no. 21499.)

[3] Dubbelt's career and personality are dealt with in chapter Five.   [4] Trotsky, p. 48.

[5] Ukaz no. 9355, *loc. cit.* p. 773 (ch. 1, clause 5). This decision was also embodied in a separate ukaz, no. 9356 of the same date, *loc. cit.* pp. 782–3.

Barents Sea

White Sea

• Arkhangel'sk

FINLAND

Baltic Sea

Abo Helsingfors
Petrozavodsk
Revel' St.Petersburg
Derpt
Mitava Riga Pskov
Kovno Vitebsk
Vilno Smolensk
Warsaw Grodno Minsk
③ Mogilev
④
Chernigov
Zhitomir
Kamenets- Kiev
Podol'sk Poltava
⑤
Kishinev
Odessa Kherson
Simferopol

Vologda
Vyatka • Perm'
Yaroslavl' Kostroma
Tver'
Vladimir
Moscow
❷
Kaluga Ryazan'
Tula
Orel
Tambov
Kursk Voronezh
Khar'kov
Ekaterinoslav
DON COSSACKS
Novocherkassk

Nizhnii- Kazan'
Novgorod
Simbirsk • Ufa
Penza ❺ Samara
❻ Orenburg
Saratov

Tobol'sk

Sea of Azov

Stavropol'

Black Sea

Astrakhan'

Caspian Sea

Tiflis

.... Provinces
⊙ Gendarme Section H.Q.
● 1827
○ 1832 (1st. and 2nd. G.D. not re-numbered)

Miles 0   100   200   300
Km 0 100 200 300 400 500

MAP I: GENDARME DISTRICTS FROM 1827 TO 1832
(see Appendix D I)

Barents
Sea

White
Sea

● Arkhangel'sk

FINLAND

TOBOL'SK →

Abo Petrozavodsk
Helsingfors
❶
Baltic
Sea
Revel' ST. PETERSBURG Vologda
□ Vyatka □ Perm'
Derpt □ Novgorod
❽
Mitava Riga Pskov Yaroslavl □ Kostroma
□ Ufa
Kovno Tver Nizhnii- □ KAZAN'
VILNO Vitebsk ❷ MOSCOW Vladimir Novgorod
Smolensk Simbirsk Samara
WARSAW Grodno Minsk Kaluga Ryazan Penza Orenburg
Belostok Mogilev Tula
❸ ❹ Orel Tambov Saratov
Zhitomir Chernigov Voronezh ❼
Kamenetz- Kiev Kursk
Podol'sk POLTAVA Khar'kov
Kishinev ❺ Ekaterinoslav DON COSSACKS
Odessa Kherson Novocherkassk
Astrakhan'
Simferopol' Sea Stavropol'
of Kizlyar
Azov ❻ Caspian
Black Sea
Sea Derbent
Akhaltsykh □ TIFLIS
Shusha

..... Provinces
□ Detachment H.Q.
▣ District H.Q.
⫽⫽⫽ Provinces re-
distributed in 1841

1836 Regulations (7 Gendarme Districts)
❺ Included Astrakhan', Stavropol' and Tiflis areas
❻ District newly created from 5 th. G.D. (1832)
❼ Re-numbered from 6 th. G.D. (1832)

Miles 0   100   200   300
Km.   0   100 200 300 400 500

MAP 2: GENDARME DISTRICTS AFTER 1837
(see Appendix D II)

tions in its organizational character.[1] The chain of command was now divided in descending order of authority into Chief, District and Provincial Directorates, the Chief Directorate being commanded by the Chief of Gendarmes, District Directorates by Lieutenant-Generals or Major-Generals and Provincial Directorates by Colonels, Lieutenant-Colonels or Majors.[2] This regulation emended the previous administrative system of the Corps and the original organization of Gendarme Districts by 'Sections' was abolished. In 1827 each Provincial staff-officer had been made responsible for controlling gendarme work in the several provinces which constituted his 'Section'; by 1836 it was evidently realized that the total area subordinated to one officer was too vast and his authority was therefore now limited to one province only, with the result that two or three officers were now required to administer the area previously controlled by only one.

Strength of Corps: its powers and duties

As regards the numbers involved, the total Headquarters establishment of the Chief Directorate of the Corps (all ranks) was laid down as 87, that of the 1st and 2nd Districts as 32 and of the remaining Districts as 28. Provincial staff-officers stationed in the 1st and 2nd Districts were each allotted a personal staff of 11; those stationed in other Districts, of 9.[3] The total number of staff-officers below the rank of General, that is, those officers with specific responsibility for staff administration or local detached command, was now fixed at 7 Colonels, 32 Lieutenant-Colonels and 27 Majors. Such was the fixed establishment of staff-officers at this date. In order to assist recruitment of suitable personnel, the regulations stated that these staff-officers might hold higher or lower substantive rank provided that the establishment itself remained constant. This nucleus of 66 staff-officers was assisted, in addition to their own headquarters staff, by a total of 36 Captains (18 of whom held the lower rank of Staff-Captain), 14 Lieutenants ('poruchiki') and 14 Ensigns ('praporshchiki') in the capacity of O.C. Gendarme Detachments.[4] The essentially military character of the Corps was guaran-

---

[1] The Composition and Administration of the Corps are set out in Chs. 1 and 2 of Ukaz no. 9355, loc. cit. pp. 772–4.

(Both remained substantially the same until 1867 when a new Statute was issued abolishing the majority of the Districts and re-naming Provincial staff-officers 'Heads of Provincial Gendarme Directorates', see A. Ye. Yanovsky's article on 'Zhandarmy', Br. Efr. Enc. vol. 11, p. 718 (no sources quoted).)   [2] Ch. 2, loc. cit. Clauses 24–7, 29.

[3] See 'Prilozhenie' to Ukaz no. 9355, loc. cit. vol. 11 (pt 2), pp. 337–9. Details of comparative pay-rates are also given.

[4] Ch. 1, loc. cit. Clauses 7–10.

This total of 64 officers commanded the 57 Gendarmes Detachments of the Towns and Cities named in the 'Prilozhenie' to this Ukaz (see Appendix D 2). It must be presumed that seven

teed by one regulation stating that no civilians were ever to be appointed as Provincial staff-officers or to command Gendarme Detachments unless they had had previous military experience,[1] and by another ordering that all ranks of the Corps should wear the uniform of the Gendarme Regiment.[2]

As in any military unit the majority of the Corps of Gendarmes consisted of 'Other Ranks', that is, Non-Commissioned Officers and men (or troopers). In the Corps of Gendarmes they represented a component of cavalry troops capable of ensuring that the decisions of their officers could, at any time or place, be instantly backed by armed strength. Like all comparable forces operating in the capacity of a political police, they were not subject to the orders of any other authority. Unlike the ranks of regular Corps and Divisions, they did not operate as a collective body but were dispersed throughout the empire in detached units under the command of local Gendarme officers. They were organized in 'Diviziony' (each of which consisted of two Squadrons) and 'Komandy', that is, 'Detachments' or 'Troops'. A 'Divizion', commanded by a Colonel, consisted of 26 Officers and 404 Other Ranks who, together with a non-operational rear echelon of 97, made up a total strength of 501. A 'Divizion' was allotted an establishment of 327 horses and was attached to the G.O.C. at St Petersburg and Moscow. A 'Komanda', commanded by a Staff-Captain ('Shtabs-Kapitan') or by a junior officer holding that rank temporarily, consisted of 1 Officer and 28 Other Ranks who, with an additional non-operational 4 ranks, made up a total strength of 34 with an allotted establishment of 25 horses. A 'Komanda' was attached to each Provincial staff-officer. Slightly smaller 'Komandy' were also stationed at certain strategic Ports, Towns and Fortresses in addition to the normal establishment of Provincial Gendarme Directorates.[3] The distribution of Gendarme detachments on a provincial

Detachments were unaccounted for in the above total because they were stationed in the 3rd Gendarme District, particulars of which were not given.   [1] *Loc. cit.* Clause 17.

[2] This uniform was worn by all Generals (who were also authorized to wear regular Generals' uniform), Staff-Officers and A.D.C.'s 'with aiguillettes'. Other officers below staff rank were not authorized to wear aiguillettes, *loc. cit.*, clause 22. Civilian officials, whose employment as Secretaries was permissible in default of suitable military personnel, were required to wear the uniform of the War Ministry, *ibid.* Clause 23.

[3] Ch. 2, *loc. cit.*, clauses 28, 30; also 'Prilozhenie', *loc. cit.* pp. 340–2.
The smaller Gendarme Detachments were organized as follows:

Location	Horses	Total
Tsarskoe Selo	13	13
Odessa	18	18
Derpt and port towns of Kronstadt, Nikolayev, Feodosiya, Taganrog, Odessa	12 each	72
Fortresses of Bobruisk, Dinaburg, Izmail	22 each	66
	Total operational strength	169

'Prilozhenie', p. 342

basis enabled each General commanding a Gendarme District to have at his disposal a relatively strong and mobile force of armed troops capable of quick concentration and deployment.

The 'Powers, Duties and Responsibility of Members of the Corps'[1] closely resembled those laid down in 1827 but were now prescribed in greater detail. As regards the powers of the Chief of Gendarmes, he continued to enjoy independent authority over his Corps, being only required to report the internal transfer of his officers to the Minister of War for his information. His Chief of Staff—a post that did not exist under that name in 1827—had the same obligations and privileges as all other Corps' Chiefs of Staff. As regards duties, the activities of the Chief of Gendarmes consisted of the supervision and inspection of the Corps' work (the findings of which were also passed to the Minister of War). District Commanders were required to hold annual inspections of their Districts—which could be inspected by proxy through Special Duties Staff-Officers—and to submit annual reports to the Chief of Gendarmes by 1 September. At the next, that is, the executive level, the ukaz stated: 'The duties of Provincial staff-officers are laid down in the special instructions of the Chief of Gendarmes. As the closest local authorities ['nachal'niki'], they keep watchful surveillance over the preservation of law and order through the Gendarme detachments subordinated to them.'[2] As regards their responsibility, all members of the Corps were held answerable for their actions in accordance with their rank and duties, that is, they were subject to the normal requirements of military discipline.

Regulations covering the employment of Gendarme 'Diviziony' in the capitals and 'Komandy' in provinces, fortresses and ports[3] reveal the considerable variety of duties allotted to the lower ranks of the Corps. These mounted troops were used for ensuring that rulings or sentences imposed by the law-courts were carried out—for apprehending thieves, runaways and distillers of illicit alcohol—for discovering bandits and dispersing gatherings forbidden by law—for suppressing revolts and restoring civil obedience— for pursuing and capturing smugglers of contraband goods—for providing escorts for special ('nyeobyknovyennykh') criminals and persons under detention—for preserving order at fairs, trading centres, on religious and popular feast-days, on all occasions involving public assembly (fires, parades, ceremonies etc.). The use of Gendarme detachments was also authorized for

The total strength of each Detachment was probably slightly higher. The 'Prilozhenie' does not record the attachment to these 'Komandy' of any non-operational ranks. (Details of their individual establishment are also not given, and the rank of their Commander is not stated.)

[1] See ch. 3, *loc. cit.* pp. 775–6.
[2] *Ibid.* Clauses 47, 48. It would have been difficult to specify more exactly the duties of Provincial staff-officers in view of their extreme variety and complexity. Cf. the text of Benckendorff's 1827 Instructions, para. 5 (conclusion), Appendix C, p. 244.
[3] See ch. 4, *loc. cit.* pp. 776–7.

'night patrols' in the absence of any cavalry troops; and Gendarmes were attached as orderlies or dispatch-riders to specified officials.[1] 'Ober-Politsei-meisters' in the capitals (that is, the Heads of the Lower Police) were permitted to demand the use of Gendarmes 'for authorized objects' as also in other localities were 'Civil Governors, Commandants and Mayors; in such cases these Gendarmes were temporarily subordinated to their applicants, who were held responsible for their charges over the period requested and required to pay for any expenses involved. Gendarmes employed on detached duties by higher officials other than their own officers were paid a bonus of 10 roubles in the capitals and 5 roubles elsewhere, half of which was placed in a Lower Ranks fund and the other half added to the Gendarmes' own pay. A Gendarme could also count on receiving a bonus of 10 roubles for effecting a capture. It is clear from the regulations contained in this ukaz that the 'Other Ranks' of the Corps carried out in general the normal functions of local civil police forces with the difference that they were both mobile and military and, except as stated above, were primarily responsible only to the officers of their Corps. Their maintenance and accommodation was incumbent on the War Ministry.[2]

Recruitment into the lower ranks of the Corps was also a War Ministry responsibility and the Inspectorate Department of this Ministry was charged with the supply of suitable candidates for transfer from the Army. The qualifications demanded were that such candidates should possess an exemplary record of behaviour and good health, they should have completed five years' service without ever having been charged with offences and they were required to have an excellent knowledge of cavalry service. Regimental Commanders instructed to select recruits for the Corps were likely to make recommendations with care because, if their choice proved to be faulty, they were held personally responsible for bearing the expenses incurred by the necessity of replacement. Retired cavalrymen could enlist in Gendarme 'Diviziony' or 'Komandy' on a voluntary basis provided they obtained the permission of the Chief of Gendarmes. The incentives to transfer to (or, in the case of retired soldiers, to enlist in) the Corps were several, including such items as 'improved rations' which were issuable as soon as they set out on their new posting—the eligibility of N.C.O.s with unblemished records for commissions 'on the discretion of higher authority, whereupon they could choose whether to continue to serve in the Corps or transfer as officers to the regular Army'—the alternative choice offered to such N.C.O.s of a per-

[1] In the capitals, to the Military Governor-General (2), Civil Governor (1), Ober-Politseimeister (4) and Politseimeisters (2 each); in provincial towns, to the Military Governor (1), Governor-General (1) and Civil Governor (1); in port towns, to the Mayor (1); and in fortresses, to the Commandant (1), *ibid.* Clause 55.
See chs. 5 and 6, *loc. cit.* pp. 777–9.

manent civilian appointment in the Postal Department—the promise of 'indefinite leave' after twenty years' irreproachable service— and so on.[1] It is also permissible to surmise that the prospect of a comparatively varied and active life, to say nothing of the authority of the Gendarme uniform, acted as no small inducement to service in the Corps.

The total strength of the entire Corps of Gendarmes was not established by the 1836 ukaz at any specific number, but it is possible to estimate roughly from a calculation of the establishment figures given in the Appendix to this ukaz that at that date, on a basis of seven Gendarme Districts only, the Corps contained over 4,000 officers and men.[2] This approximate total cannot be accepted as more than partially and provisionally accurate in view of the absence of published information on the organization and strength of the 3rd Gendarme District[3] and the somewhat conjectural estimate of the strength

---

[1] See chs. 6 and 8 on Recruitment and Privileges, *loc. cit.* pp. 779–82.

Ch. 9 (Miscellaneous) dealt with the right of Gendarmes to medical attention and their liability to Court-Martial if found guilty of offences.

[2] This total is computed thus:

Establishment figures			Total
Corps HQ			87
1st and 2nd Gendarme Districts HQ	(2×32)		64
3rd G.D. HQ	(av. total estimated at 30)		30
4th, 5th, 6th and 7th G.D. HQ	(4×28)		112
Provincial Staff-Officers (all Districts)			66
Their staffs in 1st G.D. (11 provinces)	$(11 \times 11) = 121$		
Their staffs in 2nd G.D. (10 provinces)	$(10 \times 11) = 110$		
Their staffs in 3rd G.D. (estd. equiv. of 7 provinces)	$(7 \times 9) = 63$		618
Other G.D. (totalling 36 provinces)	$(36 \times 9) = 324$		
2 Gendarme 'Diviziony' in Capitals	(2×501)		1002
64 Gendarme 'Komandy' in Provinces (incl. 7 estimated to comprise the number of 'Komandy' stationed in the 3rd G.D.)	(64×34)		2176
Port, Town and Fortress 'Komandy' (estimated from number of horses allotted to each, see p. 92, note 3)			169
		Total estimated strength	4324

See 'Prilozhenie' to Ukaz no. 9355, *loc. cit.* pp. 337–42.

[3] Details of the 3rd Gendarme District were not published until 1843—eleven years after it was first instituted, see Ukaz of 18 Jul. 1843. *Poln. Sobr. Zak.* vol. 18, pp. 464–72 (and 'Prilozhenie', *ibid.* pp. 278–82), no. 17038. It differed from Gendarme Districts in Russia proper in that it was subordinated for operational purposes to the Viceroy of Poland. As regards its organization, a 'Divizion' was established at Warsaw and 'Komandy' at Plotsk, Warsaw (Varshava), Radom and Lublin. Geographically the 3rd G.D. was considerably smaller than its equivalents in Russia, but it was probably allotted a disproportionately large numerical establishment in view of the Polish Revolt of 1830–1. If a 'Divizion' was already stationed at Warsaw by 1836, the above estimate of the Corps' total strength at that date would be nearer 5,000.

The internal administration of the Kingdom of Poland was altered in 1844 and as a result

of all Port, Town and Fortress 'Komandy'. Even an approximate figure, however, shows the extent to which the Corps had grown during the first ten years of its existence; and this growth was increased shortly afterwards with the further expansion of the Corps to include eight Districts in 1837. Important additions also occurred in subsequent years with the creation of new responsibilities undertaken by the Corps, notably the formation of a new 'Komanda' at Brest-Litovsk in 1840,[1] the appointment of staff-officers to the gold mines in Siberia in 1841 and 1842,[2] the establishment in 1846 of a temporary Gendarme Squadron to control the new St Petersburg–Moscow railway,[3] the institution of a Gendarme Headquarters at Samara in 1850 (the

the organization of the 3rd G.D. was further amended by an Ukaz of 28 May 1845. *Poln. Sobr. Zak.* vol. 20, no. 19047, p. 423.

It is interesting that the subordination of the 3rd G.D. to the Viceroy of Poland was later quoted as a precedent when it was decided to subordinate the 6th G.D. to the Viceroy of the Caucasus in 1856. (See *Poln. Sobr. Zak.* vol. 31, pt 1, no. 30926, p. 835.)

[1] See *Poln. Sobr. Zak.* vol. 15 (1840), Ukaz no. 14039. Its status was similar to that of the other 'Komandy' stationed at the fortresses of Bobruisk, Dinaburg and Izmail, and it was subordinated to the Gendarme Staff-Officer in the Province of Grodno.

[2] *Ibid.* vol. 16 (1841), Ukaz no. 14537; vol. 17 (1842), Ukaz no. 15621.

[3] *Ibid.* vol. 21 (1846), Ukaz no. 19979. This Squadron was placed on detached duty at the complete disposal of the Railway Authorities. Its temporary character later became permanent and Gendarme units were increasingly used for the political surveillance of rail communications.

It appears that a 'special railroad gendarmerie' was first established at the instigation of the Minister of Communications, Count Kleinmikhel', in the spring of 1844 to deal with complaints about working conditions on the railway.

'Officially, the new hounds were to see to it that the workers were comfortably sheltered, well fed with fresh and ample food, and doctored when falling ill. The real mission was of course to keep everybody under close surveillance; the two high and six junior officers were to command the ten non-coms and seventy-two privates guarding against disorder in men's thoughts and acts.

Now, along Whistler's line, the sky-blue uniform of a gendarme was everywhere. The sight of it was dreaded...

Baron Tisenhausen was in active charge of spying. He was only a lieutenant and eager for promotion...he seemed ubiquitous and omniscient. On occasion he would disguise himself as a traveler; thus unobserved and unfeared, he would listen from a carriage to rumor and grumble. But there was a slit in his armor: he was partial to bribes...

His gendarmes looked after the serf-laborers' spiritual welfare also: six military field-churches...were erected by these police along Whistler's line. Priests and their assistants were borrowed with the churches...To show to the serfs precisely what branch of the Tsar's service bossed these churches, two emblems were painted on the holy gates of the altar screen: an all-seeing eye on the left gate, and an all-hearing ear on the right one...

Though actually wielding most of the power, officially Baron Tisenhausen was second in command. Chief of the railroad gendarmerie was Prince Belosel'sky-Belozersky...', Albert Parry, *Whistler's Father* (New York, 1939), ch. 13, pp. 161–2. (The American Major George Washington Whistler (1800–49) came to Russia in 1842 on the invitation of Nicholas to build the first Russian railways.) According to Parry, Kleinmikhel' ordered the expansion of the railroad gendarmie to twice their former number early in the summer of 1846, ch. 23, p. 260. (It was evidently this expansion that was officially proclaimed by Ukaz no. 19979, issued on 27 Apr.)

(Baron K. Ye. Tisenhausen (1802–1887), after a career in the Army, transferred to the Corps of Gendarmes as Lt.-Col. in 1837 when he was appointed Provincial Staff-Officer at Tver'. He

Максимъ Яковлевичъ фон-Фокъ.

(Съ портрета, находящагося въ „Альбомѣ Пушкинской выставки“).

3. M. Ya. von Vock, Director of Chancellery of the Third Department, 1826–1831

(Shil'der, *Imperator Nikolai Pervyi*, vol. 2, p. 285)

facing page 96

Л. В. ДУБЕЛЬТЪ *(акварель 30 г.)*.

«Его худощавое лицо съ длинными сѣдыми усами, пристальный взглядъ большихъ сѣрыхъ глазъ имѣли въ себѣ что-то волчье», характеризуетъ Дубельта П. П. Каратыгинъ *(Ист. Вѣст. 1887 г.)*. «Черты его имѣли что-то волчье и даже лисье, т.-е. выражали тонкую смышленость хищныхъ звѣрей; вмѣстѣ уклончивость и заносчивость» (отзывъ А. И. Герцена).

4. General L. V. Dubbelt and a Gendarme

(Golos Minuvshago (1913) kn. III, opposite p. 132)

facing page 97

Province of Samara was created the following year)[1] and of another at Erivan in 1851.[2] This natural development of gendarme duties, however, affected only the strength of the Corps without materially altering its organization.

At all stages of its development this organization was unique in that it represented a large deployed military unit engaged on such political tasks as the safeguarding of national internal security and the acquisition of intelligence information. Possessing this special status it contained a higher proportion of senior and junior staff-officers (the latter acting as assistants and A.D.C. to the former) than was customary in regular Army units of Corps size, and their direct contact with the Lower Ranks of the Corps was relatively limited. That is to say, they did not command Gendarme troops in the field, and an analysis of the proportion of officers to men in the Corps' strength would therefore tend to be misleading. The Lower Ranks, the N.C.O.s and Troopers of Gendarme 'Diviziony' and 'Komandy', merely constituted an armed force to execute the specific orders of higher authority. The officers who commanded these units were strictly subordinated to the senior staff-officers of the Corps—Majors and above—in whose hands its influence and real power were concentrated. It was these staff-officers who provided the Third Department in the person of Benckendorff with a constant supply of intelligence reports 'on all events without exception'.[3]

At the same time the connexion between the Third Department and the Gendarme officers who fulfilled its instructions was not publicly stated in official documents for a number of years. According to one source,[4] 'the first mention of Gendarme ranks acting as organs of the Third Department in an investigatory capacity occurs in a supreme ukaz dated 24 March 1831 announced by the Chief of Gendarmes to the Senate and occasioned by the dilatoriness of the authorities in fulfilling the demands made by ranks of the Corps of Gendarmes'. An inspection of the text of this ukaz,[5] however, reveals that it referred only to 'officials' ('chinovniki') and did not mention

held a similar post at Novgorod in 1838 and was promoted Col. shortly afterwards. In 1847 he was appointed Head of the Police Directorate of the St Petersburg–Moscow Rly (it was opened in 1851, see Parry, Epilogue, p. 335). In 1852 he was made Provincial Staff-Officer at Vyatka and promoted Maj.-Gen. In 1857 he transferred to the Ministry of Internal Affairs and in 1885 was attached to the Army Cavalry Reserve with the rank of Lt.-Gen., see *RBS*.

Prince Belosel'sky-Belozersky is not recorded in the *RBS*. According to Parry, he bribed Kleinmikhel' to allow him to supply the railway with iron from his own foundries and died during his subsequent trial for peculation, ch. 13, pp. 163–4.)

[1] *Ibid.* vol. 25 (1850), Ukaz no. 24582. (See also vol. 26 (1851), no. 24803.)
[2] *Ibid.* vol. 26 (1851), Ukaz no. 24877.
[3] Ukaz no. 449, Art. 8, see Appendix B, p. 241.
[4] Yanovsky, *loc. cit.* p. 718.
[5] Ukaz of 24 Mar. 1831. *Poln. Sobr. Zak.* vol. 6, pp. 265–6, no. 4450.

the Corps of Gendarmes by name.[1] It is nevertheless permissible to assume that this ukaz 'On the Instant Satisfaction of the Demands of officials entrusted with the Conduct of Investigations authorized by the Imperial Orders and Edicts of the Third Department of His Majesty's Own Chancellery' was in fact issued in response to complaints forwarded by the Corps' staff-officers. It was, after all, no secret that the Corps was commanded by the Head of the Third Department and it is odd that an ukaz of such importance should have refrained from referring directly to the gendarmes whom it so clearly concerned. Had these 'officials' been merely secret agents of the Third Department, they would scarcely have been authorized to make open demands for information from administrative offices—which was exactly what Gendarme staff-officers were required to do. There can therefore be little doubt that from the first the Corps of Gendarmes was intended to operate as the executive branch of the Third Department.

Officially these two related but dissimilar organizations continued to lead an apparently independent existence until 1839, when the following ukaz was announced by the Minister of Justice.

General-in-Waiting Count Benckendorff in his minute of 25 March has informed him, the Minister of Justice, that the Sovereign Emperor, recognizing it necessary that the Third Department of His Imperial Majesty's Own Chancellery and the Headquarters of the Corps of Gendarmes should be directed by one official under the chief direction of Count Benckendorff, has Imperially deigned to order: that both these directorates should be subordinated to Major-General Dubbelt of His Majesty's Suite and that he should be called the Chief of Staff of the Corps of Gendarmes and the Director of the Third Department of His Imperial Majesty's Own Chancellery.[2]

It is probable that the decision to subordinate these two offices to one and the same functionary was due less to a change of policy than to a chance circumstance. Von Vock's successor in the Third Department, A. N. Mordvinov,[3] was dismissed from his post of Director of its Chancellery on 18 March for having inadvertently authorized the publication of an almanach containing the signature of an ex-Decembrist, whereupon Dubbelt, whose influence by 1839 had now considerably increased, was left as the most senior of Benckendorff's assistants. His relations with Benckendorff were excellent and for the remainder of the reign he occupied the chief administrative post in the Third Department. His promotion to it provided yet another example

---

[1] It is noteworthy that the *Poln. Sobr. Zak.* index-reference to this Ukaz is listed not under 'Voyennaya Politsiya' (see p. 87, note 1) but under 'Sobstvennaya Ye.I.V. Kantselyariya'.

[2] Ukaz of 28 Mar. 1839. *Poln. Sobr. Zak.* vol. 14, no. 12177, p. 231.

[3] Mordvinov was the last civilian to hold such high office in the Department. His appointment is discussed in chapter Four, pp. 138 ff.

of Nicholas' preference for military advisers and may be described as having further contributed to the 'militarization' of Russia's political police force.

The final step in this direction was taken three years later when the Army Gendarme Regiment—the last Gendarme unit to remain outside the control of the Department—was subordinated to Benckendorff in 1842.[1] The control of all forces concerned with the task of disciplinary surveillance in Russia was from that date onwards concentrated in his or his subordinates' hands.

Such were the stages by which the Corps of Gendarmes attained a position of great political importance in nineteenth-century Russia.

Development of the Corps, 1826–1855

Its development within the framework of the Third Department from its institution in 1826 until the end of Nicholas' reign was characterized by its steady growth and increasing authority over the country both administratively and geographically. It would have been surprising had this development proceeded along different lines. The Corps of Gendarmes was one of the typical phenomena of its period, and another, closely connected with it, was the tendency to reaction in internal policy which became increasingly manifest as the reign advanced. As the one developed, so did the other. Not all the factors that contributed to this reactionary tendency were of domestic origin. Nicholas is generally acknowledged to have been a stern and authoritarian ruler, and as such he conscientiously regarded it as his duty to protect his country from all potentially harmful influences at work elsewhere. 'Elsewhere' in this context signified Western Europe, where successive political events encouraged him in his belief that dangerously liberal trends of opinion could easily spread their infection to Russia. This conviction was strengthened by the outbreak of disaffection in Poland so soon after the Paris rising of 1830, and by the gradual increase of revolutionary discontent in Europe which finally culminated in the events of 1848. Against this background of political ferment abroad, Nicholas felt impelled to take firm measures at home; for who should say that sporadic incidents of civil disobedience (the peasant mutinies, the frequent murder of landowners by their serfs and so on) were not symptomatic of a rebellious spirit that might disrupt his entire empire? In order to safeguard against such a disaster he relied whole-heartedly on the loyalty of a special Higher Police subordinated to the leading Department of his own Chancellery. As a result, no other branch of his administration enjoyed such favour. No other branch so increased its authority that its importance quickly outweighed that of any other government institution. Its autocratic master could at any time send

[1] Ukaz of 5 Mar. 1842. *Poln. Sobr. Zak.* vol. 17, no. 15357, p. 156.

7-2

for specific information from his 'Gendarme Colonels' stationed in all parts of the country and could then proceed to take any independent action that seemed to him appropriate. The Third Department thus came to represent 'an institution capable of by-passing other institutions or of acting outside their sphere of competence'.[1]

Official and unofficial reactions

The acquisition of such widespread power by this favoured branch of semi-secret police would seem to be far removed from the modest beginnings of the Corps in 1826. Yet in an autocratic régime this development was inevitable. No amount of sentimental appealing and moralizing on the part of Nicholas and Benckendorff could conceal from the Russian public in general and from Russian officials in particular that, in the opinion of their Tsar, they were neither trusted nor trustworthy and that they were therefore to be placed under the surveillance of specially selected envoys with Imperially confirmed authority.

It is hence not surprising that public opinion was generally hostile to this new institution and not in the least comforted by the seemingly noble sentiments which, to judge by Benckendorff's directive, allegedly prompted its actions. 'Naturally the pathetic artificiality of this Instruction made the worst impression everywhere. Everyone knew that the disinterested assistants for whom Benckendorff hoped were not be to found. What was felt and recognized daily was an irritating system of control...'[2] This view of a later historian is fully confirmed by the evidence of the contemporary memoir-writer Vigel' who, having explained that 'every staff-officer of this Corps, in the province in which he was stationed, was required to superintend the just conduct of law-court administration, to direct the attention of Governors to all instances of disorder in general, peculation on the part of the civil service, cruel treatment indulged in by landowners, and to report on such incidents to his own authorities'—an accurate appraisal of the duties involved—proceeded to subject this new organization to apt criticism. 'Its purpose, of course', he wrote, 'seemed to be an excellent one, but to fulfil it where was one to find men possessing the qualities of conscientiousness, impartiality, experience and perspicacity? Did there really not exist governors, urban and rural police and, finally, attorneys whose job it was to superintend the legal conduct of affairs? Had there indeed hitherto been no order in Russia whatsoever? Did lawlessness really reign supreme throughout its extent? And if so, could all this be put to rights by a handful of army officers selected

[1] A. D. Gradovsky, *Sobranie Sochinenii* (SPB, 1907), vol. 8, p. 520.
[2] Schiemann, vol. 2, ch. 3, p. 99.

at random? To grant such persons complete confidence meant undermining that of all local authorities, senior and junior.'[1]

This natural reaction to the announcement of the institution and duties of Gendarme officers was doubtless common to many people at the time, although Vigel' did not conceal the fact that the Corps apparently succeeded in marshalling a full complement of recruits by the end of 1826, 'no matter how difficult it was from the very beginning to entice certain respectable persons to enlist in it. The sky-blue uniform which differed in colour from all other military uniforms as being, so to speak, the distinctive dress of the informer, produced a feeling of revulsion even in those who finally made up their minds to wear it.'[2] It is equally possible to surmise, however, that the noble—if somewhat naïve—ideals propounded by Benckendorff genuinely appealed to the sincerely patriotic officer who may well have hoped that he personally could not at any time be accused of stooping to the ignoble practices of secret police agents in the past.

Nevertheless it must be admitted that the career of a Gendarme officer also offered considerable material advantages to all members of this Corps irrespective of their moral qualities. Both Stogov (enlisted 1833) and Lomachevsky (enlisted 1837)—believed to have been the only Gendarmes who left published memoirs—referred to the inducement of higher pay, and both these officers were promoted shortly after their transfer to the Corps.[3] And apart from these attractions there were others no less tempting.

Many staff-officers who entered the Gendarmes found it agreeable to live in a province in complete independence without any definite occupation and in a position to constitute a threat to all. They would accept denunciations from persons of the very worst character, outcasts of society, and dispatch these to St Petersburg with their own comments and additions. If it proved on investigation that their comments were ill-founded, well, did they care? They might in their enthusiasm be mistaken and, if they were, they were not held in any way responsible. But where were provincial authorities, to say nothing of private individuals, to look for protection against them, when Benckendorff himself, their Chief, was to some extent appointed watch-dog over other Ministers? All peaceful provincial country life was alarmed by this state of affairs. Once can imagine what...may this word be forgiven me...what demoralization was bound to ensue as a result.[4]

---

[1] Vigel', vol. 2, p. 276.   [2] *Ibid.*

[3] 'In selecting various branches of service I found that there was more pay in the Gendarmes and decided to seek a transfer' ('Zapiski E. I. Stogova', *R. Star.* (1903), vol. 114, p. 307). Stogov's comment after having arranged his transfer to the Corps is interesting: 'And so it happened: I am a Gendarme, that is, a policemaster of morals' ['nravstvennyi politseimeister'], *ibid.* p. 308. This was doubtless the light in which such officers chose to regard themselves.

Lomachevsky refers to the prospect of *triple* pay and the possibility of being transferred away from the capital (where life was too expensive to live without debts) as the motives for his entering Gendarme service, *op. cit., loc. cit.* p. 245.

[4] Vigel', *loc. cit.* pp. 276–7.

This was obviously the view of an unfriendly critic and, for all that it may well have been largely based on hearsay evidence, it probably represented a majority opinion. It was undoubtedly true that provincial Gendarme officers did enjoy complete freedom of action, witness Stogov:[1] 'I arrived in Simbirsk, I think, on the 8th of January 1834 and, in entering on my duties, acted independently and myself took responsibility for everything I did. In Simbirsk I was first by right,[2] and my word had weight and significance. Dubbelt and Count Benckendorff were my screen in St Petersburg.' And what primarily disturbed the Corps' many enemies was not so much the contention that Gendarme officers possessed no 'definite permanent occupation' as the knowledge that the considerable powers conferred upon them gave them an unassailable right to interfere in the permanent occupations of others. There is equally little doubt that this was Nicholas' intention.

Benckendorff's own view of the impact made on society by the introduction of the new Higher Police force was reported to the Tsar in a 'Picture of Public Opinion in 1829' containing the following appraisal:

When this institution was created it generally brought consternation into the mood of society, but at the present moment, thanks to the restrained and prudent activities of the gendarmerie and its relatively successful selection of officials, public opinion is almost unanimously favourably disposed towards it. Only corrupt officials are up in arms against it. Society is, perhaps, too demanding as regards the gendarmerie in imagining that the latter can dispose of all abuses, all injustices, whereas it is only in its power to draw attention to them. It is possible that the gendarmerie could act to even greater purpose if it were not faced with so much opposition and hostility on the part of local authorities. The following are thoughts on the gendarmerie expressed by certain influential persons. I quote their literal words: 'The gendarmerie has become the national doctor of morals. Recourse is had to it by every distressed and despairing person, and if other authorities did not harm it with their opposition it would lead to still greater benefit. Only those who misuse official authority ['zloupotrebiteli'] and the aristocratic nobility ['znat''] are against it. But the former are obliged to hold their tongues and the latter has no influence whatsoever among the larger public.[3]

[1] Stogov, *loc. cit.* p. 314.
[2] 'V Simbirske ya byl pervym po pravu.' These words provide direct proof that the authority of a Gendarme staff-officer could override that of a Governor-General. And, as Stogov's memoirs themselves prove, this was true in practice as well as in theory. See chapter Six, pp. 186 ff.
[3] *Krasnyi Arkhiv* (1930), no. 38, p. 132. According to A. A. Sergeyev, the author of the Introduction to the series entitled 'Graf A. Kh. Benkendorf o Rossii v 1827–30 gg. (Yezhegodnyye otchety Tret'ego Otdeleniya i Korpusa Zhandarmov)', see chapter Six, p. 200, note 3, these reports, written in French, were composed by von Vock for Benckendorff to submit to Nicholas. (See *Kr. Arkh.* (1929), no. 37, p. 139.) Hence the Russian translation 'zhandarmeriya'— not usually employed to describe the Third Department and Corps of Gendarmes—from the original French 'gendarmerie'.

It will be noted that Benckendorff did not attempt to conceal from Nicholas the generally unfavourable impression initially caused by the institution of his political police, although he naturally claimed that it was enjoying a wide measure of deserved popularity a few years later. Opposition to such a body was, after all, inevitable; and the Tsar could now afford to ignore it provided he could rely on the support of those unnamed 'influential persons' whose opinion of the gendarmerie he so obviously shared.

The Tsar's attitude to his 'corps d'élite' was one of unequivocal approval. 'As Nicholas saw it, the Gendarme Colonel, tightly buttoned in his sky-blue tunic with its silver aiguillettes, helmeted, with white gloves, and with a sword at his side, was required above all to contribute to the triumph of truth and justice throughout the whole extent of the Empire. In every provincial town he would play the part of 'the eye of St Petersburg' or that of a '"doctor of the nation's morals"'.[1] Such was Nicholas' desire but, as the same writer aptly commented: 'A praiseworthy intention, indeed, but how dangerous! Was there not an absolute contradiction between the desire, so loudly asserted by the Sovereign, of inaugurating in Russia the reign of law alone, and the institution of a privileged corps whose very functions put it above the laws?'[2] A contradiction of this kind, however, could scarcely be expected to cause any qualms to an autocrat whose legal right to personal rule, whose very word, was unassailable. And this autocrat was an indefatigable and conscientious worker. 'Just as Nicholas loved to make an unexpected appearance in government institutions in order to check whether officials were in their places at an early hour and whether external order was observed, so through the agency of his gendarmes he strove like a good administrator to inquire into all corners of Russian life and like a good administrator to keep it under his protection. He himself could not be everywhere—he was replaced and assisted by trusted servants, the staff-officers of his Corps of Gendarmes. Invested with considerable powers, they penetrated into the bureaucratic system like a wedge, exposing its faults and abuses...'[3] It followed, therefore, that as the Tsar's wishes were perforce inviolate, these special staff-officers, acting in his name as his personal representatives, could 'legally' impose their rulings on local authorities. 'Laws', runs a phrase attributed to Benckendorff, 'are written for subordinates and not for those who make them.'[4] This attitude was largely responsible for the unsavoury reputation earned by the Higher Police in succeeding years, for it did not confine its activities merely to drawing attention to abuses and injustices, as

[1] De Grunwald, p. 184. (The English translation of B. Patmore (London, 1954) creates a wrong impression by constantly translating 'gendarmerie' as 'Constabulary'.)
[2] *Ibid.* pp. 184–5.
[3] Presnyakov, *loc. cit.* p. 19.
[4] 'Zakony pishutsya dlya podchinyonnykh, a nye dlya nachal'stva.'

Benckendorff contended. Nicholas intended it to interfere in all kinds of public affairs—and interfere it did.

One further opinion of its impact on society in the early years of its existence is worth quoting, largely because of the source from which it emanated. In 1831 Nicholas granted an interview to de Sanglen, Alexander's old police chief, then in retirement.[1] In the course of conversation Nicholas asked him: 'What do you think of our gendarmes?'—'I do not know the details of this institution, and am unable to pass judgement on it.'—'You avoid answering; you may speak openly.'—'If it is your will, I am bound, as a loyal subject, to confess that this branch is not to my liking, nor is it to that of all Russia.'—'Why so?'—'Because the loyal devotion of Your Majesty's subjects is offended by this apparent evidence of the lack of confidence placed in it or because, generally speaking, the denunciations which this institution makes inevitable may incite Imperial anger and thus destroy the close connexion between the affection of the Tsar and that of the people.'[2] There is no evidence that de Sanglen was ever considered as a prospective member of the Third Department in any capacity; in 1826 he had reached the age of fifty and his name was linked with too many unhappy memories of the days of the Ministry of Police; and it is hence unlikely that his opinion was primarily motivated by a spirit of vindictiveness.[3] It seems more than probable that this opinion was generally shared. What is interesting is to note how, in the view of a man once well conversant with political police affairs, the original 1827 intention of 'bringing the voice of suffering mankind to the throne of the Tsars' was in fact—four years later—said to be having the opposite effect of alienating the one from the other.

These various opinions may to some extent be regarded as typical of the contemporary official and unofficial reaction to the creation and development of the Corps of Gendarmes in Russia.

[1] De Sanglen's published memoirs did not cover the years 1816 to 1831, when he resumed his story with an account of a slanderous campaign conducted against him by the Governor-General of Moscow, Prince Golitsyn. (This was the reason for his requesting an audience of the Tsar, 'Zapiski Ya. I. de Sanglena', pp. 558–78.)

(A series of official letters on the subject of de Sanglen exchanged in Nov. 1830 between Golitsyn, Lt.-Gen. Volkov (G.O.C. 2nd Gendarme District), von Vock and Benckendorff tend to prove that even in retirement de Sanglen was greatly disliked and distrusted. See article 'K istorii tsarstvovaniya imperatora Nikolaya I', *R. Star.* (1896), vol. 86, pp. 553–70.)

[2] 'Zapiski de Sanglena', p. 570. Nicholas' reaction to this opinion was 'I like your outspokenness. I am myself ready to die for truth', *ibid.* p. 571.

[3] 'I have chosen truth as my only guide'; 'I am not writing for my contemporaries; I am writing as though I were no longer alive; thus I do so without envy or malice . . . so let strict truth guide my pen: I may have made mistakes—I am a man—but I vouch for having had no evil intentions or designs', *ibid.* pp. 577, 578.

An editorial note states that de Sanglen kept his word. All his memoirs except certain pre-1796 accounts were published posthumously.

The Corps came into being as a new solution to the age-long problem of governmental security. As such, it was granted powers unlike those possessed by its earlier (and in some respects similar) predecessors. It developed in little over a decade into an extensive centralized organization with an administrative network embracing the whole empire. By the end of the reign its strength may well have increased to double the figure estimated for 1836.[1] The multifarious duties undertaken by the Corps were performed by a nucleus of specially selected officers subordinated to the headquarters of the Third Department. This headquarters consisted of a small staff of soldiers and civilians who, by virtue of their peculiar status, exercised immense authority.

The careers, personalities and influence of these officials form the subject of the two following chapters.

An unpublished document in the Vienna Archives, which gives a large-scale breakdown of the Russian Army in Europe, contains the following bald statement: 'Zu besondern Zwecken bestimmte Truppen...Polizei-Truppen (Gendarmerie): *Mann* 8000 *Pferde* 8000'. K. und K Haus-, Hof- und Staats-Archiv, Vienna, Karton 136 (1848), Russland Varia.

4

The Leading Personalities of the
Higher Police: in its early years

...I think that I have surely been almost the first of all Secret Police Chiefs whose death people feared and who have not been pursued to the edge of the grave by a single complaint...

from Benckendorff's memoirs, 1837[1]

'In Russia more than anywhere else every law has been ignored and for this reason those who have created the laws...have always possessed an especially important significance.'[2] This truism may serve as justification for a detailed survey of the men who were individually responsible for the institution and direction of Nicholas' secret police. In accordance with his wishes they enjoyed immense powers subject only to his personal approval and the development of these powers depended to a large extent on their private and public characters.

A. Kh. Benckendorff
Head of the Third Department of His Imperial Majesty's Own Chancellery (Chief Director after 1839) and Chief of Gendarmes from 1826 to 1844

The personality and influence of Count Benckendorff has often been inaccurately assessed, mainly because the reputation of the Third Department which tended to deteriorate as the reactionary nature of Nicholas' régime increased was inevitably bound to cast a decidedly unfavourable reflection on its first and most eminent Chief Director. The leaders of early revolutionary thought saw in him the personification of all the repressive measures adopted against them in the immediate post-Decembrist period and their hatred of the Third Department was widely shared by all nineteenth-century writers and thinkers whose freedom of action it sought to control. Thus Benckendorff's rôle in the organization of Russia's political police necessarily attracted highly unsympathetic criticism from investigators such as Lemke whose purpose it was to show how this police adversely affected the development of Russia's literary genius. The extreme hostility of left-wing political circles to the work of the Third Department in its later years was equally bound to result in the further blackening of Benckendorff's reputation. In still more recent times—our own era—an additional element of political bias

---

[1] See p. 121, note 3.   [2] Lemke, *Nikolayevskie Zhandarmy*, p. 19.

may be discerned in the works of Soviet writers describing him as 'a cruel, ignorant and ungifted general', 'a cruel general of the Arakcheyev school' and so on.[1] Such judgements, albeit constantly repeated, are so prejudiced as to be worthless. As will emerge from what follows, the Head of the Third Department may in many respects have been ignorant, but he was never wittingly cruel (had he resembled Arakcheyev, it is improbable that he would have enjoyed Nicholas' favour) and he was far from being ungifted. The weight of evidence all tends to show that he bore little if any resemblance to the secret police chiefs of Russia's past, for his character contained no element of either fanaticism or brutality. Indeed, not one of the many writers who have discussed him has attempted to deny that at all events up to his appointment as Chief of Gendarmes in 1826 at the age of forty-three he had deserved well of his country and its rulers. An examination of his subsequent career[2] proves that if he did not possess as many defenders as he himself later claimed, it was the general consensus of contemporary opinion, at any rate, that in his melancholy post he did as little evil as possible; and there were those, of whom the Tsar was understandably one, who maintained that his personal contribution to Russia's domestic history was wholly praiseworthy. And although the latter view was by no means held by the majority, it is unjust to condemn the first Chief of Gendarmes for the many shortcomings of his Department which neither he nor any man in his position could have prevented.

Aleksandr Khristoforovich Benkendorf (as his name is spelt in Russian)[3] was born in 1783, the elder son of General of Infantry Khristofor Benkendorf, or Benckendorff (1748–1823), then Military Governor of Riga. The latter was a member of an old Prussian family which had settled in Estonia and he had risen to this rank after a lifetime of military service in the Russian army. This service was not in any way distinguished, and he appears to have been remembered after his death only thanks to numerous anecdotes relating to his chronic absentmindedness.[4] (This characteristic was inherited by his son

---

[1] *Istoriya SSSR*, vol. 2. 'Rossiya v xix vyeke' pod red. M. V. Nyechkinoi (Moscow, 1940), ch. 11, p. 188; *Bol'shaya Sovyetskaya Entsiklopediya* (1947), vol. 'SSSR', p. 493.

[2] No specific biography of Benckendorff has appeared. Except where otherwise stated, the details of his career are taken from the *RBS*. The fullest account of his character (which includes the opinions of many widely differing critics) is given by Lemke, pp. 20–6.

[3] The spelling of Russian names, especially those of foreign origin, tends to vary according to the preference of individual non-Russian writers, e.g. 'Benkendorf', 'Benckendorff', 'Benckendorff'. The latter is used here because its owner himself adhered to this spelling when not writing in Russian.

[4] References to the absentmindedness of Benckendorff's father are numerous, but too incidental to be recorded in detail. A typical example of such anecdotes, however, may be found in P. I. Bartyenev, *19-yi vyek. Istoricheskii Sbornik*, 2 vols. (Moscow, 1872), vol. 2, pp. 291–2, which includes three relevant stories taken from a 'staraya zapisnaya kniga' (the work of an unknown author) found in Moscow in 1813.

—with regrettable consequences for many!) His wife was Baroness Charlotte Schilling who came to Russia as one of the ladies of honour of Princess Sophia Dorothea of Württemberg, known to history as the Empress Mariya Fyodorovna, the wife of the Emperor Paul. Alexander Benckendorff was thus—like Nicholas himself—more German than Russian. His younger brother Konstantin (1785–1828) followed the family tradition of military service and became, like Alexander, a General-in-Waiting, serving with gallantry in the Turkish Campaign of 1828 which led to his premature death the same year. The most remarkable member of the family, however, was his sister Dorofyeya, or Dar'ya (1784–1857) who, as the famous Princess Lieven, played an important part in the social and diplomatic world of her day,[1] and whose comments on that world, particularly as regards persons and events in this country, have proved of considerable value to later historical research. Her affection for her brother Alexander prompted her to remain in close touch with him for many years[2] and potentially she was one of his best sources of information on European politics.[3] It is difficult not to feel that generally speaking her intelligence and political acumen were distinctly superior to those of her brother, but having developed in the course of a busy life abroad a certain independence of outlook, she

[1] 'Princess Lieven was from every point of view an extraordinary woman. She began by being the mistress of Metternich, she ended by being the lover of Guizot. Her intimacy with George IV and Earl Grey was such as to excite comment even in the easy-going era of the Regency. She was at times the close friend of two Foreign Secretaries, Castlereagh and Canning; of three Premiers, Wellington, Lord Grey and Lord Aberdeen; of the three Royal Dukes of Clarence, Cumberland and of York. She was the avowed leader of English Society for nearly twenty years, and no foreign lady ever had such opportunities of knowing English Society at first hand, or of exercising more influence upon it'. H. Temperley, *The Unpublished Diary and Political Sketches of Princess Lieven* (London, 1925), p. 11. (There is evidence that she was also the mistress of Nicholas' elder brother, the Grand Duke Constantine, *ibid.* p. 22.)

　　She was the wife of Count (Prince 1826) Khristofor Andreyevich Lieven (1777–1838), Ambassador to the Court of St James from 1812 to 1834. For details of her relationship with Metternich, which began in Oct. 1818, see P. S. Squire, 'Metternich and Benckendorff, 1807–1834', *The Slavonic and East European Review*, vol. XLV, no. 104, Jan. 1967, pp. 152–4.

[2] 'Alexander, who was soon to enter the army, was the young Countess Lieven's favourite. Until death took him from her over forty years later they were to keep up an unbroken and affectionate correspondence.' H. Montgomery Hyde, *Princess Lieven* (London, 1938), p. 18. (The context refers to her wedding to Count Lieven in 1800.)

[3] 'Whatever hard things were said against her—and many of her friends as well as her enemies regarded her as a gossip-monger, a spy and an intriguing mischief-maker—we cannot deny that Princess Lieven established a unique position for herself during her residence in England. Probably no foreigner living in this country has ever exercised such a remarkable influence in society and affairs...', *ibid.* p. 212.

　　In the light of the importance of Princess Lieven's position and her close connexion with her brother, it is surprising that she is not even mentioned in the works of either Lemke or Trotsky, both of whom had access to the Archives of the Third Department. The probability is that she was not officially considered as an agent of the Department and her information was communicated to Benckendorff privately.

deeply offended Nicholas by preferring to live there permanently,[1] thus convincing the Tsar that, although politically her career had been a success, her character lacked one indispensable feature—unquestioning and unchanging obedience. In this respect her brother Alexander was beyond reproach; his career was not only successful—it was also eminently conventional.

Thanks to the patronage of the Empress Mariya Fyodorovna, the young Benckendorff brothers were educated in the Jesuit 'pension' of the Abbé Nicole in St Petersburg. According to one witness 'a fashionable upbringing was its sole purpose, and no one thought of including higher studies in it'.[2] Alexander Benckendorff (hereinafter referred to simply as Benckendorff) remained at this establishment only until 1798, however, when at the age of fifteen he began his military career as an N.C.O. in the Life Guards Semyonovsky Regiment. His promotion was rapid, for the same year he was commissioned with the rank of Ensign and the appointment of 'Fligel'-Ad'yutant' to the Emperor.[3] He retained this appointment on the accession of the Emperor Alexander and on the instigation of the Dowager Empress was dispatched on various Court commissions, now abroad, now inside Russia, now to the army.[4] His active service dated from 1803 when he fought with distinction in Georgia and was awarded his first decorations. The following year he was sent to the Adriatic and attached to the staff of General Anrep at

[1] 'A most painful quarrel had been developing for some years between the Princess and her husband. The iron despot, Nicholas, had decided that Dorothea should not live in Paris, and her husband, obsequiously loyal to his Czar, demanded with increasing insistence that she should return to St Petersburg, or else leave Paris. She refused to do so in 1836, and again after the visit to England in 1837', Temperley, p. 199.

An early edition of her letters in English states: 'In our ignorance of the rivalries and intrigues of the Russian Court it is impossible to estimate how far there may have been potent agencies at work in St Petersburg...The prospect, however, of living in the society of the Imperial family [officially Princess Lieven was a Lady-in-Waiting of the Empress] had little attraction for the Princess, notwithstanding the protestations of ardent devotion so frequently recurring in her letters. Whether she had formed the secret determination to reside in Western Europe... or whether she fled from a situation for which she had no ambition, it is impossible to guess. The utmost that can be said is that some time afterwards, when writing with reference to her abrupt ending of her service at Court, she made use of the expression, "The master has not forgiven and will never forgive me"...', L. G. Robinson, *Letters of Dorothea, Princess Lieven, during her Residence in London, 1812–1834* (London, 1902), pp. xiv–xv.

Princess Lieven remained in voluntary exile until her death.

[2] Vigel', vol. 2, p. 274. 'Various statesmen of the first half of the 19th century spent some time in this 'pension', such as the Princes Orlov, Golitsyn, Gagarin, Menshikov, Stroganov, Vyazemsky and others', Lemke, p. 20.

[3] 'In order to advance his own fortune, he made drawings of frigates in the Emperor Paul's album, which obtained for him the epaulettes of the aid-de-camp [*sic*] to the Czar', Ivan Golovine, *Russia under the Autocrat, Nicholas the First*, 2 vols. (London, 1846), vol. 1, ch. 10, p. 317.

[4] 'Without stopping for long almost everywhere he went, he would course over vast distances with all the ignorance that might have been expected of the education of the day, with the giddiness of youth and the thoughtlessness inherent in the Benckendorff family', Vigel', p. 274.

Corfu. In the 1806 and 1807 wars he fought on the staff of General Count Tolstoi and so distinguished himself at the battle of Preussisch-Eylau that he was again decorated and promoted to the rank of Captain. Only two weeks later he was again promoted and found himself a full Colonel at the early age of twenty-four. After the conclusion of the Peace of Tilsit he remained with Tolstoi when the latter was appointed Ambassador to Paris in October 1807.

During this period, after so adventurous a life and so meteoric a rise to relatively high rank, the young Benckendorff evidently considered himself entitled to a little relaxation. His duties at the embassy, which were principally those of a courier and cypher officer, were not so onerous as to leave him no time for diversions; and, unlike his contemporary, Nesselrode, then Counsellor of the embassy and always serious-minded, he preferred to devote himself to the latter. It was, indeed, in the pursuit of pleasure that he first became acquainted with Metternich, who was Austrian Ambassador in Paris from August 1806 to July 1809. One of Metternich's several mistresses during this period was a young actress, Marguerite-Joséphine Weymer, better known by her stage name of George, who in the years 1802–4 had been mistress to Napoleon. Benckendorff not only emulated Metternich in becoming Mlle George's lover, but even persuaded her to join him in Russia where she lived for some months under his name and protection.[1]

During his stay in the French capital, which lasted until the summer of 1808, Benckendorff is not known to have given any promise of later achievement. In money matters too he appears to have acted irresponsibly and there is evidence to show that he left Paris in some haste in order to avoid his creditors.[2] It is possible, even so, that he did not devote himself entirely to pleasure in that city and that his mind was first attracted to the idea of a national 'gendarmerie' as the result of what he personally observed there,[3]

[1] The details of Benckendorff's liaison with Mlle George are given in Squire, 'Metternich and Benckendorff', *op. cit.* pp. 135–46. See chapter Six, p. 211, note 4.

[2] 'As an A.D.C. to the Emperor Alexander, this man contracted debts in Paris in his youth and fled shamefully from that city to avoid meeting his creditors. The Queen-Mother [Mariya Fyodorovna], who was on very friendly terms with the young man's mother, paid his debts. I have had the opportunity of going over the papers of the late Alexander Kurakin who was then Russian Ambassador in Paris and I have seen his correspondence with the Queen-Mother on the subject of the young man's flight and the payment of his debts', P. Dolgoroukow, *La Vérité sur la Russie* (Paris, 1860), p. 294 (Note).

(P. A. Tolstoi was Ambassador in Paris from Oct. 1807 to Oct. 1808. After Erfurt he was replaced by A. B. Kurakin who continued in that post until 1812.)

[3] 'One of my brother-officers who was also a Fligel'-Ad'yutant was Alexander Khristoforovich Benckendorff and from this time* we were first quite well acquainted and subsequently on terms of close friendship. Benckendorff had then returned from Paris where he had been attached

* Volkonsky was appointed Fligel'-Ad'yutant on 6 Sept. 1811.

so that from the point of view of his later responsibilities the visit was not without its value—at least to himself. Probably his thoughts on the subject were still only nebulous at this stage, but they may well have contained the germ of his 1821 Memorandum.[1] For the time being, however, he was kept too busy elsewhere to devote any attention to this project.

In 1809, having apparently tired of life in St Petersburg with Mlle George, Benckendorff volunteered to join the army then operating against the Turks, 'spent the whole campaign in the vanguard of that army and always led the riskiest and most difficult expeditions', receiving another decoration for his leadership at Rushchuk. At the beginning of the 1812 War he was placed in command of the vanguard under General Winzengerode and promoted Major-General for a successful attack at Velizh. In this rank he fought continuously for the next two years, invariably proving a courageous and resourceful soldier. He commanded the rearguard of Winzengerode's Corps in the Russian retreat and succeeded then and later, on the recapture of Moscow, in taking vast numbers of prisoners and guns. He served on Kutuzov's staff during the French retreat to the Niemen, capturing three generals and over 6,000 troops. In 1813 he commanded an 'independent flying detachment' of cavalry troops operating between Berlin and Frankfurt-on-Oder, fought from Jüterbog to Dresden, occupied Lüneburg, and commanded the left wing of Winzengerode's Corps at the battle of Leipzig. In Holland and later in Belgium he achieved more startling successes in command of detached troops, and by the end of the year had been awarded an impressive array of outstanding Russian, Swedish, Prussian and Dutch decorations. The Prince Regent sent him a gold sword with the inscription 'For Valour'. He took part in the Rhine crossing of 1814 in command of all cavalry troops under Count Vorontsov and commanded the rearguard of the Corps when it moved up to Châlons. These exploits represent only a part of his distinguished service[2] which was such as to compel even an unfriendly critic to write that 'he played an active rôle in all this fighting, was excessively brave and lucky and also, like Miloradovich, got through without so much as a scratch'.[3]

to our Embassy and, as a thinking and impressionable man, had seen what advantages derived from the Gendarmerie in France', *Zapiski S. G. Volkonskago*, p. 135.

(Volkonsky's account reads as though Benckendorff at once prepared the Memorandum eventually submitted by him in 1821—see chapter One, p. 44—but it is probable that here Volkonsky's memory or accuracy was at fault.)

It is interesting, in view of the later connexion between Benckendorff and Metternich (see chapter Six, p. 212, note 1), that the latter was similarly impressed: 'Metternich avait toujours eu beaucoup d'admiration pour le système de surveillance policière, exercée par Napoléon', C. de Grunwald, *La Vie de Metternich* (Paris, 1938), p. 289.

[1] The suggestion that Benckendorff first contemplated the introduction of a Gendarmerie in Russia while still in his twenties is not mentioned elsewhere.
[2] The *RBS* article on Benckendorff lists them in greater detail.   [3] Vigel', p. 275.

After the conclusion of the Napoleonic Wars Benckendorff was appointed in 1816 G.O.C. the 2nd Dragoon Division then stationed in Khar'kov, where he spent three years in comparative obscurity until his next appointment in 1819 as Chief of Staff to the Corps of Guards, in which year he also became one of the Tsar's Generals-in-Waiting.[1] While still holding the former appointment he became a member of the Masonic Lodge of 'United Friends'. At the time these lodges contained a curious assortment of devotees, as may be judged from the fact that three of Benckendorff's co-members were Chaadayev, Griboyedov and Pestel';[2] but it is permissible to assume that he was not greatly impressed with his experiences in this milieu, for he ceased to belong to this society in 1818. Benckendorff's interests, like those of his future master, lay rather in the sphere of military service. In 1821 he was promoted to the rank of Lieutenant-General and given the command of the 1st Guards Cuirassier Division.

It was in this year that he submitted to Alexander the Memorandum on Secret Societies which included proposals for the adoption of vigorous counter-measures—suggestions which were, however, disregarded by that capricious emperor.[3] Whether or not this Memorandum was Benckendorff's own unaided work,[4] it certainly represented the first stepping-stone to the immensely powerful position he came to occupy five years later, because the proposals it contained were both appropriate and intelligent. But at the time Benckendorff himself did not enjoy the imperial favour. 'There was nothing particularly unusual about his subsequent service in Alexander I's reign [after 1819]: the emperor behaved coldly to the Chief of Staff of the Corps dearest to his heart in spite of the two memoranda submitted by him, and, perhaps for that very reason. Shortly before Alexander left for Taganrog in 1825 Benckendorff wrote to the emperor that he was very hurt by the lack of favour accorded to him'.[5]

---

[1] 'The Emperor Alexander, who was such a discriminating judge of men, although to please his mother he did indeed make him his General-in-Waiting, never desired to use him as a close member of his staff, and Benckendorff, in peace-time, commanded a Cavalry Division in Khar'kov, an almost forgotten and unknown man. There, it is said, he read nothing, wholly scorned the local civil servants and their activities, and made a practice of sacrificing the demands of military service to those of his amusement and love intrigues', Vigel', *ibid.*

[2] See A. N. Pypin, *Obshchestvennoe Dvizhenie v Rossii pri Aleksandre I*, 3-e izd. (SPB, 1900), p. 318.

[3] See chapter One, p. 44.   [4] *Ibid.* note 4.

[5] Lemke. p. 20. (For the explanation of 'two memoranda' see chapter Two, p. 50, note 3.)

Benckendorff's letter read: 'Oserais-je donc supplier humblement Votre Majesté d'avoir la grâce de me faire savoir en quoi j'ai pu avoir le malheur de manquer. Je ne saurais vous voir partir, Sire, avec l'idée accablante d'avoir peut-être démérité les bontés de Votre Majesté Impériale', Shil'der, *Imperator Aleksandr Pervyi*, vol. 4, note 257, p. 472. There is no record of any reply from the Tsar.

It is possible that this unfriendliness may have been caused by the Tsar's former suspicions

Alexander's attitude is all the more surprising in view of the further distinguished service rendered by Benckendorff at the time of the disastrous floods in St Petersburg in 1824. 'No one in the midst of this terrible portent contributed as much as he did towards saving victims on the point of drowning. Throughout the duration of this scourge (the 7th/19th of November) General Benckendorff did not cease to visit the most perilous areas, running the greatest dangers and filling the long-boat that carried him with persons who, surrounded by the waves, had abandoned all hope of rescue. This devotion and self-denial won him the respect of the sovereign and of the Russian nation. To repair the unheard-of disasters caused by this terrible storm, the Emperor appointed General Benckendorff Military Governor of a third of the city... One month after this catastrophe in which it had been expected that the commerce and splendour of the capital would be engulfed, all the ruins and damage were repaired, and it was thanks to the intelligent activity of Count Benckendorff that these results were achieved.'[1] Yet even these exploits so typical of his energy and bravery did not advance Benckendorff in the Tsar's good graces, although his appointment as Military Governor of Vasilevsky Ostrov[2] indicates that his abilities were recognized; and he was still holding this post when Alexander died.[3]

It is evident, however, that even before the tragic events of 14 December 1825 Benckendorff was on excellent terms with Alexander's eventual successor. On the 7th (19th) of that month—that is, during the interregnum—Countess Nesselrode, the wife of the Minister for Foreign Affairs, wrote to her brother, then Ambassador at the Hague, '...History knows no other similar example of two brothers so magnanimously tossing a crown from one to the other like a ball. Alexander Benckendorff enjoys the complete confidence of the Grand Duke Nicholas, and his poor head is not capable of withstanding all the importance of the moment: he talks complete rubbish with hardly a vestige of discretion. It is a pity that for the most part monarchs are mistaken in those whom they select to be with them; and later, when they

that Benckendorff's liaison with Mlle George—and her journey to St Petersburg in 1808—was not unconnected with an intrigue to supplant Mariya Antonovna Chertvertinskaya, who was Alexander's mistress at the time and for many years afterwards; see Squire, 'Metternich and Benckendorff', *op. cit., loc. cit.* note 59, pp. 144–5.

[1] Germain Sarrut and B. Saint-Edmé, *La Biographie des Hommes du Jour* (Paris, 1839)—*La Biographie du Général-en-Chef-de-Cavalerie Comte de Benckendorff*, pp. 5–6.

[2] General Komarovsky states in his memoirs that the three officers appointed Military Governors-General of the city as a result of the 1824 floods were himself (Peterburgskaya Storona), Gen. Depreradovich (Vyborgskaya Storona) and Gen. Benckendorff (Vasilevsky Ostrov), *Zapiski*, pp. 225–6.

[3] Neither Lemke nor the *RBS* record this appointment, although it was important in view of the vital rôle played by Benckendorff on 14 Dec. 1825, when he was in command of all troops quartered in that area of the city and used them against the mutineers. See chapter Two, p. 49.

notice this, they justify themselves by referring to the absence of worthy persons, whereas if only they wanted to have better advisors, it would be possible to find them!'[1] This scathing opinion of Benckendorff's abilities was never shared either then or afterwards by Nicholas, who saw in him a gallant and devoted officer whose character was the very antithesis of Arakcheyev's—a recommendation in itself. It is not known exactly when Nicholas, as Grand Duke, first became acquainted with Benckendorff, but it is likely that they had known each other for many years and Countess Lieven may have discussed her distinguished brother's career with the future Tsar during the latter's visit to England in 1816–17.[2] During the final years of Alexander's reign Nicholas undoubtedly came into close contact with him as one of the Tsar's Generals-in-Waiting. And even if Benckendorff had lacked influential friends at Court, it is probable that he would in any case have attracted Nicholas' attention. He had achieved what the militaristic Grand Duke had been prevented by his position and the wishes of Alexander from ever achieving—the fame of a successful soldier. His courage and ability in the field thus compelled Nicholas' admiration and respect. In addition, there was no reason to fear that he was anything but loyal and honest.[3] These were the qualifications which brought him to Nicholas' favour. But at the same time it cannot be denied that Countess Nesselrode's opinion was later confirmed by numerous other witnesses, for he was not as intelligent as he was honourable.

An account of Benckendorff's increasing influence after the events of 14 December and the investigations that followed them has already been recorded.[4] The initiative he showed in submitting his 'Project for the Organization of a Higher Police', together with his personal charm and devotion, resulted in his becoming the new Tsar's inseparable companion and aide. The wisdom of this choice is supported by the evidence of Prince

[1] '14 dek. 1825 g. v pis'makh gr. M. D. Nessel'rode', *Kr. Arkh.* (1925), vol. 10, p. 270.
    These letters from Countess Nesselrode to N. D. Gur'yev are translated from the original French.
[2] 'Il fallait donc songer à lui [Arakcheyev] donner un successeur, qui fût capable, par son zèle, son dévouement, son intelligence et son habileté, d'assurer la sécurité de l'empereur et de la famille impériale...Il [Nicholas] connaissait, d'ailleurs, de longue date, Alexandre de Benckendorff, parent de la vénérable comtesse de Lieven, qui lui avait recommandé ce brillant officier, homme aimable, doux, souple, insinuant, agréable de figure et de manières, plein d'esprit et de talent; Benckendorff avait su plaire au grand-duc Nicolas, et il ne tarda pas à se faire aimer de l'empereur', Paul Lacroix, *Histoire de la Vie et du Règne de Nicolas Ier, Empereur de Russie*, 7 vols. (Paris, 1864–73), vol. 2, p. 231. Lacroix does not state the source from which he deduces that Benckendorff was recommended to Nicholas by Countess Lieven.
[3] 'Benckendorff avait toujours été intègre; il le fut, pour ainsi dire, davantage, quand il eut entre ses mains la fortune, la liberté, et la vie de tous les habitants de la Russie', Lacroix, *loc. cit.* p. 232. This evidence is confirmed by other writers.
[4] See chapter Two, pp. 50 ff.

Volkonsky who, as a Decembrist, suffered as a result of the findings of the Investigatory Commission (of which Benckendorff was a member) and who may therefore be considered a relatively unbiased witness. In referring to Benckendorff's Project for the institution of a 'gendarmerie' he states that 'Alexander Khristoforovich...[was] fully convinced, I am sure, that its activities would be directed towards the protection of persons from persecution, towards their timely preservation from errors. This was the purpose of his noble heart and enlightened mind...'[1] And to some extent this view was shared even by Countess Nesselrode, whose opinion of him had not otherwise changed, in recognizing that Nicholas could have chosen a worse adviser. On 19/31 March she wrote: 'The man whom the Emperor sees daily and with whom he converses with complete candour is Alexander Benckendorff, whose duty it is to inform him of everything said in society which might damage his reputation. He is a very respectable person, full of good intentions, but he is characterless and amazingly frivolous; but nevertheless he is full of enthusiasm for good, and I therefore prefer that he should be in such close contact with the Emperor rather than anyone else who might make things a thousand times worse...'[2] That two such dissimilar witnesses could agree on the nobility of Benckendorff's intentions provides adequate proof of their existence.

There can be no doubt, however, that Benckendorff's mind lacked both objectivity and originality. In all his thoughts and actions after Nicholas' accession he clearly did no more than reflect the views of the new Tsar, as may be seen from his memoirs[3] on the conduct and conclusions of the Investigatory Commission.[4] The biased nature of his views may be judged from such comments as '...there had never been a tribunal in Russia which inspired greater respect and at the same time enjoyed greater independence' and '...it was the wish of the judges and of the emperor himself to be as forbearing as possible', to select only two examples from an account which even so excessively restrained a historian as Shil'der felt impelled to criticize as 'expressed in terms with which unprejudiced history cannot agree'.[5] There

[1] *Zapiski Volkonskago*, p. 136. It is noteworthy that throughout his memoirs Volkonsky never speaks of Benckendorff otherwise than as of a close friend and a most efficient and courageous soldier. He goes on '...and later, as an outcast, I am bound to say that throughout my exile the sky-blue uniform did not convey to our minds the idea of persecution, but rather of protection both of ourselves and everyone else from persecution', *ibid*.

[2] *Kr. Arkh.*, *loc. cit.* p. 285.

[3] These particular memoirs were not published independently, but certain excerpts were included by Shil'der in his History of Nicholas I, *op. cit.* vol. I. (Details of Benckendorff's memoirs which have been published separately are given on p. 118, note 1.)

[4] Shil'der, *Imperator Nikolai Pervyi*, vol. I, pp. 440–1.

[5] *Ibid.* p. 440. Lemke's comment on Benckendorff's account of the Commission's work was: 'Only great effrontery could permit Benckendorff to write this abominable piece of cheap banality' ['...etu uzhasnuyu poshlost''], p. 21.

is no reason to suppose, however, that Benckendorff did not record such opinions in all good faith; he never ceased to believe most sincerely in the correctness of his emperor's actions. He was present at the execution of the five Decembrist leaders on the morning of 13 July, and his description of his reactions on that occasion may be quoted as a typical example of his outlook: 'I was not attracted to it by mere curiosity [he wrote] but by sympathy: these were mostly young persons, noblemen of good families; many of them had formerly served with me, and some of them such as, for instance, Prince Volkonsky, had been my immediate companions. My heart ached; but soon the feeling of regret aroused in me by the thought of the blow that had struck so many families gave way to feelings of irritation and disgust. The revolting and misplaced converse and jokes of these unfortunates bore witness both to their profound moral deterioration and to the fact that their hearts were accessible to feelings of neither repentance nor shame...'[1] Benckendorff could hardly have failed to show his sympathy for many of the Decembrists[2] and his understanding of their motives; and there is evidence that he personally always treated them fairly. (The son of the Prince Volkonsky mentioned above, describing his father's life under arrest at this period, referred to 'the kindly memory left by General Benckendorff, always straightforward and polite, although entering into all the details of the evidence'.[3]) At the same time he did not allow his personal feelings to affect his judgement of individuals whom he regarded as criminal conspirators, and he therefore insisted on the imposition of capital punishment on five of the accused in order to make an example of them.[4] It is fair to comment that this was precisely the view of Nicholas himself. Both were undoubtedly convinced that there was no justification for recommending to mercy men whose complicity in state treason was incontestably proved; and that the protection of the state hence demanded the severest of penalties. Besides, Benckendorff's importance now far exceeded that of a mere General-in-Waiting; by his appointment as Chief of Gendarmes on 25 June and Head of the Third Department on 3 July he had become the second most powerful

---

[1] Shil'der, *loc. cit.* p. 452.

[2] Lemke states that 'from the point of view of the accused his conduct was sufficiently reasonable because he was apprehensive of incurring the disapproval of those homes that were well aware of his former friendly relations with some of the heroes of the 14th of December', but also reminds his readers that Benckendorff did not hesitate to recommend the use of the death penalty, *ibid.*

[3] *Zapiski Volkonskago*, p. 451. Volkonsky's evidence is confirmed by that of another Decembrist, M. A. Fon-Vizin, who refers to Benckendorff's 'decent conduct' during the proceedings of the Investigatory Commission, stating that he 'often showed signs of sincere sympathy and compassion for [us] prisoners', see V. I. Semyevsky, *Obshchestvennye Dvizheniya v Rossii v I-uyu polovinu XIX vyeka* (SPB, 1905), vol. 1, p. 198.

[4] A. O. Smirnova, *Zapiski* (SPB, 1897), pt 1, p. 89.

man in Russia. It was thus his duty to ensure that the Decembrist movement should have no successors.

The news of Benckendorff's appointment to the most influential post in the country probably came as no surprise to those in Court circles who were aware of his intimacy with the Tsar. But it must be doubted whether it gave cause for satisfaction to any but the members of his own family[1] and Nicholas himself. Elsewhere, although Benckendorff's reputation for honesty provided some consolation and it was generally acknowledged that Nicholas' choice could have lighted on a less deserving recipient, the public reaction to the news of his promotion appears to have been unfavourable. 'Who could then have thought [wrote Vigel'] that soon the fate of so very many intelligent honourable men would completely depend on this empty-headed creature? The new Tsar, of course, was not deceived by his boundless devotion to him: Benckendorff would have let himself be cut into pieces for his sake; but should he not also have paid some heed to the man's abilities? No one had fewer of the qualities required by someone who was to occupy an important governmental position.'[2]

It was entirely in accordance with Nicholas' character, however, that he should have preferred to such high office a man whose loyalty was so far superior to his ability and intelligence. In Benckendorff's company the Tsar could rest assured that he had a true friend whose only desire was to perform his master's will. All Benckendorff's subsequent honours stemmed from this realization; and these honours were considerable. In December 1826 he was made a Senator and awarded 25,000 desyatins of land in the province of Bessarabia to be the property of himself and his descendants in perpetuity;[3] in 1829 he was promoted General of Cavalry; in 1830 he was appointed a member of the Council of State and in 1832 was raised to the rank of Count. He was also decorated with the highest decorations his Sovereign could confer

---

[1] Princess Lieven in a letter to her brother from London dated 1st/13th Aug. 1826 wrote: 'I have heard with much interest and more pleasure of the new duties imposed upon you by the Emperor's confidence. Your position is a difficult one, but I can well understand that one gives one's self entirely to such a master—and when one's heart is in one's work difficulties disappear.' Robinson, pp. 85–6.

[2] Vigel', vol. 2, p. 275. One of the Decembrists, in discussing the character of the members of the Investigatory Commission, commented on Benckendorff's unfailing loyalty to Nicholas in the following terms: 'Alexander Khristoforovich Benckendorff—the flesh and blood of the dynasty —was incapable of separating the duty of personal attachment [to the Tsar] from his duty to his country, albeit that country was not his own.' A. V. Podzhio [Poggio], 'Zapiski Dekabrista', *Golos Minuvshago* (1913), Kn. 1, p. 140. (The foreword to this article by A. I. Yakovlev gives Poggio's dates as 1797–1873, *ibid.* p. 134.)

[3] Benckendorff was married on 12 Nov. 1817 to Yelizavyeta Andreyevna Zakharzhevskaya as her second husband. (She was originally married to P. G. Bibikov, d. 1812.) She was appointed a 'Stats-Dama' in 1839 and survived her husband, dying in 1858. But no male children were born to them and the title of Count passed on Benckendorff's death to his nephew, Konstantin Konstantinovich B.

upon him—the Order of St Vladimir Class I after the Turkish Campaign of
1828 and the Order of St Andrei Pervozvannyi in 1834.

As the Tsar's closest confidant he accompanied Nicholas on the latter's
numerous journeys inside Russia and abroad, during which he always occupied the seat beside the emperor in his carriage. He became at one and the
same time his master's friend and bodyguard. When Nicholas wished to
travel incognito, he would do so in the assumed capacity of A.D.C. to his
favourite, and Benckendorff's memoirs[1] are of particular value for the light
they throw on Nicholas' character and interests, although they contain
almost no information on the Third Department or the part played in its
development by their author. They prove, however, that the two men were
inseparable until 1837, when a serious illness undermined Benckendorff's
strength and their relationship grew less intimate.[2] Even so he was chosen to
suppress disorders that had broken out among the Lithuanian peasants in

[1] These memoirs ('Zapiski grafa A. Kh. Benkendorfa') have never been published in full in one
edition. The majority appeared as separate articles in three different historical journals between
1865 and 1903. These articles are listed here according to the years covered by the memoirs:
1828, R. Star. (1896), vol. 86, Jun., pp. 471–510 (these memoirs were written in 1834, see
p. 497); *1829, ibid.* vol. 87, Jul., pp. 3–27; *1830, ibid.* vol. 88, Oct., pp. 65–83; *1831, ibid.*
pp. 84–96; *1832, R. Star.* (1898), vol. 93, Feb., pp. 281–95; *1835, Ist. Vyestnik* (1903), vol.
XCI, Jan., pp. 37–65; *1836, R. Arkh.* (1865), no. 2, pp. 130–9; *1837, Ist. Vyestnik, loc. cit.,*
Feb., pp. 447–69. (All these articles were contributed by N. K. Shil'der with the exception of
that printed in *R. Arkh.* which was contributed by M. A. Korff.)

Excerpts from Benckendorff's memoirs relating to the period before 1828 were not published
separately but are included in Shil'der's History of Nicholas I. As this work covers the reign
only up to 1831, its editors explain (vol. 2 (Appendices), p. 617): '...we consider it...
appropriate to include excerpts from the Memoirs of General-in-Waiting Count Benckendorff
copied by N. K. Shil'der from the original mss. They cover the period from 1832 to 1837 and
include extremely important material for the biography of Emperor Nicholas...' These
excerpts are printed in vol. 2, pp. 647–764. It will be noted that Benckendorff's memoirs
covering the years 1833 and 1834 are only to be found at this reference.

It is interesting that Nicholas himself read these memoirs and frequently added marginal
corrections to their text. Benckendorff's style is generally undistinguished and marked throughout by the most fulsome flattery and sentimental eulogies of every aspect of Nicholas' character,
appearance and achievements. (Baron Korff records that Nicholas commented to Orlov that
he found in them a very faithful and vivid—though badly written—account of his reign; and
that Orlov had personally passed this comment on. It is also confirmed by Nicholas' son, later
the Emperor Alexander II. See *R. Star.* (1899), vol. 100, p. 490, Dec.) The memoirs
are, however, disappointingly reticent on the subject of the writer's control of Higher Police
affairs.

(Apart from the *Zapiski*—complete details of which have not previously been listed—
Benckendorff also wrote various articles of a purely military character relating to his own
experiences during and after the 1812 War. These articles were printed in the *Voyennyi Zhurnal
Glavnago Shtaba.*)

[2] 'The separation [caused by Benckendorff's illness in 1837] had its effect, and shortly afterwards
Count Benckendorff's star began to dim; and towards the end of his career...even coldness
set in and he left for abroad for several months', P. Bartyenev in a footnote to a letter dated
31 Jul. 1837 written by Benckendorff to Prince Vorontsov in which he laments his separation
from the Emperor. *Arkhiv Knyazya Vorontsova,* p. 344.

1841 and was the emperor's representative at Riga in 1842 when regulations were drawn up by a Council of Nobles to attempt a solution of local peasant problems. Only Benckendorff's death in 1844 put an end to a friendship which might, had Nicholas' character been different, have influenced the Tsar to act with less arbitrariness and severity.

Benckendorff's character, it must be admitted, did not prove sufficiently strong to resist the demands made upon it by Nicholas' will and the circumstances of his reign. Yet despite the reputation for harshness earned by the Department he headed there is no doubt that Benckendorff did occasionally venture to persuade Nicholas to modify his severity and his 'good name and humane kindness'[1] found many defenders. One of the best known of these, P. P. Karatygin, quotes an instance of this kind when, at the beginning of the 1830s, Benckendorff influenced the Tsar to show mercy in cases where a disproportionate punishment had already been awarded. ' "As it is, Sire, there are already too many persons who hate you. . ." "But *one* friend I have!" said the Emperor, embracing Benckendorff, "and thank you!" ' whereupon the sentences in question were reduced.[2] The same feelings of gratitude to Benckendorff prompted Nicholas' later behaviour in 1837 during the former's illness, when it was thought that Benckendorff was on his death-bed. The Tsar wrote to him at his country estate of Fall' in Estonia, addressing him always as 'mon cher ami' and invariably signing himself as 'A vous pour la vie, votre tendrement affectionné Nicolas'; and on the sick man's return to St Petersburg he would visit him twice a day. It was on this occasion that Nicholas' sincere distress led him to say, on coming out of the Count's bedroom, 'There dies a man who has never caused me to quarrel with anyone and who has reconciled me with many of you. I want you all to know this', and, according to one source, there were tears in the Emperor's eyes.[3] The degree of respect and affection that existed between Nicholas and Benckendorff fully explains the latter's predominant position in the control of Russia's internal affairs.[4]

[1] See *RBS* article on A. Kh. Benkendorf.

[2] P. P. Karatygin: 'Benkendorf i Dubel't', *Ist. Vyestnik* (1887), vol. xxx, p. 167, Oct. This author records that after Benckendorff's death Nicholas always kept a bust of him in his study, *ibid*.

[3] 'Zapiski E. I. Stogova', *R. Star.* (1903), vol. 114, p. 312. The Tsar's words on this occasion became widely known, but sources differ slightly as to the exact wording, e.g. 'In the course of 11 years he has not caused me to quarrel with anyone, and he has reconciled me with many', see *RBS* article. Other versions with similar minor variations also exist.

[4] 'Matters entrusted to no one else were confided to him. Thus, for example, on more than one occasion complaints were made to Nicholas of the lack of restraint of his brother Mikhail, who used to lose all control in moments of irascibility and passion caused by the most insignificant service shortcomings on the part of members of the Guards Corps under his command. The Emperor once ordered Benckendorff to have a word with the Grand Duke on this subject. . . Mikhail Pavlovich listened to him calmly, concealing his anger at the all-powerful courtier', Lemke, p. 24.

This position was naturally, however, one of immense difficulty for Benckendorff as he was bound to incur the extreme dislike of all highly placed courtiers and officials who enjoyed less favour. As early as March 1827 he wrote to Baron Diebich: '...if only good should come of it, I shall be completely consoled because my one aim is the common weal, but it is difficult to get things done; the wrath of the highest officials, namely, the Governors-General of both capitals, increases daily against me by reason of the fact that public opinion is in favour of the establishment of the Higher Police and, I will venture to say, of my direction of it. So long as it is only feasible, I shall protect the Emperor from all possible kinds of unpleasant-nesses; this will add to the number of my grey hairs, but I shall never com-plain; when intrigues finally exhaust my patience I shall apply for my brother's appointment in command of some cavalry unit—there, at any rate, when the guns are thundering, intrigue remains behind the front.'[1] There are no grounds for supposing that Benckendorff was not perfectly sincere in believing that public opinion was favourable to his Department, but it says little for his perspicacity that he could overlook the strong probability that the hostility to it of 'the highest officials' was widely shared by most sections of the community. As for his personal popularity, it is permissible to conjecture that the public, like Countess Nesselrode, was merely consoled by the know-ledge that he, instead of some more aggressive figure, occupied so high a post.

This negative view of the Head of the Third Department continued to prevail a decade later,[2] but Benckendorff does not appear to have been aware

[1] Shil'der, vol. 2, pp. 37–8.
[2] 'March 2–4 [1837]...Count Benckendorff has fallen ill. There is no hope of his recovery. The public is showing great sympathy for his illness. All are afraid of losing him, knowing that he can be kind to the distractions and errors of young people. Standing at the head of the secret police and in a position to do much harm, he hurts no one. During his illness the Emperor has visited him twice daily. It is said that should he die, Count Orlov or Count Chernyshov will be appointed in his place; the latter is apparently feared in society; even more feared is the appoint-ment of the Governor-General of Lithuania, Prince Dolgorukov', 'Dnevnik P. G. Divova', *R. Star.* (1900), vol. 104, p. 488. (Senator Divov (1763–1841), after a long career in govern-ment service, was appointed a member of the Investigatory Commission in 1826 and thereafter remained in close contact with Court and official circles. His diary thus represents a valuable and reliable source of contemporary information.)

Count A. F. Orlov (1786–1861), who became the second Head of the Third Department in 1844, was a member of the Council of State and in fact temporarily replaced Benckendorff on this occasion. (Benckendorff wrote: 'I invited Count Orlov to call and asked him to take over the most outstanding of my duties', *Ist. Vyestnik* (1903), vol. XCI, Feb. p. 447.)

Count A. I. Chernyshov (1786–1857) was Minister of War throughout the reign.

Prince N. A. Dolgorukov (1792–1847) was appointed Governor-General of the Grodno, Belostok and Minsk Provinces (retaining the rank of Military Governor of Vil'no) in 1834, posts which he held until 1840 when he was appointed Gov.-Gen. of the Khar'kov, Poltava and Chernigov Provinces. He was the elder brother of Prince V. A. Dolgorukov (1804–68) who became third Head of the Third Department in 1856.

of it. Writing after his recovery from the illness of 1837, he recorded with pride the daily visits of the Tsar to his bedside, the callers from every class of society, the prayers held in churches of all denominations and the personal messages received from the monarchs of Prussia, Austria and Sweden; and then sentimentally and characteristically wrote:

I had the good fortune in my own lifetime of hearing my own eulogies, which were the greatest reward which can be vouchsafed to a man on this earth, consisting of the tears and regrets of poor unknown orphans, of every mark of sympathy generally[1] and in particular of the lively commiseration of my Tsar, who showed me by his grief and tender solicitude the best and noblest sign of his gracious favour. In the post I occupied this, of course, represented the most brilliant account of my eleven-year-old tenure of office, and I think that I have surely been almost the first of all Secret Police Chiefs whose death people feared and who have not been pursued to the edge of the grave by a single complaint.[2] This illness was a real triumph for me, the like of which none of our high officials had yet experienced. Two of my colleagues who were very highly placed indeed and who had never concealed their hatred of my position—and possibly were also somewhat envious of the relationship in which I stood to the throne—both told me that they would capitulate in the face of this unanimous sympathy on the part of the public; and ever since they have been my constant friends. But most of all this triumph was enjoyed by the Tsar, who saw in it the approval of his own choice and of the steadfastness with which he had supported me and my position against every ill-disposed suggestion.[3]

Lemke comments with some justice that 'only Benckendorff could imagine that all the deference which surrounded him was sincere and due to his per-

[1] According to an account of Benckendorff's illness published abroad in 1842 by a French visitor to Russia and accepted as true by Baron Korff—the author is not named—the sick man said to the Emperor during one of the latter's visits: 'Sire, I can die peacefully: this crowd which waits and asks for news of me will be my advocate; it feels that my conscience is clear!', 'Iz Zapisok Barona (vposlyedstvii Grafa) M. A. Korfa', *R. Star.* (1899), vol. 100, p. 486.

[2] There is an echo of this eulogistic sentiment to be found in the memoirs of an English traveller who, speaking of Count Benckendorff as 'another most conspicuous character both in Russian history and in the Petersbourg world', wrote: '...In his more especial Department as head of the secret police he has earned for himself a confidence and affection which certainly no *chef* in this ominous capacity ever enjoyed before, and it is matter of universal congratulation throughout the empire that this office is placed in such hands', Lady Eastlake (Elizabeth Rigby), *A Residence on the Shores of the Baltic described in a series of letters*, 2 vols. (London, 1841), vol. 2, p. 248. Lady Eastlake made a journey to Estonia in 1838 where she stayed at Fall' ('Fall' is in the possession of Count B. [*sic*], the man who, after the Emperor, wears the diadem in Russia', *ibid.* p. 144) and, though she does not appear to have met Benckendorff either there or in the capital during the winter of 1838–9, she was greatly impressed by what she discovered about him. She was in no way a credulous observer and her book concludes with a 'reluctant conviction that, at this present time, Russia is the country where the learned man wastes his time, the patriot breaks his heart, and the rogue prospers'. (According to the late Count Benckendorff, by the time of the Revolution the Fall' estate had passed into the possession of Prince Peter Volkonsky, a descendant of one of Benckendorff's daughters.)

[3] *Ist. Vyestnik, loc. cit.* p. 449 (p. misprinted 944); or Shil'der, vol. 2, pp. 736–7.

sonal merits and qualities'.[1] The weight of evidence on Benckendorff's character and abilities all tends to prove that he lacked the mental grasp necessary for the proper fulfilment of the onerous duties of Head of the Third Department. 'Neither this high post nor all the favours constantly conferred upon him by the Emperor...could make a genius out of a man who, though noble and worthy, was a not unusual person',[2] wrote Baron Korff, whose personal knowledge of Benckendorff was profound and who, furthermore, had no reason to harm his late colleague's reputation.[3] His appreciation is thus of particular interest and represents a more valuable guide to the understanding of Benckendorff's character than the adulatory 'necrologue' published at his death.[4]

Instead of being the hero of rectitude and right-thinking which it represented Benckendorff to have been, he was rather in fact a man whose goodness was negative. Besides the amount of good that was done in his name there was also much that was arbitrary and evil. With no knowledge of affairs, with no inclination for study, a man whose special characteristics were forgetfulness and perpetual absent-mindedness—traits which repeatedly gave rise to various anecdotes highly entertaining to their audience or those who witnessed them but very far from being amusing to those who were their victim—and lastly, a man immoderately devoted to women, he was never either businesslike or efficient and was always the tool of those who surrounded him. I shared his company for four years in the Committee of Ministers and for ten in the Council of State, but on not one single occasion did I hear him speak on any subject whatsoever, even though many of the subjects under discussion were originated by him and others must have been of personal interest to him. It would often happen at the conclusion of a session at which he had been present from beginning to end, he would ask me how such and such a motion of those he himself had moved had been decided, just as if he himself had been absent from the meeting.

On one occasion in the Council of State the Minister of Justice, Count Panin, delivered himself of a very long speech. After it had already lasted half an hour,

[1] Lemke, p. 25. He further suggests (p. 114) that Benckendorff partially engineered his own illness to cover his unpopularity with Nicholas at having played a dubious rôle in the last days of Pushkin. But no evidence is quoted in substantiation of this charge.

[2] *Iz Zapisok Korfa, loc. cit.* p. 485.

[3] Baron (later Count) Korff (1800–76), State-Secretary, Member of the Council of State, had a distinguished career under Speransky in the Second Dept. of H.I.M. Own Chancellery, of which he eventually became the Chief Director in 1861.

As his evidence gave a generally unfavourable picture of Benckendorff, he stated in a footnote: 'I consider it my duty to observe here that the Count's relations with me were always of a most amicable nature and not one instance of unpleasantness ever occurred between us: consequently, in this sketch of his portrait I have not been guided by any prejudices against him but solely by the voice of truthfulness, possibly even with a certain indulgence in his favour', *ibid.* p. 486.

[4] 'In his person the Emperor has lost a faithful and devoted servant, the fatherland has lost a useful and worthy son, mankind a zealous champion', see Korff, *ibid.*

Benckendorff turned to his neighbour, Count Orlov, and exclaimed: 'Sacré Dieu, voilà ce que j'appelle parler!'—'But my dear fellow, do you not realize that it is you he has been opposing for the last half-hour!'—'Indeed?' answered Benckendorff, who only then understood that Panin's speech had in fact been the reply opposing his motion. Five minutes later he said, with a glance at his watch: 'A présent adieu, il est temps que j'aille chez l'Empereur' and left the other members to disentangle his argument with Panin as they might see fit.

There was a constant stream of similar anecdotes, and as a result he not infrequently harmed the very persons whom he intended to help, and afterwards failed to understand why what had happened was precisely the opposite of his views and wishes. It should further be stated that with all his pleasant manners, with that chivalrous something in his tone and words, and with a certain fashionable liveliness in conversation, he had only the most superficial education,[1] learned nothing, read nothing and did not even possess a reasonable knowledge of how to write properly, witness all his autographs in French and German that have been preserved together with his signature on Russian documents, in which only in the very last years of his life, probably owing to a dutiful hint from someone in his immediate entourage, did he cease to sign himself 'pokorneishei sluga'.[2,3]

Benckendorff was, of course, the faithful and devoted servant of his tsar in the fullest and highest meaning of the word and did not do anybody any harm on purpose; but he could be useful only to the extent that this corresponded to the views and suggestions of his immediate circle: for he possessed no more personal initiative than he possessed natural talents or elevated opinions. In a word, just as he himself was a person whose goodness of character was negative, so too his usefulness was exclusively negative: it lay in the fact that the post invested with such colossal power was occupied by a man whose apathy paralysed it and not by someone else who might have been not only less kindly than he was but also a person whose one aim was that of actively advancing his own interests. His name, it is true, always stood at the head of all industrial and speculative enterprises of the day; he was a director of all possible shareholding companies and the promoter of many of them; but all this was done not with the purpose of acquiring fame nor simply

[1] In this respect he was greatly the inferior of his younger brother Konstantin who, in addition to considerable personal bravery, 'was unusually well educated for his day and spoke five languages'. See *RBS* article on Konstantin Benkendorf. Alexander Benckendorff's intellectual capacity was undoubtedly much inferior. A recent historian describes him as 'a man of small intelligence and education', S. G. Pushkaryov, *Rossiya v xix vyeke (1801–1914)* (New York, 1956), p. 41.

[2] 'Your most humble servant.' Grammatical error in the Russian.

[3] Lemke comments that Benckendorff's ignorance of French was 'genuinely astonishing'; and quotes his note on a letter from Pushkin in which the poet requested him to petition the Emperor for the loan of a considerable sum of money. Benckendorff's note read: 'l'Empereur lui propose 10,000 roubles et 6 moi de congé au bout de quel il voira s'il doit prendre son congé ou non', p. 23; nor can this be regarded as an isolated instance. Shil'der reproduces the facsimile of a letter written by Benckendorff on 26 Aug. 1826 to the wife of one of the Decembrists which reads: 'Madame—J'ai eu l'honneur de montrer la lettre que vous avéz bien voulue me confier; Sa Majesté l'empereur m'a chargé, de vous prévenir, que vous aviéz l'entière permission de joindre votre epoux à l'endroit de sa destination', *op. cit.* vol. 1, opp. p. 462.

out of a desire to do good in the public interest, but rather because all speculators and societies primarily appealed to the Count with a view to obtaining in him a powerful protector. In his lifetime he acquired considerable wealth on many occasions but then squandered his gains time after time and towards the end of his career left his affairs in the most pitiful condition.

Nevertheless there is no doubt that for twelve years or more Count Benckendorff was one of the emperor Nicholas' chief favourites not only because the latter was accustomed to him but also because he respected in him, with all his weaknesses, the feelings of an absolutely devoted sincere gentleman of mild and equable character who always endeavoured to mollify rather than to inflame his monarch's passionate nature...[1]

This account of Benckendorff's personality by a responsible statesman who knew him well and over a period of years must be accepted as authoritative. It is confirmed by such differing sources as his 'literary collaborator' (Grech),[2] by one of his 'victims' (Herzen) and by one of his own staff-officers (Stogov).

Grech was normally a strong supporter of Nicholas' policies in general and of the Third Department in particular, yet in his memoirs he referred unequivocally to its first Head as 'a muddle-headed courtier', 'the kindly but inane Benckendorff', 'Benckendorff the ever smiling', 'the tactless Benckendorff' and so on.[3]

Herzen, who was summoned into his presence in December 1840, wrote in a famous passage:

There was nothing in itself displeasing in the appearance of the Chief of Gendarmes;[4] he resembled the usual type of Baltic noblemen and of the German aristocracy in general. His face was worn, tired, he had that deceptively kind expression which is often peculiar to evasive and apathetic persons.

It is possible, indeed, that Benckendorff did not do all the harm he might have done as head of this terrible police which stood outside and above the law, which had the right to interfere in everything—I am ready to believe this, especially when

---

[1] *Iz Zapisok Korfa, loc. cit.* pp. 485–8. Korff goes on to discuss (pp. 488–90) Benckendorff's waning popularity and influence after 1837, together with the details of his financial position, his mistresses and the final episode of his infatuation for a society lady who, it was said, succeeded in converting him on his death-bed from Lutheranism to Catholicism. (According to a footnote, Emperor Alexander II commented: 'All this is extremely exaggerated and is a malicious slander.') Korff also records the details of Benckendorff's death and burial—at Fall'—and the discovery of his memoirs—'In view of a certain lack in Benckendorff of industry, patience and literary ability, I was completely unprepared to learn that he had left memoirs'—but makes no further comments on his character.

[2] Lemke even refers to Grech as 'Benckendorff's eulogist', p. 25.

[3] N. I. Grech, *Zapiski o moei Zhizni* (ed. Moscow–Leningrad, 1930), pp. 390, 394, 419, 459.

[4] Benckendorff made the same impression on the censor Nikitenko who was summoned to meet him in Dec. 1842. Nikitenko describes him as 'an old man of venerable appearance'. A. V. Nikitenko, *Zapiski i Dnevnik 1804–1877*, izd. 2-oe. 2 vols. (SPB, 1904), vol. 1, p. 330.

I recall the insipid expression of his face—but he did not do any good either: for this he lacked the energy, the will and the heart. The fear of saying a word in the defence of persecuted individuals is as bad as any other crime when one is in the service of so cold and merciless a man as Nicholas.

How many innocent victims passed through his hands, how many perished through inadvertence, through absentmindedness, because he was busy with official red-tape, and how many gloomy thoughts and grievous memories perhaps wandered through his head and tormented him on the steamer where, a prematurely drooping and senile old man, he sought in a betrayal of his religion the intercession of the Catholic Church with its all-forgiving indulgences.[1]

Perhaps the only criticism that can be made of this otherwise excellent appreciation is that Herzen tentatively ascribed to Benckendorff at the end of his career certain feelings of remorse. From what is known of the latter's character, Benckendorff in fact remained until his death unaware of his own shortcomings as well as of those of his Department.

There can be no doubt that Benckendorff's subordinates constantly took advantage of their Chief's incompetence. Colonel Stogov, who transferred to the Corps of Gendarmes from the Navy at the end of 1833,[2] has left first-hand evidence of life in the Third Department under his direction. He enjoyed the friendship of Benckendorff's leading military assistant, Dubbelt, and more than once reported directly to Benckendorff in Dubbelt's place.

The report passed off well. The Count continually called me Stokgof [sic]—I did not contradict him, when you are with a German it is as well to be a German. I often performed Dubbelt's duties at the Count's audiences and entered into the part of a man of affairs, and when I got to know the Count—I used to invent boldly when I was ignorant of something and all went well...Personally Benckendorff was a brave man, but he had little understanding of administrative business. The Count was the kindest possible creature, and I do not know of a single instance in which he harmed anyone.[3]

Stogov's attitude to his Chief was thus a mixture of deference, affection and amusement. He records several incidents of the chronic absentmindedness for which Benckendorff had become notorious[4] and if in name and position

---

[1] A. I. Gertsen, *Byloye i Dumy* (izd. Ogiz, Leningrad, 1946), p. 240.

[2] E. I. Stogov (1797–1880), see *RBS* article.

[3] 'Zapiski E. I. Stogova', *R. Star.* (1903), vol. 114, pp. 310, 312.

[4] One of the best known of these told how Benckendorff once went to call on the French envoy and, failing to find a visiting card in his pocket, was unable to recall his own name. Returning on foot, he happened to meet Count Orlov who called to him 'Count Benckendorff!' 'The latter was overjoyed, waved to Orlov as though he had found something and, repeating to himself "Count Benckendorff", returned to the envoy's house and entered his name. The whole of Piter [popular name for St Petersburg] repeated this anecdote and the Emperor knew of it', *R. Star., loc. cit.* pp. 311–12. (This story is also quoted by Trotsky, p. 118.)
That it was no isolated instance is proved by Stogov's memoirs of the Emperor's visit to

the Head of the secret police was a formidable figure, he clearly held no fears for his own junior officers. In the absence of equally reliable evidence to the contrary, it is fair to assume that Stogov's views were shared by many of his brother officers.

Stogov also recorded how Benckendorff conducted his everyday duties in the Department and the attitude to him of many of the petitioners who appealed for his assistance:

The Count was a dandy, every morning a barber would tidy his few hairs. From 9 o'clock onwards his office was already full of petitioners. At 10 o'clock he would emerge informally in a frock coat without epaulettes and would listen to every applicant; with ladies he was exceedingly polite. It once happened that a lady, for greater conviction, knelt before him and I saw how the Count trembled, changed expression and hurried forward to raise her to her feet—he could not endure a woman's humiliation. Going round the petitioners, he would prepare to drive to the palace, and meanwhile new petitioners would collect. At 11 or half past 11 the Count would emerge in uniform, would again go round all the petitioners, listen to them and accept petitions. Knowing the Count, we were well aware of the utter futility of his audiences. He would listen to a petitioner kindly—without understanding a thing; of course he never saw the petitions again; but the public was very pleased by his kindness, patience and consolatory words...Knowing the Count's duties, it was forgivable for him not to take over control of administrative matters, he had to know in detail everything that had been said and done on the preceding day throughout all Russia...[1]

Like the members of the public who were misled by Benckendorff's affability of manner, Stogov too was prepared to make considerable allowances for his many other deficiencies.

Within the evidently narrow limits of his ability, Benckendorff probably did make sincere attempts to deserve a reputation for philanthropy. If Dubbelt's description of him to Herzen as 'a man of angelic kindness'[2] was somewhat exaggerated, the facts quoted by Karatygin in his memoirs prove that he did not lack genuine admirers and even beneficiaries.[3] He probably

Simbirsk in 1837 accompanied by Benckendorff. 'The Emperor approached where we were standing...Count Benckendorff, in presenting me, said: "The Gendarme staff-officer stationed in the Province of Simbirsk (looking at my epaulettes), Lieutenant-Colonel...Lieutenant-Colonel..." I see that the Count is crumpling the memorandum I had handed him in his right hand, but has forgotten both my name and it. The Emperor smiled and said graciously: "You are Stogov"...', 'Ocherki, Razskazy i Vospominaniya E. I. Stogova', *R. Star.* (1878), vol. 23, p. 675.

[1] *R. Star.* (1903), *loc. cit.* p. 312. [2] Gertsen, *Byloye i Dumy*, ed. cit. p. 239.
[3] P. P. Karatygin (1832–88), the author of an interesting article on Benckendorff and Dubbelt published in *Ist. Vyestnik* (1887), vol. xxx, pp. 165–79, Oct., was the son of a well-known actor and writer of 'vaudevilles' who had been a personal friend of Benckendorff. The son records various stories of the Count and his work which he learned (p. 165) from his father. These include an incident in 1832 (pp. 168–72) telling how Benckendorff accepted without

acted with all possible kindness whenever he felt impelled to do so, but it must be doubted whether some of Karatygin's praises[1] were fully deserved and whether in general he was equal to the demands imposed upon him by his office. His mind lacked a proper sense of proportion and he seems to have been unable to distinguish clearly between cases of genuine subversion on the one hand and relatively petty and even juvenile instances of 'free-thinking' on the other. The numerous stringent measures adopted quite arbitrarily against the latter category tend to prove that Herzen was correct when he referred to the 'many victims' who passed through Benckendorff's hands.

A well-informed Englishman who was resident in Russia in the 1830s and 1840s describes[2] among other cases of this sort that of a young officer who,

demur the unsubstantiated story of a young Russian named Pokrovsky who might otherwise have been accused of a serious crime. Pokrovsky was in fact guilty of nothing but bad luck, but in order to avoid a scandal, it was necessary for Benckendorff to conceal the truth from his own staff. The story thus remained a secret between him and the young Pokrovsky who, when in later life he heard Benckendorff abused, felt impelled to declare 'Gentlemen, I am not an agent of the Third Department; once, in all my life, I was in contact with it, in fact, while Count Aleksandr Khristoforovich was alive...In God's name do not slander his memory: he was my benefactor; I owe him the saving of my honour and life itself.' According to Karatygin, this case was by no means unique (p. 172).

[1] For example, it is difficult to reconcile with what is known of Benckendorff's abilities Karatygin's assertion that 'the Count possessed a capacity, necessary to his job, which developed amazingly as he grew older—that of penetrating a person from the expression on his face and the sound of his voice', *Ist. Vyestnik, loc. cit.* p. 172.

[2] (C. F. Henningsen), *Revelations of Russia: or the Emperor Nicholas and his Empire in 1844. By One Who Has Seen and Describes*, publ. anonymously in 2 vols. (London, 1844), vol. 2, ch. 4, p. 90.

Charles Frederick Henningsen, a typical soldier of fortune, was born in 1815 of a Swedish father and English mother. After serving with the Carlist Army in Spain, he saw further military service with the Russian Army in the Caucasus. In 1849 he was fighting with Kossuth and commanded the fortress of Comorn. He then fought under William Walker in Nicaragua in 1856, when he was promoted Major-General. In the American Civil War he commanded the 3rd Regt of Wise's Brigade in the Confederate Army and saw service in Virginia. He died in Washington in 1877. *Mod. Engl. Biography*, publ. by Fred. Boase (Truro, 1892), vol. I, p. 1431. *The Dict. of American Biography* (London–New York, 1932), vol. VIII, pp. 543–4 clarifies the anomaly of a foreigner apparently serving with both the Russian Army and Kossuth by stating that in fact Henningsen fought in the Caucasus with Schamyl [*sic*] against the Russians before continuing to oppose them outside Russia in the capacity of Kossuth's confidential secretary.

(British Foreign Office archives contain a letter dated 5 Feb. 1843 from the Third Department to the British Ambassador Lord Stuart de Rothsay. It is signed by Benckendorff, who tells the Ambassador that 'le tribunal général de la police a terminé l'enquête judiciaire au sujet des faux dont le Sr Henningsen, sujet de S.M. Britannique, s'est rendu coupable' and states that the latter's dossier has been conveyed to the criminal court which will pronounce sentence. Public Record Office, Series F.O.181, vol. 180 (notes from Russian Ministers 1842–3). Vol. 173 (Notes to Russian Ministers 1841–3) contains a reply from the Ambassador dated 26 Mar./ 7 Apr. in which he thanks Benckendorff for 'tout l'intérêt qu'elle [Votre Excellence] a témoigné à l'égard du Sieur Henningsen' and requests his further assistance 'vu sa jeunesse [H. was then 28] et son inexpérience et la longue détention qu'il a déjà subie'. The Ambassador also suggests that the Easter season might provide possible grounds for the exercise of clemency. From this

'in the privacy of a very small circle', repeated some humorous lines he had composed on the subject of the many ukazes which constantly appeared. These lines ended 'Tout se fait par ukaze içi—C'est par ukaze que l'on voyage—C'est par ukaze l'on rit.' He was summoned to the Third Department. 'My young friend [said the Count] you have got a very pretty talent for writing verses, we hear. You recited some very charming poetry last night, in which you contemplated the possibility of a journey. I announce it to you. (Vous avez prévu un voyage. Eh bien! je vous l'annonce.) The Feld-Jaeger and his post waggon were waiting at the door to convey him into exile.' The author's comment on this and comparable stories was 'These are a few out of five hundred similar instances which immediately occur to us...' and it is hardly possible to absolve Benckendorff from the charge of having personally approved a policy which perpetually involved the use of such Draconian punishments. Authenticated examples of their application are too numerous not to make it certain that many of Benckendorff's decisions lacked due discrimination.

It remains to assess the degree of influence he exerted on what Herzen called 'the secular inquisition founded by Nicholas'.[1]

The 'Jubilee Report' of 1876 refrained from any comment whatsoever on the personalities at the head or on the staff of the Third Department.[2] Only Lemke and Trotsky have investigated this aspect of its development in any detail and, understandably, both have depicted Benckendorff's rôle and character in the most unfavourable light. Lemke's appreciation includes the evidence of most of the sources quoted above, from which he naturally deduces that little good can be said of Benckendorff either as man or states-man. He discounts the favourable views recorded by the Decembrist Prince Volkonsky on the grounds that, in the first place, Volkonsky knew Benckendorff only before 1825 when he himself was still a young man and insufficiently experienced in assessing people; and that, in the second place, Volkonsky was bound 'to esteem a man who conducted himself well, at all events on the surface, towards the Decembrists, his own friends and companions'.[3] Lemke makes no mention of the even more favourable evidence published by Karatygin: possibly he considered it too biased to merit

correspondence it is clear that Henningsen's anti-Russian activities led to his capture and captivity and that he was deported, although there is no further information about him from this source and his book discloses nothing relating to the 'faux' of which he was charged.)

   The Dict. of American Biography described him as 'a scholar and linguist of unusual ability ...His writings deal accurately and fearlessly with the social, cultural, military and political aspects of people and countries...Written in a direct, lucid, serious and convincing vein, where fact excludes fancy, they are both valuable and entertaining...'

[1] Gertsen, p. 235.
[2] The section of Adrianov's History which deals with the Third Department (*op. cit.* pp. 97–101) is equally silent on this subject.   [3] Lemke, p. 26.

inclusion in his work. It is probable, however, that Lemke's view was primarily affected by his study of the obstructive rôle played by Benckendorff in the flowering of Russian literature and education, as is evident from his quotation of the latter's opinion that 'we should not be in too much of a hurry to educate her [Russia], lest the people should become the equal of monarchs in their sphere of intelligence and then encroach upon the latter's power to its deterioration...'[1] Obscurantism of this kind, typical as it may have been of its day, convinced Lemke of Benckendorff's harmful influence on Russian life in general and its literature in particular. Trotsky's more recent appreciation of Benckendorff is equally damning. He throws no new light on what is known of Benckendorff's character, but his brief summary of his career is interesting.

For seventeen years Benckendorff headed the Third Department, but, strange as it may seem, did not succeed in winning, let alone the affection, even the hatred of those whom the Third Department oppressed. This may be explained by the fact that it soon became very clear to everyone that Benckendorff really played a very insignificant rôle in gendarme affairs. He was a man of feeble will, not endowed with the slightest gifts of a statesman...His subordinates quickly realized that they could please their chief with prompt and resolute answers, no matter how far removed from reality, and all went well. Benckendorff himself remained unalterably convinced of the admirable efficiency of the Department entrusted to his care and of his own irreplaceability.[2]

In Trotsky's view, Benckendorff was a mere nonentity whose sole distinguishing characteristic was that of servility to the Tsar, a characteristic equally shared by his successor Count Orlov.[3]

The relative unimportance of Benckendorff's part in the development of the Third Department must be admitted. It is clear that his rôle in it was usually limited to the precise execution of Nicholas' wishes and demands. All that can fairly be said of his influence as Chief of Gendarmes is that he tried, mainly by personal example, to raise the status of Higher Police officials on to a higher plane. Their reputation had sunk so low during Russia's earlier history that this in itself represented an advance and was to some extent successful. Even Herzen could write, in a reference to his arrest in 1834, 'One could not be a spy, a trafficker in others' depravity, and at the same time an honest man, but one could be a gendarme officer without losing all human dignity'; and, recalling a later encounter with the Third Department in 1840, he referred to gendarmes as 'the flower of courtesy' who considered

---

[1] Shil'der, vol. 2, p. 287; Lemke, *ibid.*
[2] Trotsky, pp. 118, 120. (Benckendorff in fact died in 1844 and thus headed the Third Department for eighteen years.) Trotsky quotes no specific sources for these conclusions.
[3] Trotsky, p. 121.

their actions dictated by 'a sacred obligation' and 'the duty of service'.[1] Benckendorff was neither well educated nor intelligent, but he possessed certain positive qualities of unselfishness which had been lacking in his only comparable predecessor—Alexander's Minister of Police, Balashov. He was honest, sincere, hard-working, unshakably loyal and, at least to outward appearances, respectable. He did not want his countrymen to think of him as a kind of Grand Inquisitor. If he was hypocritical in his opinions and actions, he was probably not aware of being so. He was undoubtedly by nature a kindly man[2] and he made an excellent personal impression on a wide variety of persons. One foreign resident in Russia described him as 'talented, gentle, insinuating in manner, and with advantages of person', claiming that he 'had the art of making himself generally beloved...'[3] An Austrian diplomat reported that he was 'one of those men who are so honourable, so chivalrous and possess such courteous manners that they ennoble all those who come within their sphere of influence'.[4] Even Pushkin commented: 'Au fond c'est un brave et digne homme.'[5] But for all his apparent goodness, and

---

[1] Gertsen, pp. 108, 237.

[2] Without giving his source, de Grunwald states that Benckendorff treated his own serfs with great kindness, making them pay insignificant dues; and apparently, when he wished to dispose of them to another owner, they begged him to keep them and suggested trebling the amount of their payments. Constantin de Grunwald, *La Vie de Nicolas I-er* (Paris, 1946), p. 187. (Subsequent references to de Grunwald apply to this work.)

[3] J. H. Schnitzler, *Secret History of the Court and Government of Russia under the Emperors Alexander and Nicholas*, 2 vols. (London, 1847), vol. 1, p. 270.

Another reference in this work mentions Benckendorff as 'a man, if not extremely moral, at least honest, besides being active, enlightened, of uncommon intelligence, and an agreeable companion...', vol. 2, p. 206. (The author (1802–71) was a native of Strasbourg and spent the years 1823 to 1828 in Russia as a private tutor. He later acquired a reputation as an historian, statistician and encyclopaedist. There is nothing in the above-mentioned work to suggest, however, that he was acquainted with Benckendorff other than by hearsay—which possibly explains his reference to him as being 'of uncommon intelligence'.)

Schnitzler's view of Benckendorff's good qualities is to some extent confirmed by the memoirs of another foreigner resident in Russia for a far longer period. Discussing the 1840s he wrote: '...fear pervades everybody when the remark is heard, "The chief of the secret police has sent for you!" The terrible Count Benkendorf is no longer an object of terror. Was, then, the man so terrible? Not the man, but the office. Count Benkendorf was never a bad man; but that those near him never felt comfortable, is equally certain...Moss and grass now grow over the weaknesses which neither befitted the statesman nor his office [this is probably a reference to B.'s known partiality for the opposite sex]; yet I could wish that he was still among the living —not for my sake, but for that of millions. A man possessing feelings of humanity, and free from every idea of brutality, is a meteor in Russia. Most assuredly it disappeared too soon!...' *Recollections of Russia during Thirty-Three Years' Residence by a German Nobleman*, revised and translated, with the author's sanction, by Lascelles Wraxall (London, 1855), p. 252. (The British Museum used to possess a copy of the 2nd ed. of this work in German (Braunschweig, 1855), but it has been missing from the shelves since 1910.)

[4] 'Le Comte de Woyna à Metternich, 6 décembre 1841'—dispatch quoted from the 'Vienna Secret Archives' by de Grunwald, *ibid*.

[5] *Pushkin. Pis'ma*, ed. by B. L. Modzalyevsky, 3 vols. (Moscow–Leningrad, 1926–35), vol. 2, p. 60 (1826–30). (Letter to Prince P. A. Vyazemsky dated approximately 25 Jan. 1829.)

unfortunately for the institution he headed and the effect it was to have on the history of Nicholas' reign, his political shortsightedness was combined with a certain fatuous sentimentality.

Colonel Stogov records that Benckendorff's final injunctions on dispatching him to the provinces were 'You must be loved and necessary in society. If a gendarme is not loved, he is useless. In extremities be decisive and bold, and when things are quiet...fall in love!'[1] Idiotic 'instructions' of this kind could only be given by a man whose whole approach to the question of bettering public morals was fundamentally unrealistic. On the one hand he required his agents, primarily in the persons of Gendarme staff-officers, to pry into every nook and cranny of national life, be it political, social, moral or domestic; on the other, he insisted that in doing so they should acquire popularity. The inherent contradictions of such aims made it inevitable that much of the work of the Third Department, no matter how well intended, failed to achieve its purpose. For this Benckendorff must be held largely responsible. At the same time he was infinitely less responsible than Nicholas himself, who could at any time have changed the policy, methods and officials of his Higher Police. As Benckendorff remained at its head until his death, it must be assumed that Nicholas was satisfied both with the Department itself and with Benckendorff's direction of it. The real target for the popular resentment of the Third Department and its practices should not have been Benckendorff at all, but his master.

Benckendorff was served by three outstanding subordinates during his long tenure of office—M. Ya. von Vock, A. N. Mordvinov and L. V. Dubbelt. Regrettably little is known of the first two of these officials.

M. Ya. von Vock
Director of Chancellery of the Third Department 1826–31

Maksim Yakovlevich von Vock has already been mentioned in these pages, first as Chief Assistant to de Sanglen in the Special Chancellery of the Ministry of Police in 1811, then as Head of the Special Chancellery in that Ministry until 1819 and of the Ministry of Internal Affairs for the remainder of Alexander's reign.[2] During this period he evidently established for himself a reputation for intelligence and honesty which he was to maintain until his death. There appears to be no record of his life, family or education before 1811, but the fact of his having retained his difficult and responsible office from 1812 to 1825 gives some indication of his abilities. Vigel' refers to him as 'a man with whom I was acquainted: for our fathers were friends and we

---

[1] 'Zapiski Stogova', p. 314.
[2] See chapter One (in particular p. 37, note 4; p. 43, notes 1, 3; p. 45, note 6); chapter Two, *passim*.

were both educated by the same tutor...He was a German dreamer who considered free-thinking natural and in accordance with the law and was ready rather to take up arms against its opponents. Generally speaking he was never disposed to seek evidence against anyone.'[1] This kindly opinion of von Vock was shared by another of his contemporaries, Grech, who wrote 'I was acquainted with the Director of the Special Chancellery...von Vock from 1812 onwards and enjoyed his friendship and kind regard. He was a man who was clever, noble, tender-hearted, educated, honest and just in his work.'[2] The possession of these excellent qualities might explain why he nearly fell victim to the political intrigues and rivalries resulting from Alexander's reluctance to place the direction of all secret polices under one central authority,[3] but he managed to survive all dangers until—with the outbreak of the Decembrist revolt—his career entered a new phase.

Despite the fact that the Special Chancellery had been unable to prevent this conspiracy, evidently no blame was attributed to von Vock and his services were immediately required to investigate the circumstances that had given rise to it. In this connexion one of his tasks was to examine the personal records of all government employees who admitted membership of any secret society. The memoirs of a former junior official of the Ministry of Internal Affairs contain details of his cross-examination by von Vock, 'the head of the secret police [sic]', on this subject. His description of von Vock is of some interest because it represents the only known source of information on his appearance and methods. 'He put me facing the window and, gazing intently into my eyes, began to question me. He had a huge wart covered with hairs on his right eyebrow and constantly twitched it; this gave his face a strange and even somewhat terrifying appearance and he seemed to rely on this when conducting cross-examinations...' Nevertheless, the results of this particular inquiry revealed nothing incriminating and the young man's account of his exoneration ends: 'I hasten to say that von Vock was an admirable man, clever and well educated; in the performance of his duties he

---

[1] Vigel', vol. 2, p. 258. (His name—and Vigel''s evidence—in fact represents all that is known of von Vock's German origin.)

Waliszewski, writing of the end of Alexander's reign, states: 'La sévérité des policiers avait, en effet, un palliatif, dans la tolérance plus ou moins affectée du souverain, dans leur propre corruptibilité, ou même, bien que très exceptionnellement, dans les inclinations personnelles de quelques-uns d'entre eux, comme ce fut le cas de Kissiélév, et, dans un autre genre, de l'Allemand von Fock, un censeur fantaisiste, indulgent à toutes les licences de l'esprit.' K. Waliszewski, *Le Règne d'Alexandre I-er*, 3 vols. (Paris, 1923–5), vol. 3, p. 210. The index lists him as 'Fock (Maxime Iakovlévitch), censeur russe', *ibid*. p. 440.

[2] Grech, *Zapiski*, p. 711. Elsewhere in his memoirs Grech also refers to him as 'most noble', 'philanthropic', 'gentle and kindly', *ibid*. pp. 421, 506, 705.

[3] 'During the latter years of Alexander's reign he was in disfavour by reason of the plots and calumnies of Magnitsky and other scoundrels who tried through him to overthrow Kochubei', Grech, *ibid*. See also chapter One, p. 43, note 3.

combined strict justice with all possible kindness. Such an official, especially during the time of a superior like V. S. Lanskoi, was indeed a blessing in that troubled period'.[1]

The circumstances of von Vock's acquaintance with Benckendorff during the six months that elapsed between the accession of Nicholas and the creation of the Third Department have been described already.[2] His past qualifications convinced Benckendorff of his worth and whether or not, as Vigel' suggests, the Third Department was created mainly on his initiative, the administrative details of its formation and development were undoubtedly entrusted to him as 'an old police wolf who had begun his service as far back as the days of Balashov and under the direct control of de Sanglen'.[3] Both his competence and his personality appealed to Benckendorff and the two men quickly became not only colleagues but also friends. The best evidence of this is provided by the series of letters which von Vock wrote to his chief in the late summer and autumn of 1826.[4] An editorial introduction to the publication of these letters in 1881 explains von Vock's position and resources at this period in the following terms:

Extensive acquaintances and connexions in the highest society of St Petersburg enabled him to see and know everything that was said and done among the aristocracy of the day, in the literary and other circles of the capital's population. To assist him in observing the mood of other classes of this population, various agents were recruited; some actually worked in the Higher Police, while others operated 'con amore' under the influence—or so they asserted—of the unsullied conception of disinterested service to the interests of their country... Among these agents one sometimes even came across persons of the society world; there were men of letters—and prolific ones at that—and one would sometimes meet ladies old and young who moved in the highest circles of society and who, in all probability, worked as 'observers' from no less noble motives...[5]

It is clear that von Vock thus enjoyed a unique position in St Petersburg in the early years of Nicholas' reign. His long connexion with Alexander's

---

[1] 'Vospominaniya O. A. Przhetslavskago (1818–31)', R. Star. (1874), vol. 11, pp. 680–1. (Józef Przecławski (1799–1879) served in the Ministry of Internal Affairs from 1824. Subsequently he worked from 1833 to 1840 in the Second Dept. of H.I.M. Own Chancellery on the compilation of Polish laws. He eventually became a Censor and a Council Member of the Ministry of Internal Affairs. As a pro-Russian Pole, he edited a journal—Tygodnik Peterburgski—which he began publishing in 1829 and which enjoyed official favour for thirty years, see RBS.)

There is one extant portrait of von Vock, reproduced from Al'bom Pushkinskoi vystavky (Moscow, 1899) by Lemke (opp. p. 32) and Shil'der, vol. 2, p. 285. It is an undated drawing of a severe-looking but distinguished man in civilian dress wearing decorations. He is thin-lipped, big-nosed and with a large wart—but on the left eyebrow. See plate 3.

[2] See chapter Two (in particular pp. 56–7).

[3] Trotsky, p. 125.   [4] See chapter Two, p. 63, note 6.

[5] R. Star. (1881), vol. 32, pp. 165–6.

Special Chancellery had not resulted in his becoming personally unpopular and there is evidence that during his career he won the respect of his superiors.[1] The remarkable absence of hostile witnesses indicates that this respect was generally shared by all who came into contact with him.

After the formation of the Third Department he became its first Director, subordinate only to Benckendorff. In this capacity he was responsible for the selection of the Department's staff, for their organization, and for collating the information they obtained. Von Vock was Benckendorff's Chief of Staff in all but name, but, despite the para-military character of the new 'Higher Police', the senior officials of the Department seem to have been little concerned with the direction of the Corps of Gendarmes. There was good reason for this. Von Vock, as far as is known, had had no military experience since the beginning of his police career in 1812,[2] and there is no published evidence to show that he had any control over the instructions issued to the Generals commanding Gendarme Districts—even though the reports submitted by their staff-officers must necessarily have engaged his attention. It is likely that orders to the Corps of Gendarmes were therefore issued by Benckendorff alone after consultation with von Vock, who dealt primarily with the recruitment and organization of secret agents and with the countless political, social and cultural 'cases' in which the Third Department took an interest.

None of the reports submitted by von Vock to his Chief were published during the Tsarist régime, but after the Revolution several of them were printed as a series of articles in *Red Archives* under the title of 'Count A. Kh. Benckendorff on Russia in 1827–30'. Their contributor, A. Sergeyev, stated that these reports were evidently the work of von Vock, 'Count Benckendorff's right hand', and were then re-submitted by Benckendorff to the Tsar. Sergeyev confirms von Vock's extensive acquaintance with St Peterburg society, adding that he relied on 'a magnificently organized network of agents...which provided him with a vast amount of information.'[3] The

---

[1] 'Together with Vock's reports, P. M. Doragan [von Fock's nephew who on 19 Apr. 1875 contributed them to *R. Star.*] has also presented us with several original letters from Count V. P. Kochubei covering the years 1823–6 and from A. Kh. Benckendorff [in 1828] to M. M. [*sic*] Vock. Both former and latter are insignificant as regards their contents, but it is obvious from their general tone that Vock enjoyed the favour...both of his former chief Kochubei and of Benckendorff, who was on the most friendly and confidential terms with him'. Ed. note, *R. Star.*, *loc. cit.* p. 560 (note).

[2] It is possible that von Vock had some military experience before this date. In the Notes to *Pushkin. Pis'ma*, there is a reference to him as 'a former soldier' ['byvshii voyennyi'] in a brief explanation of his rôle in the Third Department, *op. cit.* vol. 2, p. 426 (1826–30). I have found no similar references elsewhere and assume that any military service he experienced must have occurred only in his early years.

[3] A. Sergeyev, introd. to 'Graf A. Kh. Benkendorf o Rossii v 1827–30gg'., *op. cit.*, *Kr. Arkh.* (1929), no. 37, p. 139.

excellent style and presentation of the early Annual Reports of the Third Department (which are discussed in a later chapter)[1] indicate that von Vock rather than Benckendorff was primarily responsible for their preparation.

It seems probable, indeed, that many decisions affecting the policy of the Department were taken by von Vock without reference to Benckendorff. This view is held by Vigel' who wrote, in his appreciation of von Vock: 'Generally speaking, and to give him his due, he was not in the least mean and, I repeat, he sought no one's downfall. His illiterate superior would sign papers almost without ever reading them and thus blindly and unintentionally would sometimes ruin people; and for this reason von Vock found it extremely convenient to throw a large part of these false denunciations into the fire without bringing them to his notice, all the more so because their ever increasing number was not proportional to the number of those working in this office. Benckendorff only escaped his control when under some strong external influence...'[2] This evidence fully accords with what is known from other sources of Benckendorff's incompetence, and it is therefore fair to deduce that von Vock's intelligence and generosity exerted a favourable influence on the early development of the Third Department.

Von Vock's sympathies were not confined to cases of solely political importance. He was also ready to further the cause of literature by providing practical assistance in cases of need even to writers who were quite unknown and could not be suspected of serving the specific interests of the Third Department. In 1830, for example, he was approached by Bulgarin on behalf of the young Gogol', then materially distressed after his journey to Lübeck, and it was thanks to von Vock that Gogol' was granted a minor post in the Ministry of Internal Affairs.[3] His readiness to help in such cases may well have contributed to the good reputation he enjoyed in contemporary circles.

He was not, however, a man whose character and talents particularly commended themselves to the Tsar, and this may to some extent explain why the details of his career are so little known. His position in the Third Department was naturally overshadowed by that of Benckendorff, who was so close an intimate of Nicholas that the latter can rarely have needed to summon von Vock in his place. The Emperor's attitude to von Vock is recorded by Pushkin who wrote in his diary on the 4th of September 1831: 'The other day there died in St Petersburg von Vock, the head of the Third Department of the Emperor's Chancellery (the secret police) [sic], a kind, honest and resolute man. His death is a public calamity. The Emperor said: 'J'ai perdu Fock; je ne puis que le pleurer et me plaindre de n'avoir pu l'aimer.' The

[1] See chapter Six, pp. 199 ff.   [2] Vigel', vol. 2, p. 277.
[3] See V. V. Kallash, 'Biograficheskii Ocherk N. V. Gogolya', introd. to *Sochineniya i Pis'ma N. V. Gogolya*, 9 vols. (SPB, 1907), vol. I, p. 33.

question : who will replace him? is more important than the other question: what shall we do with Poland?'[1] It is possible that Nicholas felt little sympathy with a man whose life had been spent in a predominantly non-military sphere and with whom he therefore had little affinity. Even so he must have appreciated von Vock's ability as an organizer.

Pushkin, on the other hand, in view of his singular relationship to the Third Department, could appreciate von Vock's influence from a very different standpoint, and his evidence is therefore valuable.[2] He had good reason to be aware of the close watch kept on all questions concerned with literature in general and with writers in particular; and it is all the more to von Vock's credit that, despite the many restrictions placed on the poet's freedom of action, Pushkin could nevertheless pay him so unequivocal a tribute.[3] He clearly realized that the loss of so relatively liberal-minded an official was deplorable. In a letter to Prince Vyazemsky he wrote: 'You write of a journal. But what a hope! Who will permit us to have a journal? Von Vock has died, and the next thing we may learn is that his place will be taken by N. I. Grech. We'll be in a fine fix...'[4] Pushkin's view of von Vock thus fully confirms the favourable opinions expressed by Grech himself who claimed in his memoirs that 'the Emperor and Russia are indebted to him for many excellent thoughts and deeds (from 1825 until 1831, the year in which he died on the 27th of August, the day Warsaw was subdued); Benckendorff owed him the reputation he gained for intelligence and a knowledge of his profession'.[5]

It might be possible to accept this appreciation as final[6] were it not that Trotsky questions its accuracy, for all that he describes Grech as 'a man sufficiently well versed in the internal mutual relationships of the Third Department'. Trotsky suggests that von Vock's professional experience was

---

[1] A. S. Pushkin, *Poln. Sobr. Soch.*, 9 vols. (Acad. ed. 1937), vol. ix, p. 473. (Pushkin does not state the source from which he heard the Emperor's words.)

[2] 'For eleven of the best years of his life the great poet A. S. Pushkin was, it may be said, in daily contact with the Head of the Third Department. Benckendorff, Vock and Mordvinov—these were the men set on to his every word and step...', Lemke, p. 467. Lemke's book includes a section dealing with Puskhin's relations with the Third Department, pp. 467–526. See also B. L. Modzalyevsky, *Pushkin pod Tainym Nadzorom* (Petrograd, 1922).

[3] Pushkin's opinion cannot have been influenced by any special favours he received. On one occasion in 1830 he requested von Vock's support in opposing 'The Northern Bee', but von Vock answered evasively, claiming that he was not biased in favour of any one group of writers; see Lemke, pp. 504–5.

[4] *Pushkin. Pis'ma*, vol. iii (1831–3), p. 46, Letter dated 3 Sept. 1831.

[5] Grech, *Zapiski*, p. 711.

[6] It is not qualified by Lemke whose information on von Vock is, however, limited, including only a reference to the general testimony of his having been 'a man of undoubted education and good breeding' (see Shil'der, vol. 1, p. 464), a quotation from the Editor of *R. Star.* (see chapter Two, p. 63, note 6) and the mention of his death in Pushkin's diary (p. 27). He does not attempt any estimate of von Vock's rôle in the Third Department.

in fact ill-suited to the requirements of the new Higher Police. He points out that von Vock had come to the Third Department 'fully armed with the police methods of the Alexander period', but that a new period had now opened and Nicholas, in elevating the police to the rôle of the highest state organ in the country, was attempting to alter its character. As proof Trotsky quotes the handkerchief legend, Benckendorff's 1826 memorandum and von Vock's letters to his Chief in the late summer of that year showing that, in the interests of this altered policy, efforts were being made to recruit men of a different calibre into the new Department. He goes on: 'Vock quickly sensed the new fashion and began to adapt himself to it. . . it was in the Vock period that the process began of creating the noble and sensitive policeman in the blue uniform; but Vock was unable to achieve the creation of this type: too strong in him was the attachment to the old methods of work, to agents recruited from the dregs of society, bought by money and threats.'[1] Trotsky does not substantiate this opinion by references to Archives documents, and it is possible that he merely assumes von Vock to have been a convinced adherent of earlier police practices without acknowledging the fact that any efficient secret police organization must obtain information from all available sources in every walk of life. Neither von Vock nor any other official in his position could have entirely discarded the services of low-grade agents, however much it may have seemed preferable to employ under a new régime men of a better class and character. Also by all accounts von Vock was intelligent enough to have been fully capable of assessing the true value of all the information he received. It is thus permissible to doubt whether von Vock can fairly be blamed for having instituted or encouraged any of the more distasteful features of the Third Department's work which were characteristic of its later development after his death; it is just as likely, from the little that is known of him, that he helped to prevent their emergence at an earlier date.

Von Vock played a leading if most unobtrusive rôle in the control of Russia's internal security for a total of some nineteen years. It is difficult to state with any certainty to what extent he was a cunning, able and ambitious man who saw in the establishment of a reformed, powerful and centralized secret police an unrivalled opportunity for self-advancement and, on the other hand, to what extent his career was simply that of an intelligent, disinterested and high-minded patriot. Either interpretation of his character is possible. Nicholas' coldness to him, which not one of the few writers who have mentioned him has attempted to explain, may have arisen not so much from a dislike of the police methods of the preceding reign as from a suspicion that this capable and generally respected official, known to have fostered

[1] Trotsky, pp. 126, 128.

liberal views in the past, might be inclined to act in the future with something less than the desired severity. All that can definitely be established is that von Vock, as the chief civilian organizer of the Third Department during its initial phase, earned himself a consistent reputation for honesty and competence among his contemporaries.

A. N. Mordvinov

Director of Chancellery of the Third Department 1831–9

Von Vock's place was taken by Alexander Nikolayevich Mordvinov, of whom it is likely that even less would be known than of his predecessor had not his later career in the Russian civil service been relatively distinguished. Nothing is known, for example, of his early service—whether he was transferred to the Third Department from the old Special Chancellery in 1826 or was recruited into it after its creation.[1]

He was born in 1792 and is believed to have been working in the Third Department by 1829 in some unstated capacity.[2] It is possible that he attained no position of prominence before 1831, when an altercation between the Minister of Education Prince Lieven and his brother-in-law Benckendorff led to the formation of a special committee which decided that henceforth a representative of the Third Department should be consulted on all questions relating to the censorship of literary productions.[3] Mordvinov was chosen to be this representative. The responsible nature of such an appointment suggests that by this time he had become the senior official of the Department, and he succeeded to von Vock's post on the latter's death with the rank of Actual State Councillor.

Mordvinov retained this position for eight years, receiving the additional appointment of State-Secretary at the end of 1834. He remained Benckendorff's closest assistant, reporting to the Emperor in Benckendorff's absence and frequently replacing him in interviews with Pushkin, a figure of particular interest to the Third Department. It is likely that as Director of the Department in the 1830s he was chiefly concerned with the authorization of

[1] 'Information about him is very scarce', Lemke, p. 62; 'Unfortunately we possess no information on Mordvinov's rôle in the Third Department', Trotsky, p. 128. (It is noteworthy that no ukaz announcing his appointment is included in the *Poln. Sobr. Zak.*)

[2] Lemke states he has reason to believe that a note from von Vock to Benckendorff on the subject of Pushkin's unauthorized journey to the Caucasus in this year was written by Mordvinov from von Vock's draft. 'In Vock's lifetime Mordvinov was a very ordinary official of the Third Department and of course would not have dared to write to his Chief over Vock's head', Lemke, p. 493.

[3] See Lemke, pp. 56–62. (The other members of this committee were Count Nesselrode, Gen.-in-Waiting Vasil'chikov and Minister of Justice Dashkov.)

publications—in 1833 Nikitenko refers to him as a Censor.[1] Nothing is known of his administrative work in connexion with the Department's agents. As Benckendorff's deputy, however, he was responsible for the direction of all cases under investigation. In 1836 General Perfil'yev,[2] G.O.C. the 2nd Gendarme District (Moscow), was corresponding with Mordvinov directly on the subject of the famous Chaadayev letters; and in the capacity of Benckendorff's assistant he was appointed a member of the Investigatory Commission on Chaadayev.[3] There seems, however, to be no published account of his personal views on this or any other comparable occasion.

Mordvinov's character is equally unknown. After all his researches in the archives of the Third Department, Lemke could still claim no more than 'the probability of supposing that if he was less talented than his predecessor, he was at least no less respectable'.[4] Trotsky abstains from expressing any opinion and merely quotes a passing reference to him in Herzen's memoirs as 'belonging to the choicest breed of inquisitors'.[5] The nineteenth-century émigré Dolgorukov states that 'In the first years of the existence of this organization, the principal functionary, M.M....[sic], who, in view of the incompetence and stupidity [étourderie] of his superior, was in full control, was a man of rugged character, but intelligent and scrupulous. In 1837 he was removed by one of those bureaucratic intrigues so frequent in Russia...'[6] Dolgorukov is not, however, a reliable witness and it seems possible that he may have been confusing Mordvinov's character with that of his predecessor. Apparently Mordvinov left no marked impression on contemporary society.

The 'bureaucratic intrigue', mentioned by Dolgorukov in fact took place in 1839 and was not occasioned by any shift in internal departmental policy but simply by an unlucky oversight on Mordvinov's part. In March of that year the Third Department authorized the publication of an almanach entitled *A Hundred Russian Authors* and including a portrait of Marlinsky. The Tsar took exception to the fact that a facsimile of this writer's signature was reproduced beneath the portrait, showing that Marlinsky was the pseudonym of the Alexander Bestuzhev who had been implicated in the Decembrist conspiracy. Even though Bestuzhev had been killed in the Caucasus two years previously, Nicholas insisted on an investigation of this

---

[1] Nikitenko, *Zapiski*, vol. I, p. 226.
[2] Stepan Vasil'evich Perfil'yev (1796–1878), regular officer till retirement in 1823 with rank of Col. Joined Corps of Gendarmes in 1827; promoted Maj.-Gen. to command 2nd G.D. in 1836; promoted Lt.-Gen. in this appointment in 1847, see *RBS*; also chapter Six, p. 194, notes 1, 2.
[3] See Lemke, pp. 416–17, 425.
[4] Lemke, p. 62.
[5] Trotsky, p. 128; Gertsen, *ed. cit.* p. 109. (The reference occurs in a description of the author's first arrest in 1834. He never met Mordvinov, however, and does not mention him again.)
[6] Dolgoroukow, p. 295.

instance of lax censorship and, as a result, Mordvinov was summarily dismissed.[1] Although he was soon afterwards employed elsewhere in the public service, becoming a Senator seven years later, he was never subsequently reinstated in the Third Department.[2]

The removal of Mordvinov marks the end of the first phase in the administration of the Higher Police—a phase distinguished by the decline of the influence exerted on its development by civilian officials.

This process, though gradual, was natural enough. Nicholas preferred dealing with soldiers and Benckendorff's own experience had been almost exclusively confined to military rather than civil affairs. During the first few years of the Third Department's activities Mordvinov, as von Vock's assistant, was only a subordinate official and is not known to have possessed the long experience of his superior. Furthermore, the organization of the Corps of Gendarmes—the primary executive arm of the Higher Police—was greatly expanded during the years when Mordvinov held office, until by 1836 it had become the strongest weapon of internal security in the country. Consequently the influence of its Chief of Staff, Major-General Dubbelt, increasingly tended to outweigh that of his civilian counterpart.[3] And there is no evidence that Mordvinov enjoyed the personal friendship that Benckendorff had extended to von Vock.[4]

As a result of this shift of emphasis within the headquarters of the Third Department Mordvinov gradually lost ground. 'A number of cases are known which were dealt with not by the actual Director of Chancellery but by the cunning Major-General. People knew this and sometimes addressed themselves directly to the Chief of Staff in cases which were, in fact, no concern of his.'[5] It is therefore not surprising that a man already so influential should have been the obvious choice as successor to Mordvinov when the latter was sacrificed as scapegoat for a fancied error of judgement. Only a few days after Mordvinov's dismissal Dubbelt was appointed Director of the Third Department in his place, a position he was to combine with his previous duties as Gendarme Chief of Staff.

[1] See Ye. I. Dubel't, 'Leontii Vasil'evich Dubel't. Biograficheskii ocherk i yego pis'ma', *R. Star.* (1888), vol. 60, p. 492, Nov.; Nikitenko, pp. 293–4; Lemke, pp. 119–20.

[2] After his dismissal on 18 Mar. 1839 Mordvinov remained in temporary retirement. He soon re-entered service, however, and was made Civil Governor of Vyatka, a post he held from 1840 to 1842. He then became Director of the Department of Taxation and Levies in the Ministry of Finance, and was appointed a Senator in Oct. 1846. He died in 1869. (The few known facts of his career recorded in this Chapter are taken from *Pushkin. Pis'ma*, p. 595 and *Ist. Prav. Sen.* vol. 5, p. 138.)

[3] 'Already during his tenure of office Mordvinov began to retire into the background in comparison with Dubbelt, whom he had himself recommended...', Trotsky, p. 128.

[4] This may have been partly due to the difference in age between them; von Vock had been six years older than Benckendorff whereas Mordvinov was nine years younger.

[5] Lemke, p. 124. (An actual instance of this in 1837 is quoted, *ibid.*)

The ukaz[1] announcing this new appointment on 28 March 1839 did more than raise Dubbelt to the highest administrative office in the Third Department. By combining the leading military and civilian posts and by conferring the functions of both on one man, it doubled the significance of the appointment. For this, if for no other reason, the third and last of Benckendorff's chief assistants exerted a far greater influence on the development of the Higher Police than either of his predecessors.

[1] See chapter Three, p. 98, note 2.

5

The Leading Personalities of the Higher Police: after the reorganization of 1839

Dubbelt is an original character, he is probably cleverer than the Third and indeed than all the three Departments of His Majesty's Own Chancellery.   from Herzen's memoirs[1]

If not to everybody's taste—For all of us it is the same—Yet kindness, honesty, nobility, All are united in his name.   Zhukovsky on Dubbelt in 1842[2]

L. V. Dubbelt

Director of the Third Department and Chief of Staff of the Corps of Gendarmes 1839–1856

Leontii Vasil'evich Dubbelt[3] served a total of twenty-six years in the Third Department. He was Chief Assistant to Benckendorff until the latter's death in 1844 and to Benckendorff's successor Orlov until both retired in 1856. But although it would thus appear that he held a subordinate position in the Higher Police, the part he played in its development was undoubtedly greater than either of theirs. De Grunwald says of him:

Ni Benckendorff, ni Orlov ne sont, en réalité, les vrais inspirateurs de la police impériale. Une silhouette inquiétante se dessine derrière ces courtisans: celle du général Dubbelt, chef d'état-major au corps des gendarmes, policier de vocation, espèce de Fouché russe...C'est lui le vrai détenteur du pouvoir occulte; c'est lui qui accumule les dossiers accusateurs, c'est lui qui recouvre tout l'Empire d'une toile invisible d'espionnage et de délation pour étouffer la moindre opposition, la moindre manifestation de la pensée libre; c'est lui enfin qui donne au système gouvernemental de Nicolas son empreinte définitive et transforme la Russie en une vaste caserne où règnent la discipline et l'ennui.[4]

This is a just assessment of Dubbelt's rôle in the police régime of Nicholas' Russia and his career and character therefore deserve detailed study.[5]

---

[1] Gertsen, *ed. cit.* pp. 237–8.
[2] See Ye. I. Dubel't, 'Leontii Vasil'evich Dubel't. Biograficheskii ocherk i yego pis'ma', *R. Star.* (1888), vol. 60, p. 497. (The writer was one of L.V.D.'s descendants, see Editorial Note, *ibid.*)
[3] His surname in Russian is spelt Dubel't. In Western languages it is transliterated as Dubbelt, Dubelt, Doubelt and even Douvelt. I have adhered to the first of these spellings as being that most commonly used by historians, although D. himself, when not writing in Russian, signed his name 'L. Doubelt', see Public Record Office, Series F.O. 181, vol. 157 (Notes from Russian Ministers), Letter dated 22 Oct./3 Nov. 1840.   [4] De Grunwald, *La Vie de Nicolas*, p. 189.
[5] Except where otherwise stated, the details of Dubbelt's career are taken from Ye. I. Dubel't's introduction to his letters, *loc. cit.* pp. 491–7; and also from an article on him by V. Zherve

Dubbelt was nine years younger than Benckendorff and, like him, was not of pure Russian origin. He was born in 1792 of a Russian father[1] and Spanish mother. The former, Vasilii Ivanovich Dubbelt, was a dvoryanin of whose life and career nothing seems to be known save that during a visit to Spain he abducted a princess of the grandee family of Medinaceli and fled with her to Italy, where they married. They subsequently travelled to Russia, where two sons were born to them, of whom Leontii was the elder. According to various sources his mother was a highly educated and 'extremely good-natured' lady, and the young Dubbelt received all his early upbringing at her hands until in 1801 he was placed in the Gornyi Korpus, where he remained for nearly six years.

His military career began in 1807 when war with France necessitated an increase in the recruitment of young officers, and Dubbelt was gazetted ensign to the Pskovsky Infantry Regiment at the early age of fifteen. He saw active service the same year and again throughout the War for the Father-land. He fought in the battle of Borodino where he was wounded in the leg, and accompanied the Russian army abroad as A.D.C. to two Corps Com-manders, Generals Dokhturov and Rayevsky. By 1815 he had reached the rank of Major and been awarded a number of decorations including the Prussian order 'For Merit'. The same year he was appointed Duty Staff-Officer in the 3rd (afterwards 4th) Infantry Corps and in 1817 promoted Lieutenant-Colonel for distinguished service in this post. The following year, when this unit was stationed in Kiev and still on the staff of General Rayevsky, he married the niece of N. S. Mordvinov, Anna Nikolayevna Perovskaya; and in 1819 was transferred in the same capacity to the Moskovsky Infantry Regiment. His first independent command was that of the Starooskolsky Infantry Regiment to which he was appointed in 1822.

It is interesting that at this period, when vague political theorizing was much in vogue among army officers, Dubbelt may have been attracted by this trend in much the same way as Benckendorff had flirted with Masonry a few years earlier. N. I. Grech wrote in his memoirs: 'It is worthy of note that one of the first loud-mouthed liberals in the Southern Army was Leontii

[Gervais], *RBS*. (The former gives the date of his birth as 1793, but this is not confirmed elsewhere.)

[1] No explanation is given by the above or other sources of his non-Russian surname. According to Professor Unbegaun, 'Dubbelt' is undoubtedly a German name, though whether of Baltic or other origin is less certain. The biographical sketch by Ye. I. Dubel't states that Dubbelt's father was descended 'from the Russian nobility' ('iz russkikh dvoryan'), p. 491, but Professor Unbegaun comments that this may well mean only that his name was recorded in one of the books of the Russian nobility, the so-called *Dvoryanskaya Kniga*, a privilege which conferred rank without requiring its holder to be Russian-born. It is therefore likely that Dubbelt's family on his father's side was not Russian, but only russified; and that his paternal ancestors were of Germanic blood.

Vasil'evich Dubbelt, later to become famous as the Chief of Staff of Gendarmes. When those guilty of complicity in the revolt were arrested, everyone asked—"Why have they not detained Dubbelt?"'[1] It seems nevertheless unlikely that Dubbelt was genuinely sympathetic towards the Decembrist cause, and as he was promoted full Colonel in 1826 it may reasonably be assumed that his loyalty was never in question.

His career in the regular army lasted only until 1828, however, when he had a disagreement with his Divisional Commander, General Zheltukhin. The details of this disagreement are unknown, but as a result Dubbelt left the service 'for domestic reasons', although he was permitted to retain his uniform and was granted a pension.

After this setback Dubbelt remained without occupation for a whole year, but he found a life of inactivity intolerable and financially embarrassing. It is clear from a letter to his wife[2] from St Petersburg dated 8 January 1830 that to save expenses he was forced to deny himself minor luxuries while awaiting the answer to his application for further employment in government service; and that the period of waiting cost him much anguish.[3] His letters also make it clear that he was acquainted with A. N. Mordvinov, then only a junior official of the Third Department, and that his intention was to join the Higher Police with the double aim of restoring his fortunes and embarking, at the age of thirty-eight, on a new and promising career.

While awaiting the decision of higher authority, he received a letter from his wife the contents of which distressed him and he evidently considered it necessary to justify his course of action:

'Do not be a gendarme', you say! But do you understand, does Alexander Nikolayevich [Mordvinov] understand the essence of the matter? If I, on entering the Corps of Gendarmes, become an informer and a tell-tale, then my good name will of course be stained. But if, on the contrary, without getting involved with matters concerning the internal police, I defend the poor, protect the unfortunate; if, acting openly, I am in a position to secure fair treatment for the oppressed, if I can see to it that law-suits be decided in the courts in accordance with rectitude and justice—what will you call me then? What will Alexander Nikolayevich call me?

[1] Grech, *Zapiski*, p. 459. This evidence is valuable because Grech was always well disposed towards Dubbelt; and later writers have not denied it.

[2] The only private letters of Dubbelt that have been published are those contributed to *R. Star.*, *loc. cit.* pp. 498–514, by Ye. I. Dubel't. They consist of 14 letters written to his wife between 1830 and 1846. Their contents are insignificant except in so far as they throw some light on Dubbelt's state of mind on applying for a post in the Corps of Gendarmes and on his general personality.

[3] 'In order to economize, I have decided not to drink tea'...'I pray God every day that my case should be decided quickly. The processes through which it has to pass are so intricate and slow that they remove all hope of its quick solution', *ibid.* pp. 499, 499–500. (It is evident from the contents of these letters that the Minister of War, Count Chernyshov, had to give his consent before any serving or retired officer could be transferred to the Corps of Gendarmes.)

—Shall I not then be worthy of respect, will not my position be a most excellent, a most noble one? So, my friend, this is the aim with which I shall enter the Corps of Gendarmes; nothing shall deflect me from this aim and, in agreeing to enter it, I have requested L'vov to inform Benckendorff that he should not submit any application on my behalf if I am to be made responsible for fulfilling duties of a dishonourable character and that I would not agree to join his Corps if I am asked to perform tasks which a kindly and honest man would shrink from even considering. . . You may rest assured that not for anything in the world will I blot my good name. However, to set your mind even more at rest, I will look for another post and, if I find it, I will put a stop to Benckendorff's application, for it will be some time before it reaches the Emperor. . . [1]

It is clear from this letter that Dubbelt originally envisaged the possibility of being appointed Gendarme Staff-Officer at Tver', partly because his family estate of Ryskino was situated in that district and also because in that post he could count on receiving additional allowances and would enjoy a wide degree of independence. Besides, there was no vacancy on Benckendorff's headquarters at the time of his application, 'the post of Duty Staff-Officer being then occupied by Colonel Mukhanov'. Dubbelt also disclaimed any desire to be attached to Benckendorff 'on special duties' on the grounds that 'these duties were definitely not of a savoury nature', but as events turned out the Duty Staff-Officer, Sukharyov,[2] fell ill before Dubbelt's departure to Tver' and Benckendorff thereupon proposed that he should remain in the capital as Sukharyov's temporary replacement. Dubbelt was not slow to accept this offer and, whatever misgivings he may have felt before entering gendarme service, they were quickly forgotten and he was confirmed in this appointment in 1831[3] in his old rank of full Colonel.

Although in this capacity he occupied an important position as chief assistant to Benckendorff, it was apparently some time before he succeeded in fully restoring his depleted finances. Colonel Stogov's memoirs, in an

---

[1] *Ibid.* pp. 501, 502. No other letter on this subject is included in this series.

[2] As there was only one Duty Staff-Officer of the Corps of Gendarmes at a time, it is possible that Dubbelt mistakenly wrote 'Mukhanov' for 'Sukharyov'. (The latter name and appointment are quoted in Ye. I. Dubel't's article, *loc. cit.*)

There is no reference to L'vov, Mukhanov or Sukharyov in any of the published 'Reports on the Activities of the Corps of Gendarmes' from 1828 to 1832, although a Colonel L'vov is mentioned in an ukaz dated 31 Mar. 1839 ordering his appointment as officer responsible for His Majesty's own escort in conjunction with the duties of Secretary to Benckendorff, see *Poln. Sobr. Zak.* vol. 14, pp. 336–7, Ukaz no. 12189. It is possible that he is the L'vov who in 1843, as Major-General, became G.O.C. the 7th Gendarme District, see chapter Six, p. 205, note 4.

[3] The 'Report on the Activities of the Corps of Gendarmes for 1830' states that 'Colonel Dubbelt, who is now performing the functions of the Duty Staff-Officer of the Corps, has been attached to Mr Senator Count Gur'ev, who has conducted an investigation into the case of the former Governor-General, Minitsky' (*Kr. Arch.* (1930), no. 38, p. 147). (In later reports Dubbelt is not singled out for mention, but each Report is countersigned by him as having been submitted to the Emperor.)

account of their author's acquaintance with Dubbelt at the end of 1833, contain the following passage: 'Dubbelt and I soon became friends; he was still a colonel and chief of staff, was often short of money and used to borrow 300 to 400 roubles from me.'[1] The absence of other references to Dubbelt's pecuniary difficulties suggests, however, that they were only temporary.

Dubbelt owed his position and quick promotion to the fact that Benckendorff recognized in him a loyal and efficient deputy whose exclusively military background doubtless served as an additional recommendation. Dubbelt's published letters contain few references to his colleagues[2] at Benckendorff's headquarters and understandably do not discuss the nature of his duties, but it is permissible to assume that apart from the everyday conduct of official inquiries and reports he was mainly concerned with questions relating to the administration and expansion of the Corps of Gendarmes between 1832 and 1837. As the Corps was staffed by regular officers and men, this task could only be entrusted to a soldier. The steady growth of the Corps in the 1830s may be considered the main reason why Dubbelt and not Mordvinov became Benckendorff's closest collaborator.

By 1834 Dubbelt had so far gained the confidence of his Chief that he could freely approach him on questions not directly concerned with official business. Even so high a courtier as N. S. Mordvinov (his wife's uncle) received the status of Count largely as the result of Dubbelt's requests to his superior.[3] In 1835 he was appointed Chief of Staff of the Corps of Gendarmes (a new official post) and promoted 'for distinguished service' to the rank of Major-General. The following year saw the publication of the revised regulations for the Corps[4]—regulations which established its organization for the remainder of the reign and for which Dubbelt was primarily responsible. In all matters relating to the preservation of internal security Dubbelt was second only to Benckendorff, and in cases of an operational as opposed to a consultative character his importance outweighed that of Mordvinov. (After Pushkin's death, for instance, it was Dubbelt who was entrusted with the task of removing the poet's body from the capital and preventing any public disorder. Dubbelt attended on this occasion with twenty other gendarme officers and later personally examined all Pushkin's papers.[5])

---

[1] 'Zapiski E. I. Stogova', p. 308. (Stogov's memory was at fault in describing Dubbelt as Chief of Staff at this moment as this title was only officially granted him two years later.)

[2] For example, he does not once mention von Vock; and his letters throw no light at all on the relationship of civilian to military officials inside the Third Department. (It is clear from one reference, however, that he was on good terms with Mordvinov and regularly dined with him, see letter dated 31 Aug. 1838, *R. Star.*, *loc. cit.* p. 510.)

[3] See letter dated 30 Jun. 1834, *R. Star.*, *loc. cit.* pp. 505–6.   [4] See chapter Three, p. 90.

[5] See Lemke, *Nikolayevskie Zhandarmy*, p. 524. (The figure twenty is almost certainly an exaggeration.) During his lifetime Pushkin corresponded only with Benckendorff, von Vock and Mordvinov; and had no direct dealings with Dubbelt. (Hence the absence of references to him

By 1837 his influence had so greatly increased that the sub-editor of the 'Journal of the Ministry of Public Education', A. A. Krayevsky, who wished to obtain permission to publish an historical article by Zhukovsky, took the unusual step of submitting it not to the censorship authorities nor even directly to the Third Department, but to Dubbelt through his assistant M. M. Popov.[1] Dubbelt evidently regarded this move as entirely proper. He approved the text in general but raised a number of minor objections,[2] which were prudently heeded by Zhukovsky. (The article in question did not appear until 1849.) It is noteworthy that the account of Krayevsky's approach to Dubbelt contains no mention whatever of Benckendorff, and it is therefore fair to deduce that in the opinion of certain well-informed contemporaries Dubbelt was already the most influential official of the Third Department and in full possession of Benckendorff's confidence. Obviously this confidence was also shared by the Tsar and in 1838 Dubbelt was made a member of the Imperial Suite.[3]

His biggest promotion, however, occurred in 1839, when the sudden dismissal of Mordvinov resulted in his appointment as Director of the Third Department whilst remaining Chief of Staff of the Corps of Gendarmes.[4] This decision to combine the two senior posts in the administration of the Higher Police and to entrust them to one man represented a major development in its organization; and in practice it placed Dubbelt in a position of immense authority. He also inherited other functions of a non-military

in Pushkin's writings.) Curiously enough, after his death 'Fate brought Pushkin's descendants into closer contact with Nicholas' gendarmes: the daughter of the great poet Natal'ya Aleksandrovna (by her second marriage the Countess Merenberg) married Dubbelt's son.' *Ibid.* p. 526.

[1] I. A. Bychkov, 'Popytka napechatat' "Cherty Istorii Gosudarstva Rossiiskago" V. A. Zhukovskago v 1837 godu', *R. Star.* (1903), vol. 116, pp. 595–600.

[2] Dubbelt objected to some of Zhukovsky's generalizations on historical development, summing up his own views in the following typical words—'In my opinion the Tsar is a father, his subjects are his children, and children should never sit in judgement on their parents—otherwise we shall have a France here, a vile ["poganaya"] France', *loc. cit.* p. 596.

[3] It is possible that this appointment may have owed something to a tactfully conducted interview which Dubbelt had with the Grand Duke Mikhail Pavlovich at Oranienbaum. The latter had seen a letter written by Dubbelt to Benckendorff on the subject of the Grand Duke's treatment of his inferiors and was angry with its writer. Dubbelt, however, succeeded in pacifying him and was subsequently invited to dine at the palace. According to Dubbelt's account the evening was a success. See letter dated 31 Aug. 1838, *R. Star., loc. cit.* pp. 507–8.

[4] The text of this ukaz is given in chapter Three, p. 98. The new title of 'Director' ('Upravlyayushchii') of the Third Department replaced that of 'Director of Chancellery of the Third Department', as held by von Vock and Mordvinov. After 1839 the Head of the Third Department (first Benckendorff and then Orlov) was known as the 'Chief Director' ('Glavno-Upravlyayushchii'), see Lemke, p. 126.

Lemke records that as this internal reorganization 'was completed on the day of the Annunciation [25 Mar.], whereby Nicholas desired to offset its importance, wits were quick to proclaim that these "good tidings" in fact announced the forthcoming birth of a new torture-chamber', *ibid.*

character such as membership of the Central Directorate for Censorship and of the Secret Committee on Dissenters. But chiefly he owed his redoubtable position to the fact that he was far more intelligent and energetic than his Chief. As Benckendorff grew older, and particularly after his severe illness of 1837, he became increasingly apathetic and willingly left the conduct of routine business in the hands of his efficient deputy.[1]

Dubbelt, however, was a loyal deputy. He repaid Benckendorff for his patronage by according him unlimited devotion and their relations were always close and friendly. Benckendorff for his part fully appreciated the qualities of his protégé. On one occasion, in the early years of his Higher Police career, Dubbelt threatened to resign because he believed that the Tsar did not wholly trust him; whereupon Benckendorff informed Nicholas of Dubbelt's intention and 'holding two papers in his hand, placed one of them on the table with the words—"Then will Your Majesty be pleased to sign the order for his resignation?" When the Emperor inquired what were the contents of the other paper, the Count replied: "It is my resignation, should you sign the first one." '[2] As may be seen from his letters, Dubbelt's affection for Benckendorff lasted until the latter's death. In 1844 Dubbelt wrote to his wife: 'You know, my dearest, how I love my Count and God is my witness that for each year of his life I would give away one of my own'; and he described Benckendorff's death with genuine emotion: 'I have wept so much that now my head aches terribly; I am just off to Demidovsky Dom to hold a memorial service for him.'[3]

On his death-bed Benckendorff bequeathed to the Emperor all his colleagues, thanked all his subordinates for their labours and Dubbelt in particular for his friendship. 'Thus died [wrote Dubbelt] one of the kindest men, one of the most faithful of the Emperor's servants—give his soul peace, O Lord! Count Orlov, fortunately for Russia, has consented to take his place. What will happen to me I do not yet know. The Count could not be more gracious to me, but as yet I have been unable to penetrate his innermost thoughts, and I have not wished to do so—I have wept and am still weeping now.'[4]

Possibly Dubbelt's apprehensions with regard to his immediate future were not without foundation. A foreign diplomat recorded in his memoirs that 'The position of General Dubbelt, who was disliked by all for reasons closely connected with his official duties, was considered to be extremely

---

[1] 'Count Benckendorff had undermined his health and from 1837 took an apathetic interest in his duties, which were left in the hands of L. V. Dubbelt...', P. Bartyenev, Editorial Note to article 'Instruktsiya Grafa Benkendorfa chinovniku 3-go Otdeleniya', R. Arkh. (1889), 7, p. 398. [2] Ye. I. Dubel't, loc. cit. p. 493.
[3] Letters dated 19 May, 15 Sept. 1844, R. Star., loc. cit. pp. 511, 513.
[4] Letter dated 17 Sept. 1844, ibid. p. 514.

shaky at the time of A. F. Orlov's nomination; it was even thought that he would not long retain his post.'[1] It soon became obvious, however, that Benckendorff's death had no effect on either the policy or the staff of the Third Department.[2] Dubbelt's own position was in fact strengthened by Orlov's distaste for police work and he continued to play the leading rôle in all matters relating to the country's internal security for the remainder of Nicholas' reign. During this period his influence on the national administration tended to become even more important as the policy of the government grew more and more reactionary; and the events of the year 1848 and the 'Petrashevsky Affair' in Russia had the result of making Dubbelt's services appear even more indispensable. He sat on every Investigatory Commission and was a member of the Censorship Committee of 2 April 1848 presided over by Prince Menshikov. There can be no doubt that the Emperor regarded him as the man chiefly responsible for carrying out the many repressive measures which darkened the final decade of his reign, and it was during his tenure of office that the Third Department acquired its lasting reputation as an instrument of oppression.

Dubbelt's services came to an end in 1856 when Orlov's long absence in Paris at the conclusion of the Crimean War necessitated his replacement. The new Tsar Alexander II proposed that Dubbelt should be nominated in his stead, but the latter declined on the grounds that so important a post should be occupied by a high official with wealth and a title. The new Emperor called him Don Quixote and appointed Prince V. A. Dolgorukov as Orlov's successor. In reward for his past services Dubbelt, who had already been promoted from the rank of Lieutenant-General to that of General of Cavalry, retired with the orders of St Vladimir 1st Class and Alexander Nevsky with diamonds. He was permitted to retain his Corps of Gendarmes uniform and was granted the additional privilege of attending on the Emperor once a week in a consultative capacity. Alexander, like his father, trusted him implicitly. Dubbelt aged quickly in his retirement, however, and died in 1862.

Dubbelt's character is to this day something of an enigma and has been the subject of controversy. Compared with that of his two superiors it was

---

'Imperator Nikolai I i ego spodvizhniki. (Vospominaniya grafa Ottona de Bre, 1849–52)', *R. Star.* (1902), vol. 109, p. 128. These memoirs were first published under the title of *Denkwürdigkeiten des Grafen Otto von Bray-Steinburg* (Leipzig, 1901).

   (Otto Camillus Hugo Gabriel, Graf Bray-Steinburg (1807–99), the son of a French émigré who was the Bavarian envoy to St Petersburg from 1808 to 1822, had lifelong connexions with Russia and was himself Bavarian Minister there between 1843 and 1859. His memoirs contain descriptions of all the leading Russian Ministers of this period, *loc. cit.* pp. 115–39. The *Neue Deutsche Biographie* (Berlin, 1953) describes him as 'sober and reserved, not a man of outstanding character but a solid and high-principled official', vol. 2, p. 564.)

[2] 'The system introduced in Benckendorff's day was conserved in every respect and reports were merely submitted by a new Chief in place of the one who had died', Trotsky, p. 120.

undoubtedly more complex, and he was indisputably more intelligent than either. He resembled Benckendorff in his unquestioning devotion to the principles of autocracy and the person of the Autocrat, in his insistence on preserving the forms of outward courtesy in all circumstances and also in the sentimentalism which many of his critics called hypocrisy. Unlike Benckendorff, however, he was genuinely feared and widely distrusted. He was suspected of using his position to obtain wealth as well as power, and his venomous and unconcealed dislike of writers and thinkers earned him many enemies. Yet Zhukovsky's epigram on him did contain some elements of truth.

Probably the best known description of Dubbelt is that given by Herzen, who was summoned into his presence in December 1840: 'His gaunt face, shadowed by long pale whiskers, a tired gaze, and especially the furrows in his cheeks and on his forehead were clear evidence that many passions had striven in that breast before the sky-blue uniform had mastered, or at least concealed, all that it contained. His features had in them something of the wolf and even of the fox, that is, they expressed the shrewd intelligence of wild beasts, and at the same time evasiveness and arrogance. He was always deferential.'[1] Dubbelt's punctilious behaviour to Herzen on this occasion was no doubt typical of his normal conduct in such cases. Herzen was amazed at his opening sentence—'Count Alexander Khristoforovich has provided me with an opportunity of making your acquaintance'—as though their meeting were a purely social one; and when Herzen ventured to protest that his household was distressed by the intrusion of Dubbelt's gendarmes, the latter exclaimed 'Oh, my goodness, how unpleasant! How clumsy they all are!'[2] But such politeness scarcely reassured its recipient who, having incurred the Tsar's displeasure, had been summoned to the Third Department only to be informed of his forthcoming exile.

Herzen's evidence, although generally accepted,[3] might be considered unduly biased were it not that it bears considerable resemblance to that given by Karatygin, one of Dubbelt's avowed sympathizers, who said of him: 'He was in many respects a remarkable personality: an excellently educated man, perspicacious, intelligent and not in the least malignant, but, because of the post he occupied and partly because of his appearance, he was an object of terror for the majority of the inhabitants of St Petersburg. His gaunt face with its long grey whiskers, the penetrating gaze of his large grey eyes had something wolfish about them. An ironic smile and a certain mordant sarcasm which he affected when interrogating suspects were frightening; but

[1] Gertsen, *ed. cit.* p. 238.   [2] *Ibid.* pp. 238, 239.
[3] Trotsky, for example, records his opinion that Herzen's analysis of Dubbelt was an accurate one, p. 130.

to writers, actors, artists and peaceable citizens in general Leontii Vasil'evich was affable, kindly and obliging.'[1] Karatygin admits that Dubbelt frequently interfered in questions concerning theatrical productions, but maintains that no other course was open to him and that he was as great a friend of the theatre as circumstances permitted. As regards his behaviour to those who for some reason had incurred official displeasure, Karatygin records various instances of Dubbelt's methods. He claims that, where possible, suspects were treated kindly and even luxuriously during their detention inside the Third Department and that it was Dubbelt's practice to issue ironic warnings rather than resort to more severe methods of punishment. If investigations failed to produce satisfactory incriminating proof of a detainee's guilt, he was admonished and released. In one such case Karatygin commented: 'Burdin [a suspected member of the "Petrashevsky Affair"] was in fact innocent; but if Dubbelt, as is traditionally believed, had been a man of the type of A. I. Ushakov or Sheshkovsky,[2] he would not of course have spared even a man whose guilt was unproved. In many cases his position allowed of no superfluous and inappropriate kindness, since it obliged him to be stern, sometimes even cruel; but when it was possible for him to show feelings of humanity and sympathy, he always showed them...'[3] (This is to some extent confirmed by an entry in Nikitenko's diary referring to the exile of Nadyezhdin in 1836 after the publication of Chaadayev's 'Letters': 'He [Nadyezhdin] speaks gratefully of Benckendorff and especially of Dubbelt.'[4])

An occasional display of clemency, however, can hardly have affected Dubbelt's formidable reputation among his contemporaries, and Karatygin's evidence is less valuable than that of a man who had good reason to regret falling into the hands of so redoubtable a figure. I. V. Selivanov, a dvoryanin arrested in 1849 shortly after his return from a visit to Paris on a charge of having expressed liberal views on the subject of the obligations of landowners to their peasants, included in his memoirs a detailed account of his experiences in the Third Department.[5] His treatment was remarkable for its excellence. His cell was clean and comfortable, he was supplied with good food and drink from a neighbouring inn and Dubbelt paid him a personal visit to inquire whether he was warm enough, whether he smoked tobacco or cigars and whether he had any special habits.[6] But this solicitude for his well-being

[1] Karatygin, *Ist. Vyestnik*, *loc. cit.* p. 174.
[2] Both these men were Heads of the Secret Chancellery during the second half of the eighteenth century, see chapter One, pp. 15, 16.
[3] Karatygin, *loc. cit.* p. 179.   [4] Nikitenko, vol. 1, p. 280.
[5] I. V. Selivanov, 'Zapiski Dvoryanina-Pomyeshchika', *R. Star.* (1880), vol. 28, pp. 289–316.
[6] *Ibid.* pp. 306, 307. Such treatment was evidently the customary practice. A suspected 'Petrashevets' arrested in 1849 at the age of 25 wrote in his memoirs: 'In the Third Department we were regaled with dinner, tea and cigars, but none of us had any desire to partake of anything.' D. D. Akhsharumov, *Iz Moikh Vospominanii (1849–1851)* (SPB, 1905), p. 7.

can have been small recompense for the subsequent unpleasantness of his interrogation. Selivanov admitted under Dubbelt's cross-examination that in his view the position of the landowner in Russia was unenviable because his moral responsibilities were so great. 'This nonsense is instilled into you by scoundrels like Bakunin, Herzen and others', was Dubbelt's reply. When Selivanov objected to the inclusion of Herzen in this accusation 'My Dubbelt flared up like powder, his lips trembled, even froth showed on them.—"Herzen!" he shouted furiously.—"I have 3,000 desyatins of forest at my disposal and I know of no tree vile enough to hang him on! Enough, go! To-morrow you will be given written questions."'[1] Realizing the uselessness of resistance,[2] Selivanov eventually decided to sign a false statement of his guilt prepared with the help of Dubbelt's sympathetic assistant Popov, although he believed himself innocent of any offence and was clearly the victim of a denunciation. No specific accusation was preferred against him; he was merely informed that, like Herzen some years earlier, he was to be exiled for a limited period to Vyatka, and not until he reached his destination did he discover that he had been sentenced 'for wrongful thinking expressed in literary writings and private correspondence'.[3] It was typical of Dubbelt's methods that outwardly he should have treated Selivanov with unfailing courtesy and kindness—he instantly granted a request that the latter should be allowed to visit his father on his way to exile—while at the same time deciding his fate in an entirely arbitrary manner.

Selivanov's explanation of his own conduct is particularly interesting for the light it throws on Dubbelt. 'Perhaps many people will say: why did he admit to something to which his story contains no reference?—and will reproach me for lack of character. Let these gentlemen put themselves in my position and remember what fear the Third Department then inspired; let them remember. . .that this Popov advised me not to anger Leontii Vasil'evich on whom my fate completely depended; let them remember the rumours then current to the effect that Dubbelt invented conspiracies to frighten the government and thus prove his own indispensability. It is clear from the above account that Dubbelt had to find somebody guilty so as not to have to confess to his own lack of perception. . .by concocting a case which proved to be non-existent. . .'[4]

[1] I. V. Selivanov, *op. cit.* pp. 308–9.

[2] In his written answers Selivanov accused minor officials of covering their own arbitrary actions by referring to orders received from higher authority and thus stirring up the people against the government. '"Please, do not argue", the little man [Popov] told me quietly. "But write rather that you repent and regret having written this." "How can I. . .when I've written the opposite?" "Oh Heavens", he interrupted, "obey me. Leontii Vasil'evich will be angry if you do not write what I tell you." Seeing the all-powerfulness of Dubbelt, I reflected that it was dangerous to argue with such a man.' *Ibid.* p. 311.

[3] *Ibid.* p. 479.   [4] *Ibid.* p. 315.

If Selivanov's story of his encounter with the Third Department is accurate, it disproves Karatygin's statement that Dubbelt exonerated suspects in cases where incriminating evidence—judged by Western and not Russian standards—could not be produced.

Yet such cases did occur. A Lieutenant-Colonel N. N. Zhedyonov published in 1890 an account of his arrest as a young officer in the capital at the end of 1848 which in many respects fully substantiates the details given by Selivanov. Zhedyonov, who was equally unconscious of having committed any offence, was treated with the same courtesy and kindness.[1] It transpired, however, that his arrest was due to a particularly absurd denunciation and Dubbelt's reaction on this occasion was of a different order. Convinced that Zhedyonov did not know even the names of his so-called fellow conspirators, Dubbelt confronted him with his accuser and dealt the latter a vigorous slap as reward for his slander.[2] Zhedyonov was released and subsequently received compensation for his wrongful arrest by being taken by Dubbelt to an audience with the Tsar, who commended him for his loyalty and made a handsome present of money to his mother.

It is probable, however, that Dubbelt was by nature more inclined to listen to denunciations when they were directed against writers or members of the landed gentry who had lived abroad—especially if he thought he could detect in their ideas the hated influence of foreign liberalism. After the revolutions of 1830 and 1848 he had a particular loathing of France, and this may have contributed to his decision to exile Selivanov quite as much as any desire to concoct conspiracies. Conversely, the fate of a young and manifestly blameless Guards officer may well have struck him as a case deserving his sympathy and protection.

Dubbelt undoubtedly possessed the quality of making himself affable to persons who for various reasons came into contact with the Third Department. He not only saw to it that such persons received courteous treatment during their period of detention at the Department's headquarters; he also sought to ingratiate himself with them during cross-examinations. According to the historian Kostomarov, who was arrested in 1847 and exiled the following year, Dubbelt interrogated suspects in the gentlest possible language, always addressing the person concerned as 'my dear friend'. 'He would substantiate his arguments with dexterously chosen quotations from Holy Writ, with which he was evidently very conversant; and he was exceedingly clever at baiting traps with words.'[3] It was thanks to such behaviour—

---

[1] 'Leontii Vasil'evich has ordered that you should be asked whether you would like to be sent cigars, books or journals', N. N. Zhedyonov, 'Sluchai v Peterburge v 1848 g. Razskaz byvshago gvard. ofitsera', *R. Star.* (1890), vol. 67, p. 301.

[2] *Ibid.* p. 299.

[3] N. I. Kostomarov, 'Avtobiografiya', *Russkaya Mysl'* (1885), Kn. 5, p. 127.

curiously reminiscent of Sheshkovsky's in the late eighteenth century—that Dubbelt acquired his reputation for hypocrisy. Arbitrary sentences of imprisonment and exile were no less severe for being announced to their recipients in soft tones and to the accompaniment of pious aphorisms. Nevertheless Dubbelt succeeded in leaving a personally favourable impression of himself on many unlikely persons. Even Dostoyevsky, who saw him during cross-examinations on the 'Petrashevsky Affair' in 1849, referred to him as 'a most agreeable man.'[1]

By scrupulously adhering to 'correct methods', however, Dubbelt was simply acting in accordance with the reformed policy of the Higher Police laid down by Nicholas at the beginning of his reign. But as the reign advanced and Nicholas' internal policy tended to become more and more repressive in character, so the power of this police increased proportionately, with the result that its original 'nobility' was preserved only on the surface. 'Outward hypocrisy...became the official tone of the Third Department. And it was in fact Dubbelt who finally completed the formation of the gendarmerie system and also perfected the creation of the "noble gendarme" type.'[2] At the same time Dubbelt believed that the Higher Police could hardly hope to maintain adequate control over society merely by setting an example. If it was to be effective as a political force, it must inspire not only respect but also fear.

Dubbelt himself was widely feared; as much by the innocent as by the guilty. The mere thought of angering him was sufficient to persuade Selivanov that repentance for some unspecified misdemeanour was preferable to an attempt at self-justification. Zhedyonov's reaction on finding himself in the hands of Dubbelt was one of extreme apprehension.[3] Even persons who were not themselves the objects of the Third Department's attention were conscious of a feeling of uneasiness if for some reason or other they found themselves in Dubbelt's company. This may be judged from the account of a courtesy visit paid to him by V. A. Kokorev, who was about to take up an official appointment as tax-collector ('otkupshchik') in St Petersburg. Notwithstanding the extreme politeness of his host, Kokorev confessed to considerable disquiet in his presence.[4]

[1] 'Prepriyatnyi chelovyek', A. N. Milyukov, 'Fyodor Mikhailovich Dostoyevskii', R. Star. (1881), vol. 30, p. 706. (The article contains an account of Dostoyevsky's arrest which he recorded in 1860 in an album belonging to Milyukov's daughter.)

[2] Trotsky, pp. 131–2.

[3] 'So I am under arrest! And where?—in the Third Department building...For what offence? For how long—God alone knew. There was no evidence whatever to justify arresting me, indeed there could not be...but nevertheless, I was being looked upon as a state criminal.' Zhedyonov, loc. cit. p. 300.

[4] 'Well, Mr Kokorev, what are your impressions on leaving me?' 'The respect I feel for Your Excellency obliges me to speak openly...' 'Well, then?' 'You have visited the performances

This feeling was commonly shared by the majority of Dubbelt's contemporaries. For all that to outward appearances he was deferential and
obliging, the general public suspected that this behaviour was expressly
assumed to conceal his natural fierceness and ruthlessness. None of his
actions during his long tenure of office served to modify this opinion and
St Petersburg society christened him 'le général Double'[1]—a title which
doubtless owed as much to the two-faced nature of his conduct as to the
chance coincidence of his surname.

But if Dubbelt's character did contain some features which made him a
formidable Inquisitor, others suggest that he was not a whole-hearted supporter of all practices condoned by Higher Police officials.[2] It is even possible
that there were times when he felt a certain repugnance for his chosen profession, a certain disgust for the 'duties of a dishonourable character' which
came his way.[3] No other explanation can be found for the scorn with which
he regarded amateur informers. According to Karatygin, 'he was well aware
that a denunciation in the hands of rascals was extremely often a weapon of
vengeance... anonymous denunciations almost always received scant attention; signed denunciations and those made in person were most carefully
checked, and, if they were found to be correct, their authors always got less
than they bargained for'; and when Dubbelt paid his agents, he always did
so in multiples of three—'in memory of the thirty pieces of silver.'[4] Karatygin
gives several instances of this practice—on one occasion Dubbelt paid a student
300 roubles for some volunteered information; but nevertheless made him
renounce his studies and enrol as a member of a Gendarme 'Division'.[5] This

given by Zam? Zam goes into the lion's cage, strokes the king of beasts on the mane, and the
public holds its breath as it enjoys the spectacle. But what's it like for poor Zam? Of course, the
only thing he's thinking to himself is: "May the Lord get me out of here as quickly as possible".'
'Iz Zapisnoi Knizhki Russkago Arkhiva', *R. Arkh.* (1892), vol 30, pt 2, p. 491. This outspokenness
evidently pleased Dubbelt, who afterwards invariably afforded Kokorev his protection, *ibid.*

[1] 'Ocherki i Vospominaniya Knyazya N. S. Golitsyna', *R. Star.* (1890), vol. 68, p. 378. (The
nickname was doubtless well known. The émigré writer Golovin, in a story entitled 'The Spy',
describes an incident of political kidnapping abroad (possibly founded on fact), the organization
of which he attributes to 'General Dvoinoi [sic]'. Ivan Golovine, *The Russian Sketch-Book,*
2 vols. (London, 1848), vol. 1, pp. 133–94.)

[2] 'The "cunning general" was not an entirely ordinary character. Evidently, deep down inside,
he had something that remained, under the cover of his uniform, unknown perhaps to his
contemporaries and to posterity', Lemke, p. 122.

[3] Even so hostile a witness as Golovin indirectly supports this view. He reproduces the dialogue
of an interview between 'General Duvelt [sic]' and an unnamed Frenchman of his acquaintance
on the occasion of the latter's visit to Russia. The cross-examination ended thus:
'Shall you enter into the French service?'
'My past and present affairs may be in your province, the future concerns myself alone.'
'I am really ashamed of having asked you all these questions, but my duty required it.'
Ivan Golovine, *Russia under the Autocrat, Nicholas the First,* 2 vols. (London, 1846), vol. 1,
pp. 108–9.

[4] Karatygin, *Ist. Vyestnik, loc. cit.* p. 172.   [5] *Ibid.* pp. 172–3.

kind of rough justice was typical of Dubbelt's sardonic sense of humour and he did not hesitate to employ it whenever he thought the occasion suitable.

By virtue of his position Dubbelt naturally came into contact with writers of all kinds, and here too his dry humour sometimes took odd forms. Bulgarin, for instance, often suspected of collaboration with the Third Department, was nevertheless made fun of by Dubbelt who would send for him whenever he overpraised the government, telling him that it had no need of his praises. Once, when Nicholas ordered that Bulgarin should be given 'a parental piece of advice', Dubbelt actually made him stand in the corner for half an hour with his face to the wall.[1]

The uncertain outcome of any interview with Dubbelt probably contributed in no small degree to the fear with which he was regarded, and the knowledge that his decisions were final did not serve to lessen his reputation for severity.

At the same time he was not by nature an unemotional man. He was genuinely attached to Benckendorff as well as to the Emperor, and, as he recounts in a letter to his wife, the sight of Bryullov's picture of the Crucifixion moved him to tears and he described his feelings with undoubted sincerity.[2] Even those who were not convinced of his merits in an official capacity were ready to concede that at any rate in his domestic circle 'he was incontestably a most sincere and kindly man.'[3] One is forced to the conclusion, however, that Dubbelt's outlook permitted the display of kindness only in cases which in his opinion could not constitute the slightest danger to the state; and in so repressive an age such cases were relatively few.

The question of Dubbelt's honesty has never been satisfactorily resolved. By the end of his career he had amassed a considerable personal fortune, but it is difficult to establish the exact means by which it was acquired. While he probably supplemented the high official salary paid to him over a long period of years by indulging in private speculation, it is impossible to state with any certainty whether or not all such speculation was strictly legitimate. Owing to his position he automatically became a target for the attacks of countless enemies whose favourite charges against him were those of greed and peculation. Russian exiles abroad were particularly vociferous.

[1] Karatygin, *loc. cit.* p. 168. (Karatygin exonerates both Grech and Bulgarin from the charge of having been 'literary agents' of the Third Department, claiming that they merely sought to reduce the effect of the censorship exercised by Dubbelt and hence aimed at securing protection. 'Bulgarin, a coward by nature...made friends with officials from all the Sections of the Third Department and with gendarme officers', pp. 167–8. Grech in his memoirs says that Bulgarin was never 'employed on secret cases' and he confirms that Bulgarin greatly feared gendarmes. 'When he saw...a horse with a sky-blue saddle-cloth, he would take off his hat and bow', *Zapiski, op. cit.* p. 714.)

[2] Letter dated 31 Aug. 1838, *R. Star.*, *loc. cit.* pp. 506–7.

[3] Editorial Note to Dubbelt's letters, *R. Star.*, *loc. cit.* p. 497.

General Douvelt was his [Benkendorf's] factotum, who took with both hands, and it was therefore more than once in contemplation to dismiss him; but Count Benkendorf having declared that in that case he would immediately quit the service, the Court shut their eyes, waiting for the time when the Count should do the same; but after his death they forgot to open them.[1]

He [Mordvinov]...was replaced by a general officer endowed with remarkable intelligence, but whose aim in life consisted of enriching himself at any price. The best method of making a fortune being to make use of malpractices for this purpose and of official dishonesty to conceal his peculations, this man appointed himself the most ardent protector of all abuses...[2]

These writers quoted no specific instances in support of their accusations and their views were doubtless both prejudiced and embittered. But Dubbelt was widely believed to have accumulated a considerable private fortune.

According to the memoirs of Prince N. S. Golitsyn (a well-known military writer and professor), rumours to this effect even reached the Emperor who authorized Orlov to investigate the truth of the matter. The inquiry in no way disconcerted Dubbelt who, while not denying the existence of this fortune, claimed that it belonged not to him but to his wife, in whose name it was registered. Golitsyn does not record his opinion of this claim, merely asserting that one of the sources of Dubbelt's wealth was the gaming house of a certain Lukull Politkovsky well known to St Petersburg society. Here, he maintained, the public was openly enticed to extravagant social gatherings which acted as a cover for secret gambling for high stakes in the rear apartments of the house. Huge sums of money were lost in this way. According to Golitsyn Dubbelt was one of Politkovsky's partners and a leading member of this 'secret society'.[3] This evidence of one of Dubbelt's sources of wealth has been accepted by later writers.[4] But although, if true, it provides an adequate explanation of the wealth Dubbelt was accused of amassing, it certainly does not prove that he became rich by dishonest means in either his official or unofficial life. Dubbelt may well have regarded this form of private speculation as a profitable investment entirely divorced from any of his official functions. Golitsyn's evidence was neither refuted nor confirmed by

[1] Golovine, *Russia under the Autocrat, Nicholas the First*, p. 320.

[2] Dolgoroukow, *op. cit.* p. 295. (D. for some reason refrains from mentioning names, but there is no doubt to whom he is referring here. Cf. 'this superior [after 1844] left all business to the general officer I have just mentioned, and there then began for Russia an epoch of sinister memory which lasted until the death of the emperor Nicholas and of which I cannot think without a profound sentiment of disgust and horror...', p. 297.)

[3] N.G. [*sic*], 'Leontii Vasil'evich Dubbelt', *R. Star.* (1880), vol. 29, pp. 127–8. (The index carries him as *Knyaz'* N.G., p. 1162; and these initials clearly refer to Prince N. S. Golitsyn whose memoirs were later published under his full name in *R. Star.* (1890), vol. 68, and which repeat much of the information, e.g. the details he gives of the Petrashevtsy Affair, contained in his earlier article.)   [4] See Lemke, p. 123; Trotsky, p. 138.

Ye. I. Dubbelt in his prefatory note to the publication eight years later of some of his eminent relative's letters; indeed, his biographical sketch of their author contains no mention whatever of Dubbelt's finances.

This account does deal, however, with the general question of Dubbelt's moral integrity in both its private and public aspects, and quotes various examples of his incorruptibility. It records, for instance, how a certain millionaire, Count Pototsky [Potocki], who had been exiled first to Vologda and then to Penza, came to St Petersburg on leave at the end of the 1840s and offered Dubbelt 200,000 roubles if he would intercede with the Emperor with a view to releasing him from surveillance. Dubbelt refused this offer, warning the millionaire that he would bring it to the Emperor's attention. As a result the Count received a letter from Orlov, then Chief of Gendarmes, which the latter wrote by Imperial command to inform him that 'not only he, Count Pototsky, but also the Emperor himself did not possess sufficient money to bribe Dubbelt'.[1] This was evidently the reputation which Dubbelt had long desired to establish, for in one of his letters to his wife in 1844 he tells how, when a certain Rogozhin attempted to win support for the Dissenters with a present of 100 souls and 2,000 desyatins of land or, if preferred, 50,000 roubles in cash, '...I told Mr Rogozhin that Nikolai Pavlovich has not enough money to bribe me with and that in general I advise the Dissenters not to give cash presents to anyone, for those who can do something useful for them will not accept their money and those who do accept it are not in a position to give them any help.'[2] (Rogozhin continued to press his offers, but they all met with the same stern reply.)

Ye. I. Dubbelt also claims that his relative's straightforward honesty was not limited to public affairs alone, and quotes two cases in support of this contention. In the first Leontii Vasil'evich had advised a widow named Lestrelen to invest 30,000 roubles in a financial concern which promptly lost them and Dubbelt then felt it his duty to refund the money. In the second Leontii Vasil'evich summoned an apprehensive young officer to his presence and, once assured of his identity, proceeded to pay him 17,000 roubles which, he told him, he had owed the young man's late father—a debt of which there had been no record on paper.[3] And, as if to show that such generous behaviour was appreciated not merely by its beneficiaries, the same source records the lines written by Zhukovsky in praise of Dubbelt the man.[4] On the other hand, it must be admitted that every incident related by this source

---

[1] Ye. I. Dubel't, *R. Star.*, *loc. cit.* p. 493. Referring to this letter, the author states: 'This precious document which, as it emanated from so fair a judge of merit as the Emperor Nikolai Pavlovich, bears such high testimony to the personality of Leontii Vasil'evich, is preserved even to the present day in the archives of the former Third Department of H.I.M.s Own Chancellery', *Ibid.*

[2] Letter dated 18 Apr. 1844, *R. Star.*, *loc. cit.* p. 510.

[3] Ye. I. Dubel't, *loc. cit.* p. 496.　　　　　　　　　　[4] *Ibid.* p. 497.

is undoubtedly, if understandably, strongly prejudiced in Dubbelt's favour and hence gives a very one-sided picture of his character.

In general, the evidence regarding Dubbelt's honesty is so scanty and so contradictory that it is hard to arrive at any definite conclusions. It seems probable, however, that Dubbelt was too intelligent to risk compromising his position by accepting bribes. He had succeeded in winning the confidence of his superiors and especially of the Emperor himself who took a close personal interest in all Higher Police matters; and he cannot have failed to realize the extreme importance to himself of retaining such confidence. If Dubbelt had taken any improper advantage of his unique appointment, his many detractors would surely have welcomed so excellent an opportunity of bringing about his dismissal by attempting to discredit him in Nicholas' eyes. To do this, however, they would have needed circumstantial proof of his dishonesty. Dubbelt in his turn fully appreciated the importance of proving to the world in general that his administration of the political police was both efficient and disinterested; and on one occasion, when a dishonest employee of the Third Department wrote an anonymous denunciation to Nicholas accusing his seniors of peculation, Dubbelt at once demanded that his 'chancellery' should be subjected to the strictest possible investigation. This audit 'was entrusted on imperial orders to Prince A. F. Golitsyn, who was then President of the Commission for Petitions. The Prince found the whole conduct of official business to be in exemplary order.'[1] Dubbelt's insistence on the holding of this inquiry was well rewarded, for the Emperor was so satisfied with its findings that he conferred a high decoration on him despite the latter's protestation that his service was as yet too short to warrant this honour. It is difficult to avoid the conclusion that Dubbelt valued the Emperor's goodwill above all else. Those who charged him with pocketing vast sums of money failed to substantiate their allegations and apparently did not distinguish between his salary as a public servant and his income as a private individual. Their accusations were indiscriminate and dictated by an obvious bias; and their authors also seem to have ignored the fact that Dubbelt could only continue to exercise his immense power by giving constant proof of his official integrity and dependability.

A far more reliable guide to Dubbelt's personality is provided by his own memoranda recorded at random over a long period. These *Notes* were not published until 1913[2] and their existence was evidently unknown before

---

[1] *Ibid.* p. 494. The exact date of this inquiry is not stated.

[2] 'Zamyetki L. V. Dubel'ta', contributed and annotated by L. F. Panteleyev with introductory foreword by S. Mel'gunov, *Golos Minuvshago* (Moscow, 1913), Kn. III, pp. 127–71. (These 'Zamyetki' were written in Russian and are reproduced from Dubbelt's ms.; they cover the period 1830 to 1862, see footnote, *loc. cit.* p. 131.)

(Five brief letters from Dubbelt to Prince Chernyshov in May 1849 are included in a later

then.[1] Although they represent little more than a series of disconnected reflections on the various topics that interested their writer, it is not enough to dismiss them without closer examination as mere hypocritical aphorisms, for they inevitably reveal much of what Dubbelt genuinely believed. He laid claims to being an idealist in thought and deed. In a lengthy passage dealing with his private hopes and beliefs he wrote: '...[I desire], in a word, that in all my doings there should shine the abundant grace of God. I desire the impossible, but I desire it',[2] and he saw nothing incompatible between this lofty ambition and the policy he in fact pursued as the man mainly responsible for a political police in a reactionary régime.

There is, indeed, no reason to doubt that Dubbelt saw in police service the possibility of fulfilling the ideals he respected and this appealed to something in his nature which responded to the kind of philanthropic sentimentality so favoured by Benckendorff. '"I know no better feat" [wrote Dubbelt] "no greater pleasure than to proffer a hand to a poor man and to guide a blind youth, blind from his youth and inexperience"'; and he upholds his chosen profession in the following terms: 'The duties of the police consist in protecting persons and property; in preserving the tranquillity and safety of each and every person; in averting all kinds of harmful deeds and in controlling the exact functioning of the laws; in taking all possible measures for the public welfare; in defending and helping the poor, widows and orphans; and in the tireless pursuit of criminals of all categories. Let people prove to me that service of this kind does not merit the respect and gratitude of one's fellow-citizens.'[3] This definition is strongly reminiscent of the idyllic picture sketched by Benckendorff in his 1826 Memorandum; and indeed both the above quotations aptly illustrate the mentality of Nicholas' leading advisers on police affairs.

Nowhere does Dubbelt attempt to analyse either the principles or the work of the institution he controlled, obviously believing its supra-legality

---

issue of *Golos Minuvshago*. The first four deal with a man detained on suspicion of loitering near the palace and believed to have connexions with Polish malcontents. The fifth informs Chernyshov that the Emperor has no objections to Madame Sukhozanet's journey to certain countries abroad. These letters throw no extra light on Dubbelt's character. 'Donesyeniya L. F. [*sic*] Dubel'ta kn. A. I. Chernyshovu', *Golos Minuvshago* (1914), Kn. IV, pp. 222–3. A footnote on p. 222 by the Editor, V. I. Semyevsky, states that these letters were reproduced from copies preserved in the papers of N. K. Shil'der.)

[1] Neither Lemke nor Zherve (author of article on Dubbelt in the *RBS*) mentions them. Mel'-gunov confirms Lemke's view of Dubbelt as a 'not entirely ordinary character' (p. 128), but contends that both Herzen and Karatygin may have erred in their appreciation of him (p. 131); his view is that Dubbelt was simply a hypocrite and he describes the *Notes* as 'thoughts utterly lacking in depth' ('eto polnago ubozhestva mysli'), *ibid*. This is also the opinion expressed by Trotsky, who claims that these 'memoirs...were written for the consumption of others and are very flat and aphoristic', pp. 130–1.

[2] 'Zamyetki', *loc. cit.* p. 131.   [3] *Ibid*. pp. 133, 134.

to be in all circumstances right and proper. The only comment he makes on his own position reads: 'The Director of the Third Department of His Imperial Majesty's Own Chancellery should lay down for himself an invariable rule: "que chaque accusé doit être regardé comme innocent, jusqu'à ce que l'accusation portée contre lui soit démontrée par des preuves directes et suffisantes" [sic].'[1] Dubbelt may well have believed in this admirable precept in theory even if in practice the ideal fell far short of the reality; which explains why he has been thought hypocritical.

His political outlook was entirely uncomplicated. 'The first duty of an honest man is to love his country above all else and be the most loyal subject and servant of his Emperor', he wrote, and his attitude to Nicholas was always one of uncritical devotion: 'People said of Alexander Pavlovich that he was a man upon the throne; of Nicholas it should be said that he is an angel upon the throne—a real angel...I do not like his having gone abroad [in 1844]; there are many of those useless Poles there, and he takes so little care of himself! I have given Count Benckendorff a pair of loaded pistols and asked him to put them quietly in the Emperor's carriage...Despite all the severe appearance of the Emperor Nikolai Pavlovich he is a man of the gentlest, kindest heart; his feelings are always sublime, noble—he is a real knight "sans peur et sans reproche" [sic].' Dubbelt was not only genuinely attached to the person of the Emperor, however; he was also a convinced supporter of the autocratic system Nicholas embodied—'Sovereigns are necessary, like a driver for a herd of goats, like a rudder to a ship.' Such opinions[2] constantly repeated throughout the *Notes* make it easy to understand why, from the point of view of Nicholas, the choice of Dubbelt as Director of the Higher Police was an excellent one.

Dubbelt was a man of strong likes and dislikes. If his eulogies of Nicholas in particular and the state of Russia in general are entirely uncritical, he reveals an almost pathological hatred of those elements which he considered harmful to his country. Foremost among the latter were foreigners. In one passage he urges his sons: 'Do not become infected with the senselessness of the West—it is a disgusting rubbish dump from which nothing will come your way but a stench', and he interpreted 'senselessness' to mean all the liberal freedom-loving notions cherished in Western Europe. For this reason he was naturally anxious that such perverted ideas should not be allowed to infiltrate into Russia. 'Foreigners are snakes whom Russia warms with her sunshine and as she does so they creep out and bite her.' Unfortunately, as he saw it, too many travellers from abroad, not being favourably impressed by their observations of life in Russia, subsequently recorded their reactions in print; and Dubbelt was obviously angered by their outspoken criticisms.

---

[1] *Ibid.* p. 135.   [2] *Ibid.* pp. 132, 137, 141–2, 160.

'We should not let a single foreigner into Russia—that's all there is to it; and the real trouble is that this can't be done...Not a doubt of it, it's a fine place, Europe—just like a rotten apple! Only the trouble is that one can throw an apple out of the window, but as to throwing the lot of them into the sea—that's impossible.' Nor were these inconvenient visitors the only foreigners whom Dubbelt detested; and a diatribe against 'those wretched Austrians', whom he accused of ingratitude for Russian help in crushing the Hungarian revolt of 1849, suggests that it extended to any nationality which did not owe allegiance to Nicholas. This comprehensive xenophobia is a theme to which Dubbelt constantly reverts[1] in his *Notes*.

This hatred appears to have been at least partially dictated by a somewhat smug sense of pride in his own country, so that any criticism of it he regarded as an outrage. 'All these absurdities [stories in the foreign press of harsh life in Russia] are simply ridiculous when one sees what goes on in their countries and how peaceful it is in ours...One's heart rejoices and swells with pride when one compares Russians with these worthless foreigners...Individual cases mean nothing; take the whole physiognomy of the state; contentment, peace, tranquillity, industriousness. Who is unhappy in Russia? Only the sponger and the man who cares nothing for the views of others...I am convinced that Russia is great, strong and rich because (1) she has an autocratic Emperor; (2) she has the landowner who enjoys rights over the peasant; (3) she has the peasant who feeds himself, the landowner, the townsman, the merchant, the soldier, the statesman and the Emperor himself.'[!][2]

According to Dubbelt's way of thinking, nothing must be allowed to jeopardize this admirable state of affairs. 'All this is because our people is not spoiled by fictitious freedom and the rights of man that conform to nothing, rights founded on the destruction of one's neighbour...Overthrow our existing order—see what will happen! If the peasants were freed, they would get their freedom without land, because not a single landowner will give away his land voluntarily, and our government is too just to take our property away from us and deprive us of our last crust of bread—it will not remove from us the land which we have inherited from our forefathers.' Western ideas of freedom were thus anathema to Dubbelt, who saw in them the cause of all Europe's difficulties in the past. '...and blood flowed in rivers always and everywhere where the people were free...Our people is intelligent because it is tranquil, and tranquil because it is not free—though here, however, it should be said that if the peasants are not given freedom, at any rate the landowners should not persecute them—landowners who do should be packed off to Siberia.' Dubbelt consistently believed that any changes in Russia's political system were dangerous and he relied on the

---

[1] 'Zamyetki', *loc. cit.* pp. 132, 133, 153, 155, 162.   [2] *Ibid.* pp. 153, 154, 158, 159.

landowner to defend it—'The landowner is a most loyal, unsleeping watch-dog who preserves the state.' Such[1] were the ultra-reactionary opinions that governed all his actions.

In particular they affected his views on education, of which he approved only in so far as it supported the existing régime. 'In our Russia men of learning should conduct themselves like apothecaries whose stock includes both beneficial...remedies and poisons—and they should give rein to their learning only as the government prescribes.' Therefore, he argued, education should lead to a sympathetic understanding of the government and in that case he naturally did not oppose it. 'It is not education that is at fault, but distorted views of it'...'Education doesn't hurt people, only its false direction.' Dubbelt undoubtedly believed, however, that all education should be subject to strict control, since otherwise its misapplication might tend to disturb the tranquil development of Russia's internal history. He was es-pecially anxious that the peasant should not be exposed to such dangers. 'Not knowing their letters [he wrote of them] their imagination is not inflamed by reading magazines and all kinds of dirty literature arousing the very worst passions.'[2]

Dubbelt does not devote space in his *Notes* to the work of the leading literary figures of the day, but it is permissible to assume that his suspicions of education in general led him to distrust all expression of 'independent' thought. He appears to have lacked any appreciation of literature, which during his period of office was subjected to a most repressive scrutiny.[3] Although he sometimes treated certain writers with unexpected kindness even when they had fallen foul of the censorship regulations,[4] he approved their work only if it conformed to a strictly loyal pattern. 'You are now on a good footing', he said to the playwright Polevoi in 1838 after the latter had submitted a work commended by the Emperor, 'this is much better than wasting your time playing the liberal.'[5] These words are typical of Dubbelt's attitude to writers, and it remained unchanged by the years. Even at the very end of his life he was disgusted when a monument was erected to the Ukrainian poet Taras Shevchenko, of whose career and personality he

---

[1] *Ibid.* pp. 149, 158, 160, 161.   [2] *Ibid.* pp. 133, 155, 163, 154.

[3] In 1839 Dubbelt objected to the publication of some newly-discovered mss. of Pushkin with the comment: 'Enough of that rubbish...was printed in his lifetime without needing to con-tinue hunting out his unpublished stuff after his death...' He was equally forthright on the subject of Belinsky, whose untimely death in 1848 he regretted with the words: 'We would have let him rot in a fortress.' Only at the end of his career did Dubbelt show any leniency. In 1855 he consented to the publication of an unexpurgated edition of Gogol''s Complete Works, but in Gogol''s case this official approval is easier to understand.

[4] The editor Nadyezhdin (exiled in 1836 after the publication of Chaadayev's *Lettres Philo-sophiques*) 'speaks gratefully of Benckendorff and especially of Dubbelt'; V. K. Sokolovsky (exiled in 1837) also 'speaks well of Benckendorff and Dubbelt', Nikitenko, vol. 1, pp. 280, 289.

[5] *Ibid.* p. 292.

strongly disapproved. 'If in such cases, before their final decision, orders were given to apply to the Third Department of the Emperor's Chancellery to discover, so to speak, what lies beneath the surface, our versifiers would not find it possible to distort the truth and so insolently deceive the government.'[1] He had no doubts that the Department he directed could justly be regarded as a repository of wisdom.

As a rule Dubbelt's defence of his uncompromising views is pursued with considerable logic, although in one passage his *Notes* reveal a remarkable instance of inconsistency. Referring to the general distress 'worse than the cholera' caused by two recruit call-ups in one year (1848), he observes: 'The landowners and the people grumble and I think that, if the Emperor were told how this exhausts the national strength, he would spare his subjects who are, of course, dear to him; but he stands so high that he himself does not see the sufferings of the people...If our good Emperor knew what a misfortune it [military service] is for all, if he saw these fits of fainting, these tears, if he heard these shrieks of despairing wives and mothers, his heart would be moved and, in his fatherly mercy, he would devise some other method of filling the ranks.'[2] It does not appear to have occurred to Dubbelt that it was above all his duty to report these sufferings to Nicholas, for was not the Third Department primarily intended to act as a direct link between the Tsar and his people? And his suggestion that Nicholas' sensitive heart would urge him to employ other methods of recruitment was obviously unrealistic, for what other methods were available? Dubbelt himself had no solution for this problem.

Indeed, as far as may be judged from the *Notes*, he did not regard himself as a policy-maker. Only in moments of exasperation did he feel impelled to record his personal advice on specific issues,[3] and for the most part he preferred to limit himself to generalizations.[4] This cannot be attributed to any particular caution or discretion on Dubbelt's part because he did not hesitate to express his dislike of the behaviour of both Grand Duke Mikhail Pavlovich and Count Kleinmikhel'. His *Notes* give the impression of being written by a man who cared for no one but the Emperor, all of whose decisions must be accepted as correct and final. Dubbelt did not seek to be a power behind

[1] Dubel't, 'Zamyetki', *loc. cit.* p. 171. [2] *Ibid.* pp. 145, 146.
[3] In a reference to the Petrashevtsy he wrote: 'One cannot be sufficiently amazed that there are such brainless people who like foreign disorders [the 1848 revolutions]. Were I the Emperor, I would send all these wiseacres there to join those who think like them...Send them out of Russia as people unworthy of living in their own country, as a sore and a plague dangerous to touch. Such measures would achieve marvellous results; however, it is not my place to pass such judgement', *ibid.* p. 161.
[4] This is especially true with regard to information on the Higher Police. Dubbelt does not discuss a single Third Department official apart from Benckendorff and Orlov, and does not mention a single officer of the Corps of Gendarmes.

the throne; he sought only to serve the throne's best interests by blind obedience to its occupant, and when he retired he was satisfied that he had done so.[1]
'In our bear's den [he wrote] there is order, obedience, love for the Emperor,
love for one another (well, perhaps, not altogether that), love for one's duties!
Whereas in their enlightened countries of perfection there is famine, rebellion, hatred, barricades, civil strife, all disasters, all harmful passions which
lead to hell and proceed from it.'[2] This is possibly the most characteristic
example of Dubbelt's outlook in both style and content.

In assessing the part played by Dubbelt in the expansion of the Higher
Police, it is important to consider the change of atmosphere that had taken
place since 1826. During the first quarter of the century the liberal movements maturing in Western Europe penetrated into Russia and resulted in
the Decembrist revolt. The direct consequence of this was Nicholas' determination to establish a Higher Police organization under his immediate control and thus effectively prevent the further development of 'liberal ideas'
inside his empire. At its head he placed an eminently respectable general
whose chief merit was that he enjoyed Nicholas' friendship and was blindly
subservient to Nicholas' wishes. But although Benckendorff was well-
meaning, loyal and reliable, he was neither outstandingly intelligent nor
able; and it was these last qualities which distinguished Dubbelt, in whom
Nicholas also found a man who was as hidebound a conservative as he was
himself. Dubbelt was an ideal Chief of Staff for the Corps of Gendarmes
because he genuinely believed that the political *status quo* in Russia must
remain unchanged and he had a corresponding loathing for foreign ideas
with their implicitly dangerous dreams of freedom. Dubbelt played his part
faithfully. He understood what Nicholas required of him and his organization of the Higher Police shows how conscientiously he sought to satisfy
these requirements. He never had any intention of directing this department
with the object of establishing a kind of Reign of Terror; and Lemke's
reference to him as 'this Malyuta Skuratov in a sky-blue uniform'[3] expresses
a highly prejudiced opinion. The repressive control exercised over writers
in Nicholas' reign undoubtedly gave rise to widespread discontent and sometimes to cases of ill-merited persecution, but Dubbelt himself was merely
executing Nicholas' orders in the conviction that he was acting in the country's
best interests. Once the existence of a political police has been accepted in
principle as necessary, it is unjust to blame beyond their due those men whose
duty it was to organize it and who at the same time honestly tried to improve

[1] '26 Aug. 1856. God sees that I have served without any ambitious aims, for the benefit of my
Emperor, my country and my fellow-citizens. Now I return to insignificance...', *ibid.* p. 169.
[2] *Ibid.* p. 151.
[3] Lemke, p. 546. Malyuta Skuratov was one of the cruellest 'oprichniki' of Tsar Ivan IV, see
chapter One, p. 14.

its character. 'Men are not angels [wrote Grech in 1851] and among them many are devils, consequently a police, and a strict police, is necessary both for the state and for all honest persons, but its actions should be just, discriminating, should inspire confidence in the honest and innocent... Nikolai Pavlovich is stern and exacting, but noble and frank. In employing such men as Count Benckendorff, Maksim Yakovlevich von Vock and Leontii Vasil'evich Dubbelt, he has removed from the Higher Police all that was wicked, deceitful and vengeful...'[1] That this view was that of a man whole-heartedly biased in favour of Nicholas' régime cannot be denied, but it is equally true that Grech was excellently placed to know much of the Third Department and its leading officials. Trotsky, writing in 1930, supports Grech's contention that Dubbelt was instrumental in eradicating some of the features that had disfigured the political polices of Russia's past. Commenting on Dubbelt's methods, he points out that he 'gladly recruited to his service military or naval officers provided they possessed the right outlook and seemed likely to benefit from their re-education in the spirit of the gendarmes' and concludes that 'Dubbelt did in fact raise the Corps of Gendarmes to a certain height and the attitude of society towards its members was a reasonably tolerant one.'[2] Such an appraisal hardly confirms Lemke's 'Skuratov' definition of Dubbelt as a kind of ogre.

The fact remains, however, that Dubbelt's name has long been linked with a period of Russian history remarkable for its reactionary character. The hatred and criticism it earned, when not directed (as it should have been) against Nicholas, inevitably found in Dubbelt an obvious target for its venom. Dubbelt was ideally suited by nature to attain notoriety as the Director of a political police, but most of the blame heaped upon him was due less to his own character than to the post he filled. In that post he was not free to act in any other way. And believing as he did that sovereigns were necessary for their peoples just as drivers were necessary for herds of goats, he may well have consoled himself with the sardonic reflection that a driver needs a stick and that a stick to be effective must be used. It will be seen later whether his direction of the Corps of Gendarmes was as effective as Nicholas could have wished.

[1] Grech, p. 104. (For date, see introduction by Ivanov-Razumnik, p. 18.)
[2] Trotsky, pp. 135, 136.

A. F. Orlov

*Chief Director of the Third Department of His Imperial Majesty's Own Chancellery
and Chief of Gendarmes 1844–1856*

Dubbelt had only one superior after the death of Benckendorff in 1844—
Count Aleksei Fyodorovich Orlov.[1]

Orlov was one of the most prominent Russian statesmen in the reign of
Nicholas. An illegitimate son of the youngest of the famous Orlov brothers
of the preceding century (Fyodor Grigor'evich), his early career in the army
was as distinguished as that of Benckendorff. Like him, Orlov took part in
much of the fighting in the Napoleonic Wars as a cavalry officer, was quickly
promoted for his valour and by 1825 was a General-in-Waiting and the
Commander of both the Life Guards Cavalry Regiment and the 1st Brigade
of the Guards Cuirassier Division. He was a strict disciplinarian and, unlike
Benckendorff, he never at any time displayed sympathy with the liberal
views held by many of his brother-officers in general and by his younger
brother General Mikhail Fyodorovich Orlov in particular, who ended
his career as a Decembrist exile. Aleksei Orlov, again like Benckendorff,
owed his later success as courtier and statesman to the prominent rôle
he played on 14 December, when his regiment was the first to swear
allegiance to Nicholas. The same month he was made a Count of the Russian
Empire.

Throughout his reign Nicholas made use of Orlov as his personal plenipotentiary abroad. He was appointed Ambassador to Turkey and to Austria,
proving himself a skilful negotiator; and he was the Tsar's chief diplomatic
envoy on a number of foreign state occasions.[2] In 1836 he was made a member of the State Council.

It is typical of the confidence placed in him that when a revolt broke out
in the Military Settlements in 1831 it was Orlov whom Nicholas selected to
restore order, and he did so with remarkable firmness and presence of mind.
(This was the first of Orlov's 'police' appointments.) Two years later he
took part in the negotiations with Metternich at Münchengrätz one of the
results of which was a Russo-Austrian agreement to extradite each other's
state criminals.[3] But with these exceptions Orlov had no direct connexion

---

[1] A. A. Petrov, article on A. F. Orlov (1786–1861), *RBS*. Except where otherwise stated, the
details of his career are taken from this article. (On returning to Russia after the signing of the
Treaty of Paris in 1856, Orlov was appointed President both of the State Council and the
Committee of Ministers by Alexander II, who raised him to the rank of Prince on the occasion
of his coronation.) Orlov held office as Head of the Third Department and Chief of Gendarmes
from 17 Sept. 1844 to 5 Apr. 1856, see Adrianov, p. 99.

[2] He was the Russian representative at the funeral of the Austrian Emperor in 1835 and was
sent to England to congratulate Queen Victoria on her accession in 1837. He accompanied
the Tsar on his visit to England in 1844.   [3] See chapter Six, p. 212.

with questions relating to internal security until 1837, when he temporarily replaced Benckendorff during the latter's severe illness.[1]

When Benckendorff died, Nicholas appointed Orlov in his place as the second Head of the Third Department and Chief of the Corps of Gendarmes. He accepted this office only in response to the Emperor's insistent demands and a threat, in the case of his refusal, to appoint Kleinmikhel'; and Orlov occupied the post reluctantly.[2] According to one source Nicholas said of him 'Nobody is so indispensable to me'; and whether or not it is true, according to the same source, that Orlov even declared 'I do not comprehend the utility of this institution',[3] he certainly regarded the duties it involved with some repugnance.

The news of his appointment was greeted with an equal lack of enthusiasm by the general public. The Bavarian Minister noted that in many households Benckendorff was remembered with respect 'whereas the nomination to this post of Orlov aroused in many people apprehensions', for evidently since the crushing of the Military Settlements revolt 'the Russian people connects with Orlov's name a superstitious fear'. The same diplomat commented, however, that these apprehensions proved groundless and stressed Orlov's good qualities of honesty and capability despite the fact that 'he is rather a good executor than an adviser'.[4] Such a man was obviously to Nicholas' liking. He was already an established statesman by 1844 and, although he may have been attracted by the possibility of increasing his wealth (he enjoyed indulging this fancy[5]), it is more likely that he assumed it merely in deference to the Tsar's wishes and had no particular ambition to become the Chief of Gendarmes. This is confirmed by a dispatch from the Austrian Ambassador to Metternich in 1846—'Count Orlov often speaks of the aversion he feels for the duties of the supreme chief of police, he says over and over again that he only accepted and continues to fulfil them out of personal devotion to the Emperor.'[6]

On becoming Head of the Third Department Orlov was also appointed Commandant of the Imperial Headquarters in succession to Benckendorff, and he held all these posts until after the death of Nicholas. He enjoyed the Tsar's closest friendship and confidence; and in the last years of his reign there was no important Committee or Commission of which Orlov was not either the President or a member. But despite the fact that after 1844 his

[1] See chapter Four, p. 120, note 2.
[2] Bartyenev, *R. Arkh.* (1889), July, p. 398.
[3] Golovine, *loc. cit.* p. 323. (G. commented: 'May the Count one day see its total inutility, and contribute to its abolition.')
[4] Bray-Steinburg, *Vospominaniya, loc. cit.* p. 128.
[5] See 'Zapiski Vladimira Ivanovicha Dyena', *R. Star.* (1890), vol. 67, p. 184.
[6] 'Colloredo à Metternich, 31 août 1846', dispatch quoted from the 'Vienna Secret Archives' by de Grunwald, p. 188.

duties were mainly concerned with the Higher Police, his long experience of foreign affairs made it inevitable that Nicholas should also have chosen him to conduct further special negotiations abroad. He took part in conferences in Berlin and Olmütz in 1852 and in Vienna in 1854; and after the conclusion of the Crimean War he was chosen by Alexander II to represent Russia at the Peace Conference of 1856. Indeed it was owing to his long absence in Paris in this capacity that on 27 June that year he was succeeded as Chief of Gendarmes by Prince V. A. Dolgorukov.

As Orlov had taken little if any interest in the Higher Police as a political institution, it is hardly surprising that his appointment as its Head had no noticeable effect on its development. Benckendorff on his death-bed had bequeathed to the Emperor all his subordinates, and Orlov, as far as is known, accepted this bequest without reservations. Besides, any changes in either the personnel or the policy of the Third Department and Corps of Gendarmes would have involved their new Chief in a number of irksome tasks; and Orlov was never the man to exert himself unduly. The Bavarian Minister wrote: 'To the distinctive features of his character belongs sloth, which impels him to avoid important tasks instead of seeking them. Orlov loves to stand aloof and he only appears where his presence is indispensable... The current business of the Department Orlov directs is conducted by General Dubbelt, who is well acquainted with the affairs which he controlled almost independently during the latter years of Benckendorff's direction of the Third Department... Orlov, in accordance with his natural sloth and dislike of work, needed more than anyone an assistant distinguished for his dexterity, industry and knowledge of his job. For this reason Dubbelt did not lose his former influence...'[1]

Dubbelt's reaction to his new Chief is uncertain, for the only reference to him in his *Notes* reads: 'One should try to have a proud unbending character, but a kindly sensitive heart. After the decease of Count Benckendorff, I have met this virtue to the highest degree in Count Orlov.'[2] There is no reason to suppose that the appointment either surprised or displeased him. Orlov's reaction to Dubbelt as his leading assistant may at first have been one of suspicion because, according to Lemke, reports for the Tsar on the most important cases were drawn up by a junior official, M. I. Pozen, and then submitted by Orlov as his own.[3] But evidently Orlov quickly recognized Dubbelt's worth and was therefore content to leave all routine business in

---

[1] Bray-Steinburg, *loc. cit.* p. 128. Lemke also supports the view that Dubbelt owed the stability of his official position to Orlov's laziness, p. 159. (Orlov's apathetic character was probably known to most of his contemporaries, one of whom wrote that he 'had enjoyed the esteem of society so long as he was not in public life, but once in power he was generally discredited and despised... his laziness is unequalled'. Dolgoroukow, p. 296.)

[2] Dubel't, 'Zamyetki', *loc. cit.* p. 133.   [3] Lemke, p. 159.

his hands—a decision which may have earned him much of his unpopularity, especially among writers who strongly objected to the necessity of having to submit their work for the Third Department's approval.

Orlov was not himself interested in the world of literature. 'He positively ignored its existence and read absolutely nothing.'[1] In so far as writers engaged his attention at all, he naturally adopted the reactionary views officially popular during the last decade of the reign and is reported to have stated bluntly at a session of the Council of Ministers: 'Every writer is a born conspirator.'[2]

This dislike for any form of literary work also extended to the administration of his own office. According to Lemke, 'If in Benckendorff's time a considerable number of his "letters", "minutes" and "directives" were drawn up by Vock, Mordvinov and Dubbelt, and their Chief signed them without reading them, in Orlov's time this became almost without exception the rule. His name always concealed the pen of Dubbelt or, on occasions, of some other official of the Third Department...' Lemke also notes a certain falling-off in the work of the Department after 1844. The old conspiratorial methods favoured by Benckendorff with a view to encouraging pro-government writers were less frequently practised under Orlov. 'This may be explained, on the one hand, by his apathetic state of mind...and, on the other, by the intelligence of Dubbelt, who understood what sort of price could usually be set on literature produced under the orders of Nicholas' government.' Orlov was primarily interested in transferring as many of his burdens as possible on to the shoulders of others.[3]

Orlov's distaste for his official duties, however, did not altogether prevent him from taking them seriously. He personally interviewed suspects, one of whom, Selivanov, although convinced of the injustice of his sentence, pays tribute to the outward forbearance of the Chief Director's manner.[4] But this

---

[1] Lemke, p. 159. [2] Dolgoroukow, *ibid.*

[3] Lemke, pp. 159, 160. (In another of his works, in which he discusses 'The epoch of the Censorship Terror from 1848 to 1855', Lemke states: 'There is no doubt that Count Orlov had occasion to think seriously about how to rid himself of what promised to become exceedingly onerous and troublesome duties connected with the surveillance of literature and the censorship —duties accepted by the Third Department at its foundation in 1826. His intelligent adviser, the unforgettable L. V. Dubbelt, clearly foresaw what a burden and, possibly, what a responsibility the Third Department would carry if, occupied as it now was with a mass of political cases, it were also to continue dealing with censorship matters. The result of this was Orlov's firm desire to concede this latter activity to someone else...', *Ocherki po Istorii Russkoi Tsenzury i Zhurnalistiki XIX stolyetiya* (SPB, 1904), p. 194.

Orlov's desire was fulfilled with the formation in 1848 of the so-called 'Buturlin Committee' to deal with censorship matters. The Third Dept. was represented on it in the person of Dubbelt, see *RBS*, article on Dubbelt.)

[4] 'His voice had nothing hostile in it; his face was kind and had an expression of mildness...he did not look like a scoundrel; in appearance he was a simple, kindly man and by nature was incapable of evil', Selivanov, 'Zapiski', *loc. cit.* p. 312.

treatment was normally typical of officials of the Third Department. It had always been intended that this branch should impress members of the public with the correctness of its behaviour. If they were under suspicion, they were treated with seeming courtesy; if they were not, and merely required assistance, Third Department officials were meant to be accessible to all comers. According to a sympathizer this policy, which began with Benckendorff, was similarly pursued by his successor.[1]

But Orlov was undeniably bored by political police work. Trotsky, in comparing him with Benckendorff, goes so far as to say that 'in intelligence and experience he was even his inferior. His sole merit was his friendship with the Tsar. As far as practical work went, Orlov was remarkable for his complete idleness and in fact he left no imprint on the physiognomy of the Third Department.'[2] It is for this reason that he scarcely merits more than a superficial examination. He was an impressive figurehead, but in other respects may fairly be regarded as a highly placed statesman saddled with a post for which he felt no personal inclination. As de Grunwald comments: '. . . le goût personnel d'Orlov le porte vers la diplomatie: il se sent beaucoup plus à l'aise devant les dignitaires de la Haute Porte, à la Cour d'Autriche et au couronnement de la Reine Victoria, que parmi ces policiers qu'il dirige avec une paresse nonchalante et qu'il méprise au fond de son cœur'.[3]

A. A. Sagtynsky

Very little is known of the few officials who staffed the Third Department under Benckendorff and Orlov. No complete list of these officials giving names and appointments has been published. The names of von Vock and Dubbelt were mentioned in ukazes issued in 1826 and 1839 respectively, but both cases were exceptional. Even the ukaz of 1829 which put the total staff of the Department at twenty persons[4] did not state who were the several 'Ekspeditors', Senior and Junior Assistants and so on. However, there was a departure from this practice of anonymity in 1841; and various contemporary and

---

[1] Grech, pp. 587–8. He stresses the contrast between the Emperors Alexander and Nicholas in their approach to petitioners. 'I shall say directly and from my heart: both he [Nikolai Pavlovich] and all his internal administration was better than Alexander's. Alexander was alien and inaccessible to his people; he made gestures and flirted but did not get on with the job: I have in mind his final years. . . You visit some minister, demand if not justice at least an explanation, an answer. No answers were given: shoulders were shrugged. All you got was "Go and see Count Aleksei Andreyevich [Arakcheyev]". And he was as inaccessible as a Chinese mandarin. Under Nicholas people sometimes acted harshly, but quickly and decisively. In the case of a denunciation, blunder or misunderstanding, you go to von Vock or to Dubbelt or direct to Benckendorff and Orlov, you explain the case, justify yourself or receive a reprimand and there it ends.'

[2] Trotsky, p. 120.

[3] De Grunwald, p. 188.   [4] See chapter Two, p. 60, note 3.

later accounts have included passing references to three officials who served in the Department at this period, Sagtynsky, Popov and Pozen.

In 1841 it was decided to alter the nomenclature of some of the posts in the Department's headquarters administration and also to increase its establishment to a total of twenty-eight (including the Chief Director). The Senate ukaz announcing these changes[1] created the new title of 'Official for Special Commissions' to be held by four persons whose names were stated, as also were those of two minor employees appointed to be 'Junior Officials'. The former were to rank as 'Senior Officials' in the Department's hierarchy.[2]

Actual State Councillor A. A. Sagtynsky was thus officially taken on the strength of the Third Department in his new rank in 1841, although it is clear from the text of the ukaz that he must have been working in it during the 1830s and may even have been one of von Vock's original staff. He evidently enjoyed the confidence of Benckendorff. The contents of demi-official letters from the Chief of Gendarmes to Prince Vorontsov show that Sagtynsky acted as the former's courier and was sent on various missions inside Russia. For example, in 1839 he was instructed to draw up a report on the situation in Kiev and also to interview the Minister of Finance in connexion with the peculations of certain minor officials; in 1841 he was sent to investigate the situation in Bessarabia and consult with Vorontsov, without whose approval he was to take no action.[3] By December 1840 he was probably the senior official of the Department after Dubbelt, and in this capacity received Herzen when the latter was 'invited' to its office. 'Behind a large table sat all by himself a thin grey-haired old man with a sinister face... He

---

[1] Ukaz of 17 Apr. 1841. *Poln. Sobr. Zak.*, 2-oe Sobr., vol. 16 (pt 1), pp. 318–19, no. 14468. Details of the new establishment for some reason twice received the Imperial ratification—on 20 Mar. (*ibid.* p. 200, no. 14380) and on 13 Nov. (pt 2, p. 40, no. 15017). An Appendix to the latter contains a table showing the new titles, official gradings ('razryady'), salaries and allowances of the 28 officials of the Department, pt 2, p. 242.

[2] These four officials had previously been attached to the Department 'on special Imperial orders, over and above the former establishment', Ukaz no. 14468, *loc. cit.*; and were probably mentioned by name on this occasion as officially forming part of the Department's new establishment. Their names were given as Actual State Councillor Sagtynsky, State Councillor Popov, Collegiate Councillor Shveitser and Kammer-Yunker of H.I.M.'s Court Collegiate Assessor Kashintsov. The two Junior Officials also mentioned were College Secretary Golubtsov and Collegiate Registrar Bormotov. Of these, the *RBS* carries only Popov (see p. 174, note 3) and Kashintsov. (N. A. Kashintsov (1799–1870), temporarily attached to the Third Department n 1832 and engaged on the task of 'observing' periodicals published in Moscow. He eventually reached the rank of Actual State Councillor, date unspecified. According to Nifontov, the Third Department archives for 1848 contain numbers of his reports on current conditions, and he is described as being at that time 'a constant agent-informer of the Third Department.' A. S. Nifontov, *Rossiya v 1848 godu* (Moscow, 1949), p. 113, footnote.)

[3] *Arkhiv Kn. Vorontsova*, ed. cit. pp. 378, 379, 386, Letters dated 31 Oct. 1839, no. 168; 30 Jun. 1841, no. 174. (Count M. S. Vorontsov (1782–1856), a personal friend of Benckendorff, had been Gov.-Gen. of New Russia and Viceroy of Bessarabia since 1823. He was appointed Viceroy of the Caucasus in 1844.)

had a star on his breast from which I concluded that he was some kind of spy Corps Commander.'[1] This suggests that Sagtynsky had a long career behind him, and he received Herzen again in the autumn of 1846—'...beside me stood Sagtynsky, who had received me five years before in that same Third Department, even more grey-haired and considerably aged.'[2]

There are grounds for believing that after the dismissal of Mordvinov in 1839 Sagtynsky was the senior civilian official on Benckendorff's staff. He was present at Benckendorff's death-bed when the Count was returning by sea from Kiel and transported his body to Revel for burial at Benckendorff's country estate, after which he returned to the capital to convey to Dubbelt their late Chief's dying wishes.[3]

His subsequent work in the Third Department was not confined to questions of internal security alone. In Benckendorff's lifetime he suggested, on the recommendation of a Third Department agent in Paris, Ya. Tolstoi, that certain French journalists should be paid for articles favourable to Russia; and he is described as 'an official for special commissions on the staff of the Third Department who specialized in political investigations abroad'.[4] It is certain that his connexion with Tolstoi lasted at least until 1848.[5]

Throughout his service he remained unknown to the general public,

[1] Gertsen, *ed. cit.* pp. 235–6. The notes confirm that this old man was A. A. Sagtynsky (no other details given), p. 858; and Dubbelt mentions his name in his interview with Herzen, p. 238. Sagtynsky, in conversation with Herzen, asked him: 'How do you know that among those you talk to there is not on every occasion some scoundrel who asks nothing better than to come round here a minute later with a denunciation?' Herzen says in a footnote: 'I assure you on my word of honour that the honourable old man used the word "scoundrel" ["merzavyets']', p. 236.

[2] *Ibid.* p. 348. (Herzen's comment on leaving Russia is of interest. '...I swore a solemn oath not to return to that city [St Petersburg] of autocracy, of sky-blue, green and other coloured uniforms, of bureaucratic disorder, of servile insolence, of gendarme "poetics", a city where Dubbelt alone is deferential—and anyway he is the director of the Third Department', p. 349.)

[3] Dubel't, 'Pis'ma', Letters dated 15 and 17 Sept. 1844, *R. Star.*, *loc. cit.* pp. 513–14. (D., or the transcriber of his letters, spelled Sagtynsky 'Sakhtynsky'.)

[4] 'Russkaya Kul'tura i Frantsiya', *Literaturnoe Naslyedstvo* (Moscow, 1937), vol. 2. This vol. contains (pp. 563–663) a long article by E. Tarle on Tolstoi's reports to the Third Department covering the period 1836–54. The article includes a reproduction of a memorandum from A. A. Sagtynsky to Benckendorff, p. 583; also Tarle's description of his duties, *ibid.*

Yakov Nikolayevich Tolstoi (died 1867), a private citizen, was employed to refute anti-Russian opinions in the French press, becoming an attaché of the Russian Embassy after 1848. Writing under the pseudonym of J. Yakovlef, he published in Paris in 1844 *La Russie en 1839 révée par M. de Custine ou Lettres écrites de Francfort*. (His work as a 'literary agent' of the Third Department is discussed by Lemke, pp. 105–9.)

Tarle's article shows that all Tolstoi's reports were filed by the 1st Section ('Ekspeditsiya') of the Third Department (which dealt with all cases relating to the Higher Police and collated information on persons under surveillance, see Adrianov, p. 98). It is therefore possible that before 1841 Sagtynsky was its 'Ekspeditor', i.e. Head of Section.

[5] Tolstoi, 'knowing Orlov's taste for gossip', corresponded with him directly; but also continued to write to Sagtynsky, addressing him in 1848 as 'Dear and precious friend' and signing himself 'Your lifelong friend, devoted to the grave, Ya. Tolstoi', Tarle, *loc. cit.* pp. 613–14.

although he was present at the interrogation of suspects by Dubbelt or Orlov at the Third Department headquarters. The young Lieutenant Zhedyonov recorded that at his cross-examination in 1848 there was also present 'a secret police head, a civilian general with two stars',[1] whom he identified as de Sanglen! He was not aware of this 'general's' true identity, but it is permissible to assume that the man in question was Sagtynsky, who was definitely present at the interrogation of Selivanov in 1850.[2]

The few existing references to Sagtynsky give some measure of the relative obscurity in which the personalities and careers of even the higher officials of the Department were shrouded. Few of their contemporaries knew anything of them.

M. M. Popov

M. M. Popov,[3] however, is something of an exception to this rule and became well-known in certain circles thanks to his personal interest in literature and his connexion with Belinsky. Like de Sanglen he began his career as a teacher. After graduating from Kazan' University in 1821 he taught Natural Science and Literature in the Penza Gymnasium where he had received his early education; and it was at this university that he became a friend of Belinsky. He joined the Third Department in the beginning of the 1830s[4] and by 1837 was acting as Dubbelt's assistant on questions concerned with censorship.[5] In the Department he was first a Senior Official and then (in 1841) an Official for Special Commissions. In 1840 he was given the rank of State Councillor, in 1845 that of Actual State Councillor and in 1858 that of Privy Councillor. He continued to work in the Third Department under Prince Dolgorukov until his retirement in 1865, and died in St Petersburg in 1871 or 1872, blind.

If his exact functions during his long service cannot be stated with any accuracy,[6] it is at least noteworthy that favourable recollections of him were

---

[1] Zhedyonov, *loc. cit.* p. 298. This, as the editor points out, was clearly a wrong identification as de Sanglen was never employed in or by the Third Department; but even he does not appear to have known who this 'civilian general' was.

[2] Selivanov, *loc. cit.* p. 313. 'I have said nothing of the gentleman who was with Count Orlov in the room where I was told of their decision. He was a Pole, I think, Sykhtinsky [*sic*].' This opinion of Sagtynsky's origin is not confirmed elsewhere.

[3] Mikhail Maksimovich Popov (died 1871), *RBS*; see also *Br. Efr. Enc.* vol. 24, p. 564; Editorial Note, *R. Star.* (1882), vol. 36, p. 435. The two last-mentioned put his death at 1872.

[4] It is possible that he was recruited even earlier. A 'Secretary Popov' is referred to in a letter from von Vock to Benckendorff in 1826, *R. Star.* (1881), vol. 32, p. 169, Letter dated 17 Jul. 1826. The index of this vol. identifies this Popov with M.M.P., but the *RBS* does not confirm.

[5] Bychkov, *R. Star.* (1903), *loc. cit.* pp. 596, 598.

[6] 'As regards his activities in this position [i.e. in the Third Department] no information has been preserved in the memoirs of his contemporaries; it is known only that Belinsky did not break off his relationship with him in St Petersburg either and he maintained it right up to his death', *RBS.*

retained by those who had contacts with him or knew of him. 'Generally speaking, Popov was comparatively kindly and obliging, especially to writers and journalists';[1] 'Popov combined a wealth of knowledge with a kindly heart.'[2] He was referred to by Zhedyonov as 'the noblest kindest soul';[3] and this was evidently also the opinion of the Gendarme General Kutsinsky, who conducted Selivanov to St Petersburg from his estate at Penza. Selivanov was told not to be afraid, as his case was in Popov's hands and that he was 'not only a man of high honour, but even a holy man.'[4] Even Dubbelt's arbitrary handling of this case[5] did not alter Selivanov's belief that Kutsinsky had told the truth, for Popov on this occasion took it upon himself to throw into the fire some of the answers Selivanov had written to a questionnaire. 'His treatment of me shows how much honesty and, I would say, even self-sacrifice there was in this man, if he determined to destroy questions which were probably composed by Dubbelt himself.'[6] It is difficult not to feel that Popov's character was a singular one. He was clearly afraid of the redoubtable Dubbelt, yet was unwilling not to try and help where he could. Possibly he felt some natural distaste for the duties that came his way, which would explain why, in an age that tended to persecute literature, writers themselves had cause in this instance to be grateful to one of their persecutors.

The style in which Popov wrote to Belinsky just before the latter's death provides a good example of the manner adopted by the Third Department towards men of letters. His first note dated the 20th of February 1848 read: 'Leontii Vasil'evich Dubbelt would like to make your acquaintance and asks you, dear Vissarion Grigor'evich, to call upon him between 12 and 2 on a day convenient to you...It is the more pleasant for me to fulfil my superior's instructions that in so doing I too shall have the pleasure of seeing you.' Belinsky, however, was distressed by this invitation, despite its courteous language, and on the 27th of March Popov wrote again to reassure him: 'I have heard that my previous note gave you rather a fright, dear Vissarion Grigor'evich. There is no other reason for the invitation than that Leontii

---

[1] Editorial Note, *R. Star.* (1882), vol. 36, p. 435.

[2] Knyaz' N. N. Yengalychev, 'Vissarion Grigor'evich Belinskii', *R. Star.* (1876), vol. 15, p. 50.

[3] Zhedyonov, *loc. cit.* p. 299.

[4] Selivanov, *loc. cit.* p. 306. 'The justice of this was confirmed by experience, as the reader will see later.' Selivanov describes Popov as 'a man no longer young, of small stature, with unusually quiet, simple and extremely good-natured manners and speech', p. 310.

(General Kutsinsky (not carried in the *RBS*) is first described by Selivanov as 'a general of about fifty with an open and noble countenance', p. 303; he later called on Kutsinsky to thank him for his kindness, telling him that the sentence was one of exile to Vyatka—'"Well, thank Heaven", he replied, embracing me, whereupon I noticed that several tears fell on my face. He, a gendarme general, wept that a man almost a stranger to him was being sent only to Vyatka', p. 313. It is interesting that Kutsinsky evidently considered Selivanov's sentence a very mild one, as he kept repeating 'Well, thank God, thank God, that it has ended so happily', p. 314.)

[5] See p. 152, note 2.   [6] Selivanov, p. 310.

Vasil'evich wishes to make your acquaintance. You, as a man of letters, enjoy renown; people often talk of you; it is very natural that the Director of the Third Department and a member of the Censorship Committee should wish to know you personally and even become friends with you. Now, on his instructions, I most humbly ask you whether you will not be good enough to call on him at the Third Department...Believe me that you will be accorded the most kindly and cordial reception...'[1] Belinsky was then too ill to accept these invitations, and it is probable that his fears of the Third Department were not without justification—Dubbelt later regretted his death, saying 'we would have let him rot in a fortress'—but Popov is believed to have written in all sincerity and there is no reason to think that he did not genuinely desire to help his old pupil if necessary.

Popov himself had literary aspirations and wrote a number of articles on literary and political figures of his day—Pushkin, Zhukovsky and many statesmen of Nicholas' reign. But these articles throw no extra light on either the work or the officials of the Third Department.[2]

M. I. Po{en

M. I. Pozen, the official already mentioned as having sometimes drafted reports for Orlov, is entirely unknown. According to Nikitenko, he was dismissed at the end of January 1845, but from what appointment is not stated.[3]

The relative dearth of information on the few senior officials of the Third Department suggests that, from the point of view of their influence on policy and methods, they played a quite insignificant rôle compared with that of Dubbelt and were not responsible for any major decisions during the first thirty years of the Department's existence.[4]

---

[1] 'Priglasheniya v Tret'e Otdelenie V. G. Belinskago v 1848', *R. Star.* (1882), vol. 36, pp. 434–5. (Editorial Note states that the originals of these letters were kept by Belinsky's widow and presented to *R. Star.* by N. Kh. Ketcher.) The information given by the Editor on Popov's character is accepted by the *RBS* and the *Br. Efr. Enc.* (latter has incorrect ref.: vol. 31 should read vol. 36).

[2] These are listed in the *RBS* article. Even one entitled 'K kharakteristike imperatora Nikolaya I i istorii yego tsarstvovaniya', *R. Star.* (1897), vol. 90, pp. 27–54, makes no mention of either Benckendorff, Dubbelt or Orlov.

[3] Nikitenko, vol. 1, p. 357.

[4] This may be judged from the fact that their exact functions and importance are not discussed by either Lemke or Trotsky.

Л. В. Дубельтъ.

5. General L. V. Dubbelt, Chief of Staff of the Corps of Gendarmes, 1835–1856,
and Director of the Third Department, 1839–1856

(Lemke, *Ocherki po Istorii Russkoi Tsenzury i Zhurnalistiki XIX stolyetiya*, p. 398)

facing page 176

КАНЦЕЛЯРИЯ III ОТДЕЛЕНИЯ
Акварель неизвестного художника, 1840-е гг.
Институт литературы Академии наук СССР, Ленинград

6. The Chancellery of the Third Department

('Russkaya Kul'tura i Frantsiya', *Literaturnoe Naslyedstvo*, vol. 2, p. 575)

facing page 177

6

The Organization and Operation of the Higher Police: 1826–1855

When we consider for one moment the prodigious authority of the secret police, the mysterious nature of its proceedings, the proneness of all to whom power is delegated in Russia to oppression and extortion, it is easy to imagine what advantage its agents must take of their peculiar situation, and of the universal terror they inspire.

from the memoirs of an Englishman in Russia in 1844[1]

Supra-legal status

The immense authority exercised by the Higher Police in Nicholas' reign was directly due to the Tsar's unshakable belief in his own infallibility. He convinced himself that his personal intervention in any issue, however trivial, must lead to its satisfactory solution, and it was this conviction which impelled him to allot more authority to his 'Own Chancellery' than he was prepared to accord to any other advisory or executive branch of his administration. Thus the Tsar's private office as 'an extreme development of personal government' became from the year of his accession the central pivot of the whole administrative system, controlling every aspect of the country's life. As Nicholas never had the slightest intention of abrogating any of his power and was reluctant to delegate it even to his most trusted officials, it was inevitable that he should look upon his Chancellery as 'the closest instrument of his personal authority', existing for the chief purpose of implementing all his wishes. Its Departments, therefore, from the constitutional point of view, were 'organs of "extraordinary" government, outside the scope of the activities of the normal system of governmental bodies, having plenary powers of a wider and freer character, since they possessed the support and supreme authority of the autocrat who acted as he thought fit, sometimes legally but sometimes also above the law'.[2]

Convinced of the advantages to Russia of his own benevolent paternalism, Nicholas thought it right that the Third Department should act independently of all other authorities, since the task of its representatives was to carry out his immediate personal instructions. Believing that by virtue of his peculiar status an autocrat could not be subject to any constitutional restrictions, it

[1] Henningsen, vol. 1, p. 206. See chapter Four, p. 127, note 2.
[2] Presnyakov, 'Samoderzhavie Nikolaya I', *loc. cit.* pp. 15, 16.

naturally followed that the principle of autocracy must never be contested. Dubbelt, who was as faithful an imitator of his sovereign as could be found anywhere, expressed this view succinctly when he wrote: 'Russia may be compared to a harlequin's costume, the panels of which are sewn together with a single thread and hold together gloriously and handsomely. This thread is autocracy. Pull it out and the costume will fall to pieces.'[1] All the work of the Third Department was conducted with the express aim of averting this calamity.

The consequence of this policy was that the Higher Police could and did regard itself as exempt from the laws applicable to all other administrative bodies. Its competence extended to any field selected by its senior officials with the approval of Nicholas, and they hence occupied a position of un-rivalled authority. Although no specific ukaz was ever issued to establish the supra-legal powers enjoyed by the Third Department over the administra-tion—the ukaz of 3 July 1826 merely established its right to control security matters and provide the Tsar with information 'on all events without exception'—in practice its authority to act as well as to supervise was generally recognized by contemporary society to be unquestionable. The memoirs of N. M. Kolmakov provide an excellent illustration of this:

In view of the fact [he wrote] that the police could take direct action against any person under investigation, by itself, without interference from any quarter, and that the Law Courts possessed no executive organ—the police, or the executive authority in general, stood in the opinion of society as it were above the Law Courts...The Ministry of Internal Affairs and the Third Department...were believed by contemporaries to be somehow in closer proximity to the Emperor than the Ministry of Justice...these institutions, in disregarding the views of the Ministry of Justice, often permitted themselves to have recourse to various excep-tions from the general conduct of judicial cases. The consequence of this was interference in court cases, and the courts hence represented a somewhat weak instrument for the discharge of justice. Thus both in the general view and in actual fact they were not independent.[2]

Kolmakov, it should be said, did not criticize the Higher Police as an institu-tion, being prepared to admit its sincerity of purpose, but his evidence indi-cates that none of the actions undertaken by this Department was ever sub-ject to investigation by the Courts and that, on the contrary, the Courts

[1] Dubel't, 'Zamyetki', *Golos Minuvshago, loc. cit.* p. 133.
[2] 'Staryi Sud. Ocherki i Vospominaniya N. M. Kolmakova', *R. Star.* (1886), vol. 52, pp. 527, 528. These memoirs were written in 1886, *loc. cit.* p. 544.
   (The author does not comment on the relationship between the Min. of Int. Aff. and the Third Dept., but evidently mentions the former because its Minister controlled the day-to-day work of the *Lower* Police.)

themselves were as much the object of its surveillance as any other official
or unofficial body.

The Third Department..., under the immediate control of General Leontii
Vasil'evich Dubbelt, pursued, according to its way of thinking, what seemed to be
evil and, in its endeavours to do good, in many cases discharged the functions of
the courts without the slightest reservations.

Thus, it defined the degree of guilt of persons involved in cases of a non-political
character, it took their property under its protection, if they owed money it assumed
the normal duties of official administrative bodies and not infrequently investigated
such questions as who had made a fortune and how, who had suffered in the process
and in what way. In a word, the Third Department's sphere of competence in
judicial affairs was extremely extensive.[1]

Researches conducted by later investigators have established that this
sphere of competence in fact embraced not only judicial affairs but affairs
relating to all branches of the administration. Kolmakov's evidence[2] 'is fully
confirmed by an acquaintance with the Third Department's archives. There
was no aspect of Russian life which avoided the control and influence of this
unforgettable institution.'[3]

The consequence of this policy, however, as Kolmakov points out, was
that the Higher Police could not fail to earn the unpopular reputation of a
supra-legal branch empowered to pry into the affairs of everyone.

The aspirations of this Department seemed at first glance, according to the conditions of the day, praiseworthy to a limited number of persons, for they were
intended to protect citizens from all potential and existent evils, but the ways and
means practised in the course of its activities which were not liable to restrictions
imposed by the Law Courts bore heavily upon many well-intentioned persons for
whom laws were not merely an empty sound but a hallowed principle, as indeed

---

[1] *Ibid.* pp. 530–1. Kolmakov states that the Third Department kept a particularly close watch on
the activities of lawyers: 'Rare was the man who did not pay a visit to the Third Department
for explanations with General Leontii Vasil'evich Dubbelt...The slightest complaint on the
part of a client of a lawyer's lack of conscientiousness, whether it was true or false—all this was
a favourite object of Gen. Dubbelt's attention. Some of them underwent exile from the city
and others, afraid of similar penalties, sought protection for themselves by enrolling in the
service of the Department both for their own advantage and for the sake of the appearances.'
Ibid. p. 534.

[2] Kolmakov quotes actual instances of the Third Department's interference in judicial matters,
pp. 531, 533–4.

[3] Lemke, *Nikolayevskie Zhandarmy, op. cit.* p. 16. (In quoting Kolmakov's memoirs L. refers to
their inclusion in *R. Star.* (1881), IX (i.e. Sept.), p. 190. This is in fact an incorrect reference,
since it refers to one of von Vock's letters to Benckendorff (6 Aug. 1826) and has no connexion
with Kolmakov or his evidence. De Grunwald also quotes 'N. Kalmakov' [*sic*] (p. 185), but
in doing so has evidently copied L.'s incorrect reference without checking it; he gives it as
R. Star. (1881), *vol.* IX. Vol. 9 of *R. Star.* was published in 1874.)

they should have been. These ways and means were of an oppressive character, sometimes marked by personal arbitrariness, and incurred just complaint.[1]

The status of the Higher Police was thus anomalous. Created for the purpose of preserving the sanctity of the laws, it could obstruct or disregard their operation with the authority of the Tsar. Anomalies caused Nicholas no anxiety:[2] throughout his reign he was convinced that all decisions were legal provided that he had pronounced them and he believed that these decisions therefore required no further justification. It followed that since the Third Department formed part of his own Chancellery, its actions could not be questioned by anyone but himself. There can be no doubt that Nicholas never intended that restrictions of any kind should be placed on the work of this favoured branch. This may be judged from his reaction to a report submitted by the Head of the Third Department in 1838 on the subject of certain abuses in the Department of Communications. Benckendorff reported that its Director, General-in-Waiting Count Tol', was not disposed to accept warnings and observations with the same goodwill as other Ministers accepted them. Nicholas' comment on this read: 'All ministers are *obliged* to accept information emanating from you; their goodwill is therefore quite unnecessary.'[3] There is no reason to suppose that this was not his attitude from 1826 onwards. The 'Jubilee Report' remarks with some justice that 'the imperial will' thus expressed 'considerably facilitated the activities of the Department aimed at exposing the abuses of administrative organizations and officials, since it permitted it to act openly and in cases of necessity insistently'.[4]

It may thus be seen that the Third Department and the Corps of Gendarmes exercised an influence with which no other 'ordinary' government body could hope to compete.[5] Those who served in this special Higher Police

---

[1] Kolmakov, *ibid.* p. 532.

[2] In Oct. 1827, in answer to a query concerning the punishment of two delinquents, Nicholas replied: 'The guilty persons should be driven twelve times through a file of 1,000 men. Thank God we have had no instances of the death penalty in this country and it is not for me to introduce it', *R. Star.* (1883), vol. 40, p. 660. He evidently imagined that it was possible to survive so savage a punishment, although cases of such survival were very rare, and on this occasion 'a report of their death was not slow in arriving', see Lemke, p. 4. The same lack of consistency is discernible in the words he addressed to deputies of the St Petersburg nobility in Mar. 1848 —'Gentlemen! I have no police, I dislike it: you are my police', *R. Star.* (1883), vol. 39, p. 595 —at a time when the activities of the Higher Police had become more and more repressive.

[3] Adrianov, p. 100. (It is probable that Adrianov was quoting here from the 'Jubilee Report' of 1876, Bogucharsky, *Vyestnik Yevropy, op. cit.* p. 97); see also Lemke, p. 15.

[4] Bogucharsky, *loc. cit.* pp. 97–8.

[5] 'From the point of view of state law—these [the Depts. of Nicholas' Chancellery] were organs of "extra-ordinary" government, outside the scope of the activities of the normal system of governmental establishment, having plenary powers of a wider and freer character, since they possessed the support and supreme authority of the autocrat who acted as he thought fit,

were aware that they possessed unequalled authority and were expected to use it. So long as they also possessed the confidence of their superiors, they could legally and supra-legally insist on the immediate fulfilment of their demands by any of Nicholas' subjects within the Russian Empire.

Increase of authority and staff

This immense power conferred on the Third Department in the summer of 1826 tended to increase with the expansion of the Corps of Gendarmes between 1827 and 1837. Relatively few ukazes directly relating to the Higher Police were published during the reign but from these may be traced the steady acquisition of more and more authority. For example, although by the new 1826 Regulations (published less than a month before the creation of the Third Department) the Minister of Public Education was made responsible for Censorship,[1] it was not long before the Higher Police began to encroach upon that Minister's prerogatives. Early in 1828 the Censorship Regulations were modified and although the Minister's consent was still required before any works of drama could be printed, they could not be performed without the sanction of the Third Department.[2] In February of the following year the Minister of Internal Affairs instructed Civil Governors that in future all reports on special events in the provinces must be sent to the Third Department instead of to him;[3] and in March Civil Governors were informed by Benckendorff that no foreign passports could be issued to Poles without his knowledge.[4]

The extent to which the Higher Police assumed precedence over the Ministry of Internal Affairs may be judged from a further order from Benckendorff to its Minister by which the latter was instructed to arrange for 'one copy of all journals and other publications issued in Russia to be presented to the Third Department',[5] and it is also clear from this order that by the end of 1829 the Third Department was acquiring more and more control over Censorship matters.

Nevertheless, despite its immense authority, its 'officials' evidently en-

---

sometimes legally but sometimes also above the law. Of all these "departments", in accordance with the whole spirit of a protective and suspicious epoch, the Third was especially important', Presnyakov, p. 16.

[1] Ukaz of 10 Jun. 1826. *Poln. Sobr. Zak.*, 2-oe Sobr., vol. 1, p. 551, no. 403. This ukaz embodied the so-called 'Iron-clad Regulations' ('Chugunnyi Ustav') which sought to impose strict control on the expression of public opinion.

[2] Ukaz of 22 Apr. 1828, *ibid.* vol. 3, p. 463, no. 1979.

[3] Ukaz of 28 Feb. 1829, *ibid.* vol. 4, pp. 132–3, no. 2701.

[4] Ukaz of 1 Mar. 1829, *ibid.* p. 136, no. 2705.

[5] Ukaz of 25 Sept. 1829, *ibid.* p. 682, no. 3192. (The provisions of this ukaz were later repeated to Civil Governors by the Acting Minister of Internal Affairs, see Ukaz of 25 Mar. 1831, *ibid.* vol. 6, p. 266, no. 4451.)

countered much dilatoriness on the part of the administration in fulfilling its various instructions and in 1831 Benckendorff arranged through the Acting Minister of Justice that an ukaz be passed by the Senate 'for the instant satisfaction of the demands of officials entrusted with the conduct of investigations authorized by Imperial orders and the edicts of the Third Department of His Majesty's Own Chancellery'.[1] By these ukazes the Higher Police consolidated its control over the internal life of the country, and, with the exception of one further ukaz in 1834 ordering that information on all 'lower ranks' appointed to government educational establishments be forwarded to the Third Department,[2] this control was evidently considered sufficient to enable it to operate satisfactorily for the remainder of the reign.

In 1829 the Headquarters staff of the Third Department was fixed at a total of twenty persons, excluding its Head and its Director of Chancellery.[3] (Revised regulations governing the civil uniform of officials in all the Departments of the Emperor's Chancellery—dark-green with sky-blue collar and cuffs—were issued in 1834[4].) The staff of the Third Department remained at this figure until a new establishment was published in 1841[5] when the new rank of 'Officials for Special Commissions' was instituted.[6] In this

[1] Ukaz of 24 Mar. 1831, *ibid.* vol. 6, pp. 265–6, no. 4450.
[2] Ukaz of 16 Jan. 1834, *ibid.* vol. 9 (pt 1), p. 43, no. 6719.
[3] Ukaz of 29 Dec. 1829, *ibid.* vol. 4, p. 964, no. 3389. The 'Prilozhenie' to this ukaz (*ibid.* p. 63) sets out the official titles and salaries of this staff, which was organized under 4 'Ekspeditors', i.e. Heads of Sections, with 4 Senior and 6 Junior Assistants. It also included a Censor of Theatrical Productions and his Assistant; and 4 junior office clerks. The annual budget for this staff was 53,000 roubles, of which 18,000 were allotted for office expenses, accommodation, heating, lighting and watchmen. (The salaries of the Head of Dept. and the Director of Chancellery were not given.)
[4] Ukaz of 27 Feb. 1834, *ibid.* vol. 9 (pt 1), p. 173, para. 59, no. 6860. (It may be seen from the 'Shtaty i Tabeli' to this Ukaz, *ibid.* (pt 2), p. 26, that, according to the official 'categories'— 'razryady'—of civil servants in the Administration, Heads of Departments of H.I.M. Own Chancellery occupied a relatively junior position. There were ten 'categories' in all: the 1st included the President of the State Council and Ambassadors; the 2nd included Ministers and Members of the State Council; the 3rd included Senators and State-Secretaries. Heads of Depts. of H.I.M. Own Chancellery were included only in the 4th 'category' unless they already held the rank of State-Secretaries. But it is clear that the Head of the Third Dept., by virtue of his peculiar status, must in fact have exercised more influence than many Senators and Ministers.)
[5] Ukazes of 20 Mar., 13 Nov. 1841, *ibid.* vol. 16 (pt 1), p. 200; (pt 2), p. 40, nos. 14380, 15017. The 'Prilozhenie' to the latter, *ibid.* p. 242, gives the new official titles, 'categories' and salaries of the Third Department staff. It then consisted of 1 Director, 4 Senior Officials, 4 Assistant Senior Officials, 9 Junior Officials, 1 Censor of Theatrical Productions and his Assistant, 3 Junior office clerks and 4 'Officials for Special Commissions' (ranking as Senior Officials). No salary was given for the Director. Currency reform having occurred, the annual budget is quoted at 35,245 roubles, of which 5,200 were allotted for expenses as above.
According to the 'Jubilee Report' of 1876 this budget 'over the course of something over thirty years remained almost unchanged between 40 and 43 thousand roubles', Bogucharsky, *loc. cit.* p. 118.
[6] Ukaz of 17 Apr. 1841, *ibid.* vol. 16 (pt 1) p. 318, no. 14468. (See also chapter Five, p. 172, notes 1, 2).

year the total number of officials was fixed at twenty-eight, including its Chief Director (Benckendorff) and Director (Dubbelt), who had assumed these revised titles in 1839.[1] In 1842 the number of Sections inside the Department (four)[2] was increased to five, the new Section consisting of three officials—the Censor of Theatrical Productions, his Assistant and a new Junior Official.[3] After this date no further ukazes on the total establishment of the Department were issued until the following reign.[4] It is known, however, that three more officials were appointed in 1849 for the maintenance of the archives and a further six in 1850; by 1855 the number of officials employed on its Headquarters staff had risen to forty.[5]

Location of headquarters

The Headquarters building itself was permanently situated in St Petersburg. It seems to have had no premises of its own until the summer of 1831, when notices appeared in the press of accommodation available in the house of one Shal' on the Moika Canal 'with convenient annexes, yards and a handsome newly-cultivated garden'. 'Shortly afterwards there appeared at the gates of the house the dashing figures of gendarmes in heavy helmets', and it was to this address that Benckendorff came every morning from his house on Malaya Morskaya Street (now No. 18).[6] Dubbelt lived in the house owned by Madame Annenkova on Teatral'naya Square from the beginning of the 1830s and suspects were sometimes not only taken to this address for cross-examination by him but were even detained there for brief periods. (The writer Polevoi, for example, was questioned at this house.[7]) The Headquarters of the Third Department remained on the Moika for a few years only and were then transferred to a building on the Fontanka Canal beside the Tsepnoi Bridge. Herzen was conducted there in 1840 and refers to 'the house previously occupied by Kochubei; it was there, in an annexe, that the secular inquisition created by Nicholas was located.'[8] From the 1840s onwards this building housed 'the Central Office for Espionage', as Herzen called it,[9] and from here the Department acquired its ironical reputation of being 'famous for its

[1] See chapter Three, p. 98.
[2] Adrianov, p. 98.
[3] Ukaz of 23 Oct. 1842, ibid. vol. 17 (pt 2), p. 42, no. 16116. (Details of the 'categories' and salaries of these three officials are given in the 'Shtaty i Tabeli' to this Ukaz, ibid. p. 178.)
[4] In 1862 (see Ukaz no. 38600).
[5] Adrianov, pp. 98–9.
[6] A. Yatsevich, Pushkinskii Peterburg (Leningrad, 1931), pp. 163, 166.
[7] Ibid. p. 62. Dubbelt lived at this address until the beginning of the 1840s, when he acquired a house of his own on Zakhar'evskaya Street, ibid.
[8] Gertsen, ed. cit. p. 235; for date, see Notes, ibid. p. 858.
[9] Yatsevich, p. 166.

righteous judgement'.[1] Shal''s small house on the Moika retained its connexion with the Department when Count Orlov purchased it for his own use, even preferring it to the vast mansion he already possessed on the Lityeinyi Prospekt, and all those arrested on suspicion of complicity in the 'Petrashevsky Affair' were taken to the Moika address for questioning.[2] It is thus evident that both Dubbelt and Orlov used their private residences as well as the Department's headquarters for the conduct of official cross-examinations, although their staff normally worked only at the latter.

This staff possessed two main sources of information—the regular reports submitted by uniformed officers of the Corps of Gendarmes deployed throughout the empire and acting, as it were, as the plenipotentiary executive branch of the Higher Police organization; and the more secret *ad hoc* investigations, observations, rumours and denunciations which were supplied by countless amateur and professional agents.

Functions of provincial staff-officers

The Corps of Gendarmes was never intended to represent anything but a para-military body of staff-officers acting in many respects openly. As one of the tasks allotted them was the acquisition of information on any topics of potential interest to the government, they were naturally bound to make use of all available sources including secret agents; but they did not themselves belong to this category. Their object was not primarily that of spying on their fellow-men, but of assisting both the administration and the private citizen to live and work in safety; and it was intended that they should be available and accessible to all grades of society. In the case of public disturbances or official malpractices of any kind, they were empowered to take such action as they considered appropriate in the knowledge that they could disregard the possible opposition of any local authorities. The poor state of communications and the immense distances between the capital and some of the provinces thus meant that members of the Corps enjoyed unparalleled authority in their posts.

A contributor to *Russkaya Starina* at the end of the century correctly states that '...provincial gendarme officers with their completely independent status...possessed special privileges and powers which were long supported by the Chief of Gendarmes, Count Benckendorff...These officers, despite their insignificant rank of Major and even Captain, were held in extreme fear by Governors because a diary kept by Gendarmes, filled with

---

[1] From the satirical poem 'Popov's Dream' written by Count A. K. Tolstoi in 1874. A 'meticulously checked text' of the original may be found in *R. Star.* (1882), vol. 36, p. 703.

[2] Yatsevich, *ibid.*

events occurring in the province, not excluding domestic details, did not spare either them or provincial Marshals of Nobility or even the higher clergy, and, when periodically brought to the attention of Benckendorff, influenced the fate of everyone.'[1] In support of this statement this contributor tells the story of a Gendarme officer, 'Sh.' [sic], stationed at Saratov in 1830. It is based on the officer's unpublished diary and the evidence of a Gendarme Major Greben'kov who had served as a senior N.C.O. at the time of the events described.[2] The article contains a detailed account of the Governor's libidinous improprieties as a result of which one of their victims appealed to 'Sh.' for his protection, which was successfully afforded her.[3] Subsequent events, in particular an epidemic of cholera, proved the efficiency and popularity of the Gendarme officer, but also provided the Governor with an opportunity of getting rid of his enemy by poisoning him.[4] The Gendarme's reports, however, reached Benckendorff, the Governor was relieved of his duties and a senior gendarme officer was sent to take charge of documents in the possession of the dead man's widow, who was granted a full pension by the Emperor with free education for her children.[5] This incident proves that a gendarme officer might in the pursuance of his duty find his life jeopardized by senior officials fearing exposure.

[1] V. A. Shompulev, 'Iz Dnyevnika Zhandarma 30-kh godov', *R. Star.* (1897), vol. 90, pp. 261–9.

[2] The author refers to the Governor as 'Governor "G."' (appointed to Saratov at the end of the 1820s, p. 261), to the Gendarme officer as 'Sh.' ('a forty-year-old giant' of Hungarian origin 'who bore with dignity the sky-blue uniform', p. 265); and states that Major Greben'kov 'in his turn served as a Gendarme "nachal'nik" at the end of the 1840s in one of the provinces nearest to St Petersburg', p. 269.

I have been unable to trace either 'Sh.' or Greben'kov.

[3] *Ibid.* pp. 263–5. Two reports on the Governor's behaviour were sent by 'Sh.' to Benckendorff on 9 Mar. 1830, p. 265.

[4] 'Sh.' contracted cholera on 7 Aug. but recovered from it. While still weak he was treated by 'Doctor L.' sent by the Governor. '. . . convulsions and terrible stomach pains clearly indicated poisoning. Two Gendarme N.C.O.s who were devoted to him and were continuously present at his bedside were so struck by the unexpected death of their beloved officer that they could find no other explanation for it but poisoning', p. 267. The Governor then attempted to procure the arrest of these N.C.O.s, p. 268.

[5] *Ibid.* pp. 268–9. The senior officer's name is given as 'Gendarme General Maslov'. He was evidently the Lt.-Col. Maslov mentioned in the Supplement to the 1828 Report as having 'assisted the discovery of widespread malpractices in the Province of Saratov' and the Col. Maslov mentioned in that of 1830 as having been 'appointed Director of the 5th District' (which then included Saratov) in that year, see Appendix E, pp. 252, 254.

Among the documents 'of special interest' referred to here were 'forms with Benckendorff's signature which authorized Gendarme "nachal'niki" in certain circumstances to dispatch various persons to Benckendorff in St Petersburg by Imperial Order. This was done only a few years after the Decembrist revolt, especially in cases concerning the Province of Saratov, in view of the presence there of the families of two of the leading Decembrists and the exile to Siberia of several of the less important Guards officers belonging to this province', *ibid.*

Memoirs of Colonel Stogov and Major Lomachevsky

The memoirs of Gendarme Colonel Stogov show that the removal of a Governor through the agency of confidential reports to Benckendorff was no unusual occurrence. Stogov was appointed to Simbirsk in January 1834 and quickly became convinced that the Governor, 'Z.', was both ignorant and lazy. 'I had written a detailed report to the Chief about everything that had happened, and lo and behold in three weeks' time came an ukaz announcing the dismissal of Governor Z. and an imperial order that "in future he is not to be appointed anywhere". My credit rose in Simbirsk...'[1] The new Governor, Zhirkyevich,[2] was appointed in March 1834. Although both polite and scrupulous, he was not well received by Simbirsk society and eventually quarrelled with its Marshal of Nobility.[3] Stogov therefore felt himself again compelled to take action: 'On very many occasions I wrote to the Chief that Zhirkyevich was a phenomenon among governors, but in Simbirsk he was out of place. I wrote that Zhirkyevich was capable of governing three provinces, I defended his noble honesty, tireless energy, but as Governor he was completely unloved by the nobility, which was capable of respecting a Governor only when he stood at the head of society and shared their pleasures. Zhirkyevich was removed.'[4]

[1] 'Zapiski Stogova', p. 327.

[2] I. S. Zhirkyevich (1789–1848), appointed Governor after a successful military career. In his memoirs he tells how Nicholas said to him: 'I suppose you know the circumstances in which I have considered it necessary to replace Governor Zagryazhsky in Simbirsk...[he] did not know how to maintain his rank as he should have done.' 'Zapiski I. S. Zhirkyevicha', *R. Star.* (1878), vol. 22, p. 417.

Zhirkyevich was also received before leaving the capital by Benckendorff and the Head of the 1st Gendarme District, Polozov. Benckendorff was very friendly and said to Zhirkyevich: 'I have two requests to make of you; I now have two of my staff-officers there whom I ask you to take under your protection; and also that you should be in direct contact with me concerning anything out of the ordinary and any misunderstandings which may occur...', *ibid.* p. 420. (These two officers were Major Stogov and Lt.-Col. Flige—the latter on temporary attachment on cases relating to state peasants, *ibid.* vol. 23, p. 37.)

(Maj.-Gen. Daniil Petrovich Polozov (1794–1850), after distinguished service in the Artillery, retired from the Army in 1831 as G.O.C. the 2nd Artillery Division and six months later joined the Corps of Gendarmes on Benckendorff's staff. In 1833 he succeeded Lt.-Gen. Balabin (see chapter Three, p. 82, note 1; p. 83, note 1) as G.O.C. the 1st Gendarme District. He was promoted Lt.-Gen. in 1837. (See *RBS.*) His name is mentioned in the Supplement to the 1832 Report and he was still G.O.C. the 1st G.D. in 1843. Baron Korff described him as 'an honest and most noble man', *R. Star.* (1899), vol. 100, p. 54.)

[3] Stogov describes this incident, which occurred in public, in the following words: 'I see that Zhirkyevich has grown very angry, trouble will break out in a big way, people are standing close all round; I decided to enter upon my rights and, not looking at either of them, I said: "Your Excellencies, Mr Governor and Mr Marshal of Nobility! On the basis of secret instructions ratified by the Emperor, I request you to cease a conversation which humiliates the chief authorities of the district; here is not the place for it, the public surrounds you!" Both my friends held their tongues...', *loc. cit.* p. 330.

[4] *Ibid.*

It is clear that the successful operation of gendarme activities depended to a large degree on the personal authority and character of individual staff-officers. Their work could only achieve the desired results with the co-operation of local officials, as Stogov realized when first appointed staff-officer in the Corps. 'In Simbirsk I was the Emperor's confidential agent; on my tact depended my strength, that is, public confidence and respect, without it I was an empty doll, a marionette.'[1]

It hence became necessary to select for gendarme service only such men as possessed the required force of character, and the 1830s were the period when 'extremely cultured, shrewd and well-educated officers were recruited into the Corps of Gendarmes: they were the Tsar's eye who kept watch over provincial administrative officials and investigated all kinds of abuses...'[2] As a consequence, society as a whole was reasonably well disposed towards at least some members of the Corps during the early years of its existence. Herzen (who, as Trotsky points out,[3] cannot be accused of any particular sympathy for this category of persons) wrote in his memoirs: 'The majority of them were quite kindly individuals, were not spies at all, but persons who were enrolled purely by chance in the ranks of the gendarmes. Young noblemen who had learned little or nothing, had no personal fortune and did not know where to lay their head were gendarmes because they found nothing else to do. They performed their duties with all military accuracy...'[4]

Provincial gendarme staff-officers, however, found themselves in a somewhat invidious position, as the nature of these duties was inevitably resented. Stogov, who had had no previous experience of gendarme work, describes the situation on his arrival at his post in the following words: 'Confidence in and respect for the gendarme uniform had been destroyed. My predecessor was Colonel Maslov, a man typical of the old type of policeman. He had wanted to be a detective, he had thought it admirable to rummage about in dirty trifles and show off his knowledge of family secrets. He looked for

---

[1] *Ibid.* p. 314.

[2] Introduction by Edit. of *R. Star.*, M. I. Semyevsky, to article 'Erazm Ivanovich Stogov. Yego posmertnye zapiski', *R. Star.* (1886), vol. 52, p. 77. He comments: '... subsequently the Corps of Gendarmes earned a somewhat different character', *ibid.*

(These 'zapiski' are not relevant to Stogov's service in the Corps and deal only with his childhood and early career in the Navy, 1797–1816. They were contributed to *R. Star.* by his daughter, I. E. Zmunchilla, with an account of his last days. She wrote: 'The main trait of my father's character was unusual strength of will and firmness... The ideal of his whole life was the late Emperor Nicholas I', *loc cit.* p. 125. There is a portrait of Stogov as an old man (he died in 1880) opposite p. 128. [3] Trotsky, p. 136.

[4] Gertsen, *op. cit., ed. cit.* p. 107. He substantiates this statement by quoting a story told him by a gendarme officer of an incident in 1831. In that year the officer in question, then a young man, had been sent with two gendarmes to detain a Polish landowner suspected of rebel connexions. He discovered the suspect hiding on his estate but, moved by the appeals of the latter's wife, reported that he was not to be found, thus enabling the Pole to flee abroad. *Ibid.*

opportunities to fasten on to everyone, he terrified them, made "incidents" out of things, wanted to rule through fear and was repellent to everybody... Thus I appeared before a society prejudiced against the gendarme uniform embodying as it did the character of an informer and an intolerable meddler even into people's private lives.'[1] Stogov does not disguise the fact that he too was obliged to regard much of his work as secret,[2] but he relied on his tact and social sense to secure his entry into local society on better terms. As he says, 'I danced attendance on influential old ladies and played boston with them...from the very first evening they started saying that I was a very nice person, albeit in a sky-blue uniform...'[3] Stogov's main source of information on local conditions was the officer who commanded the Gendarme Detachment;[4] and he makes no mention of ever having employed civilian secret agents. It is permissible to assume that sufficient news reached his ears without the need to organize such aids. Once furnished with the necessary information, Stogov took direct action without recourse to any authority but his own: 'I knew everything that went on in Simbirsk but no one knew that I knew it and therefore I was received cordially. Officials were caught out accepting bribes, taking them first from this quarter, then from that...I never made trouble, I would summon the man to my office, 'wash his head for him', put the fear of God into him and order him to return the money to the offended person.'[5]

Like every gendarme staff-officer, Stogov knew that he had authority to act as the personal representative of the Tsar and that he could therefore issue orders to anyone, no matter how highly placed. When, in the quarrel that took place between Governor 'Z.' and the Marshal of Nobility, the latter demanded to know what right Stogov had to interfere in other people's affairs, Stogov laughed and replied 'Gendarmes were created for the very purpose of interfering in other people's affairs'; and when asked who it was who gave him this right, he replied 'Secret instructions ratified by the Emperor'.[6] No Russian subject, whether public official or private citizen, could question the right of interference in all matters possessed by members of the

---

[1] 'Zapiski Stogova', *R. Star.* (1903), *loc. cit.* p. 314.

[2] Stogov reproduces in dialogue form his first conversation with Governor 'Z'. '"With what intention have you come here?"—"To contribute to the elevation of Your Excellency's authority"—"What do you require from me?"—"Only personal respect for me and, when I need something to be kept secret, that you should keep it so...I can only be of use when my actions remain secret"', *ibid.* p. 315. In practice the Governor found this impossible and Stogov reported the facts to the Chief of Gendarmes directly, expressing the hope that he would shortly possess grounds for the Governor's dismissal, p. 318.
Ibid. p. 316.
'My O.C. Detachment was Captain Podgorny, he was over sixty and knew all the gossip in Simbirsk; he confided to me all the details of Simbirsk life', *ibid.* Capt. P. is mentioned in the Supplement to the 1832 Report.

[5] *Ibid.* p. 319.   [6] *Ibid.* pp. 323, 324.

Corps of Gendarmes and, being unable to verify what exactly these 'secret instructions' were, he was obliged to comply with any order given by a gendarme.

If a provincial Governor was honest and conscientious, if his relations with the senior Gendarme officer attached to his district were good, then the latter's services could greatly benefit the local administration. The memoirs of Governor Zhirkyevich show that this was true, for example, in the case of Stogov. Shortly after his arrival in Simbirsk he was visited by Stogov (then a Major) who 'gave me in conversation...certain information which indicated the way that I should act in future'; and after an incident involving some mutinous peasants restored to obedience by the mutual efforts of Governor and Gendarme, Zhirkyevich wrote that 'My gratitude in this matter wholly belongs to E. I. Stogov and in that spirit I reported to my authorities'.[1] His memoirs also clearly illustrate what must have been a typical relationship between the two most influential officials in a province. The Vice-Minister for Internal Affairs, Count Stroganov, visited the Governor during 1834 and asked him about the state of his relations with the Gendarmes and whether he was frank with them. Zhirkyevich replied: 'I do not know whether one can and should be frank with gendarmes. They are attached with the purpose of keeping watch on us, let them report what they like about me, I don't worry about it for I've nothing on my conscience.'[2] (This was no exaggeration, for Zhirkyevich's honesty was never impugned.) Stogov was evidently a useful assistant, however, and with the Governor's approval was instrumental in suppressing acts of civil disobedience among the provincial peasantry.[3] Zhirkyevich's behaviour to Stogov was invariably correct and when Nicholas accompanied by Benckendorff visited Simbirsk in 1836, the latter took the Governor by the arm and said: 'I thank you on behalf of my gendarme staff-officer, you have used him properly and this has given me much pleasure.'[4]

Stogov's account of his experiences in his first post[5] is valuable because it reveals the extent to which gendarme staff-officers could control provincial affairs and officials. He reported direct to Benckendorff and does not once mention the General commanding his particular Gendarme district. He was

[1] 'Zapiski Zhirkyevicha', *R. Star.* (1878), vol. 23, pp. 39, 42, 43.
[2] *Ibid.* p. 48.
[3] 'Zapiski Zhirkyevicha', *R. Star.* (1890), vol. 67, pp. 92–4.
[4] *Ibid.* pp. 119–20. (The Editor of *R. Star.* describes Stogov as 'an extremely intelligent and resourceful man', footnote, p. 119.)
[5] He was afterwards appointed in 1840 Head of Chancellery to the Gov.-Gen. of S.W. Russia, D. G. Bibikov, spending fifteen years in Kiev. He wrote of this period: 'I enjoyed great power in three provinces. The Emperor entrusted me personally with cases, by-passing the Governor-General, and always talked graciously to me', 'Zapiski Stogova', *R. Star.* (1878), vol. 23, p. 703; see also *RBS.*

hence in very close contact with the highest authority in the country. But although his powers of 'interference' were thus as great as those of his predecessor, an attempt was evidently made in the 1830s to appoint officers who sought wherever possible to avoid causing unnecessary offence.

This is confirmed by the memoirs of A. I. Lomachevsky, who joined the Corps at the end of 1837 and was appointed to Minsk in 1838.[1] Like Stogov, he records that at the time local society was not well disposed towards gendarme officers,[2] but claims that his own efforts improved this situation. He was chiefly employed on settling misunderstandings of a religious nature that had arisen between the Uniat and the Polish clergy; and evidently achieved some success, one Uniat priest telling him years later (in 1865): 'You were the first person to teach me to respect the sky-blue uniform and not be frightened of it.'[3] Lomachevsky's memoirs also illustrate the unfriendly atmosphere that existed between senior officers of the Corps and the local Governor-General,[4] but tend to show that the former were feared more

[1] A. I. Lomachevsky, 'Zapiski Zhandarma', *Vyestnik Evropy* (1872), Mar., pp. 244–88; Apr., pp. 723–57; May, pp. 296–326.

Asinkrit Ivanovich L. (*c.* 1810–18?) transferred to the Corps of Gendarmes from the regular army and served in it for several years before assuming the post of Director of the Postal Department at Minsk. He contributed articles to *R. Star.* (1874), vols. 9 and 10, on early police service in St Petersburg, but they contain no information on Nicholas' Higher Police. His 'Zapiski', covering the years 1837–43, are mainly concerned with his interpretation of the so-called 'Vil'no Events' of 1840, *loc. cit.* Mar., pp. 242–3 and *RBS*.

(The 'Vil'no Events' described by L. in the Apr. and May instalments concerned a suspected conspiracy or secret society with Polish sympathies allegedly operating in that city. L. finally proved that one member of the Commission investigating this affair had fabricated false evidence and that no conspiracy in fact existed.)

[2] L.'s predecessor, Lt.-Col. Flige, had caused resentment by his 'interference in the affairs of people who ignored him' (*loc. cit.* Mar., p. 246) and L. reports that he himself was 'a stern critic of his colleague's methods' (Apr., p. 729). The Corps of Gendarmes at this period evidently also included some unusually obtuse officers—L. quotes a certain 'Major Va—yev' [*sic*], 'remarkable for his absurd reports', who, 'having made it an unalterable rule to be absolutely frank with his superiors, considered it his hallowed duty to bring to their attention the fact that from a certain date he had taken to wearing a wig' (Mar., p. 246).

This story is quoted by Trotsky (p. 136) to illustrate the blind obedience of gendarme officers to their superiors' desire for information on all topics.

[3] Lomachevsky, *loc. cit.* Mar., p. 253.

[4] L. sums up the situation in his province thus: 'The Prince [Gov.-Gen. N. A. Dolgorukov] was not fond of gendarmes, he disputed the usefulness of their institution and constantly quarrelled with Drebush and his predecessor Dmitrii Semyonovich Yazykov over the information and criticisms they brought him. . .', *loc. cit.* Mar., p. 255. (This Gov.-Gen. was transferred elsewhere in 1840 (*ibid.*), although L. does not state whether this was due to gendarme reports.)

(D. S. Yazykov (1793–1856), after a distinguished military career, joined the Corps as Lt.-Col. in 1827 and was appointed Acting G.O.C. the 4th Gendarme District with HQ at Vil'no in 1832, with the rank of full colonel. In 1835 he was promoted Maj.-Gen. and confirmed as G.O.C. this District. The same year he left the Corps and was appointed Director of the Dept. of External Trade; after this date he held no further gendarme posts, see *RBS* and Supplements to the 1827–9 (Appendix E), 1830, 1831 and 1832 Reports. See p. 192, note 1. A. F. von Drebush (1783–1855) joined the Corps in 1829 as Lt.-Col. after a career in the civil

for what they might do than for what they did. Their reputation in certain circles was possibly worse than deserved and, to judge by the following passage, their methods of obtaining information often had nothing sinister about them.

Then, as now, gendarmes were publicly called a secret police and people were convinced that they had hired agents everywhere.—'Tell me, Asinkrit Ivanovich,' I was once asked, in a moment of frankness, by the provincial Marshal of Nobility Oshtorp, 'how do you know everything that goes on in our province? You undoubtedly have your agents everywhere who give you all the necessary information. It must be so. I should like to know . . . to what category of people your agents belong? Who are they?'—'You really want to know my agents', I replied. 'Allow me to name with great readiness the best of them—you yourself!' 'How can you say so!' replied Oshtorp, almost leaping from his chair. 'Very simply. Knowing you for an honest and well-intentioned person, I do not doubt that all injustice which reaches your ears will disturb you, and you will doubtless not wish . . . to conceal it and say nothing. Hence I listen . . .'[1]

Lomachevsky's account of his service at Minsk and Vil'no suggests that a gendarme officer with initiative could use his influence to good purpose despite a lack of previous experience in local administration.

The more I became acquainted with the principle of my new service, the more convinced I became that if I limited myself merely to the routine execution of the instructions of my authorities, refraining altogether from endlessly investigating the variety of complaints and requests with which people applied to me in person and in writing, then neither the Government nor society would derive much benefit from my services . . .[2]

With which discovery Lomachevsky turned his attention to the 'obvious trifles'[3] which filled much of a conscientious gendarme's life—the securing of a deserved appointment, the prevention of wrongful arrest, the investigation of serf maltreatment and similar cases on which he was required both to report and act.[4]

service and again reverted to a civil appointment in 1831, when he was made Acting Civil Governor of Minsk. He was appointed G.O.C. the 4th G.D. in 1836 and became a Senator in 1839, see *RBS*; he was succeeded as G.O.C. this District by Maj.-Gen. P. I. Freigang (not carried in the *RBS*), see Lomachevsky, Mar., p. 256 and Appendix E, p. 253.)

[1] *Ibid.* Mar., p. 263.
[2] *Ibid.* p. 256.
[3] 'I should too greatly weary the most sympathetic reader if I decided to acquaint him with my everyday occurrences, with these obvious trifles; but who would not agree that our whole life is composed of trifles?', *ibid.* p. 257.
[4] *Ibid.* pp. 257, 258; 260, 272; 264–5.

Gendarme duties

In the absence of other memoirs left by men like Stogov and Lomachevsky, it is permissible to conclude that in addition to the task of collecting items of information on local events, gendarme officers stationed in the provinces did indeed spend much of their time investigating cases of minor importance to the state. This is equally shown by the contents of the only official reports to the Tsar on 'The Activities of the Corps of Gendarmes' that have so far been published.[1] (These reports, covering the early years of the Corps' existence, represent the best available illustration of its comprehensive pursuits.) Supervision of the call-up of recruits, the maintenance of public order on all occasions, the detection and arrest of all kinds of criminals, inspection of local conditions, prevention of official malpractices—these were the tasks on which gendarme officers were chiefly employed, and they were also dispatched on specific missions at the Emperor's behest. But just as frequently their everyday 'cases' concerned the investigation of private individuals suspected of ill-treating their serfs, defrauding their relatives or embezzling property. Officers of the Corps in fact fulfilled many of the functions of the ordinary police officers who constituted the 'Lower Police' subordinated to the Ministry of Internal Affairs,[2] but, as a result of their superior status and their reliance on the direct support of the Chief of Gendarmes, they could exercise far greater influence on local affairs. This was undoubtedly the purpose of the Tsar, who wrote on the report of the Corps' Activities for 1831: 'I express my sincere thanks to Mr Chief of Gendarmes for his tireless labours and for that excellent spirit which he has succeeded in implanting in the officers of this corps; its activities wholly correspond to my intentions.'[3]

[1] They were included as Supplements to the 'Annual Reports' on the internal state of Russia submitted by the Head of the Third Department, see p. 200, note 3. (They covered the years 1827–9, 1830, 1831 and 1832, and a full translation of the first of these supplements is given in Appendix E.) Attached to these Supplements were two further reports, the first dealing with 'The State of Various Military Ranks', i.e. a parade state, and the second detailing 'The Activities of Junior Ranks of the Gendarmes', see edit. footnotes. None of these reports has been published.

[2] Officers of the 'Higher Police' were evidently sometimes transferred to senior posts in the 'Lower Police', cf. the case of Gendarme Major Bazin, who was appointed 'Politseimeister' (i.e. Chief of Police) of Kiev in 1830, see Report for 1830; also that of Gendarme Major Bryanchaninov, O.C. 1st Section of 2nd G.D. (Moscow) in 1830, see B. L. Modzalyevsky, *Pushkin pod Tainym Nadzorom* (SPB, 1922), p. 6, footnote. Bryanchaninov was 'Politseimeister' of Moscow in 1836 in the rank of Colonel, see Lemke, p. 416. It is likely that such transfers were not always permanent; Lt.-Col. Rutkovsky, mentioned in the first Supplement (see Appendix E, p. 252), was appointed 'Politseimeister' in Vil'no in 1831 but was again serving in the Corps of Gendarmes as a full Colonel in 1838, see *RBS*.

[3] *Kr. Arkh.* (1931), no. 46, p. 141, footnote. It continues: 'There is a further note in the handwriting of Col. Dubbelt: "written in H.M.'s own hand. 6 Jan. 1832." (signed) Polkovnik Dubel't.'

7. General Count (later Prince) A. F. Orlov, Second Head of the Third
Department and Chief of Gendarmes, 1844–1856

(Adrianov, *Ministerstvo Vnutrennikh Dyel. Istoricheskii Ocherk*, opposite p. 88)

facing page 192

Cour d'assises de Cronstadt, autrement dit bureau du visa des passeports.

Autre position dans laquelle il faut souvent attendre si l'on trouve le passeport en règle et reconnaître qu'il ne tient qu'à un fil qu'on n'y puisse entrer.

Après cela, il ne resta plus qu'à laisser soigneusement sonder ses opinions

Voyageur nouvellement arrivé en Russie, trouvant, comme M. Custine, qu'à Pétersbourg la surveillance est telle que les murs ont des oreilles.

Noble étranger auquel de hautes protections ont fait obtenir du czar l'extrême faveur de visiter ses musées nationaux.

8. The Higher Police through foreign eyes

(Histoire dramatique, pittoresque et caricaturale de la Sainte-Russie commentée et illustrée par Gustave Doré, p. 141)

facing page 193

Some individual careers

An examination of the careers of certain of the Corps' officers reveals that in every known instance they transferred to it from some branch of the regular armed forces, and Herzen's opinion that men became gendarme officers 'because they had found nothing else to do' seems unduly prejudiced. Higher pay, increased privileges and authority were the chief inducements to enlist in the Corps and satisfactory moral qualities appear to have been the sole necessary qualification.

Although the majority of the Corps' members were Russians, a few officers had names of non-Russian origin. It is even possible that foreign nationals were not automatically excluded from the category of potential recruits. In 1829, for example, Nesselrode wrote to the British Ambassador to ask whether there were any objections on the part of H.M. Government to the enlistment in the Corps of one Richard Huet, a British subject, explaining that 'les autorités militaires ont cru pouvoir déférer au désir du pétitionnaire'. Lord Heytesbury replied that according to English law no special permission was required and that there was nothing whatever to prevent Huet 'entering the Gendarmerie [sic] if the military authorities be willing to receive him'.[1] Whether or not Huet succeeded in doing so, Nesselrode's inquiry shows that there was at least no *prima facie* reason why foreigners should not serve in this as in any other Russian military or para-military organization.

Several senior Gendarme officers subsequently attained positions of some importance in the administration.[2] Their experience of Higher Police work

---

[1] Public Record Office, Series F.O. 181, vol. 71 (Notes from Russian Ministers 1826–34), Letter dated Sept. 1829. The British Ambassador's reply is contained in Vol. 80 of this Series (Notes to Russian Ministers 1829–37), Letter dated 20 Sept. 1829. Nesselrode's letter explains that Huet had submitted two documents, one signed by H.M. Consul-General at Odessa, Bayley, and another from the Richelieu Lycée at Odessa 'où il s'était trouvé placé en qualité de maître de calligraphie'. Lord Heytesbury's dispatches to the Foreign Office do not mention this case and I have been unable to discover whether Richard Huet succeeded in joining the Corps. He is not mentioned among the officers quoted in the published reports on its activities, but possibly he only became a member of its non-commissioned ranks.

[2] Had this not been the case it is unlikely that anything would now be known of their careers. The *RBS* includes few of the officers mentioned in the Supplements (see p. 200, note 3), although this may partly be explained by the fact that certain vols. of the *RBS* did not appear. For example, of the five Generals of the Corps listed in these Appendices—Volkov, Balabin, Lesovsky, Apraksin, Polozov—the *RBS* carries only Lt.-Gen. P. I. Balabin, G.O.C. the 1st Gendarme District, and his successor Lt.-Gen. D. P. Polozov; and only the bare fact of their appointments is recorded, see p. 186, note 2, in addition to the details of their earlier military careers.

There are passing references in Lemke to Lt.-Gen. A. A. Volkov, who was the first G.O.C. the 2nd G.D. from 1827 until his death, insane, in 1833, when he was replaced by Lt.-Gen. Lesovsky who held this appointment until 1836, see pp. 48, 49, 67, 88, 96, 153, 416, 482. Lesovsky was the first senior gendarme officer to be appointed to Poland as Maj.-Gen. in

and the degree of confidence placed in them made them suitable candidates for high civil posts, and it was not unusual for Gendarme Colonels to be appointed Civil Governors after only a few years' service in the Corps. Colonel Perfil'yev, who entered it in 1827 at the age of thirty-one, became Civil Governor of Ryazan' four years later; Colonel Ogaryov became Civil Governor of Arkhangel'sk in 1831 after only two years' service; Colonel Zhemchuzhnikov, after promotion to General in the Polish campaign, was made Civil Governor first of Kostroma and then (in 1834) of St Petersburg.[1] In some cases elevation to a Civil Governorship was permanent, in others it was only temporary, its holder reverting to a Gendarme command after a limited period of office; and it is evident from the career of Colonel Rutkovsky that a Civil Governorship could also be held without any relinquishment of gendarme rank.[2] Some officers with distinguished gendarme service later became Privy Councillors or Senators, and General Timashev, who succeeded Dubbelt in 1856 as Chief of Staff of the Corps, achieved ministerial rank after temporary office as Governor-General and became Minister for Internal Affairs in 1868.[3]

Membership of the Corps could therefore represent a valuable stage in a career of public service because gendarme officers had unrivalled access to all available knowledge relating to the conduct of public (and private) affairs.

1830, see Supplement for that year, although Poland was not officially established as the 3rd G.D. until 1832, see chapter Three, p. 89, note 1. (Herzen mentions both these generals in his memoirs, stating that Volkov had gone mad believing that the Poles wished to offer him the crown of Poland; Volkov's successor, Lesovsky, is described as a Pole, 'a decent, well-disposed man who, having wrecked his fortune on card-playing and a French actress, philosophically preferred the post of a gendarme general in Moscow to a debtor's prison in that city', *Byloye i Dumy*, ed. cit. p. 78.) Maj.-Gen. Count V. S. Apraksin (1796–1833) was orinally a 'fligel'-ad'yutant' in Nicholas' suite in 1830 (see Shil'der, vol. 2, p. 310) and was then attached to the 2nd G.D. in 1831 and 1832, see relevant Supplements.

None of these officers is recorded in the *Br. Efr. Enc.*

[1] S. V. Perfil'yev (1796–1878), I. I. Ogaryov (1780–1854), M. N. Zhemchuzhnikov (1788–1865): see *RBS* and references to their gendarme service in Supplements for 1827–9, 1830 and 1831.

[2] Ogaryov remained a Civil Governor for the rest of his life, transferring from Arkhangel'sk to Perm' in 1837; Perfil'yev served as Civil Governor only until 1836, when he was promoted Maj.-Gen. and posted to the 2nd G.D. which he commanded from that year (see Lemke, p. 416) for the remainder of the reign; K. L. Rutkovsky (17??–1856), a Gendarme Lt.-Col. in 1828, was appointed Civil Governor of Plotsk in 1831 but promoted Col. in the Corps of Gendarmes in 1838. He apparently held both appointments until his retirement in 1847. See *RBS* and Supplements for 1827–9, 1830, 1831 and 1832.

[3] Ogaryov—P.C. 1843; Yazykov—P.C. 1847; Zhemchuzhnikov—P.C. 1840 (Actual P.C. 1858), Senator; von Drebush—Senator; Buksgevden—Senator. (Gen. Count P. F. Buxhoeveden (1790–1863), after retiring from the Army as Col. in 1829, joined the Corps in 1840 as Maj.-Gen. and G.O.C. the 4th G.D. from 1842 to 1850, see *RBS*.)

Gen.-in-Waiting, Gen. of Cav. A. Ye. Timashev (1813–93), after a career in the Army, was Chief of Staff of the Corps from 1856 to 1861, see *Br. Efr. Enc.* (no article in the *RBS*).

The use of secret agents

The reports submitted by Gendarme staff-officers as the 'executive branch' of the Higher Police represented one of the two main sources of information at the disposal of the Third Department. The other was of a more clandestine variety and consisted of countless secret agents whose existence was widely acknowledged or suspected by contemporary society. An English writer describing in general terms the organization of the Higher Police in the 1840s accurately reported that 'Some thousands of avowed officers...of this armed force [the Corps of Gendarmes] are thus exclusively devoted to this service, under the grand-master's orders; but its secret agents, correspondents, and spies, direct and indirect, are supposed to outnumber many score of times those who wear its livery'.[1] No archive material on the recruitment, employment or organization of these secret agents has, however, been published and it is possible that little exists.[2] Trotsky states that even in the following reign the Department possessed only scant information on such prominent figures as Lavrov and Chernyshevsky; and that this was due to the low level of agents employed, relying solely on observation, reports and rumours. 'There existed no "internal system of agents" so valuable later on for keeping records of information received. And no real "secret assistants", that is, provocateurs, existed either. Information provided by "external observation", "reports and rumours", postal interception, evidence discovered by house-searches and "frank disclosures" by an accused person who either repented or was induced to repent by some means or other— these were the sources at the disposal of the Third Department at the beginning of the '6os.'[3]

It is fair to conclude that in Nicholas' reign, when there was relatively little reason to fear the successful emergence of revolutionary theories, the organization of a secret agent system was even less efficient. Volunteer spies, frequently inspired by personal grievances, submitted information which proved to be as much as 90 per cent false and, judging by the number of harmless letters opened by the Higher Police, postal interception often failed to yield results. The constant surveillance kept on suspects was just as unproductive, as is

---

[1] Henningsen, vol. 1, p. 199. A French writer a few years later gave a similar description—'La haute police s'exerce dans l'intérieur de l'empire par un corps de gendarmerie, dont un détachement est affecté à chaque chef-lieu du gouvernement avec un officier d'état-major et un aide de camp; elle emploie en outre un nombre considérable d'agents secrets', L. Léouzon le Duc, *La Russie Contemporaine* (Paris, 1853), p. 388.

[2] 'Unfortunately the scant literature on the history of the secret police is particularly scant where information on its "private" agent system is concerned. We are not therefore able at the present time to give an at all accurate picture of the police surveillance of the day. But on its results alone one can judge that it was conducted in a somewhat primitive manner', Trotsky, p. 50.

[3] *Ibid.* pp. 50–1.

shown by an instance in 1849 when closer investigation fully exonerated the man concerned. (Dubbelt's explanation on this occasion was that the suspect 'seems to be somewhat deranged mentally', which Trotsky claims was a frequent excuse for action by the Higher Police.[1])

There is evidence for believing that no successful organization of political detection existed and that this may have been partly due to the poor state of office records kept by the Department. In his Annual Report for 1828 Benckendorff informed the Tsar that 'in the three years of its existence it has kept a card-index of all persons who in one way or another have risen above the level of the crowd',[2] but as this record has not survived there is no means of assessing its quality. It can hardly have been methodically maintained, for the Department's *Index of Persons*, which is preserved in the Archives, only registered the surnames of persons on whom actual files were kept, so that if inquiries were made about a person on whom no file existed, the Department replied that they had no information on him. It would thus appear that when a member of the Headquarters staff in the capital or a gendarme staff-officer in the provinces required specific knowledge of any suspect, he had to rely either on his own observations or on the chance discoveries of agents employed *ad hoc*. At the same time close attention was paid to voluntarily submitted denunciations, which were encouraged on the grounds that any item of information however trifling might be important. It was this policy which gained the Department its reputation for being ubiquitous although the rumours and gossip thus reported proved worthless in the majority of cases.[3]

The relatively small Headquarters staff was so occupied with the immense task of sifting all the petty information it received that potentially serious subversive activities stood an excellent chance of passing undetected. This in fact occurred in 1848 with the case of the 'Petrashevsky Affair', the only prominent 'conspiracy' of the reign, which, despite the increase of internal espionage at this period, was discovered not by agents of the Third Department at all, but by the Head of the St Petersburg Detective Police, Sinitsyn, who reported it to the Minister of Internal Affairs, Count Perovsky.[4] Ever since its creation the Higher Police had been resented by the officials of this Ministry,[5] who naturally tended to regard it as a professional rival. Perovsky was delighted to have an opportunity to prove to the Tsar that his Ministry had stolen a march on the Third Department and purposely omitted to keep

---

[1] Trotsky, p. 52.   [2] *Kr. Arkh.* (1929), no. 37, p. 162. (See p. 200, n. 3.)

[3] The methods employed by the Third Department in its secret agent system are summarized here from the description given by Trotsky, pp. 51–3.

[4] 'Ocherki i Vospominaniya Knyazya N. S. Golitsyna', *R. Star.* (1890), vol. 68, pp. 376, 378. (Sinitsyn is not recorded in the *RBS*.)

[5] See von Vock's letter to Benckendorff dated 10 Aug. 1826 quoted in chapter Two, pp. 66–7.

Orlov informed of the progress of his investigations. Nicholas eventually summoned Orlov and taunted him with the accusation that his watchdogs had no sense of smell, declaring that 'their noses were bunged up', but Orlov was quick to insist on the right of his Department to participate in the inquiry; and when the suspects were arrested both it and the Ministry of Internal Affairs sent their representatives in the persons of Dubbelt and Liprandi, the Ministry official mainly concerned.[1] The Higher Police could not allow itself to be deprived of a major rôle in any case which it chose to regard as significant.

Constant interference by the Third Department in all kinds of activities must be considered the chief reason not only for its unpopularity but also for its inefficiency. Its officials were overworked not because political subversion was rife throughout the empire but because by Nicholas' wish so many non-political cases engaged their attention. Information on these cases was sought as fervently as if great issues depended on its acquisition, although Trotsky reports that in going through the Archives one is struck by 'the abyss of trivial matters, quite unimportant to the state, which occupied the gendarmes'. They meddled in everything, 'family life, business deals, personal quarrels, inventions, escapes from monasteries—all was of interest to the secret police'.[2] Agents of one kind and another played as great a rôle in the investigation of these cases as did their uniformed colleagues and were probably far more numerous, but there is no published evidence that they drew a regular salary as part of the Department's permanent staff. It is reasonable to assume that all its secret agents, whether voluntary, part-time or professional, were employed to provide the Department with information on specific cases, were given no executive authority, and can be considered to have formed a large section of the Higher Police only in the sense that their work was directed by its senior officials.

The rôle of Nicholas

The quantity of miscellaneous information obtained by the Department both from gendarmes and from agents was submitted to the Tsar for his comments and decisions, and Nicholas devoted much time to it. Presnyakov states that he 'paid close attention to their reports...and personally decided on suitable penalties for offenders, only rarely ordering that this or that person should stand trial. He read these reports carefully, often correcting in pencil the minor slips of the writer, he would investigate details, ordering further surveillance and fresh reports, inquiries in the provinces, memoranda

---

[1] See I. P. Liprandi, 'Zapiski', *R. Star.* (1872), vol. 6, pp. 70–86; Trotsky, pp. 54–8; de Grunwald, p. 264. [2] Trotsky, pp. 110, 111.

on individuals and events from various ministries and departments. In reviewing Third Department cases one feels oneself more in the atmosphere of a large police section than in a supreme government department.'[1] This personal direction of Higher Police business by Nicholas is a characteristic feature of its work; he disliked delegating any of his own authority in this favoured field. 'Almost all the cases of the Third Department were decided by the Emperor, and the gendarmes were far from being able to tell beforehand, on all occasions, how this or that affair would develop...'[2] Indeed, the Archives prove that Nicholas resented the slightest action which in his view usurped his prerogatives. In 1828 a 'complaint' addressed to him personally was opened instead by a Gendarme Lieutenant-Colonel, who was severely reprimanded in consequence.[3] In practice, however, the scope of Third Department activities was normally so voluminous that much of its work had perforce to be left in the hands of its senior officials.

Nicholas was never deterred from doing what he conceived to be his duty by the petty nature of cases concerning the Higher Police. This was especially noticeable when these involved any of his subjects abroad who refused to return to Russia when ordered. To quote an actual instance, in 1830 the eighteen-year-old M. A. Kologrivov, who had been continuing his education in Paris, was reported as having fought on the barricades against the supporters of Charles X. He disobeyed Nicholas' order that all Russian subjects should leave for home, and subsequently joined a detachment of Spanish insurgents under General Mina. This case was dealt with on the highest level. A special memorandum on it was compiled by Benckendorff for the Committee of Ministers, the young offender was sentenced to be tried *in absentia* by a personal ukaz signed by Nicholas and the case was heard out of turn 'because of its importance.'[4]

Such meticulous attention to detail, whether important or not, was typical of Nicholas' determination to be informed of everything; and the minutes he wrote on Third Department reports show that he was not satisfied with anything less than factual evidence. Benckendorff's Annual Report for 1827, in its appreciation of the state of morale of the middle class younger generation ('a most gangrenous section of the empire') states 'We already note the

[1] Presnyakov, 'Samoderzhavie Nikolaya I', *loc. cit.* p. 18.
[2] Trotsky, p. 121. [3] *Ibid.* pp. 122–3.
[4] See *Kr. Arkh.* (1937), no. 83, pp. 107–20. The details of this case are recorded in an unsigned article entitled 'A Russian Volunteer in the ranks of the Spanish Insurgents in 1830'. The sentence passed on Kologrivov originally included public exposure of his name and offence to be circulated in both capitals, his letters to be burned, deprivation of social rank after his return, sentence of hard labour and relinquishment of all goods and property to his legal successors. After 18 months in Spain K. requested permission through the Russian Legation in Berlin to return to Russia; this was granted and he returned in 1832, whereupon he was forced to enlist as a private soldier.

inception of several secret societies...whose main principle is the blind subordination of members to invisible leaders'. Nicholas' marginal comment was 'Où, qui sont les individus?'[1] He wanted names and dates, facts and figures, and to this extent his influence on the Department's work should have been beneficial. Trotsky states that he took an interest in every single denunciation 'however absurd', and quotes the case of one Lukovsky who in 1835 produced a ridiculous tale of two secret societies (one Russian, the other Polish) with headquarters in England. Their intention, he claimed,was to infiltrate subversive literature into Russia *via* India, Persia, Georgia and Astrakhan', but not one member of either society was mentioned by name. On this denunciation Nicholas wrote: 'All this is very vague, there is not one single positive fact; the only thing that is true in all this is that the English hate us.' Yet even so the fear of overlooking a possible conspiracy impelled him to add: 'However, in our century nothing must be left without attention.'[2]

It was Nicholas' passion for accumulating knowledge on every kind of incident that resulted in the countless special inquiries undertaken by the Higher Police in addition to the reports regularly submitted by gendarme staff-officers 'on all events without exception'. The most futile rumours were investigated.[3] Particular emphasis was laid on the preservation of family morality, which Nicholas regarded as of paramount importance to the life of the state,[4] and if it might be contended that such investigations were hardly vital to the security of the country, in Nicholas' view it was imperative that law and religion should always triumph and that official misdemeanours be punished.

Such was the Tsar's will: the Third Department was invariably the chief instrument of its execution.

The annual reports

An official source states[5] that the fundamental aim of Third Department activities was the preservation of the bases of Russian state life; and, like any other secret or semi-secret police, it was created with the purpose of

---

[1] *Kr. Arkh.* (1929), no. 37, p. 150.   [2] Trotsky, pp. 77–8.

[3] On one occasion (no date given) Nicholas was informed of a peasant rumour of buried treasure in a certain area. A Gendarme Lieutenant-Colonel was instantly dispatched to discover the facts, which turned out to be wholly unsubstantiated. Nicholas' reaction was to declare that those responsible for the gossip were mad! 'There were thousands of similar cases', see Trotsky, pp. 115–16.

[4] In 1851 Dubbelt received a report that a certain Guards officer had run away with a married woman. He informed Orlov, who informed Nicholas, who demanded that the runaways be instantly seized. The whole Third Department apparatus was mobilized for this purpose. It was successfully achieved and the guilty officer was sentenced to 6 years in the Alekseyevskii Ravelin, see Trotsky, pp. 116–17. (An account of this incident is recorded by P. Ye. Shchegolev in an article entitled 'Lyubov' v Raveline' in *Alekseyevskii Ravelin* (Moscow, 1929).)

[5] Adrianov, p. 100.

maintaining the political *status quo*. But, as the 'Jubilee Report' records,[1] the secret societies whose members plotted the Decembrist rising had included almost all the existing revolutionary elements in Russia and therefore, once these conspirators were discovered and sentenced, law and order was guaranteed for a long period. 'This explains why Third Department activities in strictly political cases were limited almost exclusively during the first years after its creation to dealing with questions concerning the convicted Decembrists...[2] Political surveillance soon established the fact that their criminal intentions had left hardly any trace on society...Even so its activities were energetically directed to a close and comprehensive study of the contemporary situation in Russia and to the discovery of those aspects of...public life which did not correspond to the country's requirements and might, if only in the distant future, threaten its tranquillity...' The latter part of this analysis is well illustrated by the contents of the early Annual Reports which generally speaking represent lengthy reviews of current events and popular morale rather than accounts of specific inquiries by the Higher Police into individual malpractices of a political nature.[3]

---

[1] Bogucharsky, *loc. cit.* pp. 91, 92. (These facts are closely paraphrased by Adrianov, *ibid.* but without acknowledgement.)

[2] The text here refers to the 'Orenburg Case' (footnote states to have been the work of a provocateur, Ippolit Zavalishin, described in article 'Provokator 20-ykh godov XIX vyeka', *Kievskaya Mysl'* (1914), no. 38) and to 'an insignificant attempt to form a secret society in Moscow' (footnote states to have been the case of the brothers Kritsky, described by M. K. Lemke in *Byloye*). It refers to them as 'the only, one might say, exceptional cases which claimed attention during the first five years of the Department's existence'. Such cases (the 'Kritsky brothers' in 1827 and the 'Sungurov affair' in 1830–1) were quickly proved to be isolated instances of no political importance, see M. K. Lemke, 'Tainoye obshchestvo brat'yev Kritskikh', *Byloye*, No. 6 (SPB, 1906), pp. 41–57; references in Herzen's *Byloye i Dumy*, pp. 73 (Kritsky brothers), 79–80 (Sungurov); B. Eikhenbaum, 'Tainoye obshchestvo Sungurova', *Zavyety* (SPB, 1913), Mar., pp. 15–37 and May, pp. 45–63.

[3] The full text of the first six of the Third Department's 'Annual Reports' have been reproduced from the original documents in the 'Arkhiv Revolyutsii i Vnyeshnei Politiki' in Moscow. The first four were published together with a general introduction and footnotes by A. Sergeyev under the title 'Gr. A. Kh. Benkendorf o Rossii v 1827–30gg. (Yezhegodnye otchety Tret'ego Otdeleniya i korpusa zhandarmov)', *Kr. Arkh.* (1929), no. 37, pp. 138–41 (Sergeyev's introduction), pp. 141–56 (*1827*), pp. 156–69 (*1828*); *ibid.* (1930), no. 38, pp. 109–33 (*1829*), pp. 133–45 (*1830*). The second series of these Reports appeared shortly afterwards in the same periodical with a further brief introduction by Sergeyev in which he draws attention to the value of these Reports for historical research. The title of this series is 'Gr. A. Kh. Benkendorf o Rossii v 1831–32gg.', *Kr. Arkh.* (1931), no. 46, pp. 133–4 (introd.), pp. 134–40 (*1831*), pp. 146–54 (*1832*). Four 'Reports on the Activities of the Corps of Gendarmes' have also been published; they were originally submitted as Supplements to the 'Annual Reports' for 1827–9, 1830, 1831 and 1832, *Kr. Arkh.*, no. 37, pp. 169–74; no. 38, pp. 125–7; no. 46, pp. 141–5, 154–9. No further 'Annual Reports' or their Supplements have appeared in full since 1931.

Sergeyev states that the first four 'Annual Reports' were the work of von Vock and were written in French. After 1831, the year of his death, they were 'drafted in Russian, copied out by a clerk, and their general character underwent certain alterations; but the "assessments of morale" ["nravstvenniye obozreniya"]...are very reminiscent of Vock's first "reviews". In

The first Annual Report submitted to the Tsar at the end of 1827 begins with the statement: 'Public opinion has the same importance for the authorities as a topographical map has for an army commander' and its writer was therefore careful to stress the reliability of the Report's contents—'All the information has been checked several times with the aim of ensuring that the opinion of any particular party should not be accepted as the opinion of a whole class.' The Report goes on to present a shrewd analysis of the social classes of the day listed under the headings Court, High Society (subdivided into Contented and Discontented), Middle Class (subdivided into Landowners, Merchants, Men of Letters and Younger Generation), Civil Servants, Army, Peasants, and Clergy; with a final section on Morale in the Provinces. The first two of these classes are dismissed as exerting little influence on society as a whole, but prominent persons in High Society are mentioned by name with a description of their opinions. Nicholas, to judge by his side-lining, was more interested in the state of the Middle Class, which is described as 'the soul of the empire', 'generally loyal' and 'approving the creation of the Gendarmes', although 'we should not conceal from ourselves that murmurs of discontent are heard in various sections of each of the groups included in this class'. (The Younger Generation is analysed with particular care, and its enthusiasm for secret societies—no names are given— is attributed to influences from Vienna and Paris.) The most scathing criticism of all is reserved for the class of Civil Servants ('Chinovniki'), nothing being said in its defence. 'This layer of society is probably the most perverted morally. In it respectable persons are rarely encountered. Embezzlement, forgery, legal chicanery—that is their trade. Unfortunately, they are the ones in charge of the administration...' Only the Army's morale is considered relatively satisfactory. The Peasants are restless, the Clergy is badly administered and 'good priests are very much of a rarity'. In general, states the concluding paragraph, 'all Russia impatiently awaits changes...The machine requires to be rewound afresh. The keys to this necessity are to be found in Justice and Industry.' As regards the provinces, morale in the Baltic states was said to be excellent, although the same could not be claimed for Poland.

The outspoken character of this and subsequent Reports admirably illustrates the magnitude of the tasks that confronted Nicholas, for what changes could he bring about without the assistance of a reliable administrative system? Even the most efficient and irreproachable political police could

later reports there appear sections containing material of a statistical nature (on peasants' and workers' disturbances, on fires, exiles, "noteworthy incidents", entry into the country of foreigners, censorship etc.)...Taken as a whole, the reports present a picture of the gradually increasing and extraordinary tension of the administrative system...', loc. cit. no. 37, p. 139.

scarcely hope to achieve much success against such widespread corruption, although its evident purpose was to oppose it as far as possible.

The contents of the 1828 Report show that its investigations into Russia's administration were at any rate effective enough to earn the hatred of many high officials including Ministers. 'Some have even tried to persecute persons whom they have thought to be loyal to Higher Police organs, they have tried to place them in a false position and damage their reputation.' But the Report contends that although such persons were undoubtedly hostile to the 'gendarmerie' '. . . the people as a whole support this institution. . . Private and confidential letters bear witness that in provincial districts where no gendarmes are stationed all classes desire their presence, seeing in them defenders who will protect them from the acts of injustice wrought upon them by the authorities. . .'[1] Nicholas marked this passage as deserving notice and it doubtless confirmed his view that the Higher Police was fulfilling a most necessary and beneficial function in the state. The 1828 Report is less concise than its predecessor, mentions few names and is vague in its denunciation of the 'so-called liberals' on whose activities the Department is 'keeping careful watch'. Apart from the latest information on the Polish situation, however, it was evidently the deplorable state of officialdom that chiefly engaged its attention.

This is equally true of the 1829 Report, which is particularly valuable as an illustration of the most important work undertaken by the Higher Police because it includes a detailed summary of that Department's views on all Ministries and Directorates. These views are in almost every instance unfavourable and Benckendorff did not hesitate to subject even the highest officials to frank criticism. In discussing the work of the Ministry of Finance, for instance, he notes that the Minister (Kankrin) is 'energetic and hardworking, but obstinate' and that his assistant (Druzhinin) is 'very capable, but unfortunately venal'. The harshest strictures of all are passed on the Minister of Internal Affairs (Zakrevsky), 'a complete ignoramus', interested only in preserving the outward form of good administration, and this section admirably exemplifies the inevitable rivalry that existed between the Higher Police and this Ministry. 'All information conveyed to him [Zakrevsky] by the gendarmerie he passes on to Governors, telling them at the same time from whom the information emanates; this hinders gendarme work and incurs the objections and anger of local authorities. No matter how often it is explained that this information is passed to him in confidence and is exclusively intended for his personal attention with a view to enabling him to take appropriate action—he declines to change his ways. This is due solely to the fact that he nurtures a misplaced hatred for an institution which, in his opinion, encroaches

[1] 1828 Report, p. 162.

on his own sphere of competence.'[1] Zakrevsky and his successors may well have had more reason than some of their colleagues to dislike the Higher Police, but whether because of a lack of co-operation with it or because (as is equally probable) of the especially sorry condition of civil administration in the country, the Ministry of Internal Affairs is singled out for specific criticism, in particular with regard to the state of public health.[2] The poor results achieved by other Ministries are, however, revealed almost as forcefully. Even when some restrained praise is accorded, as in the case of the War Ministry, its Minister (Chernyshov) is abused. Indeed, only the Postal Department is reported to be efficiently run and much better informed of what goes on than the ordinary police; and, although Benckendorff does not say so, it is reasonable to assume that its information was normally shared with the Higher Police. The latter's increasing control over writers may be judged from the section of the Report dealing with the Ministry of Public Education: 'The Third Department has kept under vigilant surveillance any young persons who have striven to become political reformers and have desired to edit newspapers with this purpose. Information obtained by the Third Department in this connexion has been substantiated in the majority of cases. There are a great many worthless fellows to be found among the newspaper scribblers in Moscow, but certain repressive measures have been of considerable use.'[3]

The influence of literature on certain classes of the public is discussed in greater detail in the 1830 Report, together with items of more topical interest such as the effect on Russian society of the current cholera epidemic, the 1830 Revolution in France, the Polish rising and, in particular, the dangers of liberalism. (Pushkin's 'revolutionary verses' are adversely criticized). The Report claims that large numbers of 'intriguers' had been trying to sow a spirit of unrest in people's minds by asserting that in their view 'the gendarmerie is the only reason for all evils'. Convinced of this, such individuals had done their utmost to injure everything connected with the Third Department; and although society in general held the opposite view, it 'nevertheless does experience a certain feeling of anxiety and there are well-intentioned persons who, in order to avoid insults flung at them by intriguers, have resigned from the gendarmerie and are afraid to offer it their services'.[4] This acknowledgement of the Higher Police's growing unpopularity was doubtless largely the result of its constant interference in all aspects of public

[1] 1829 Report, p. 120.
[2] Count A. A. Zakrevsky (1783–1865), after serving as Gov.-Gen. of Finland, had been Minister of Internal Affairs since 1823. He was eventually dismissed for failure to ensure adequate quarantine measures against cholera in South Russia in Nov. 1831. Further attacks on him are also contained in the 1830 and 1831 Reports.
[3] 1829 Report, p. 127.   [4] 1830 Report, p. 143.

and private life, but the Department does not seem to have been greatly perturbed by hostile comment in the country as a whole; reports of morale in the provinces are satisfactory and only individual disturbances caused by administrative shortcomings have been noted. 'Thus only the two capitals need both active and continuous surveillance by the Third Department.'[1] Nevertheless, the Report ends with a lengthy catalogue of potential opposition elements—a catalogue which includes civil servants, men of letters, officers, landowners and 'all the serf class, which considers itself oppressed and yearns for an alteration in its condition'.

The Higher Police thus satisfied the Tsar of the vital need for its own existence, yet at the same time sought to assure him by careful flattery that his autocratic rule was generally appreciated. 'Never has a monarch possessed so many means of attaching a nation to himself. Firm, bold, honest, sincere, noble-minded, he was created to be beloved, adored. The prosecution of vice and malice, the rewarding of the deserving, the scorn with which he regards intriguers, great severity combined with mildness, but no harsh measures, particularly no captious fault-finding, which is feared more than tyranny itself.

'This is what the Third Department hears on all sides and what it is bound by its duty to lay before the feet of the sovereign.'[2]

The further progress of the cholera epidemic, the disorders in the Novgorod Military Settlements and the development of events in Poland occupy the leading place in the 1831 Report; and the last-mentioned is also dealt with in detail in the 1832 Report. But it is clear from the contents of both that the investigations carried out by the Third Department at this period were still chiefly concerned with Russia's internal administration. In both, the work of the various Ministries is subjected to a detailed analysis which, although critical, is nevertheless objectively presented. There are no further references to the part played in the national life by the Higher Police, but the contents of these two Reports make it clear that its investigations were highly necessary if any improvement of the state apparatus was to be effected.

Generally speaking, the Third Department's early Annual Reports provide a lucid description of Russia's internal history at this period. Like any good intelligence digest they are outspoken and in many instances their criticism is constructive. The opinions expressed are noticeably prejudiced only when the topic under review is the character and behaviour of Nicholas himself as seen by his subjects; and even in this case there are exceptions to the general rule of adulation—'...the duty of truthfulness compels us to add that notwithstanding...the Emperor is feared and considered severe'.[3] Nicholas must have felt that, whatever the shortcomings of most branches of

---

[1] 1830 Report, p. 144.   [2] *Ibid.* p. 145.   [3] 1832 Report, p. 146.

his government—and even in the capital the ordinary police was still in a deplorable condition[1]—he nevertheless possessed in his Higher Police organization a loyal and efficient safeguard.

Activities at home

Apart from the constant surveillance of the administration, the tasks undertaken by the Third Department inside Russia for the rest of the reign were primarily intended to keep the Tsar informed of the latest developments in all the most important problems of the day—the Serf Question, the Urban Proletariat, Dissenters, Army Morale, and the Law Courts.[2]

The 'Jubilee Report', although naturally a biased source of information, does succeed in proving that the Department drew a number of correct conclusions from their investigation of these questions. For example, it was 'convinced of the necessity, even of the inevitability, of the liberation of the serfs'.[3] There is evidence that it sincerely espoused their cause and sought to protect them both from their landlords and from local officials.[4] (The Third

[1] 'All agree unanimously that the local police force is so insignificant that one might say it does not exist...even the simplest class despises it...complaints and admittedly just complaints are unending...', 1832 Report, p. 153.

[2] The work of the Third Department on these questions is described in the 'Jubilee Report' of 1876 (Bogucharsky, *loc. cit.* pp. 94–9) which evidently provided the basis (unacknowledged) for Adrianov's brief summary of the Department's activities, pp. 100–1.

[3] Bogucharsky, p. 94. The 1839 Report stated that 'the whole spirit of the people is directed towards one aim—liberation' and that 'the serf system is a powder-keg laid beneath the state and is the more dangerous that the army is composed of these same peasants...', *ibid.*

(According to Sergeyev, the later Reports—after 1832—included 'wider and more detailed information' on the incidence of serf risings during the reign, *Kr. Arkh.* (1931), no. 46, p. 133.)

[4] Bogucharsky, p. 95. This is fully substantiated, for example, by an article entitled 'The 1842 Disturbances among the Chuvash Peasantry' which appeared in *Kr. Arkh.* (1938), no. 87, pp. 89–128. It was doubtless published to stress the appalling treatment of non-Russian minorities within the Russian empire by local authorities during the reign of Nicholas, but omits to comment on the obvious truthfulness and objective approach to this subject of a Colonel of Gendarmes. (The article is based on the reports of Gendarme Staff-Officers to Benckendorff.) As early as 11 Aug. 1831 a long preliminary report by Col. Maslov (Stogov's predecessor) had characterized the Chuvash people as 'still plunged in extreme ignorance, but by nature kindly, unselfish and peace-loving...This people...ought to be flourishing, were it not bound over to be administered by authorities who have no better respect for it than for beasts of burden...' After listing the many abuses perpetrated against the Chuvash peasant, Maslov asked: 'What must he think of the ruling people and the religion he has recently accepted when he sees such tricks practised by his masters spiritual and temporal?' (pp. 92, 95). Against this background and the dissatisfaction caused by Kiselyov's attempted Land Reforms of 1838 a number of revolts broke out in 1842. The Acting G.O.C. the 7th Gendarme District, Col. L'vov, reported that these disturbances were caused by 'the unintelligent regulations enforced by minor officials...and the excessive demands for money levied on the peasants' (pp. 101–2). (L'vov was confirmed as G.O.C. the 7th G.D. with the rank of Maj.-Gen. by Jan. 1843 (p. 123). He is not carried in the *RBS*.)

The impression made by this account of events is that certain efficient Gendarme officers

Department devoted many years to the study of this important question.) The condition of industrial workers in St Petersburg was examined by a special commission set up in 1841 under the chairmanship of Gendarme Maj.-Gen. Buxhoeveden, as a result of which a series of administrative measures were adopted for the improvement of their status; and it was on the basis of this commission's recommendations that a permanent hospital for heavy workers was established first in St Petersburg and later in Moscow.[1] With regard to Dissenters, the Department acknowledged the undoubted harm resulting from proselytization on their part but on more than one occasion drew attention to the considerable injury inflicted on the state by a too severe persecution of sectants.[2] It kept an especially close watch on Army affairs, constantly pointing out the existence of current abuses and, in particular, recommended the abolition of the then popular practice of punishing offenders by the extremely brutal and humiliating 'shpitsruteny' ('rod-beatings through the ranks').[3] The Department's interference in questions relating to the Law Courts was chiefly directed to the task of speeding up the hearing of legal cases and ensuring that judicial measures were fairly applied. Particular attention was paid to the multitude of petitions and complaints from private persons who were unable to obtain satisfaction from legal offices.[4]

sincerely attempted to alleviate the lot of the serfs. Trotsky, writing before the publication of this article, was also struck by the unexpected interest shown by the Third Department in the working classes and commented: 'The reader should not be amazed at a situation which seems at first glance strange: in the rôle of defenders of peasant liberation we find not free-thinkers, Decembrists or Petrashevtsy, but Nicholas' gendarmes; and these enemies of the serf-owning classes are not reduced to the ranks or exiled to Siberia, but are rewarded with ranks, medals and power. Has there been no mistake? Did the gendarmes not ascribe to themselves post-factum [T. points out that these claims first appeared in the "Jubilee Report"] a sympathy for the question of reform—when at the beginning of the Nicholas régime people were exiled or driven through the ranks merely for thinking about such a question? No, it was quite true. The gendarmes did indeed come to the conclusion that reform was necessary, but they arrived at this conclusion by their own method of reasoning', p. 64.

According to Trotsky, the gendarmes were chiefly afraid of increased peasant risings; they were fully aware of the prevailing desire for liberation among the serf class and believed that, if it continued unsatisfied, then the security of the state might be endangered, p. 65.

This is doubtless a fair conclusion, although the contents of Col. Maslov's 1831 report make it clear that the sole purpose of at least one Gendarme Staff-Officer's endeavours was to secure better treatment for a browbeaten class which at the time could not be considered a real menace. The entire article makes interesting reading for adherents of the view that Gendarme Colonels invariably abused their immense authority; this view was probably chiefly held by local officials whose own abuses these officers successfully exposed.

(Extensive extracts from the Chief of Gendarmes' Annual Reports relating to the Peasant Question may be found in Ye. A. Morokhovyets, *Krest'yanskoe Dvizhenie 1827–1869* (Moscow, 1931).)

[1] Bogucharsky, *ibid.* (For Maj.-Gen. Buxhoeveden see p. 194, note 3.)
[2] *Ibid.* pp. 95–6.   [3] *Ibid.* p. 97.
[4] *Ibid.* pp. 98–101. (See p. 224, note 1.)

The Higher Police in general did not limit itself merely to indicating current abuses in all these fields. It also recommended measures to raise the level of the country's internal development. In 1838 it drew attention to the advantages of building a railway between the capitals, overriding the opinions of both the Minister of Finance and the Director of Communications; in 1841 it reported on the necessity of improving the government's concern for public health; in 1842 it recommended the lowering of high tariffs which were obstructing the development of trade; in 1838 and 1847 it severely criticized the onerous character of recruit call-ups.[1] In each of these cases it provided the Tsar with facts and conclusions enabling him to form an accurate estimate of public opinion on specific questions of internal policy; and, even making due allowance for these possibly exaggerated claims of the Department's efficiency and perspicacity, the informed and practical character of its reports must be set to the credit of a branch which otherwise, as is widely believed, did little or nothing to enhance the reputation of Nicholas' reign.

Activities abroad

Secret and semi-secret 'internal espionage' organized by the Third Department understandably constituted the major part of its activities throughout the reign. Political events outside Russia, however, resulted in the extension of these activities to other countries.

It will be recalled that the ukaz of 3 July 1826 which created the Third Department did not specifically authorize it to submit intelligence reports on events outside the Russian empire, but at the same time its brief to provide information 'on all events without exception' allowed the freest possible interpretation. The business of diplomatic espionage, mainly conducted by foreigners recruited abroad, had been distributed throughout various government offices and was not concentrated in that of the Third Department until events in Poland provided the necessary impetus.[2] As early as the autumn of 1827 the Department began to submit reports on the sorry condition of Polish morale,[3] but its information emanated from Polish sources and the Higher Police did not exercise any control over the Kingdom of Poland. It is surprising, in view of this Report and that of 1828 which also showed

---

[1] *Ibid.* p. 98. [2] Trotsky, pp. 58–9.

[3] 1827 Report, *Kr. Arkh., loc. cit.* p. 155. The Report is outstandingly frank about conditions in Poland: 'Justice is sold to the highest bidder by all state employees from those in the Governor-General's office downwards. Not one blessing or favour conferred by the monarch has spread to these provinces', *ibid.*

(The chief official in Poland was N. N. Novosil'tsev (1761–1836), the former personal adviser of Alexander, who from 1812 was the leading figure in the administration of the Polish provinces on the staff of the Grand Duke Konstantin Pavlovich. He was transferred to St Petersburg after the 1831 rising, *ibid.* footnote.)

that efforts by the Third Department to improve the situation had successfully been frustrated,[1] that no early decision was taken to include Poland
among the Gendarme Districts already created. (Possibly Nicholas felt that
the decision to do so would be too great an affront to his subjects in that
country.) The situation there, however, continued to worsen, and the Reports of 1829 and 1830 contain further evidence of Polish unrest, criticisms
of the actions taken by the Regent, Grand Duke Konstantin Pavlovich,
and reports of the general dissatisfaction caused by the failure to recall
Novosil'tsev.

Then, as a result of the outbreak of the Polish rising in 1830–1, the position changed. The suppression of the rising led to the belated creation of the
3rd Gendarme District in Poland,[2] and the Third Department's preoccupation with events in that country and their consequences led to a considerable
expansion of its activities.[3] These were concerned not only with reprisals
against Poles of all classes,[4] but also with the increasingly important question
of Polish émigrés who had been accorded refuge in, principally, France,
England and Belgium. The formation of Polish Committees in these
countries alarmed the Russian government, and from 1832 onwards the
Third Department began to send its agents abroad for the purpose of

[1] 'The creation of the Gendarmerie infused several drops of hope into the hearts of Poles who
thought that the Emperor would take an interest in their lot. Colonel Rutkovsky [see p. 192,
note 2; p. 194, note 2; his name indicates that he was of Polish origin] was sent to Vil'no and
there acquired general favour and respect; but as soon as it was noticed in Warsaw that he was
trying to see things in their true light and was a fighter for justice, he was at once removed...
protection is still being afforded to certain officials known to be corrupt...', 1828 Report,
loc. cit. pp. 167–8.

[2] See chapter Three, p. 88, note 4; p. 89, note 1. It is interesting that the 'Jubilee Report' states
that, as gendarme surveillance did not extend to Poland before 1831 (Bogucharsky, p. 92), the
Department could not be informed of Polish conspiracies. In fact, the 1827–30 Reports show
that it was well aware of the situation, and hence Nicholas himself was responsible for not
insisting on the creation of a Gendarme District in Poland some years before the rising took
place. On the other hand, the 1815 constitution was superseded only on 14 Feb. 1832 when the
Organic Statute of that date proclaimed the Kingdom of Poland 'an indivisible part' of the
Russian Empire, see M. T. Florinsky, Russia. A History and an Interpretation, 2 vols. (New
York, 1953), 7th impression 1961, 2, p. 762. In addition, the Viceroy was hostile to Third
Department activities in Poland: 'The Grand Duke Constantine's attitude towards the
Gendarmes was somewhat sceptical; he did not admit them into the Polish provinces which he
governed as he saw fit' (Trotsky, p. 75). See also 'Perepiska velikago Knyazya Konstantina
Pavlovicha s Grafom A. Kh. Benkendorfom, 1826–8', R. Arkh. (1884), no. 6, pp. 245–320,
passim; 'Pis'ma velikago Knyazya Konstantina Pavlovicha k Grafu A. Kh. Benkendorfu,
1829–31', ibid. (1885), no. 1, pp. 20–42, passim.

[3] 'These [Polish] provinces demand the most vigilant surveillance on the part of the government', 1831 Report, p. 138; 'These two classes [Polish landowners and Catholic clergy] are
unlikely to forget and will not for years abandon their criminal dream of freeing themselves of
their legal government and will continue to hate it'...'The state of morale in the Kingdom
of Poland is unsatisfactory...', 1832 Report, pp. 147, 148.

[4] According to Trotsky, Third Department files at this period were full of Polish names, details
of their owners' exile, sentences of hard labour, escapes and so on, ibid.

studying these Committees on the spot and building up a network of reliable observers.[1]

It was from this origin that stemmed the organization of a secret agent system abroad to provide the Third Department with accurate information on the internal political situation of European states and, in particular, on their attitude to Russia. In the absence of other equally definitive sources, the 'Jubilee Report's' summary of these activities must be quoted as evidence of the Department's concern with events abroad. After stating that information obtained, which was 'checked by various methods', was constantly presented to the Emperor, it goes on:

Time has shown how well this information was substantiated and how many of the Department's recommendations were justified. Thus even in the '30s it was noting the insincerity of Austria's attitude to Russia, discovering her plans to reach a rapprochement with France to counterbalance the growing might of our fatherland, and was constantly reporting on her equivocal policy with regard to the Poles. As early as 1839 the Department was drawing attention to England's distrust of Russia's Asiatic policy and that Power's apprehensions deriving from the increase of our influence in Asia and the growth of our export trade in the East. Eight years before the February revolution it saw in Louis Philippe the last bulwark of Monarchism in France and more than once foretold that after him a republic would be instituted in that country even if it lasted only a year, and that serious disturbances would take place—disturbances which would react on the whole of Western Europe. In 1846 the Department was drawing attention to the dissemination of destructive revolutionary theories in Switzerland and Germany, where they were least of all restrained; it foresaw the early outbreak of revolution and expressed fears that as the result of Germany's proximity to us the moral infection might also penetrate into our borders.

However, surveillance abroad was chiefly concentrated on the intrigues of Polish nationals and their attempts to bring about a rising in Poland and the Western provinces...[2]

The Third Department thus entered the field of foreign espionage in the 1830s with the primary aim of keeping watch on the work of Polish émigrés and their emissaries; and this in its turn led to increased surveillance of some of Russia's southern areas, notably the Caucasus, which had previously not been subjected to strict Gendarme control.[3] Extreme fears of anti-Russian

[1] Bogucharsky, pp. 92–3.
[2] Bogucharsky, p. 93. It is noteworthy that Adrianov omitted the whole of this passage from the paraphrase of the 'Jubilee Report' which he included in his work on the Ministry of Internal Affairs (1902). Evidently it was not thought fitting that its disclosures of espionage abroad should be made public at that time.
[3] The 'Jubilee Report' states that 'the dispatch of Chaikovsky to Turkey as emissary made it necessary to strengthen surveillance on the southern frontier and to institute a secret police in

activities in Western Europe, which was generally inclined to sympathize with the Polish cause, consequently made it imperative that Russia should be as well informed as possible of European reactions, and this task was entrusted to the Higher Police as the most reliable and suitable organ of the state.

Benckendorff and Metternich

Little is known of the Department's attempts to organize a foreign espionage system, and if the archives today contain any particulars of its chief agents none have as yet been published.[1] There is evidence, however, that some effort was made to obtain the consent of Austria to a degree of co-operation in Higher Police matters and, in particular, to influence the usually hostile foreign press in Russia's favour,[2] a task which Nesselrode considered to be officially beneath the government's dignity. The securing of this co-operation is described by Benckendorff himself:[3]

During our stay in Teplitz [Nicholas' visit to Austria in 1835], Prince Metternich tried to establish contact with me and showed me all possible signs of his confidence. The year previously I had sent to Germany one of my officials[4] with the aim of refuting by factual and well-written newspaper articles the blatant absurdities printed abroad about Russia and its monarch and in general of trying to counteract the revolutionary spirit which pervaded journalism. Prince Metternich was very interested in this course of action. Being certain, he said, that he had no official more capable of performing this mission than I had, and saying that this man had had occasion to make himself personally acquainted with him, he asked me to transfer him to Vienna so that they could use their combined strength to the advantage of Russia and Austria and help to extend the principles of benevolent monarchy. I agreed to this the more readily since I did not wish it to be suspected that our government, being too highly placed for journalistic polemics, was implicated in the matter. As a result of this my official, who had been travelling round Germany as a com-

the Caucasus and in the Novorossiisk Region, especially in Odessa and Bessarabia', pp. 93–4. (See chapter Three, p. 89, note 4.)

(The emissary in question was M. S. Czajkowski (1808–86) who, after escaping from Poland in 1831, was sent to Constantinople from Paris as a Polish secret agent, see *Br. Efr. Enc.*)

[1] Trotsky does not mention the existence of such agents. He refers only to the poor results of investigations conducted abroad and states that Yakov Tolstoi in Paris (see chapter Five, p. 173, note 4) was 'exposed as early as 1848', p. 59.

[2] 'We know that special 'agent-writers' were maintained by Benckendorff at this period', Lemke (on events in 1835), p. 97. He quotes no details in substantiation of this statement. See p. 211, note 4; p. 212, note 1.

[3] Shil'der, *Imperator Nikolai Pervyi*, vol. 2, pp. 713–14 (see chapter Four, p. 118, note 1). This passage is quoted by Lemke, pp. 97–8.

[4] According to a footnote by Lemke (p. 97), this official was 'Baron Shveitser'. He is not recorded in the *RBS* and Trotsky does not mention him. His name appeared, however, in Ukaz no. 14468 of 17 Apr. 1841 when, as a Collegiate Councillor (equivalent to the military rank of full Colonel), he was listed as an 'Official for Special Commissions' on the Third Department staff, see chapter Five, p. 172, note 2.

pletely private individual, took up residence in Vienna in his current appointment. In addition Prince Metternich, who constantly devoted particular attention to matters concerning the supreme or secret police,[1] suggested that I should send to Vienna one of our gendarme officers to acquaint himself with all the activities of this branch in Austria and, by introducing him into all the details of its mechanism, to combine by this means our mutual measures against the Poles. I gave my consent to this proposal too with pleasure, and on my return to St Petersburg I instantly attached Lieutenant-Colonel Ozeretskovsky[2] to Vienna, where he was received with all kindness and forethought.

Lemke's reaction to this account of Austro-Russian collaboration on political police matters was to ask: 'What could be more amusing than the idea of Benckendorff's seriously imagining himself as the teacher of Metternich...?'[3] and it is possibly true that Metternich welcomed this approach more for the opportunities it afforded to observe the Russian secret police in action than for any potential results this co-operation might achieve.[4]

[1] Metternich's desire to influence Russian policy in secret police matters had manifested itself many years earlier in his successful attempts to alarm Alexander, see chapter One, p. 43.

[2] Yakov Nikolayevich Ozeretskovsky (1804–64) began his career as a soldier and fought under Gen. Yermolov in Persia in 1828. Retiring from the Army, he first entered the Inspectorate Department of the General Staff and then joined the Corps of Gendarmes (date unspecified but probably after 1832 as his name is not carried in any of the Supplements to the Annual Reports that have been published up to that year). In the Corps he was attached to Benckendorff's staff as Lt.-Col. and became a particular favourite of his Chief. During his short career in the Gendarmes (he finally went abroad for health reasons in 1839), he was entrusted in 1835 with the task of inspecting the Solovyetsky Prison (a monastery on the island of that name in the White Sea); and the same year he was attached to Vienna, where he remained until 1838. After 1841 he became the Head of the Crimean Salt Directorate and held this post for over twenty years. His civilian career ultimately brought him to the rank of Actual Privy Councillor. He was the author of a number of literary articles on various subjects not connected with his gendarme service, see RBS.

(Some details are known of his inspection of the Solovyetsky Prison in 1835. He reported that the situation of its fifty inmates was too onerous and that many were undergoing punishment exceeding their offences (mostly 'religious and moral anti-social behaviour'). As a result of his findings the Archimandrite of the monastery was removed. O. had conversations with a number of prisoners and his impressions were personally reported to Nicholas by Benckendorff. Several prisoners were pardoned and released. See M. Kolchin, Ssyl'nyye i Zatochennyye v ostrog Solovyetskago Monastyrya v xvi–xix vv. (Moscow, 1908), pp. 25, 40, 121–2, 161 ff.

It is possible that he was also the unnamed Gendarme officer who inspected the Suzdal' Monastery in that year, see Gernet, vol. 2, p. 403.)

[3] Lemke, p. 98.

[4] According to de Grunwald 'Il est à noter que pendant le séjour à Münchengraetz [in 1833] des rapports très étroits se nouent entre Benckendorff et Metternich. Les deux hommes se connaissaient de longue date: des "intrigues galantes" les avaient rapprochés à Paris', p. 203 (footnote). He also states that 'On retrouve dans les archives viennoises ("Varia" Russland) les traces d'une longue correspondance entre Metternich et Benckendorff qui s'étend sur les années 1835 à 1844', ibid.

Metternich's own memoirs throw no light on this relationship. The Memoirs of Prince Metternich, trans. in 5 vols. (London, 1880–2), vol. 5 (1830–5)) contain no mention of Benckendorff. The 'intrigues galantes' in question have been investigated by the present writer, see chapter Four, p. 110, note 1.

There can be no doubt, however, that Benckendorff took advantage of his old personal link with Metternich to ensure a regular exchange of official and unofficial letters on topics of mutual interest to them both; and Metternich in his turn was no less anxious to make use of this channel for his own purposes. The two statesmen wrote to each other regularly over the next seven years.[1] It is interesting to note that on more than one occasion it was Metternich who saw conspiracies where none existed (especially inside Russia, of which he evidently had a somewhat limited knowledge); whereas Benckendorff, at least as regards his own country, was much less prone to such fears. Russia's backwardness, the lethargy of the overwhelming majority of her subjects and, first and foremost, the tight control over every branch of national life exercised by Nicholas—all this, duly reported by his subordinates, probably seemed to him sufficient to daunt the most ambitious would-be revolutionaries. Abroad, on the other hand, Benckendorff's sources of information were much more restricted.

It appears, indeed, that Russia did not command any effective control over political suspects outside her borders. Extradition rights over 'criminals' were secured between Russia, Austria and Prussia in February 1834,[2] but otherwise the organization of an established and permanently employed agent network abroad was strictly limited. Trotsky states that no support was given by Russian diplomats and summarizes the achievements of the Higher Police in this connexion in a single sentence—'In Austria and Prussia the Department had to rely more on the co-operation of local police organizations than on its own resources.'[3]

Surveillance of Russian émigrés abroad

But whether or not these resources were adequate for their purpose, the government felt itself obliged to take an increasing interest in organizations and individuals capable of damaging its prestige abroad, and the Polish Rising was not the only factor which influenced it to adopt more radical measures against any Russian subjects who for any reason failed to act as loyal citizens in foreign countries. The French and Belgian Revolutions of 1830 provided further incentives to ensure that Russians abroad were exposed as little as possible to the infection of foreign liberalism. An ukaz of

[1] Their correspondence, which continued until 1842 (not 1844, as de Grunwald states), has been examined in the Vienna State Archives by the present writer and analysed in two articles, see P. S. Squire, 'Metternich and Benckendorff, 1807–1834', *The Slavonic and East European Review*, vol. XLV, no. 104, Jan. 1967, pp. 135–62; and 'The Metternich–Benckendorff Letters, 1835–1842', *ibid.* no. 105, July 1967, pp. 368–90.

[2] Manifest of 6 Feb. 1834. *Poln. Sobr. Zak.* vol. 9 (pt 1), p. 103, no. 6780. It is described by Lemke as 'a little-known manifesto', p. 98 (footnote).

[3] Trotsky, p. 59.

1831 enacting that Russian youths between the ages of ten and eighteen must be educated at home or else lose the right to enter government service was followed in 1834 by additional restrictions on the authorized period of residence abroad (five years for nobles, three for other social categories), and the text of the latter ukaz shows that cases had already occurred of Russians electing to remain abroad as voluntary émigrés.[1] In 1836 an ukaz was passed authorizing the trial *in absentia* of any Russian subject who had taken an oath of allegiance to another Power; in 1840 a special tax was levied on passports issued to Russians desiring to travel abroad, and in 1844 this tax was increased and further obstacles were placed in the path of would-be travellers.[2] A special committee consisting of Nesselrode (Foreign Affairs), Benckendorff, and Perovsky (Internal Affairs) was instituted to review all cases concerning foreign passports.[3] All these measures may be regarded as the practical expression of Nicholas' reluctance to afford his subjects the opportunity of living anywhere outside his immediate jurisdiction.

Surveillance by the Third Department of Russians affected by these ukazes did not begin in earnest until 1843, when its attention was drawn to the activities of 'the first Russian émigrés, Prince Peter Dolgorukov and Ivan Golovin in France, and Bakunin in Switzerland'.[4] The career of Bakunin as an opponent of the Russian government is already well known; the other two were insignificant by comparison, having merely attained prominence by writing books which displeased Nicholas; whereupon they were at once ordered to return to Russia.[5] After 1848 a potentially more redoubtable émigré

[1] Ukazes of 18 Feb. 1831, 17 Apr. 1834. *Poln. Sobr. Zak.* vols. 6, 9, nos. 4364, 6994.

The latter states: 'Absence abroad with established passports is permitted both to the nobility and to all free grades of society, but to abandon the fatherland and to settle arbitrarily in foreign countries has never been permitted.

Meanwhile it has been revealed by information submitted to Us that there have been and are at the present time examples and cases where persons who have received passports authorizing absence abroad remain in residence there for an indefinite period and thus arbitrarily turn the absence that has been allowed them into permanent residence abroad...', *loc. cit.* p. 294.

[2] Ukazes of 15 Sept. 1836, 10 Jul. 1840, 15 Mar. 1844, *ibid.* vols. 11, 15, 19, nos. 9521, 13652, 17731. Referring to the last of these Baron Korff wrote: 'There is no need to add what a doleful impression it made in society. The more so as for many persons, by reason of the cost of passports and other conditions, it was the equivalent of a complete refusal of any journey abroad. At first many did not want fully to believe that it would be issued, and in Petersburg there was even a rumour spread about that noisy talk and gossip had compelled the government to withdraw the new law. But it was shortly afterwards printed in all newspapers, which put an end to the false hopes that only those who were not acquainted with the character of the Emperor Nicholas had thought to approximate to the truth', 'Iz Zapisok Barona (vposlyedstvii Grafa) M. A. Korfa', *R. Star.* (1899), vol. 100, p. 295.

[3] 'Iz Zapisok Korfa', *loc. cit. ibid.*

[4] 'Jubilee Report', Bogucharsky, *loc. cit.* p. 103. (Not recorded by Adrianov.)

[5] P. V. Dolgorukov (1816–68) published in Paris in 1842 a work entitled 'Notices sur les principales familles de la Russie' under the pseudonym of 'le Comte Almagro'. (It was published under his real name in Brussels the following year.) On receiving the order to return home he

than either Dolgorukov or Golovin—Herzen—also became the object of the Department's investigations.

The example of these men was considered dangerous and from the 1840s onwards no Russian citizen abroad dared to speak openly for fear lest his remarks should be incorporated in agents' reports. Even allowing for some possible exaggeration natural in an account written (in 1844) by an anti-Russian foreigner, the following description is probably accurate enough:

The Russian is not only subject to this terrible *surveillance* within the pale of the empire, but when he travels abroad it follows him like his shadow. In the drawing-rooms of London and Paris, he dreads that the eye of the secret police may be upon him. Foreigners, in their own country, laugh at his terrors, but experience has taught him too painfully how truly they are grounded. The secret police...has rendered itself all eyes; its very spies are spied upon. The highly-paid, and well-selected diplomatic missions of the Russian government, the only effective branch of its service, are as narrowly watched as it is *their* duty to watch over the travelling Russians. It has been related to the author, by a competent authority, and he believes it, that to his informant's knowledge, upwards of a hundred and fifty individuals, in Paris alone, corresponded, directly and indirectly, with this branch of the Russian administration.[1]

The same opinions are expressed by a French writer:

Chaque courrier qui arrive à St Pétersbourg enrichit les dossiers du grand maître de quelque révélation nouvelle. Le Russe voyageur est bien étonné, à son retour dans son pays, de se voir représenter dans un tableau fidèle toute l'histoire de son absence. Malheur à lui, si, entraîné par quelque influence étrangère, il s'est laissé aller à des actes ou à des paroles qui aient pu porter ombrage à l'autocrate.

La haute police russe revêt toutes les formes, vous la rencontrez dans les salons en gants jaunes et en habit noir; dans les magasins, sous la livrée du commis; au théâtre, déguisée en figurante ou en actrice; dans les rues et au sein même des émeutes populaires, contrefaisant le révolutionnaire et le patriote...[2]

---

instantly obeyed, whereupon he was exiled to serve in Vyatka. He left Russia secretly from Odessa in 1859 and thenceforth remained abroad, publishing *La Vérité sur la Russie* in Paris in 1860. [Author's name spelled Golovine.]

I. G. Golovin (1816–18?), after refusing to return to Russia in 1843 (for which he was deprived of his Russian citizenship with his property in Russia reverting to his heirs), published *La Russie sous Nicolas I* in Paris, 1845 (trans. into English 1846). He was pardoned by Alexander II, but never returned to his native land.

See *Br. Efr. Enc.* Lemke includes sections on both these émigrés, pp. 529–52, 555–72. (Both are quoted as sources for the present study.)

According to Korff, who also discusses the defection of Dolgorukov and Golovin, another prominent 'non-returnee' was Prince Gagarin, a member of the Russian Legation in Paris who left it to embrace the Catholic faith, 'Iz Zapisok', *loc. cit.* p. 294. (Prince I. S. Gagarin (1814–82) became a Jesuit in 1843 when he refused to return to Russia. He corresponded with Herzen and founded a Slavonic library in Paris, see *Br. Efr. Enc.*)

[1] Henningsen, vol. 1, p. 203.
[2] Léouzon le Duc, p. 384.

It is true that such accounts tend to contradict the more recent evidence recorded by Trotsky, but it is fully confirmed by that of the contemporary émigré Golovin, who wrote: '. . . I was conscious that I was innocent, but who would say that I had not been calumniated? Russian spies are very numerous at Paris, more so than in any other city. . .'[1] The practice of spying on Russian subjects abroad sometimes (as in the case of Golovin) had the opposite effect to that which was intended—it frightened them into remaining where they were or else into escaping later from Russia to live abroad permanently, when, if only because they needed money, they wrote accounts of their experiences which infuriated their country's government.

Nicholas profoundly distrusted all political theories current in Western Europe which advocated the cause of personal liberty, and he was always afraid of their possible influence on his countrymen. He did not wish his subjects to draw any attention to their life abroad and least of all to do so in print. This explains why, when Golovin wished to publish a work 'of a scientific nature', he was officially advised to keep the whole affair perfectly secret. 'Count Benckendorff had a twofold reason for this advice: "the Emperor's will is that his subjects shall keep quiet in foreign countries; and we by no means desire that they should publish anything whatever". . .'[2] Failure to observe this counsel inevitably incurred the Imperial displeasure and investigation of each case by the Third Department automatically ensued.

Surveillance of foreigners inside Russia

The 1840s also marked a further stage in the development of the Department's policy connected with events abroad.[3] This was the question of foreigners who visited Russia. Orders were given for the strictest observation to be kept on all foreigners during their stay within the Russian empire and, in particular, on Frenchmen.[4] Even these measures were not sufficient

---

[1] Golovine, vol. 1, p. 8. He goes on: '. . . they often gladly seize some opportunity of this kind to obtain favour, or at all events to evidence that they have earned their salary; because those spies who are too sparing of their reports are suspected, or dismissed. Informers enjoy the strictest incognito; they are never confronted with the accused, and their word has more weight than that of honest men. Persons, free from reproach, have been recalled to Russia on a bare suspicion of liberalism, and even when they have wholly escaped punishment, because neither word nor deed could be alleged against them, they have nevertheless been shackled in their future career. . .', *ibid.* pp. 8–9. (This evidence would naturally be the stronger if it were substantiated by facts capable of being checked, but G. could hardly quote names without imperilling their owners.)

[2] Golovine, *loc. cit.* pp. 13–14.

[3] The following details are summarized from the 'Jubilee Report', Bogucharsky, p. 102. (They are all omitted by Adrianov.)

[4] As early as 1835 Nicholas made it clear that he was opposed to foreigners' residing in Russia without due surveillance. He told Franz von Gerstner, a Czech engineer who had come to

to allay the government's fears and eventually entry into Russia was forbidden first to French and later to all other foreign subjects. The import of foreign books was even more rigorously controlled; many bookshops were searched in St Petersburg, Moscow, Riga and Derpt with the result that a number of unauthorized publications were confiscated and guilty booksellers were put on trial. Then, in 1844, an ukaz appeared ordering that all foreigners should present themselves to the Third Department as soon as they arrived in the capital for an interrogation and an examination of their passports;[1] and this in its turn led to an increase of the Department's interest in their comings and goings.[2]

Foreigners had, of course, always attracted the Department's attention. (The history of Russia's xenophobia is a long one). Irrespective of their nationality, all diplomats were subjected to government surveillance even when their country could not for geographical or political reasons constitute any menace to contemporary Russian security. The American envoy to St Petersburg from 1831 to 1833, Buchanan, reported to the President: 'To put my letters in the post-office here would be most certainly to expose them to the Russian government; indeed they scarcely think it necessary to do up the seals decently of those which I receive. . . We are continually surrounded by spies, both of high and low degree in life. You can scarcely hire a servant who is not an agent of the secret police.'[3] His words are echoed by a later successor, Neil S. Brown, who served as American Minister from 1850 to 1853 and who 'dared not risk anything in the mails that he was unwilling to have read; those legations that could afford to do so maintained regular couriers and never sent dispatches by post. . .'[4] It is permissible to assume that this situation confronted all diplomatic representatives in Russia.

Russia in 1834 on business connected with railway construction: 'There is one thing I will insist on. You will most likely need foreign experts to help you in this work. You may bring them from abroad but not before you consult my chief of gendarmerie about each one of them. Moreover, not a single French subject is to be brought. I do not need these gentlemen.' Parry, p. 44.

[1] Ukaz of 15 Mar. 1844. *Poln. Sobr. Zak.* vol. 19, pp. 196–7, no. 17734.
[2] The 'Jubilee Report' states that these measures included the annual dispatch of a special official to Kronstadt during the navigational season to check the papers of newly-arrived foreigners and to make the necessary arrangements for their entry into Russia and their stay in the country, Bogucharsky, p. 103.
[3] George Ticknor Curtis, *Life of James Buchanan, Fifteenth President of the United States*, 2 vols. (New York, 1883), vol. 1, pp. 149, 187, Letters to President Jackson dated 1/13 Oct. 1832, 22 May 1833. Cf. 'In Russia the police are long past any feelings of shame. At the chief post-offices, there are commissions and bureaus authorized to open any letters they please. They are so careless about this being publicly known, that the letters are frequently sealed up again with different wax', *Recollections of Russia during Thirty-Three Years' Residence by a German Nobleman*, pp. 256–8 (see p. 130, note 3).
[4] Thomas A. Bailey, *America Faces Russia. Russo-American Relations from Early Times to Our Day* (New York, 1950), p. 60.

As far as may be judged from our own Foreign Office archives, diplomats normally corresponded directly with Count Nesselrode or his Assistants on all matters relevant to their office, and British dispatches of the period do not appear to contain any information on the workings of the Higher Police, being concerned only with the normal conduct of diplomatic business and trade. However, in 1840 the British plenipotentiary, Mr Bloomfield, departed from this practice and wrote to Benckendorff directly ('Au lieu de faire une démarche officielle par le Ministère des Affaires Etrangères...') to obtain satisfaction on behalf of a British subject detained in prison. After a second unsuccessful approach, Bloomfield was forced to take the matter up with Nesselrode, but made no mention of his attempt to establish contact with the Third Department.[1] Nevertheless this contact was established intermittently during the 1840s, and the archives contain a small number of letters exchanged between British representatives and Benckendorff or Dubbelt between 1840 and 1849.[2] (There are no letters signed by Orlov.) The cases dealt with in these letters are all of minor importance and relate only to the difficulties experienced in Russia by private individuals of British nationality.

More revealing accounts of the interest shown by the Third Department in everything connected with foreigners (and indeed with Russian citizens also) are provided by the memoirs of temporary visitors to Russia, most of which were written by British or French travellers. Some of these are informative despite the fact that few were able to write with any real understanding of this branch of the administration and fewer still possessed a comprehensive knowledge of Russian. The best of them, Henningsen, gives an excellent explanation of the difficulties confronting any foreign investigator: '...in the Russian empire the mask of snow which is worn for half a year by

[1] Public Record Office, Series F.O. 181 (Notes to Russian Ministers), vol. 149 (1838–40), Letters to 'S.E. le Comte de Benkendorff' dated 30 Sept./12 Oct., 2/14 Oct. 1840. (Bloomfield's letter to Nesselrode on this subject was dated 13/25 Nov.)

[2] *Ibid.* (Notes *to* Russian Ministers), vol. 149 (1838–40), Letter from Bloomfield to Doubelt dated 23 Oct./3 Nov. 1840; vol. 173 (1841–3), Letter from Bloomfield to Benckendorff dated 9/21 Aug. 1841; *ibid.* Letter from Stuart de Rothsay to Benckendorff dated 26 Mar./7 Apr. 1843; vol. 193 (1844–9), Letter from Buchanan to Doubelt dated 22 Jun./4 Jul. 1849. (Notes *from* Russian Ministers), vol. 157 (1839–41), Letter from Doubelt to Bloomfield dated 22 Oct./3 Nov. 1840; vol. 180 (1842–3), Letter from Doubelt to Bloomfield dated 17 Jul. 1842; *ibid.* Letter from Benckendorff to Stuart de Rothsay dated 5 Feb. 1843; *ibid.* Letter from Doubelt to Bloomfield dated 5 Nov. 1843; vol. 192 (1844–9), Letter from Doubelt to Bloomfield dated 1 Aug. 1844 (apparently in answer to a letter from Bloomfield dated 4/16 May 1844 for some reason not included in vol. 193). There is also no reply to Buchanan's 1849 letter in vol. 192.

The letters sent by the Third Department to these British envoys were all written in French and signed by Benckendorff or Dubbelt in person. They are marked as coming from the '3ème bureau de la 3ème Section de la Chancellerie de S.M. l'Empereur', with the exception of Dubbelt's letter dated 5 Nov. 1843 which emanated from the '2ème bureau'. The 3rd Section of the Third Department normally dealt with foreigners, and there seems to be no obvious reason why on one occasion a different section should have been involved.

nature is only emblematical of that which disguises all her institutions...
Concealment from foreigners of everything that will not bear publicity and
praise is therefore, in their mutual intercourse, the end and aim of all connected with the government, and of all who dread its legions of spies; in
which category the whole nation may be said to be comprised.'[1] There is
therefore a marked similarity between all accounts left by foreigners of their
experiences of the secret police, and none is worth quoting in detail. They
all bear witness to the careful watch kept on their movements and, if their
information was often largely based on rumours, there can be little doubt
that this watch was organized with reasonable efficiency. To quote but a few
examples:

Conversation on all political subjects is generally avoided; and a man must be very
guarded in what he says at a public table, as spies are busy to collect information,
and General B-[sic]...is daily well-informed of everything that passes.[2]

It is said that he [Benckendorff] has his spies in every place. Few private parties
can be held without some one being present to repeat what is said. All places
frequented by foreigners...have a well-dressed spy or two appended to them, who
keep watch over the conversation of the guests, and note those with whom they
associate.[3]

Its [the secret police's] members are countless, and their path obscure; but their
works are visible; and they are ever present in cellar, kitchen, drawing-room,
stable, churches, gardens, workshops, etc.; known to many, unknown to the
majority—a fearful incubus on the nation.[4]

[1] Henningsen; vol. I, pp. 2, 3. He devotes a section of this vol. (ch. VII, pp. 187–207) to 'The
Secret Police', but is careful to explain that 'in proceeding to examine it, the reader must not
expect any full and complete account of an institution which is of its very nature secret, and of
which only a very small portion is ostensible. Yet even this ostensible portion [H. is referring
here to the Corps of Gendarmes, see p. 199], though a mere fraction, a branch, as it were, of the
whole establishment, is in itself immense', p. 191.
 Henningsen clearly had no exact knowledge of the organization of the Higher Police,
although he gives a rough sketch of the distribution of Gendarme officers (p. 199); but his
chapter is interesting for the detailed stories he records of individuals (unnamed) who suffered
at its hands. In addition he gives an excellent description of the 'Passport Office' which he
states was 'comprised in the institution of the high police' (p. 200) and also of the widespread
corruption of secret police officials (pp. 206–7).
 His account must rank as one of the fullest published by any contemporary foreigner. (For
details of his career see chapter Four, p. 127, note 2).
[2] Thomas Raikes, *A Visit to St Petersburg in the winter of 1829–1830* (London, 1838), p. 135.
 (There is a reference to him in Pushkin's *Yevgenii Onyegin*, ch. 8, Stanza XXVI, as 'A bird of
passage, travelling fleetly; /Starched, insolent, from top to toe; /His studious deportment so
/Caused all the guests to smile discreetly /That all condemned him; all, askance /Would inter-
change a silent glance', trans. by Oliver Elton (London, 1948), p. 226.)
[3] Robert Bremner, *Excursions in the Interior of Russia*, 2 vols., 2nd ed. (London, 1840), vol. I,
p. 269. (Bremner visited Russia in 1836.)
[4] *Recollections of Russia*, p. 242.

A Yankee, arriving on business in 1843, was told by the gendarmes that he had been to Russia once before, in 1820, on a trip of pleasure, and the details of that visit of twenty-three years earlier were recited to the traveller's great surprise. One felt in Russia as if in a glass cage.[1]

A Pétersbourg, les murs ont des oreilles...L'espionnage est si général dans ce pays, qu'on ne comprend pas comment il peut s'y trouver deux individus qui osent se confier l'un à l'autre les choses intimes de leur cœur ou de leur esprit.[2]

Every time that I went to Count Orloff's office for permission to travel, or permission to live in the town again, the official there took occasion to remind me by some casual observation, uttered in the politest manner, that he knew all about my movements; what relatives I had in Russia; where they were, and what they were doing; and, by adroit questioning, that I could not well avoid answering, he mentally sketched out for himself a tolerably accurate map of my past and proposed movements.[3]

Control over the movement of foreigners was exercised by the so-called 'Alien Office' or 'Bureau des Etrangers',[4] the equivalent for foreigners of the 'Passport Office' for Russian nationals (the old 'Address Office'). Through this channel the Third Department could obtain information on every foreigner, and the meticulous regulations with which they were compelled to comply made it certain that no foreigner could live or travel anywhere inside the Russian empire, or even leave it, without the approval of the Higher Police.[5]

[1] Parry, p. 94 (see p. 96, n. 3).
[2] F. Lacroix, *Les Mystères de la Russie*, 6 vols. (Bruxelles, 1844), vol. 1, pp. 64–5.
[3] Robert Harrison, *Notes of a Nine Years' Residence in Russia from 1844 to 1853* (London, 1855), pp. 299–300.
[4] 'In the first days of my stay in St Petersburg, I had occasion to visit the Alien-Office several times. It is, undeniably, one of the most interesting offices in the city...The officers are extremely polite, and generally address you in your native language...As every foreigner must present himself in person to obtain and renew his certificate to reside, a very interesting society is generally to be found here, and one has an opportunity of becoming acquainted with every stranger in St Petersburg. Here sit the English grumbling and cursing more than all at the countless inquiries of the Russian police; Germans who take it more patiently, and give contentedly the required guarantees, certificates, and signatures; governesses answering the many questions put to them, in fear and trembling; old ladies who, in their eightieth year, must talk about their birth, and say when and where, and how they came into this world...', J. G. Kohl, *Russia, St Petersburg, Moscow, Kharkoff, Riga, Odessa etc.* (London, 1842), p. 206.
     (Kohl's book throws no light on secret police activities, and is criticized by Henningsen who commented: 'Indeed, it is futile to expect any vigorous description of the Russian empire, and the condition of its people, from a German pen, because no German dates to publish it; or if he did so, it would be excluded from both Austria and Prussia...', vol. 1, pp. 5–6.)
[5] These regulations ordered *inter alia* that every foreigner proposing to leave Russia should advertise his intention in the newspapers at least three different times. Bremner commented: 'The professed object of this regulation is to prevent people from running away in anybody's debt; but its real object is to give the police time to ascertain, privately, whether the traveller may have any motives of a political or treasonable nature. Owing to this arrangement, the

The general atmosphere of surveillance and suspicion influenced the views of all foreigners who visited Russia in Nicholas' reign. In one account we read that '...in the Russian empire...this political and social inquisition is unlimited, unbounded, and unmerciful in the exercise of its authority';[1] in another that 'a system of espionage of the most disgusting and degrading character is in vogue—a system so complete as to extend throughout the length and breadth of the land, embracing society in all its ramifications, and reaching individuals of every condition in every part of the world. To this, more than to any other cause, we may trace the corruption which prevails in every department of the public service...'[2] And a diplomat records that 'L'espionnage est une maladie chronique à St Pétersbourg. L'empereur espionne le monde entier, et trouve encore le temps d'espionner chez lui, autour de lui, jusque dans sa plus secrète intimité.'[3] There can be little reason to doubt the accuracy of these impressions.

No one, Russian or foreigner, important or unimportant, escaped the attentions of the Third Department. 'I knew the head of the Secret Police [Orlov] very well [wrote Lady Bloomfield] and he told me one day he had a report every day of what went on in our house, that he knew everyone who went in or out...'[4] And this personal memoir is confirmed by another

stated time required for getting a passport is little short of a fortnight; so that travellers who go to St Petersburg on a flying visit ought to commence advertising themselves the day after they arrive', op. cit. vol. 2, p. 3.

A longer account of the various vexatious orders affecting foreigners (including the above) is given by Léouzon le Duc, pp. 400–8.

[1] Henningsen, loc. cit. p. 188.

[2] John S. Maxwell, The Czar, His Court and People (New York and London, 1848), p. 139. (Maxwell was Secretary to the American Minister, Col. Charles Stewart Todd, during the 1840s.)

[3] Marc Fournier, Russie, Allemagne et France. Révélations sur la politique russe, d'après les notes d'un vieux diplomate (Paris, 1844), p. 68.

[4] Lady Georgiana Bloomfield, Reminiscences of Court and Diplomatic Life, 2 vols. (London, 1883), vol. 1, pp. 315–16. Her account continues: 'so I laughed and said he was quite welcome to know all that happened as far as I was concerned, as he could not send me off to Siberia. He then made me a speech I shall never forget, saying, "Do you suppose it would be necessary I should speak to take away a person's character, not at all. If there was a question of that person in society, and that I shrugged my shoulders and seemed as if they were suspected, 'cette person seroit perdue'".

'It frequently happened that people were arrested in the night, and sent off without trial; and one lady who was living in an hotel received notice that she had better be on her guard as to what she said or did in her room, as she was watched. The walls of her room looked all right, but on tapping them she found one place hollow, and on further examination she discovered that the winter supply of wood was piled up in the yard against the wall of her room. In that there was a space where a man could watch everything that went on in the room without the occupant being the least aware of the fact.' Ibid.

(Lady Bloomfield was the wife of the second Baron Bloomfield (1802–79) who, after serving as Secretary of Embassy from 1839, was appointed Envoy Extraordinary and Minister Plenipotentiary to the Court of St Petersburg and served there from 1844 to 1851. He married Lady Bloomfield in 1845, see Dict. of Nat. Biogr. (1886).)

English lady long resident in Russia—'When three meet in Russia, you may safely count one of them as a spy;. . . A young *gendarme* officer used to visit at the house of one of our acquaintances; his presence always produced restraint, as they are obliged by their duty to report whatever they may hear.'[1]

Only in one respect can this system of universal espionage be said to have differed from others of its kind, and this was in the unfailing courtesy normally shown by senior police officials. A French traveller has left an entertaining account of his reception when summoned to appear at their headquarters: 'Arrivé à l'hôtel, un laquais vous rejoint discrètement, et vous conduit, sur de moelleux tapis, jusqu'au boudoir dont la portière retombe sur vous. La police vous tend la main en souriant, vous offre une cigarette, et, au bout d'une demi-heure, tout en causant France, Russie, littérature, tabac turc, Maryland, Taglioni, elle vous a confessé avec une insouciance adorable. C'est l'inquisition en peignoir rose, la question extraordinaire en gants parfumés.'[2] As we have seen, this behaviour was fully in accord with the tradition of politeness to which the Third Department normally adhered; but it can have mattered little to those who witnessed it that they were received by 'a gentleman who. . .was *amabilité* itself'[3] if they were subsequently treated to physical punishment or to sentences of exile for minor indiscretions.

To a greater or lesser degree all Russians and foreigners inside Russia (and many outside it) were affected by the actual or seeming ubiquity of Third Department agents. The secrecy of its activities only added to the dread its authority generally inspired in all classes.[4]

[1] *The Englishwoman in Russia; Impressions of the society and manners of the Russians at home. By a Lady Ten Years Resident in that Country* (London, 1855), pp. 79–80.

This author was informed that besides the secret police (by which she presumably implied its permanent officials) there were eighty thousand paid agents in the country, among them many Poles and foreigners. She also records that 'a great many women belong to this hateful profession; even some of the French milliners in St Petersburg have the reputation of being agents of police', *ibid.*

Cf. also 'No rank is excluded from the recruiting—servants, coachmen, porters, free-men, serfs, cooks, lady's maids, clergy, officials, nobility, *savans*, subject themselves to it. All public amusements are imbittered by the certainty that spies are present, who sow tears [tares] and thorns. . .'. *Recollections of Russia*, p. 252.

[2] Henri Mérimée, *Une année en Russie. Lettres à M. Saint-Marc Girardin* (Paris, 1847), p. 52. He comments: 'Qu'on se le dise, en quel pays la police a-t-elle ces formes exquises de politesse et d'élégance?', p. 54.

[3] *The Englishwoman in Russia*, pp. 83–4. She recounts the story of 'the disappearing chair' in Orlov's office (in the late eighteenth century Sheshkovsky was popularly supposed to favour the use of this ingenious contrivance for administering floggings on the floor below the suspects under interrogation), stating that to her knowledge it had been in use on more than one occasion, p. 84. The story is repeated in an anonymous pamphlet published in the same year as this lady's account, see *A peep at Russia; its history, growth, extent, population and government*, 2nd ed. carefully revised (London, 1855), p. 14.

[4] To quote Maxwell, 'Ladies and gentlemen of rank and title are well known to be the servants of this department. The regiments, theatres, coffee-houses, public gardens, steamboats and

Security within the department

Inside the Department itself the policy of disclosing as little information as possible was also carefully observed. The outside world knew little or nothing of any of its officials other than Benckendorff, Dubbelt and Orlov. The nature of their work and the posts held in it by lesser officials were naturally not announced. Even ukazes which fixed the establishment of the Department's Headquarters carefully refrained from mentioning names, although there was an isolated departure from this practice at the beginning of the 1840s.[1] The identities of individual senior assistants such as von Vock, Mordvinov and Popov were were well known in certain official quarters, (and unofficially in literary circles), owing to the constant interference by the Department in censorship matters; but otherwise those who carried out its decisions lived and worked in obscurity.[2]

Members of the Corps of Gendarmes, on the other hand, were in a different category from that of their civilian colleagues. Their position and duties, especially when they were on detached service in the provinces, made it impossible and even, in accordance with some of their functions, undesirable to conceal their identity. As they were frequently required to work in the open, their appointments, movements and personalities all became known as soon as they assumed their duties in the Corps. After many years' experience this was evidently considered to be inconvenient in certain circumstances, and on 11 October 1841 an imperial command was circulated throughout the censorship offices: 'in notices of arrivals and departures there should generally be no mention of those persons who belong to the department of the Corps of Gendarmes, even in those cases when they are arriving at or departing from the capitals *off* duty'.[3] Apart from this order, however, no other instruction appears to have been issued to provide cover for Gendarme officers during their service. Unless they adopted civilian dress for the more

private houses have each their appointed spies. Russian spies are to be found in almost every city in the world, and there is a secret bureau in the post-office where the letters of foreigners and suspected persons are always opened', p. 209.

(The statement concerning the secret department in the post-office is confirmed by Golovine, vol. 1, p. 236.)

[1] See chapters Five, p. 172, note 2; Six, p. 182, note 5.

[2] It is noteworthy, for example, that Benckendorff's memoirs do not mention by name any of his assistants in the Third Department (Lt.-Col. Ozeretskovsky did not serve in its civilian component). Dubbelt's *Notes* are equally reticent; his letters to his wife contain passing references to Mordvinov and Sagtynsky, but disclose no information about them or their work.

[3] Lemke, pp. 129–30. He describes this order as 'a small touch...remarkably characteristic of the epoch...In its utter disdain and complete ignorance of the world of journalism, everything seemed to the government to be of equal importance: a feuilleton, a leading article or an ordinary list...of arrivals and departures...', *ibid.*

efficient execution of individual assignments, their activities could not expect to escape notice. (This was one of the chief anomalies of the Higher Police organization as a whole.)

In general it must be stated that the Third Department succeeded in preserving the anonymity of its chief agents and officials when it wished to do so, and its 'internal security' was good, considering the diversity of functions it was called upon to fulfil.

Summary of interests

The tasks undertaken by the Higher Police during the first thirty years of its existence extended over an immense field. By the end of the reign it had assumed full responsibility for all the multifarious activities that can be classified under the general heading of 'Intelligence', whether these concerned the overall conduct of political investigations, the organization of a supreme police force distributed across a vast empire, or the day-to-day surveillance of Russia's internal administration. These tasks alone constituted an extensive sphere of action, yet they represented only part of the commitments undertaken. From the 1830s the Department's interests also included the field of foreign espionage, first with the object of spying on Poles and Russians abroad and then with that of obtaining through Russian and foreign agents information on persons and events outside its jurisdiction. In the 1830s and 1840s more and more foreigners visited Russia for reasons ranging from business interests to simple curiosity, and to them too the Department turned its increased attention. By the 1850s the effect of the 1848 revolutions in Europe had so emphasized the need for constant vigilance inside Russia that the Department's influence was felt in every branch of the nation's affairs. In particular its control over the censorship, its interference in the field of literature, epitomized the whole reactionary trend of Nicholas' government.

The 'daily round of life in the Third Department', however, usually proceeded in an atmosphere somewhat different from that of a supreme Intelligence Bureau.[1] It was largely concerned with events of relatively far less importance to the state, for, in addition to its major undertakings concerned with the primary tasks of preserving Russia's national security and the efficiency of her internal administration, the Department devoted a large proportion of its time to acting as a kind of superior Court of Appeal. The 'Jubilee Report' even prided itself on the number of problems which only

---

[1] Trotsky, p. 110. The same opinion is expressed by Presnyakov: 'In the daily humdrum activity of the Third Dept. what is predominant is the extent of the petty interests of everyday existence...', *loc. cit.* p. 19.

the Third Department possessed sufficient authority to decide.[1] It regarded itself, just as Nicholas regarded himself, as the final arbiter of all questions; and it pried energetically into the most insignificant details of the country's life. 'It was in this noisy pother about little affairs that the days and labours of the Third Department passed. Amid family squabbles, judicial complaints and false denunciations (apparently on Saturdays the gendarmes used to organize bonfires for the week's batch of denunciations) there was no time to protest about lack of work...Nikolai Pavlovich could be pleased: gendarmes were busy working, with unremitting enthusiasm, for the country's benefit...'[2] All the published evidence tends to indicate that this redoubtable organization, for all that it genuinely inspired fear in the citizens whose interests it was supposed to protect, was easily deflected from its chief aims by the Tsar's demand for information on every conceivable topic. At the same time, his desire that the Department should exercise a beneficial *moral* influence on his subjects made it impossible for the Higher Police to disregard any of the appeals addressed to it, any report that might possibly prove important.

Reputation

The result of such a policy was interference everywhere, and this led to the universal hatred with which the Department was inevitably regarded. Despite the outward courtesy affected by its senior officials, the good character and even genuine kindness of many Gendarme staff-officers, it earned itself the reputation of pandering to countless petty-minded informers and busybodies whose motives were as ignoble as their actions. In many cases such accusations were doubtless well founded, for the peculiar position of the agent makes him especially liable to bribery. No amount of sentimentalizing on the part of Nicholas and Benckendorff could ensure that the Higher Police relied only on the services of honest and noble-minded patriots. Had its servants all proved to be 'incorruptible and infallible'[3]—a highly unlikely contingency—it might have been possible to justify its existence in the political circumstances of the reign. But once its activities were morally suspect, as they were bound to be, this justification disappeared; and the Third Department, which left behind it 'so sinister a memory, so pernicious a trace on the social, political and cultural life of nineteenth-century Russia',[4] must be accounted one of the most unpleasant features of the country's history.

[1] These various problems, under the title of 'Requests and Complaints submitted to the Third Department', are set out in detail in this Report, Bogucharsky, pp. 99–101. A translation is given in Appendix F, pp. 256–7. [2] Trotsky, p. 116.
[3] See comment by Leroy-Beaulieu, p. 137. [4] Sergeyev, *Kr. Arkh.* (1929), no. 37, p. 139.

Conclusion

The historical event which most affected the development of the Russian political police system in the second quarter of the nineteenth century was the Decembrist Revolt. Kiesewetter states that all Nicholas' actions were influenced by the revolt,[1] and the Third Department was primarily instituted to prevent any possible recurrence of the incidents of 14 December 1825.

Before Nicholas' reign political surveillance was not organized as an essential feature of government policy. It is true that some form of secret police had long existed, but the extent to which its activities were encouraged had always depended on the individual attitude of each autocrat. In the first quarter of the nineteenth century Alexander's general distrust of all his advisers was reflected in his treatment of those responsible for Russia's internal security,[2] and this goes far to explain why her secret police system developed some years later than that of other European states such as France and Austria, in both of which a 'higher police' was already established by the end of the eighteenth century.

In France a Ministry of Police (containing a Secret Department) existed intermittently from 1796, and, thanks to the shrewdness of its Minister, Fouché, quickly became a vital part of Napoleon's administration.[3] There is evidence that for a time Alexander admired this French institution of which Russia's 1811 Ministry of Police was undoubtedly an imitation, but the methods the latter employed led to its abolition eight years later and neither Alexander nor his successor desired its reintroduction. Alexander's interest in a Higher Police subordinated to a Minister was superseded by more urgent concerns—the defeat of Napoleon and the state of post-Napoleonic Europe —and the question of internal political surveillance was left undecided until the outbreak of conspiracy had made some kind of solution imperative.

In Austria a secret police system was in existence as early as the reign of

---

[1] A. A. Kizevetter, 'Vnutrennyaya politika v tsarstvovanie imperatora Nikolaya Pavlovicha', *Istoricheskie Ocherki* (Moscow, 1912), pp. 420–1. He comments: 'From this influence developed that intolerable police oppression which hung over Russian society throughout all the thirty years of Nicholas' reign', *ibid.*

[2] Trotsky states that Alexander's lack of confidence in his police explains 'the uneven structure of police organization and the rivalry between its various organs which lasted the whole of his reign', p. 12.

[3] See E. de Hauterive, *La Police secrète du Premier Empire* (Paris, 1913).

(Fouché served as Minister of Police from 1799 to 1802 and 1804 to 1810, when he was succeeded by General Savary, see Forssel, pp. 150, 207.)

the Emperor Joseph II (1765–90) under the skilful direction of its 'Polizei-meister', Count Pergen. The latter's successors after 1803 brought it to a high degree of efficiency in the reign of Joseph's nephew, Francis II (1792–1835), who shared Nicholas' preoccupation with police matters. By September 1814, when all continental rulers of any importance met to negotiate Europe's future, the Austrian secret police was probably unrivalled.[1] However, Professor Fournier's study of the Austrian archives of this period contains no evidence that Russian secret police agents were equally active in Vienna and a mention of the arrival there of 'eine Hauptperson der russischen Geheim-polizei, General de Witt'[2] is his only reference to its existence.

Inside Russia Alexander's 'Special Chancellery' occupied no privileged or independent position in the administration. Its head, von Vock, was a minor official whose own safety was threatened towards the end of the reign by the rival intrigues of more powerful figures such as Arakcheyev and Milorado-vich, each of whom possessed a secret police of his own, and Alexander steadfastly refused to remedy this situation even when presented by Bencken-dorff with a practical plan for doing so.

Nicholas, on the other hand, understood that an efficient centralized political police, if organized under his immediate control with unquestion-able authority over the whole empire, might succeed in achieving a number of important objectives. It could ensure the internal security of his country against any further attempts at subversion; it could keep him fully and con-tinuously informed of all defects and abuses in the administration; and it could act as the supreme intermediary between himself and those he governed. In addition to these primary aims it could preserve the sanctity of the law —as Nicholas understood law—and thus make a valuable contribution to the nation's morals.

Whatever may have been the shortcomings of the Third Department in succeeding years, it was undoubtedly created in the guise of a *beneficial* institution designed to protect the ordinary citizen against any persons capable of injuring him or his country.

Such, at least, was Nicholas' avowed intention. Convinced of his personal responsibility for the welfare of his subjects, he regarded the question of their

[1] Vasyutinsky, 'Tainaya Politsiya vo Frantsii i Avstrii', *loc. cit.* pp. 245–6.
[2] A. Fournier, *Die Geheimpolizei auf dem Wiener Kongress. Eine Auswahl aus ihren Papieren* (Leipzig, 1913), p. 21. 'General de Witt' (possibly Count I. O. Vitt, Chief of the Southern Settlements at the end of Alexander's reign, see chapter One, p. 45, note 3) is not known to have had any connexion with the 'Special Chancellery', although it is likely that he, like Miloradovich, controlled a private system of agents.

(Fournier's book contains a number of 'Rapporte' and 'Interzepten' submitted by the Austrian secret police in Vienna on the conduct of various foreign dignitaries present at the Congress. Evidently very few Russian letters were intercepted and those reproduced are of a strictly unofficial character.)

security from the viewpoint of the 'father-commander', an honest soldier chosen by Providence to guide their destinies. As Presnyakov puts it, 'It was not for nothing that Nicholas called Russia "his command"'.[1] This outlook explains why throughout his reign he attempted to organize his administration according to a strictly military pattern and why his Higher Police force, as one of its favoured branches, was more military than civil. It was natural for Nicholas to believe that soldiers were more likely to achieve satisfactory results than civilians; and he may also have believed that soldiers would be less likely to misuse police authority.

Fülöp-Miller, who maintains that cruelty is the most prominent feature of the Russian national character, contends that '...Nicholas achieved the most truly Russian creation by endowing cruelty with definite form, with permanent machinery set up by the State and most exact in its working. In his reign arose the Corps of Gendarmes, that mighty organization for the secret supervision of the whole Empire, in fear of which not only private citizens but all other Government departments trembled...All police matters were concentrated in the Third Section, the chiefs of which were in a position to decide at their own discretion the fate of every Russian subject...a decree issued by the Third Section admitted of no protest, no defence and no appeal ...',[2] but this view takes no account of Nicholas' purpose in establishing these organs. While it is impossible to deny that many Russians did suffer at their hands, it is unreasonable to accuse Nicholas of 'endowing cruelty with form' as though this were part of a considered policy.

Indeed it is evident that by his refusal to re-create a Ministry of Police Nicholas rejected the principle of establishing the kind of political surveillance previously experienced in Russia. Furthermore, Benckendorff's Project of January 1826 advocating the creation of a reformed Higher Police emphasized the necessity of basing it above all else on lofty moral concepts.[3] Nicholas accepted the proposals contained in this Project with only one exception. Aware of the temptations to which both Fouché and Balashov had succumbed (the use of intrigue as a means of obtaining power), he was not prepared to countenance the delegation of such high authority to any Minister. Fülöp-Miller does not mention that the powers entrusted to the chiefs of the new Higher Police were strictly subordinated to Nicholas' personal direction, and that they were not encouraged to initiate any policy without first obtaining his approval. When these officials ventured to act on their own initiative, it may safely be assumed that they were convinced of their ability to justify

[1] Presnyakov, 'Samoderzhavie Nikolaya I', *loc. cit.* p. 19.
[2] René Fülöp-Miller, introd. to A. T. Vassilyev, *The Ochrana, the Russian Secret Police* (London, 1930), pp. 15, 17.
[3] 'Cette police devra mettre tous ses soins à acquérir une force morale, qui dans toute opération est la plus sûr [*sic*] garant du succès', see Appendix A, p. 240.

15-2

such actions to the Tsar if called upon to do so. Like Nicholas, these men genuinely believed that the influence exerted by the Third Department on society was both necessary and desirable. The reputation it subsequently gained should not be allowed to obscure the fact that the motives that led to its institution were in many respects commendable.[1]

Before reviewing the degree of success achieved by this Police in the objectives stated above, it is relevant to consider the main difference between the senior officials of the Third Department and their predecessors in earlier 'Secret' or 'Special' offices engaged on similar work. This difference lay in the fact that those who held the leading posts in the Higher Police after 1826 were almost invariably selected from among serving or retired army officers of *dvoryanstvo* status.[2] The distinguished careers and excellent characters of these officers were evidently considered adequate compensation for their total lack of previous experience in police work; and their military training ensured that they would accept orders unquestioningly without attempting to exceed them. This was entirely in accordance with Nicholas' usual outlook. Discussing it in general terms, his biographer Polievktov states: 'With few exceptions he sought not so much for collaborators as for those who would whole-heartedly execute his wishes, and he sought for them among persons who by their origin and status were alien to the political traditions of the end of the eighteenth and beginning of the nineteenth centuries...'[3]

Benckendorff personified this new type of secret police official. Despite such negative features of his character as superficiality, self-deception, *naïveté*, sentimentality and apathy, he was at heart a kindly respectable man of indisputable loyalty. He was not a politician but an influential member of the Imperial Suite to whom a very special function was entrusted. He was feared not because his personality in the least resembled that of Sheshkovsky but merely because he occupied a potentially frightening appointment.[4]

---

[1] Cf. 'What was later made of this institution, which had as its principle such excellent aims, I do not venture to say. I have only desired to present in a true light how noble and unsullied were Emperor Nikolai Pavlovich's initial steps, which are interpreted by many people without discernment', 'Iz pamyatnykh zamyetok P. M. Golenishcheva-Kutuzova-Tolstago', *R. Arkh.*, *loc. cit.* p. 221.

[2] It is noteworthy that Nicholas' political police system did not develop as the result of private initiative on the part of talented amateurs. There is no parallel in Russia to the career of a man like Vidocq in France, even though Vidocq specialized in criminal rather than political offences.
(Eugène-François Vidocq (1775–1857), see Philip John Stead, *Vidocq. A Biography* (London, 1953).)

[3] Polievktov, *op. cit.* p. 63. This view is echoed by Trotsky who quotes Herzen to the effect that 'He [the Emperor] needed agents, not assistants, men who would obey, not advise...', p. 121.

[4] The early initiative shown by Benckendorff in 1821 and 1826 and his eighteen years as Chief of Gendarmes appears to have convinced a number of writers that he was a genuinely awe-inspiring figure. Merezhkovsky, for instance, in his historical reconstruction of the Decembrist Revolt, even goes so far as to declare that 'Benckendorff frightened him [Nicholas], entangled him in a sticky cobweb of fear as a spider entangles a fly...the fly would not free itself

Making due allowances for the variations in their characters, much the same can be said of both Orlov and Dubbelt. Both men were soldiers, both were essentially the instruments of Nicholas' will and, as far as is known, desired to be nothing more. Orlov despised his post, preferring the world of diplomacy, and was content to leave the routine direction of the Higher Police to his competent subordinate. Dubbelt's more complex character at least allows the conclusion that according to his lights he was a sincere and devoted patriot whose severity was primarily prompted by a determination to protect his Tsar and fellow-countrymen from the dangers of revolution.

Responsibility to Nicholas for the execution of Higher Police Policy was concentrated in the hands of these three men, assisted by such able civilian advisers as von Vock, Mordvinov and Popov. It is some measure of the character of these officials that, despite their functions, the majority of known witnesses have readily testified to their good qualities.

On a lower level, it is permissible to conclude from the available evidence that many members of the Corps of Gendarmes succeeded in upholding the high principles laid down for them to follow. Even discounting the possibly biased accounts of their activities left by Colonel Stogov and Major Lomachevsky, the incidental testimony of statesmen such as Baron Korff or of Russians arrested by the Third Department such as Herzen and Selivanov all tends to prove that as a rule senior officers in the Corps bore little if any resemblance to the traditional type of secret police agent.[1] On the contrary, one is struck by the absence in contemporary memoirs of accusations against individual gendarme officers. This must be attributed at least in part to the fact that these officers owed their position to their qualifications of character. Their work required that they should be socially acceptable, and the public was aware that many of a gendarme's duties were performed openly.[2] Trotsky prefers to believe that the apparently excellent behaviour of the

from the cobweb. There had been Arakcheyev, now there would be Benckendorf', Dmitri S. Merezhkovsky, *December the Fourteenth*, trans. by Nathalie A. Duddington (London, 1930), pp. 152, 153.

This must be accounted a considerable exaggeration. Benckendorff's character was entirely dissimilar to Arakcheyev's and there is no evidence that he ever frightened Nicholas. Indeed, the contrary is more probable, as was believed by Herzen: 'It is said that whenever Count Benckendorff entered the Tsar's presence—and he did so about five times a day—he used to turn pale: these were the men the Emperor needed', see Trotsky, *ibid.*

[1] See evidence on General Kutsinsky, chapter Five, p. 175, note 4; General Polozov, chapter Six, p. 186, note 2; General Lesovsky, *ibid.* p. 193, note 2. Although emanating from a different kind of source (the Third Department's 1828 Annual Report), the evidence on Colonel Rutkovsky is also of interest in this context, see chapter Six, p. 208, note 1.

[2] Even a foreigner revolted by the prevalence of spying in Russia could write that the Corps of Gendarmes 'consists of soldiers of good conduct, and is officered by worthy men...[It] has no connexion with the actual system of espionage; it only receives and delivers the detected victims at the appointed spot...', *Recollections of Russia during Thirty-Three Years' Residence*, pp. 242, 243.

Corps was nothing more than a façade: 'Outwardly the gendarmes appeared in a sky-blue uniform and snow-white gloves. Just as cloudless and pure should have been their conscience. But behind the walls of the building by Tsepnoi Bridge the gloves were taken off when necessary and the hands would stretch out for the knout which was capable of leaving bloody traces.'[1] However, he quotes no facts in substantiation of this opinion and it must be considered exaggerated. As far as can be stated with any certainty, brutality was not generally practised by members of the Corps and modern secret police methods such as 'brainwashing' were entirely unknown.

Nevertheless, despite the apparent excellence both of Nicholas' motives and of the character of his Higher Police officials, it is impossible to regard the Third Department as anything but a pernicious organization. Shil'der, in discussing 'the historic handkerchief...which was to wipe away the maximum number of tears shed all over Russia', states that the hopes and expectations of contemporaries of the reign were not realized in practice. Even if the handkerchief legend was true, he says, in fact the beneficial purpose that was intended was not attained and the very opposite occurred. It was just this handkerchief that became even more bedewed with tears caused by the activities of the new institution...and the original guiding principles receded into the background; it was as though they were wiped from the memory of those called upon to direct them, and for many years ahead the evils that centuries had accumulated remained untouched.'[2] An almost identical criticism is recorded by Schiemann in his assessment of Benckendorff's 1827 'Instructions': 'The opposite of what the instructions intended was finally achieved. The Third Department was neither beloved nor respected, but was indeed feared, and thus it helped more than anything else to give the régime of Nicholas I the character of harsh despotism which is its distinguishing feature...it...transformed itself more and more into the most frightful instrument of a tyranny "draped in nobility"—a tyranny which was endured by the nation as its fate, accepted because there was no possibility of escaping it.'[3] These two opinions are quoted as typical of the general reaction to the achievements of the Third Department, and the student of this historical phenomenon is thus confronted with an obvious paradox. On the one hand, its Chiefs and many of its members appear in themselves to have been worthy individuals; on the other, their activities undeniably caused widespread distress and dissatisfaction.[4]

[1] Trotsky, p. 138.

[2] Shil'der, *Imperator Nikolai Pervyi*, vol. 1, p. 467. (Lemke concludes the first chapter of his book on Nicholas' Gendarmes and Literature with this quotation, p. 227.)

[3] Schiemann, *Geschichte Russlands unter Kaiser Nikolaus I.*, vol. 2, p. 99. (The text of these Instructions is given as Appendix C, pp. 243–4.)

[4] Writing anonymously in the 1840s a patriotic Russian civil servant stated: 'L'institution qui

To explain this anomaly it is necessary to examine the extent to which the Department achieved its main objectives during the reign.

With the exception of the Polish rising of 1830-1, which despite its significance was a localized occurrence, Russia was not threatened by any further attempts at organized political subversion after the collapse of the Decembrist movement. This major revolt found no support in society and the savage punishment of its leaders acted as a natural deterrent to would-be 'free-thinkers'. Furthermore, Nicholas' policy of extending political police control over the strategically important areas of his empire tended to ensure a long period of internal security. Nor was this achieved solely by the expedient of creating more Gendarme Districts in the 1830s with their additional complement of staff-officers. A stricter censorship of all publications, increased surveillance over Russian subjects in foreign countries and the imposition of tighter restrictions on travel abroad combined to create an atmosphere of vigilant suspicion which grew as the reign advanced. The struggle with subversion—or what was held to represent it—continued without interruption and, in Trotsky's view, 'the Third Department, despite all the defects of its organization, to a relative degree coped with the work it involved'.[1] In this respect, therefore, it may be claimed that the Department was at least successful in preventing the outbreak of political disorders which, arguably, might otherwise have occurred.

Nicholas' reign was, however, a period of stagnation in Russian history, and for the most part society regarded its development with something approaching complacency. Rebellion against the existing order was not generally contemplated. From the official point of view, the state of the nation, notwithstanding administrative shortcomings, was considered satisfactory so long as external order and discipline prevailed.[2] What mattered

blesse profondément la dignité du gouvernement ainsi que celle de la nation, c'est celle de la police secrète ou de la gendarmerie', the suppression of which 'est le vœu ardent de l'intérêt réel de l'Etat et de la nation', *La Russie en 1844. Système de Législation, d'Administration et de Politique de la Russie en 1844 par un homme d'état russe* (Paris, 1845), pp. 133, 163.

(The authorship of this work is attributed to one 'Pelchinsky'. He was possibly Vikentii Stanislavovich Pel'chinsky (?-1855 or 56), a graduate of Vil'no University who entered government service in 1827. By 1834 he had become an 'Official for Special Commissions' attached to the Ministry of Finance and from then until 1853 served as an official of the Dept. for Manufactures and Internal Trade, becoming a State Councillor in 1840. He spent much of his service abroad where he fulfilled various government commissions 'as a secret agent', see *RBS*. His name is not mentioned by either Lemke or Trotsky and it would appear that his employment abroad was not connected with the Third Department. The *RBS* article does not mention the work quoted above nor does it explain how such a man came to write it—if he did write it. Possibly its anonymity saved its author from official displeasure.)

[1] Trotsky, p. 60.

[2] All historians from Solovyov to de Grunwald stress this feature of the reign. It was particularly aptly described by the Marquis de Custine whose account of his visit to Russia so enraged contemporary official circles there: 'Plus je vois la Russie, plus j'approuve l'Empereur lorsqu'il

most was the façade, not the reality. And who could doubt that all was well under such an Emperor? As Benckendorff himself expressed it to a critic of Chaadayev's *Lettres Philosophiques* in 1836: 'Le passé de la Russie a été admirable; son présent est plus que magnifique; quant à son avenir il est au delà de tout ce que l'imagination la plus hardie se peut figurer; voilà, mon cher, le point de vue sous lequel l'histoire russe doit être conçue et écrite.'[1] Such sublime self-deception is all the more remarkable because only a few years were to elapse before events proved that Russia's present was deplorable and Nicholas' administrative system bankrupt.

The second objective of keeping the Emperor informed 'on all events without exception' was achieved in the sense that the Department submitted a constant flow of reports on the state of the administration. Indeed, to judge by the figures quoted in the 'Jubilee Report', it prided itself on the number of cases which passed through its hands. In its early years these were stated to be relatively few, but they increased with the expansion of its activities: 'Before 1838 the annual total of incoming papers alternated between 10 and 12 thousand, of outgoing up to 4 thousand, of imperial instructions up to 2 hundred issued, and every year approximately a thousand new cases were initiated. From 1839 to 1861 the annual total of outgoing papers was from 5 to 7 thousand, of reports submitted to His Majesty from 300 to 600, of imperial instructions from two hundred to four hundred and fifty issued, and new cases initiated numbered from 1,400 to 2 thousand.'[2] It cannot be claimed, however, that the results obtained by the Department were proportionate to the amount of business transacted. Official corruption continued to permeate the administration and as late as 1850 a contemporary writer compared the Russian government to the sea—'Beneath the surface the big fishes devoured the small ones, but on the surface all was peaceful.'[3] But Nicholas desired above all else the tranquillity of his empire and it must be

défend aux Russes de voyager, et rend l'accès de son pays difficile aux étrangers. Le régime politique de la Russie ne résisterait pas vingt ans à la libre communication avec l'Occident de l'Europe. N'écoutez pas les forfanteries des Russes; ils prennent le faste pour l'élégance, le luxe pour la politesse, la police et la peur pour les fondements de la société. A leur sens, être discipliné c'est être civilisé... Je hais les prétextes: j'ai vu qu'en Russie l'ordre sert de prétexte à l'oppression...', A. de Custine, *La Russie en 1839*, 4 vols. in 1 (Paris, 1843), vol. 2, p. 12; vol. 4, p. 442.

[1] M. Zhikharyov, 'P. Ya. Chaadayev', *Vyestnik Evropy* (1871), Sept., pp. 37–8. Lemke commented 'Benckendorff's view was that of the whole régime', p. 411.

[2] Bogucharsky, *loc. cit.* p. 117. (The Report continued: 'All this vast amount of business was conducted and is to-day [1876] conducted by an extremely small staff of officials who were, in addition, also entrusted with exceedingly important missions both inside Russia and abroad, missions which were undertaken not only on behalf of the Department but also on behalf of other government offices at the personal request of ministers.', *ibid.*)

[3] See Stählin, 'Aus den Berichten der III. Abteilung S.M. Höchsteigener Kanzlei', *loc. cit.* vol. 7 (1933), p. 382.

concluded that, so long as information reached him in sufficient quantity, he was satisfied that his Higher Police represented the best available instrument for attaining this end.

(It is also relevant to note here that the Third Department's reports on persons and events abroad were of undoubted use in helping him to formulate his policy in matters not relating to internal questions.)

The third objective—that of 'bringing the voice of suffering mankind to the throne of the Tsars'[1]—did achieve a limited measure of success. The powers conferred on the Department meant that a decision taken by any of its members could lead to immediate action, overriding the views of all central and local authorities. Any Gendarme Colonel to whom a just petition was addressed could, by reporting direct to his Chief, obtain an Imperial ruling against which there could be no appeal. There is evidence that members of the public used this channel to by-pass official procrastination, and undoubtedly a number of wrongs were righted, although this procedure automatically incurred the resentment of administrative authorities.[2] The amount of time and trouble expended by gendarme staff-officers on individual cases—particularly in family disputes—proves that private concerns were investigated as assiduously as public affairs. The 'Jubilee Report', while smugly disclaiming any desire on the part of the Higher Police to interfere in judicial matters, states nevertheless that the Department 'was compelled to have recourse to extremely frequent exceptions from this rule in so-called domestic cases' and claims that it, 'being in such cases the sole refuge of the offended party, took extra-ordinary measures in its defence, and in circumstances of particular importance brought them to the imperial attention'.[3]

Recriminations against the activities of the Third Department have been so frequent and vociferous in Russian histories and memoirs that the little good it did achieve deserves to be noted with especial care. The view of the nineteenth-century French historian Leroy-Beaulieu, one of the few to comment on this aspect of its work, is worth recording: 'It is scarcely possible that a great state institution, however faulty, should not do *some* good, at least occasionally. Thus it was even with the nefarious Third Section. Its "providential" mission was not *all* a delusion. Many a crying private wrong, especially in matrimonial affairs, *has* been redressed through its agency. Where laws are bad or inadequate, it is not altogether a bad calamity to have a last resort, a power that can bend or override the law.'[4] In

---

[1] See Benckendorff's Instructions, Appendix C, p. 243.
[2] See Golenishchev–Kutuzov–Tolstoi, *loc. cit. ibid.*
[3] Bogucharsky, pp. 116, 117.
[4] Leroy-Beaulieu, p. 142. This author quotes a number of actual instances where the mediation of the Third Department led to just decisions, pp. 142–3.

the opinion of contemporaries, however, the Third Department achieved little in its attempts to bring the Tsar and his people into closer contact. Already in 1841 (during the period of Benckendorff's eclipse) General Kutuzov could report, on his return from a special mission of inspection, 'There is no one person close to Your Imperial Majesty's throne but rather several who surround it, constituting a barrier through which abuses are invisible to you and the voice of the oppression and sufferings endured by your people is inaudible. It is easier to attain to the throne of the King of Heaven than to that of the King on earth, as our people says; and its words are true...'[1]

In general, therefore, the beneficial aims of the Third Department were achieved only in a very limited sphere.

There were many reasons for this lack of success. Among the most evident were the contradictions inherent in the system of political surveillance adopted by Nicholas. It was one thing to accept the high-minded if naïve principles enunciated by Benckendorff and slavishly imitated by Dubbelt, it was quite another to expect that these principles would meet with a sympathetic reception from the Russian society of the day, which naturally objected to the investigation of all its activities by a semi-secret body combining limitless authority with social pretensions. The personal respectability of many gendarme staff-officers was rightly considered irrelevant, for, whether or not such a course of action was distasteful to them, they were obliged by their duties to employ the services of lower-grade agents and informers; and it was feared that such persons would not hesitate to denounce anyone, innocent or guilty, if by so doing they could derive advantages for themselves. This alone disposed of the moral argument in favour of an institution such as the Third Department.

But as Nicholas was convinced of its necessity, the system was introduced and expanded irrespective of public opinion. To his way of thinking its purpose was admirable, its usefulness undeniable and in addition it formed an essential part of his Own Chancellery. There could therefore be no prospect of its disappearance, and from modest beginnings it quickly developed into a system of government.[2] Those it governed could not protest against its orders; they could only resent them and obey.[3] And obedience to the

---

[1] 'Sostoyanie gosudarstva v 1841 godu. (Zapiska N. Kutuzova, podannaya imperatoru Nikolayu I.)', *R. Star.* (1898), vol. 95, p. 518. (This document, dated 2 Apr. 1841, is also reproduced in M. O. Gershenzon (pod. red.), *Epokha Nikolaya I* (Moscow, 1910), pp. 169–82.) Kiesewetter describes this report as 'submitted to the emperor by General-in-Waiting Kutuzov after a tour of several provinces undertaken by the latter', p. 499. (General K. is not recorded in the *RBS*.)

[2] In the opinion of Polievktov, this was true as early as 1830, p. 201.

[3] Lermontov expressed this feeling in some famous verses written before his final period of exile in 1840:

Higher Police was what Nicholas demanded. Its popularity was a minor consideration.

A further explanation of the Department's failure lay in the fact that, with all its authority, it was unable to alter the basic character of Russia's administration. As von Vock noted in his letters to Benckendorff, corruption was deeply ingrained in its bureaucracy and, in the view of one civil servant, the Third Department's efforts not only failed to remedy this situation but even contributed to the abuses that marred official life.[1]

The accuracy of its information and the integrity of many of its agents was also questionable. As we have seen, Dubbelt himself realized this, and it was an opinion largely shared by contemporaries. Dolgorukov, for instance, expressed it when he wrote:

One of the greatest *naïvetés* of the Russian government consists in its belief that the political police enables it to know what goes on. It is wholly mistaken. The spies it employs take its money, tell it what they wish and slander their personal enemies. In a word, the government spends a great deal of money but discovers nothing, opens the door to abuses and assists the personal grudges of the agents of its police. And how could it be otherwise? A wretch who accepts cash as a spy and informer is always ready to lie; can his word be trusted? Can one accept his good faith or his statements?[2]

Hostile critics were particularly ready to accuse officials of the Higher Police of venality, arbitrary arrests, vindictive denunciations and so on, and it is not easy to assess how far they should be credited.[3] These, however, were the customary abuses of earlier secret police offices in Russia, and it cannot

'Farewell, unwashed Russia,
Land of slaves, land of masters,
Both you, sky-blue uniforms,
And thou, nation subservient to them.

Perhaps, beyond the Caucasian hills
I shall conceal myself from thy tsars,
From their all-seeing eye,
From their all-hearing ears.'

M. Yu. Lermontov, *Poln. Sobr. Soch.*, 5 vols. (izd. Academia, Moscow–Leningrad, 1936–7), vol. 2, p. 88; for date, see commentary, *ibid.* pp. 222–3.

[1] 'Si le gouvernement se proposait de recourir à cet expédient [la gendarmerie] pour extirper les abus, la vénalité des fonctionnaires: on peut déclarer franchement et positivement qu'il est dans une étrange aberration, car tous les abus proviennent des institutions défectueuses... toute institution secrète investie d'un pouvoir discrétionnaire conduit évidemment à augmenter des abus et non pas à les supprimer', *La Russie en 1844*, pp. 134, 135.

[2] Dolgoroukow, p. 293. This view was also held by Pel'chinsky: 'Quelles sont les garanties de la haute probité des agents de gendarmerie? Qui oserait hautement les affirmer?', *La Russie en 1844*, pp. 135–6.

[3] See Dolgoroukow, pp. 298–309.

be shown that the Third Department was much less inclined to them than its predecessors. Widespread doubts of its infallibility and incorruptibility must be accounted another reason for its unsavoury reputation.

Yet another lay in the general feeling of shame that such an institution should have been thought necessary or desirable for Russians. At home they were offended by the knowledge that all their actions were subject to secret surveillance; abroad they were humiliated by the sympathy or curiosity of foreigners who asked embarrassing questions.[1] It was impossible to conceal the fact that no Russian was trusted by his government to think and act as an intelligent and *loyal* individual, and the realization of this truth caused general indignation.

To sum up, therefore, Nicholas' Higher Police was discredited because its arbitrary authority was universally feared and hated. Its gendarmes were considered to be interfering busybodies whose methods were as ineffective as they were unpopular. Even though a gendarme might himself be a decent official acting in the open, his instructions from the Third Department and his sources of information were both suspect and secret. By common consent this system did nothing but breed spies and informers. Persons guilty of nothing more than minor indiscretions of conduct were arrested, imprisoned and exiled throughout the reign, there was no freedom of expression, and this resulted in a general atmosphere of suspicion and oppression which continued until Nicholas' death.

One final and important contradiction should be stressed. Although Nicholas' Third Department is normally referred to by historians as a secret police, its executive arm was organized on a non-secret basis. This policy may have been adopted to avoid the evil consequences that had disfigured similar institutions in the past, but in practice it robbed the new system of much of its efficacy. The Corps of Gendarmes had nothing in common with the French Gendarmerie[2] apart from its name and para-military character, although it has been assumed that the former was modelled on the latter. Nicholas' decision to inaugurate a para-military Corps as part of his Higher Police changed the whole character of political control in Russia, and possibly not for the better.

This view was clearly expressed in General Kutuzov's 1841 report, in

---

[1] 'Partout on entend ces mots humiliants: N'est-ce pas que votre gouvernement ne vous permet pas de voyager à l'étranger? N'est-ce pas que vous n'osez pas venir à Paris? Ensuite on est obligé de boucher ses oreilles pour éviter d'entendre partout répéter: des espions russes contre les Russes mêmes', *La Russie en 1844*, p. 136.

[2] The Gendarmerie Nationale was initially created by the Assemblée Constituante at the end of 1790 and subsequently incorporated as a disciplinary organ of the First Empire in 1801. It was a 'force militaire chargée de veiller à la sûreté publique, d'assurer le maintien de l'ordre et de l'exécution des lois', see Larousse du XXᵉ siècle (Paris, 1930), vol. 32, p. 747; and, as a branch of the ordinary police force, it did not concern itself with political surveillance.

which he stated that the economic and administrative reasons which had reduced the state to a deplorable condition were concealed from the Tsar.

. . . why are they concealed when, it is said, we have a secret police? But this is only *said*. We have a Corps of Gendarmes, and not a secret police which ought to see and hear everything while it itself is neither seen nor heard. . . When the Corps of Gendarmes was instituted, an analogous organization in France was taken as an example, but it was forgotten that in that country the gendarmes are the equivalent of our Internal Security Troops[1] and that in that country there is a higher secret police which controls the activities of the gendarmes. With us it is just the other way round—France's admirable institution is reversed: secret police agents are subordinated to the gendarmes and thus, because they are obliged to maintain contact with them, they have made themselves known to everyone . . .

As a result of the harmful trend of our century, a secret police is necessary, but, I repeat, a secret one in the full meaning of the word. Any distinction of dress, any interference in administrative affairs is at variance with its purpose . . .[2]

Nicholas' reaction to this criticism is not known. Possibly he felt that it was then too late to embark on a radical reorganization of an already established system. Possibly he preferred to adhere to his original decision and hope that succeeding years would witness an improvement in the operation of this police. In any case, the system remained unchanged. Kutuzov's objections to it, however, were well founded. Gendarmes were neither special agents nor ordinary police officers, but an unsuccessful combination of both. They were unable to work in secrecy and their dealings with petty informers of all kinds inevitably brought them into disrepute. This reputation extended to all connected with the Higher Police.

The Third Department was the most typical feature of a reactionary period in Russian history. Its immediate proximity to the Tsar placed it in a position whence it could act supra-legally in accordance with his wishes, taking no account of any other authority. This, in Nicholas' view, was right and proper—the wishes of an Autocrat must unquestionably be legal. Their execution frequently devolved upon the Higher Police, and it was this which made it so personal an instrument of Nicholas' policy. Presnyakov states:

Accumulating and serving as precedents, the Tsar's decisions assume the importance of special legislation, unsystematic, unplanned and disconnected. Proceeding from one occasion to another, it exchanged the normal functions of supreme authority for a multifarious variety of different directives in place of regular, planned work. In this way directives that were inconsistent and contradictory, casual and fragmentary, were inevitable. This could not have been prevented by exceptional

[1] 'Vnutrennyaya Strazha', see chapter One, p. 31, note 1; chapter Three, p. 80, notes 2, 3; p. 88, note 3.
[2] 'Sostoyanie gosudarstva v 1841 godu', *R. Star.*, *loc. cit.* pp. 528, 529. (It is remarkable that neither Lemke nor Trotsky nor Monas mentions the inconsistencies noted by General Kutuzov.)

genius and the ability to assimilate the maximum amount of information, but Nicholas was far from possessing such qualities...[1]

This explains why the Third Department was forced to interfere in so many different concerns, why it had to be ubiquitous. In no other way could Nicholas make his influence felt everywhere and at all times. But his mistrustfulness, his insistence on personal rule and his determination to apply it by force brought about no improvement in Russia's internal condition. On the contrary, his political police system contributed rather to a worsening of this condition. Its actions were directed against the very ideas of freedom and liberalism which might, in time, have made its existence superfluous.

[1] Presnyakov, *loc. cit.* pp. 14–15.

Personal memorandum by General-in-Waiting Benckendorff on the formation of a Higher Police under the command of a Special Minister and Inspector of a Corps of Gendarmes

Les événements du 14 Décembre et les horribles trames qui depuis plus de 10 ans ont préparé cette explosion, prouvent assez la nullité de la police de l'Empire, comme aussi, l'indispensable nécessité d'en organiser une, d'après un plan adroitement combiné et activement exécuté. Une contre-police secrète n'est presque pas possible; les honnêtes gens en sont effrayés, les coquins la devinent.

La perlustration des correspondances est déjà une contre-police, et la meilleure, par ses moyens constants, qui embrassent toute l'étendue de l'Empire. Il faut pour cela avoir, dans quelques points seulement, des chefs de bureaux de poste d'une probité et d'un zèle éprouvé: comme à Pétersbourg, Moscou, Kiew, Wilna, Riga, Kharkow, Odessa, Kazan et Tobolsk.

Il faut que la police pour être bonne et pour couvrir toute l'étendue de l'Empire ait un centre connu, et des ramifications aboutissantes à tous les points; qu'elle soit crainte, et respectée par les qualités morales de celui qui en sera le chef.

Il devrait porter le nom de ministre de la police et inspecteur des gens d'armes militaires et des provinces. Ce titre seul lui ouvre les avis de tous les honnêtes gens, qui voudraient prévenir le gouvernement sur quelques trames, ou lui donner des nouvelles intéressantes. Les coquins, les intrigants et les dupes, revenus de leurs erreurs ou cherchant à racheter leurs fautes par les délations, sauront où s'adresser.

Ce titre réunirait la coopération de tous les officiers de gens d'armes, dispersés dans toutes les villes de Russie et dans toutes les divisions de l'armée: donnerait le moyen d'y placer des gens intelligents et d'employer des hommes purs, qui souvent répugnant au rôle d'espions cachés se font un devoir de ce métier, sous l'uniforme, qui les rend coopérateurs du gouvernement.

Des grades, des croix, un remercîment, encouragent davantage l'officier, que des sommes d'argent n'encouragent des gens secrètement employés, qui souvent font le double métier d'espionner pour et contre le gouvernement. Le ministre de police devra voyager tous les ans; se trouver de temps en temps aux grandes foires, aux contrats, ou plus aisément il peut former des liaisons utiles et séduire des gens, avides d'argent.

Il dépendra de sa perspicacité de ne donner une confiance positive à personne en particulier. Le chef de chancellerie même ne doit pas connaître tous les individus employés ni tous les aboutissants.

L'intérêt personnel, la crainte de perdre une place qui doit être très lucrative, répondront de la fidélité de ce chef de chancellerie, pour ce qui indispensablement doit être connu de lui.

Les différents ministres civils et militaires les particuliers même trouvront un aide, un appuis dans une police organisée dans ce sens. Cette police devra mettre tous ses soins à acquérir une force morale, qui dans toute opération est la plus sûr garant du succès. Tout homme comme il faut conçoit la nécessité et appelle de ses vœux la vigilence d'une police conservatrice de la tranquillité, dévoilant et prévenant le désordre et les crimes. Mais tout homme craint une police de délation et d'intrigue. La première donne la sécurité aux honnêtes gens, la seconde les effraye et les éloigne du trône.

C'est donc du choix de ce ministre, de l'organisation de ce ministère, qui dépendra l'impulsion première et la plus importante de cette police et de l'opinion qu'elle imprimera au public.

La chose décidée il faudra combiner un travail, qui trop important pour être précipité, doit être le résultat de mûres réflexions d'essais et de la pratique même.

from N. K. Shil'der, *Imperator Nikolai Pervyi. Ego Zhizn' i Tsarstvovanie*, vol. 3 (prilozheniya k pervomu tomu), LV, pp. 780–1.

Notes

This Appendix is entitled—'Sobstvennoruchnaya zapiska General-Adyutanta Benkendorfa ob uchrezhdyenii Vysshei Politsii pod nachal'stvom osobago Ministra i Inspektora Korpusa Zhandarmov'

A footnote in Russian states: 'This Memorandum dates from January 1826. By imperial command it was forwarded on 12 April 1826 to General-in-Waiting Diebich and to Count P. A. Tolstoi with instructions that it should be returned after examination to his Majesty's own hands "with your opinion".'

The Russian text of the Memorandum is printed in *Russkaya Starina* (1900), Dec., pp. 615–16; and may also be found in Lemke, pp. 12–13.

Imennoi Ukaz addressed to the Acting Minister of Internal Affairs. (No. 449 dated 3 July 1826.)

On the attachment of the Special Chancellery of the Ministry of Internal Affairs to His Majesty's Own Chancellery

In recognizing the necessity of organizing under the command of General-in-Waiting Benckendorff a Third Department of my Chancellery, I order: that the Special Chancellery of the Ministry of Internal Affairs be abolished, transferring on the selection of General-in-Waiting Benckendorff a part of its officials under the direction of Actual State Councillor von Vock to the establishment of this Department.

I nominate as the spheres of interest of this Third Department of my Chancellery

1. All regulations and matters of general interest concerning the Higher Police.

2. Information relating to the number of varying sects and dissenting movements existing in the state.

3. Information relating to discoveries of false paper money, coins, seals, documents etc., inquiries into which subsequently become the responsibility of the Ministries of Finance and Internal Affairs.

4. Detailed information on all persons under police surveillance; also all regulations pertaining thereto.

5. Questions relating to the exile, disposal and accommodation of suspicious and harmful persons.

6. Inspectorial and administrative control of all places of confinement in which state criminals are held.

7. All edicts and regulations concerning foreigners residing in Russia, entering and leaving the confines of the State.

8. Information and reports on all events without exception.

9. Statistical information relating to the police.

On the basis of these principles I propose:

1. That in accordance with the above stated the Special Chancellery of the Ministry of Internal Affairs be incorporated into the establishment of the Third Department of My Own Chancellery.

2. That all matters dealt with in the Special Chancellery which are not listed above and which should remain under the control of the Ministry of Internal affairs should be distributed throughout other departments of this Ministry.

3. That all Heads of Provinces inform other persons whom it may concern that they should report to me personally concerning all the above-mentioned subjects which are dealt with by the Third Department of My Own Chancellery, to whom relevant communications should be sent.

4. That the appropriate relations should be established with General-in-Waiting Benckendorff concerning all methods likely to prove the most successful for ensuring this provision.

from *Poln. Sobr. Zak.*, 2-oe Sobr. vol. 1, pp. 665–6

Instructions given by the Chief of Gendarmes to Lieut. Shervud-Vernyi, Life Guards Dragoon Regt., 13 January 1827

'Endeavouring faithfully to fulfil the duty laid upon me by His Imperial Majesty and thus to promote the philanthropic aims of the Sovereign Emperor and his fatherly desire to maintain the well-being and tranquillity of all classes in Russia, to see them enjoying the protection of the law and the establishment of complete and universal justice, I order you as your bounden duty, sparing no pains nor that solicitude peculiar to every loyal subject, to observe the following in the furtherance of your calling:

1. Your particular attention should be directed to abuses, disorders and acts contrary to the law which may occur in all branches of administration, in all classes of persons and in all parts of the country.

2. You should ensure by surveillance that law and order and the rights of citizens are not liable to be infringed by any man's personal authority, by the predominance of force or by the prejudicial tendencies of ill-intentioned persons.

3. Before proceeding to expose any offences that may occur, you may personally confer with and even give preliminary warning to the senior officials and staffs of those authorities or tribunals (or even the individuals concerned) in which you have noted illegal activities, and may then report to me when your endeavours shall have proved vain, for the purpose of your office should be, first and foremost, to anticipate and extirpate every kind of wrongdoing; for example, should rumours reach you of the dubious morality and bad behaviour of young persons, you should warn the parents or those on whom their fate depends of these facts, or else endeavour by kindly suggestions to instil into the offenders an aspiration to good deeds and to bring them out on to the path of truth before publicly revealing their poor conduct to the government.

4. Your own noble feelings and principles should doubtless win you the respect of all classes, and your calling, strengthened by public confidence, will then achieve its purpose and be of obvious benefit to the state. Every man will see in you an official who through my agency can bring the voice of suffering mankind to the throne of the Tsars, who can instantly place the

defenceless and voiceless citizen under the supreme protection of the Sovereign Emperor.

How many cases, how many illegal and unending lawsuits can be brought to an end through your mediation, how many wrongdoers, thirsting to take advantage of their neighbours' property, will be fearful of putting their pernicious intentions into practice when they are assured that the victims of their greed have a direct and speedy approach to the patronage of His Imperial Majesty!

On this kind of basis you will swiftly acquire numerous fellow-workers and assistants, for every citizen who loves his fatherland, who loves truth and desires to see calm and order reigning everywhere, will strive to defend you at every step and assist you with his own useful counsel and thus contribute to the happy intentions of his Emperor.

5. There can be no doubt that, if only because your own heart so inclines, you will endeavour to discover the existence of such officials as are suffering from extreme poverty or are alone in the world, who serve disinterestedly the cause of truth and religion, who are unable to subsist on their salary alone—you are to furnish me with detailed information about such persons so that they may be accorded some relief and so that in this way the sacred will of His Imperial Majesty may be duly fulfilled: to seek out and mark by distinction humble and faithful servants.

You will now clearly understand what palpable advantage will derive from a precise and impartial fulfilment of your duties, and at the same time you can easily imagine what harm and evil might be caused by any actions contradictory to this philanthropic conception; therefore, of course, there can be no limit to the penalties to which any official will be subjected who, God forbid, I dare not even think of it, misuses his profession, for by so doing he will utterly destroy the object of this fatherly institution of the Sovereign Emperor.

It is impossible, however, to name here all the causes and objects to which your attention should be directed, it is impossible to outline those rules by which you should be guided in every case, but I rely in this respect on your perspicacity, and still more on the disinterested and noble inclination of your frame of mind.'

from N. K. Shil'der, *Imperator Nikolai Pervyi. Yego Zhizn' i Tsarstvovanie*, vol. 1, pp. 468–9

Note

These Instructions were also issued to Colonel BIBIKOV, Gendarme Regt. (Shil'der, vol. 3 (Prilozheniya k pervomu tomu), LVI, pp. 781–2).

Gendarme Districts 1827–32

1ST GENDARME DISTRICT

Provinces	HQ	Section no.
St Peterburgskaya	St Petersburg	1
Kn. Finlyandskoye	Helsingfors	2
Arkhangel'skaya		
Vologodskaya	Vologda	3
Olonyetskaya		
Pskovskaya		
Smolyenskaya	Smolyensk	4
Novgorodskaya		
Liflyandskaya		
Kurlyandskaya	Mitava	5
Estlyandskaya		

2ND GENDARME DISTRICT

Provinces	HQ	Section no.
Moskovskaya	Moskva	1
Yaroslavskaya	Yaroslavl'	2
Tver'skaya		
Vladimirskaya	Vladimir	3
Kostromskaya		
Ryazanskaya	Ryazan'	4
Tul'skaya		
Orlovskaya	Oryol (Orel)	5
Kaluzhskaya		
Voronezhskaya	Voronezh	6
Tambovskaya		

3RD GENDARME DISTRICT

Provinces	HQ	Section no.
Vitebskaya	Vitebsk	1
Mogilevskaya		
Volynskaya	Zhitomir	2
Kamenets-Podol'skaya		
Minskaya	Vil'no	3
Vilenskaya		
Grodnenskaya	Grodno	4
Obl. Belostok-skaya		

4TH GENDARME DISTRICT

Provinces	HQ	Section no.
Kievskaya	Kiev	1
Poltavskaya	Poltava	2
Chernigovskaya		
Slobodsko-Ukrainskaya	Khar'kov	3
Kurskaya		
Khersonskaya		
Ekaterinoslav-skaya	Ekaterinoslav	4
Tavricheskaya		
Obl. Bessarab-skaya	Odessa	5
G. Odessa		

5TH GENDARME DISTRICT

Province	HQ	Section no.	Province	HQ	Section no.
Vyatskaya			Nizhegorodskaya	Nizhnii-	3
Kazanskaya	Kazan'	1	Penzenskaya	Novgorod	
Permskaya			Astrakhanskaya	Astrakhan'	4
Orenburgskaya			Gruziya	Tiflis	5
Simbirskaya	Simbirsk	2	Obl. Kavkaz-	Stavropol'	6
Saratovskaya			skaya	or	
				Georgievsk	

from *Poln. Sobr. Zak.* (2-oe Sobr.), vol. 2, Appendix pp. 130–1, relating to Ukaz of
28 Apr. 1827, no. 1062

Gendarme Districts 1832–6

On the creation of a new Gendarme District in the Kingdom of Poland—henceforth to
be known as the 3rd—the old 3rd, 4th and 5th Gendarme Districts were renumbered
4th, 5th and 6th.

from *Poln. Sobr. Zak.* vol. 7, p. 109. Ukaz of 27 Feb. 1832, no. 5192

Gendarme Districts 1836–7

1ST GENDARME DISTRICT

Provinces constituting District	Towns and cities with Gendarme Detachments
St Peterburgskaya	St Petersburg
Kn. Finlyandskoye	Helsingfors
Arkhangel'skaya	Arkhangel'sk
Vologodskaya	Vologda
Olonyetskaya	Petrozavodsk
Pskovskaya	Pskov
Novgorodskaya	Novgorod
Liflyandskaya	Riga
Kurlyandskaya	Mitava
Estlyandskaya	Revel'
G. Derpt	Derpt

G.O.C.'s HQ—ST PETERSBURG

2ND GENDARME DISTRICT

Provinces constituting District	Towns and cities with Gendarme Detachments
Moskovskaya	Moskva
Yaroslavskaya	Yaroslavl'
Vladimirskaya	Vladimir
Kostromskaya	Kostroma
Ryazanskaya	Ryazan'
Tul'skaya	Tula
Orlovskaya	Oryol
Kaluzhskaya	Kaluga
Tverskaya	Tver'
Smolyenskaya	Smolyensk

G.O.C.'s HQ—MOSCOW

3RD GENDARME DISTRICT

Kingdom of Poland
(no details given)

4TH GENDARME DISTRICT

Kievskaya	Kiev
Vitebskaya	Vitebsk
Mogilevskaya	Mogilev
Minskaya	Minsk
Vilenskaya	Vil'no
Grodnenskaya	Grodno
Volynskaya	Zhitomir
Kamenets-Podol'skaya	Kamenets-Podol'sk
Obl. Belostok-skaya	Belostok

G.O.C.'s HQ—VIL'NO

5TH GENDARME DISTRICT

Provinces constituting District	Towns and cities with Gendarme Detachments
Poltavskaya	Poltava
Chernigovskaya	Chernigov
Khersonskaya	Kherson
Ekaterinoslav-skaya	Ekaterino-slav
Tavricheskaya	Simferopol'
Obl. Bessarab-skaya	Kishinev
G. Odessa	Odessa
Astrakhanskaya	Astrakhan'
Obl. Kavkaz-skaya	Stavropol'
Zakavkazskii	Tiflis

G.O.C.'s HQ—POLTAVA

6TH GENDARME DISTRICT

Provinces constituting District	Towns and cities with Gendarme Detachments
Nizhegorodskaya	Nizhnii-Novgorod
Tambovskaya	Tambov
Voronezhskaya	Voronezh
Khar'kovskaya	Khar'kov
Kurskaya	Kursk
Simbirskaya	Simbirsk
Saratovskaya	Saratov
Penzenskaya	Penza
Kazanskaya	Kazan'
Vyatskaya	Vyatka

G.O.C.'s HQ—KAZAN'

7TH GENDARME DISTRICT

Tobol'skaya	Tobol'sk
Permskaya	Perm'
Orenburgskaya	Ufa
Tomskaya	Tomsk
Irkutskaya	Irkutsk
Eniseiskaya	Krasno-yarsk
Obl. Omskaya	Omsk

G.O.C.'s HQ—TOBOL'SK

Notes

1st G.D.: also controls Gendarme detachment stationed at Abo and an 'Urban detachment' at Tsarskoye Selo. Derpt also has an 'Urban detachment'. 5th G.D.: Odessa has a 'Port detachment'.

rom *Poln. Sobr. Zak.* vol. II (pt 2), Appendix pp. 342–3, relating to Ukaz of 1 Jul. 1836, no. 9355

Gendarme districts from 1837

The final organization of Gendarme Districts occurred the following year with the creation of a new District in the Caucasus and adjoining territories. It was formed from three areas previously included in the 5th Gendarme District (with HQs at Astrakhan', Stavropol' and Tiflis); and was henceforth known as the 6th Gendarme District. The 1836 6th and 7th Gendarme Districts were renumbered 7th and 8th.

6TH GENDARME DISTRICT

	HQ		HQ
Gruziya, Imeretiya, Mingreliya, Abkhaziya, Guriya	Tiflis	Chechentsy, Lezginy, Kubinskaya and Bakinskaya pravleniya	Derbent
Akhaltsykhskii Pashalyk, Bambaki, Elisavetopol'skii Okrug, Armenskaya Obl.	Akhaltsykh	Kumyki, Mozdok	Kizlyar
Karabakhskaya, Shekinskaya, Shirvanskaya, Talyshinskoye khanstvo	Shusha	Kavkazskaya Obl., Zemlya Chernomorskikh Kazakov, Kabarda, Nogaitsy, Abad'a	Stavropol'

G.O.C.'s HQ—TIFLIS

from *Poln. Sobr. Zak.* vol. 12 (pt 2), pp. 974–5. Ukaz of 7 Dec. 1837, no. 10779

Thus after 1837 the Russian Empire was subdivided into eight Gendarme Districts with Headquarters as follows:

1st	— St Petersburg	5th	— Poltava
2nd	— Moscow	6th	— Tiflis
3rd	— Warsaw	7th	— Kazan'
4th	— Vil'no	8th	— Tobol'sk

Report on the activities of the Corps of Gendarmes since its institution up to 1 January 1829

The command of the Corps of Gendarmes most graciously entrusted to me by Your Imperial Majesty laid a sacred duty upon me: to endeavour by all means to achieve the useful and genuinely beneficial purpose of its creation.

In the brief period of its existence the Corps of Gendarmes has justified as far as has been possible the aims set out at its creation.

On more than one occasion I have been happy to inform Your Imperial Majesty of distinguished service rendered by individuals, of the exploits of various gendarme officials.

In now submitting to the steps of Your Imperial Majesty's throne a general review of the activities of the Corps as a whole, I should consider myself a hundred times happy if it satisfies Your Majesty's expectations.

Your Imperial Majesty is aware that the duties of Corps of Gendarmes officials are of two kinds; standing orders of those laid down by instructions, and *ad hoc* orders or those conferred by the will of Your Majesty and directives issued by Your Majesty's authorities.

Standing orders, which consist of observing public opinion, detecting hidden abuses, revealing instances of victimization of innocent persons or of unpunished crime etc. etc., have been carried out by all without exception: the vast amount of information that they have acquired especially relating to the Third Department of Your Imperial Majesty's Own Chancellery, some of which has been extremely important, bears witness to their activity, and the abuses, malpractices and even crimes which were previously undetected and are now prosecuted by law, the several striking instances of innocent persons being saved from acts of vengeance or injustice, and, I venture to say, the general state of calm are proofs of the unanimity, diligence and enthusiasm of the whole Corps in the service of Your Majesty.

I am bound in fairness to add that such happy results of the solicitousness of the supreme government—a government which has put all branches of state administration on the right path—cannot be attributed to the activities of gendarme officials only, but it is true at any rate that these officials, as the instruments and members of the higher supervisory police, have contributed to these results by taking such steps as depended on them.

Duties of a temporary nature that have been incumbent upon the GHQ and senior officers of the Corps of Gendarmes and that have consisted of carrying out investigations and inquiries of various kinds in accordance with an Imperial order or with my directions—have been accurately fulfilled.

Commissions dealing with matters relating to the Third Department of Your Majesty's Own Chancellery have also been entrusted to gendarme officials and have been brought by them to successful conclusions.

Not presuming to inconvenience Your Majesty with a detailed account of all the doings of the GHQ and senior officers of the Corps of Gendarmes— which, in addition, would indeed be impossible by reason of their multiplicity and diversity—I confine myself to an extremely brief estimate of important items for which they have been responsible, that is, apart from the fulfilment of the duties laid down in standing orders.

1. The following were employed in the supervision of the call-up of recruits and helped to prevent or discover abuses: in the province of St Petersburg for the 91 and 92 classes, also in St Petersburg proper for the current or 93 class—Lt.-Col. SHUL'MAN;
In the province of St Petersburg for the 93 and 94 classes—Col. FREIGANG (who is attached to me);

In the provinces of:	Classes
Vologda, Olonets and Archangel	91, 92 and 93—Lt.-Col. DEIER;
Estonia, Lithuania and Kurland	91, 92 and 93—Lt.-Col. BELAU;
Kaluga	91 and 92—Maj. SHVARTS (attached to Lt.-Gen. Volkov);
Tula	91—Maj. BEGICHEV (attached as above);
Moscow	91 and 92—Maj. VOLKOV;
Yaroslavl'	91—Lt.-Col. SHUBINSKY;
Moscow, Vladimir, Yaroslavl' and Kostroma	92—Lt.-Col. SHUBINSKY, Col. PERFIL'YEV, St.-Capt. VER'GOVSKY (who assisted Maj.-Gen. Buturlin)

PERFIL'YEV made one supervisory tour in the province of Kostroma during the 91 class call-up;

| Ryazan' | 91—Lt.-Col. PRIKLONSKY |
| Ryazan' and Tula | 92—Lt.-Col. PRIKLONSKY |

Assistance on both call-ups in the Ryazan' and Tula provinces was given by Capt. YANOVSKY;

In the provinces of:	Classes
Orel	91 and 92—Lt.-Col. ZHEMCHUZHNIKOV;
Orel, Kursk and Ukraine–Sloboda	92—Ensign BAZANSKY (who assisted the A.D.C. of Count Stroganov);
Vitebsk and Mogilev	91 and 92—Col. MERDER;
Vilno and Minsk	91 and 92—Lt.-Col. RUDKOVSKY

(who has now been transferred to Kiev, Chernigov and Poltava for 93);

Ukraine–Sloboda, Kursk	92 and 93—Maj. BAKHMET'YEV
(as above)	91—Col. VUICH

(assisted by Under-Ensign ANDREEVSKY who was then attached to A.D.C.-in-Waiting Grinvald [Grunwald] for the 92 class call-up);

Kazan', Perm and Vyatka	91, 92 and 93—Lt.-Col. NOVOKSHCHENOV

(who also assisted A.D.C.-in-waiting Prince Lieven in supervising the 92 class call-up);

Saratov, Penza and Simbirsk	[—]—St.-Capt. MEL'GUNOV
(as above)	91, 92 and 93—Lt.-Col. MASLOV

(who was assisted in supervising the 92 class call-up by Capt. BAZIN, who is attached to Col. Yurenev);

Saratov, Tambov, Penza and Simbirsk	93—[no name given]
Nizhni-Novgorod and Penza	91 and 92—Lt.-Col. YAZYKOV

(who was assisted by Capt. PANYUTIN on the 91 class call-up and assisted A.D.C.-in-waiting Pryanishnikov for the 92 class call-up in the province of Penza);

Astrakhan'	92—Col. SHALIM
Pskov and Novgorod	[—]—Maj. KOKUSHKIN;
Vladimir	91 and 92—Maj. BRAUN of the Moscow Gendarme 'divizion';
Tambov	91 and 92—Maj. RZHEVSKY also of this unit.

In enumerating the officials of the Corps of Gendarmes who have been employed on the supervision of recruit call-ups, it has been my purpose to show that the greater part of the whole Corps is contributing to the general benefit which is derived from this kind of surveillance and which, if one may judge by former practices that occurred in these call-ups, cannot but be perceptible to the people, who bless your Majesty for all that you enact in paternal affection for their welfare.

2. Places, in which an unusually large concourse of persons of every kind and calling has made it imperative in the interests of law and order to reinforce the methods of surveillance, have been visited by the most trustworthy gendarme officials. The institution of temporary commandants at trading centres has been beneficial, as in the cases of Major REBINDER at Dorogobuzh and Gzhatsk, Colonel MERDER at Beshenkovichi, Lieutenant-Colonel RUDKOVSKY at Bobruisk and Pinsk, Major BAKHMET'YEV at the Korennaya Fair and Lieutenant-Colonel YAZYKOV at the Nizhegorodskaya.

3. According to Imperial command, various investigatory missions have been carried out of which I am mentioning only those worthy of note.

Col. FREIGANG—was summoned to deal with the report submitted by A.D.C.-in-waiting Prince Lieven on the subject of abuses and instances of persecution directed against recruits in the province of Olonets. He exposed various cases of extortion, the poor treatment of recruits in the Petrozavodsk Hospital etc.

Lt.-Col. YAKOVLEV—was sent to the province of Olonets to conduct an investigation into malpractices in the timber industry. This commission he fulfilled successfully and with admirable enthusiasm, witness Senator Baranov, on whose ultimate responsibility this investigation was conducted. Exceedingly large sums of money were found to have been misused.

Col. SHAMIN—who placed himself at the disposal of Lt.-Gen. Izmailov during a mutiny of the latter's men; and was also attached to Lt.-Gen. Count Gur'ev for the purpose of undertaking investigatory commissions ordered by Your Imperial Majesty.

Maj. KOKUSHKIN—was sent to investigate malpractices discovered in Pskov by A.D.C.-in-waiting Reád. The findings are available in our GHQ.

Maj. BEGICHEV—was sent to the province of Orenburg to investigate the reason for unrest among the Kirgiz tribesmen—a mission he fulfilled most successfully.

Lt.-Col. YAZYKOV—was sent to conduct the most rigorous investigation into the reasons for the acceptance of 26 unfit recruits in the Makar'evskoye Prisoutstviye. He pursued this investigation in a proper manner.

Your Imperial Majesty has been duly informed, according to their individual degree of importance, of the cases of investigation prosecuted by officials of the Corps of Gendarmes in connexion with questions which are the concern of Your Imperial Majesty's Own Chancellery.

4. The activities of the following merit particular attention:

Lt.-Gen. VOLKOV—who, being in command of the Higher Police in the capital of Moscow, has rendered the government constant distinguished service; and has also undertaken special commissions of which Your Majesty is aware, such as the case of the Moscow Commissariat Commission, the

Court of Inquiry into the case of Maj.-Gen. Ushakov etc. VOLKOV's correspondence with the Third Department on Higher Police matters amounts to whole stacks of files.

Lt.-Col. ZHEMCHUZHNIKOV—who saved, so to speak, the fortune of the Podymova orphans, details of which case were duly reported to Your Majesty; and whose memoranda on abuses prevalent in the postal system—circulated at Your Majesty's desire to the Heads of Provinces—have proved of great benefit both to the Treasury and the general public;

Lt.-Col. MASLOV—who exposed a series of abuses occurring at the call-up of recruits, assisted the discovery of widespread malpractices in the province of Saratov (Serdobsky region), fulfilled with accuracy and outstanding intelligence investigations into the losses caused last winter by the incursion into the Saratov province area of Kirgiz horse-corrals and secured especially noteworthy information on the province of Orenburg. He is now leaving for a tour of inspection of state criminals; and

Maj. BAKHMET'YEV—who rendered valuable service in procuring information on the election of landowners and malpractices in the province of Ukraine–Sloboda, and also in carrying out the mission with which he was entrusted of investigating the question of a demarcation-line in the freehold lands of the Rogostsev village (province of Kursk), as a result of which a proposal for the creation of temporary courts in the above-mentioned province to investigate and decide upon matters of this sort has been submitted for approval.

5. Your Imperial Majesty is acquainted with those Corps of Gendarme officials who are attached to Your Imperial Majesty's GHQ in the army and has been informed of all their activities, including those of Lt.-Col. KEL'CHEVSKY who was entrusted at Your Majesty's desire with a special mission abroad.

In my absence Maj.-Gen. BALABIN, in addition to his command of the 1st District, has been in charge of matters relating to the Corps' HQ, and the Head of the 2nd Dept. of the 4th District, Lt.-Col. REPESHKO, has performed the function of Duty Staff Officer of the Corps. Their service and the accuracy with which they have fulfilled their duties are also worthy of attention.

I have now laid before Your Imperial Majesty a short account of duties that have been incumbent upon me as Chief of Gendarmes, who is required to report to Your Majesty and take responsibility for actions undertaken in this capacity. I now venture to add that as time goes by and the members of the Corps become more experienced and as the sphere of their operations becomes more extensive, we may expect that the benefits that the Corps has so far been able to secure will gradually increase to twice the number.

Throughout the Corps' existence, in spite of the difficulty of enlisting in its ranks persons who are capable in all respects and of severely tested moral powers, in spite, even, of those very obstacles which are usually encountered with every new enterprise, all missions have been accomplished with such success as was possible.

Local authorities now comprehend the real purpose of this institution; public opinion, accustomed to see in all measures enacted by a strong and solicitous government the prosperity of each and every individual, agrees that the Corps' existence is necessary. Men of goodwill in general and even whole classes of society trust gendarme officials and the fear of being perse-cuted for words uttered involuntarily or by accident in a circle of close friends has disappeared. All know that it is only crimes and abuses, when the government's eye lights upon them, that invariably meet with penalties. To sum up, I have grounds for feeling certain that the Corps of Gendarmes, sanctioned and approved by the attention and favours of Your Imperial Majesty, will win the right to general respect and will in the full sense be worthy of its predestined part.

In conclusion, it is my most humble duty to inform Your Imperial Majesty that, so that Your Majesty may in future be provided with the clearest and most accurate possible knowledge of the activities of Corps of Gendarmes officials, I have proposed to introduce a special report (which I shall be happy to present Your Majesty annually) which will cover every assignment allotted and comment on the success obtained therefrom; it will also include details of other noteworthy undertakings as, too, of such shortcomings and irregularities as may be committed by any official or be brought to the attention of the authorities.

It will thus be possible at a glance to pick out an outstanding official and the degree of service that he has rendered. For reasons I have mentioned above, almost three years have passed before there has been any possibility of drawing up all at once a report of this nature.

General-in-Waiting BENKENDORF

from Krasnyi Arkhiv (1929), no. 37, pp. 169–74

Requests and complaints submitted to the Third Department

The immense number of requests and complaints reaching the Third Department from private individuals convinced it of the entirely unsatisfactory nature of our judicial offices. In general this branch of activity was distinguished by its particular extensiveness, because in the '40s there was an annual influx of from two to five and a half thousand requests, apart from the petitions addressed to His Majesty delivered during imperial journeys, the number of which alternated between four and ten thousand. Requests and complaints about private matters of the most diverse variety reached the Department from persons of every class without exception of Russian subjects as well as of foreigners residing both in Russia and beyond its borders.

The objects of requests were, in particular:

(*a*) Co-operation in obtaining satisfaction with documents not expressed in correct legal form.

(*b*) Relief from payment of debt in questions concerning disputed mortgages and similar cases.

(*c*) Review of legal sentences passed in lower courts, stays of execution and abrogation of official orders.

(*d*) Restoration of the right of appeal against court decisions.

(*e*) Assistance in law-suits not covered by the existing code.

(*f*) Accommodation of children in educational establishments at the public expense.

(*g*) Legitimization of illegitimate children following the marriage of their parents.

(*h*) Award of monetary grants, pensions, leases, gratuities and decorations.

(*i*) Postponement and assessment of payment of official levies.

(*j*) Restitution of civic rights, alleviation of penalties awarded, release of detainees.

(*k*) Presentation of various projects and inventions.

Complaints were of two kinds:

1. About the actions of private individuals, and
2. about the actions of public officials and offices.

Complaints in the former category were chiefly submitted on the following grounds:

(*a*) Personal insults.
(*b*) Infringement of marital relations by husbands against their wives when the latter requested that the former should pay for their wife's and children's maintenance.
(*c*) Seduction.
(*d*) Insubordination to and abuse of parental authority.
(*e*) Improper actions of relatives in cases concerning legacies.
(*f*) Misuse of authority by legal guardians.
(*g*) Cases of forgery of wills and failure to observe the testator's wishes.
(*h*) Complaints of landowners against peasants and *vice versa*.

Complaints in the latter category chiefly concerned:

(*a*) Inactivity or slowness in paying out money orders.
(*b*) Prejudice, slowness or neglect in carrying out inquiries into civil or criminal cases, in executing legal decisions and sentences and
(*c*) failure on the part of persons in authority to pass judgement on requests and complaints.

Certain requests and complaints also contained information concerning the abuses of private individuals in cases relating to the payment of official dues, illegal timber-felling and arson of state forests, leaseholds of state distilleries, contracts and deliveries, and so on.

Every request and complaint submitted to the Third Department was dealt with only when it was found to be fully substantiated. According to their peculiarities, these cases either were presented to His Majesty with a request for the requisite decision, or were concluded by a conciliatory agreement between the petitioner and defendant, or else were transferred to the appropriate authorities for their ruling. In certain cases it proved necessary to insist on their speedy and correct decision by the authorities to whose department the specific question referred. Requests and complaints which proved to be unsubstantiated were not followed up. The number of such requests and complaints usually constituted from ten to fifteen per cent of the general total received.

from the 'Jubilee Report' of 1876, Bogucharsky, *loc. cit.* pp. 99–101

Bibliography

ABBREVIATIONS

Br. Efr. Enc.   *Entsiklopedicheskii Slovar'* pod redaktsiei I. E. Andreyevskago (izd.
           Brockhaus—Efron)
Ist. Vyestnik   *Istoricheskii Vyestnik*
Kr. Arkh.   *Krasnyi Arkhiv*
R. Arkh.   *Russkii Arkhiv*
RBS   *Russkii Biograficheskii Slovar'*
R. Mysl'   *Russkaya Mysl'*
R. Star.   *Russkaya Starina*

Adrianov, S. A. *Ministerstvo Vnutrennikh Dyel. Istoricheskii Ocherk* (SPB, 1902).

Akhsharumov, D. D. *Iz Moikh Vospominanii (1849–1851)* (SPB, 1905).

Ancelot, M. *Six Mois en Russie. Lettres écrites à M. X. B. Saintines en 1826* (Paris, 1827).

A peep at Russia; its history, growth, extent, population and government, 2nd ed. carefully
    revised (London, 1855).

Bailey, Thomas A. *America Faces Russia. Russo-American Relations from Early Times
    to Our Day* (New York, 1950).

Baranov, P. *Mikhail Andreyevich Balug'yanskii, Stats-Sekretar', Senator, Tainyi Sovyet-
    nik (1769–1847). Biograficheskii Ocherk* (SPB, 1882).

Bartyenev, P. I. *18-yi vyek. Istoricheskii Sbornik.* 4 vols. (Moscow, 1868–9).

—— *19-yi vyek. Istoricheskii Sbornik.* 2 vols. (Moscow, 1872).

—— 'Instruktsiya Grafa Benkendorfa chinovniku 3-go Otdeleniya', *R. Arkh.* (1889), 7.

Bazilyevsky, V. *Gosudarstvennye Prestupleniya v Rossii v XIX vyeke.* 2 vols. (SPB, 1906),
    vol. 1 (1825–76).

Benkendorf, A. Kh. 'Zapiski', *R. Arkh.* (1865), 2; *R. Star.* (1896), vols. 86, 87, 88; (1898),
    vol. 93; *Ist. Vyestnik* (1903), vol. xci. See also Shil'der, N. K. *Imperator Nikolai I,*
    vol. 2.

Bloomfield, Lady Georgiana. *Reminiscences of Court and Diplomatic Life.* 2 vols.
    (London, 1883).

Bogdanovich, M. I. *Istoriya Tsarstvovaniya Imperatora Aleksandra I i Rossii v yego
    vremya.* 6 vols. (SPB, 1869–71).

Bogucharsky, V. 'Tret'e Otdelenie Sobstvennoi Ye.I.V. Kantselyarii o Sebye Samom.
    (Nyeizdannyi dokument)', *Vyestnik Yevropy* (1917), Mar.

Boigne, Comtesse de. *Memoirs.* 4 vols. (ed. London, 1908).

Bol'shaya Sovyetskaya Entsiklopediya (1947).

Bray-Steinburg, Graf Otto von. *Denkwürdigkeiten des Grafen Otto von Bray-Steinburg*
    (Leipzig, 1901).

Bremner, Robert. *Excursions in the Interior of Russia.* 2 vols. 2nd ed. (London, 1840).

Brikner, A. 'Vskrytie Chuzhikh Pisem pri Yekaterine II', *R. Star.* (1873), vol. 7.

Brockhaus–Efron Encyclopedia. Pod red. I. E. Andreyevskago (SPB, 1890–1906).

Bychkov, I. A. 'Popytka napechatat' "Cherty Istorii Gosudarstva Rossiiskago" V. A.
    Zhukovskago v 1837 godu', *R. Star.* (1903), vol. 116.

Charques, R. D. *A Short History of Russia* (London, 1956).

Cherkas, A. 'Sanglen, Yakov Ivanovich de', *RBS*.

Chernyak, Ye. *Pyat' Stolyetii Tainoi Voiny. Iz istorii razvyedki* (Moscow, 1966).

Chulkov, G. *Imperatory. Psikhologicheskie Portrety* (Moscow–Leningrad, 1928).

Clarke, Edw. Daniel. *Travels in Russia, Tartary and Turkey.* 6 vols. 2nd ed. (Edinburgh, 1839).

Curtis, George Ticknor. *Life of James Buchanan, Fifteenth President of the United States.* 2 vols. (New York, 1883).

Curtiss, John Shelton. *The Russian Army under Nicholas I, 1825–1855* (Durham, N.C., 1965).

Custine, A. de. *La Russie en 1839.* 4 vols. in 1 (Paris, 1843).

Divov, P. G. 'Dnevnik P. G. Divova', *R. Star.* (1900), vol. 104.

Dmitriev, M. A. *Myelochi iz Zapasa moei Pamyati* (Moscow, 1869).

Dolgoroukow, P. *La Vérité sur la Russie* (Paris, 1860).

'Doneseniya L. F. Dubel'ta kn. A. I. Chernyshovu.' *See* Semyevsky, V. I.

Doré, Gustave. *Histoire dramatique, pittoresque et caricaturale de la Sainte-Russie* (Paris, 1854).

Dubel't, Ye. I. 'Leontii Vasil'evich Dubel't. Biograficheskii ocherk i yego pis'ma', *R. Star.* (1888), vol. 60.

Dubel't, L. V. *See* Panteleyev.

Dyen, V. I. 'Zapiski Vladimira Dyena', *R. Star.* (1890), vol. 67.

Eastlake, Lady (Elisabeth Rigby). *A Residence on the Shores of the Baltic described in a series of letters.* 2 vols. (London, 1841).

Eikhenbaum, B. 'Tainoe obshchestvo Sungurova (po nyeizdannym dokumentam iz arkhiva III otdeleniya)', *Zavyeti* (1913), 3, 5.

Englishwoman in Russia, The; Impressions of the society and manners of the Russians at home. By a Lady Ten Years Resident in that Country (London, 1855).

Florinsky, M. T. *Russia; a history and an interpretation.* 2 vols. (New York, 1953 and 7th impression 1961).

Forssel, Nils. *Fouché. The Man Napoleon Feared.* Trans. from the Swedish by Anna Barwell (London, 1928).

Fournier, August. *Die Geheimpolizei auf dem Wiener Kongress. Eine Auswahl aus ihren Papieren* (Leipzig, 1913).

Fournier, Marc. *Russie, Allemagne et France. Révélations sur la politique russe, d'après les notes d'un vieux diplomate* (Paris, 1844).

Fülöp-Miller, René. *See* Vassilyev.

Gernet, M. N. *Istoriya Tsarskoi Tyur'my.* 4 vols. (Moscow, 1951–4).

Gershenzon, M. O. (pod red.). *Epokha Nikolaya I* (Moscow, 1910).

Gertsen, A. I. *Byloye i Dumy* (izd. Ogiz, Leningrad, 1946).

Golitsyn, Kn. N. S. 'Leontii Vasil'evich Dubel't', *R. Star.* (1880), vol. 29.

—— 'Ocherki i Vospominaniya', *R. Star.* (1890), vol. 68.

Golovine, I. *Russia under the Autocrat, Nicholas the First.* 2 vols. (London, 1846).

—— *The Russian Sketch-Book.* 2 vols. (London, 1848).

Gol'tsev, V. A. *Zakonodatel'stvo i Nravy v Rossii XVIII vyeka.* 2-oe izd. (SPB, 1896).

Gradovsky, A. D. *Sobranie Sochinenii* (SPB, 1907), vol. 8.

Grech, N. I. *Zapiski o moei Zhizni* (izd. Academia, Moscow–Leningrad, 1930).

(Gretsch, N.) *Examen de l'Ouvrage de M. le Marquis de Custine intitulé 'La Russie en 1839'* (Paris, 1844).

Gribovsky, V. M. *Gosudarstvennoe Ustroistvo i Upravlenie Rossiiskoi Imperii* (O dessa 1912).
Grunwald, Constantin de. *La Vie de Metternich* (Paris, 1938).
—— *La Vie de Nicolas Ier* (Paris, 1946).
Harrison, Robert. *Notes of a Nine Years' Residence in Russia from 1844 to 1853* (London, 1855).
Hauterive, E. de. *La Police secrète du Premier Empire*. 3 vols. (Paris, 1913).
[Henningsen, C. F.] *Revelations of Russia: or the Emperor Nicholas and his Empire in 1844. By One Who Has Seen and Describes*. Published anonymously in 2 vols. (London, 1844).
'Imperator Aleksandr Pavlovich i Ego Vremya', *R. Star.* (1881), vol. 32.
'Instruktsiya Grafa Benkendorfa chinovniku 3-go Otdeleniya', *R. Arkh.* (1889), 7.
Istoriya Pravitel'stvuyushchago Senata za dvyesti lyet. 5 vols. (SPB, 1911).
Istoriya SSSR pod red. M. V. Nyechkinoi, vol. 2. *Rossiya v XIX vyeke* (Moscow, 1946).
'Iz Zapisnoi Knizhki Russkago Arkhiva', *R. Arkh.* (1892), 8.
K. und K. Haus-, Hof- und Staats-Archiv, Vienna, Series 'Russland'.
Kafengauz, B. B. *I. T. Pososhkov. Zhizn' i Dyeyatel'nost'* (Moscow–Leningrad, 1950).
Kallash, V. V. (ed.). *Sochineniya i Pis'ma N. V. Gogolya*. 9 vols. (SPB, 1907).
Karatygin, P. P. 'Benkendorf i Dubel't', *Ist. Vyestnik* (1887), vol. xxx.
'K istorii tsarstvovaniya imperatora Nikolaya I', *R. Star.* (1896), vol. 86.
Kizevetter, A. A. 'Vnutrennyaya politika v tsarstvovanie imperatora Nikolaya I', *Istoricheskia Ocherki* (Moscow, 1912).
Kohl, J. G. *Russia, St Petersburg, Moscow, Kharkoff, Riga, Odessa etc.* (London, 1842).
Kolchin, M. *Ssyl'nye i Zatochennye v ostrog Solovyetskago Monastyrya v XVI–XIXvv.* (Moscow, 1908).
Kolmakov, N. M. 'Staryi Sud. Ocherki i Vospominaniya N. M. Kolmakova', *R. Star.* (1886), vol. 52.
Komarovsky, Ye. F. *Zapiski*, izd. P. Ye. Shchegolev (SPB, 1914).
Korf, M. A. 'Dyeyateli i Uchastniki Padeniya Speranskago', *R. Star.* (1902), vol. 109.
—— 'Iz Zapisok Barona (vposlyedstvii Grafa) M. A. Korfa', *R. Star.* (1899), vol. 100.
Kornilov, A. *Kurs Istorii Rossii XIX vyeka*, 2-oe izd. (Moscow, 1918).
Korsakov, A. N. Article on Sheshkovsky, *Ist. Vyestnik* (1885), vol. xxii.
Kostomarov, N. I. 'Avtobiografiya', *R. Mysl'* (1885), kn. 5.
Kotoshikhin, G. *O Rossii v Tsarstvovanie Alekseya Mikhailovicha* (izd. SPB, 1906).
Kukiel, M. *Czartoryski and European Unity, 1770–1831* (Princeton, 1955).
Kutuzov, N. 'Sostoyanie gosudarstva v 1841 godu. (Zapiska N. Kutuzova, podannaya imperatoru Nikolayu I)', *R. Star.* (1898), vol. 95.
Lacroix, F. *Les Mystères de la Russie*. 6 vols. (Bruxelles, 1844).
Lacroix, Paul. *Histoire de la Vie et du Règne de Nicolas I-er, Empereur de Russie*. 7 vols. (Paris, 1864–73).
Laporte, M. *Histoire de l'Okhrana; la Police Secrète des Tsars 1880–1917* (Paris, 1935).
Lee, Robert, M.D., F.R.S. *The Last Days of Alexander and the First Days of Nicholas* (London, 1854).
Lemke, M. K. *Nikolayevskie Zhandarmy i Literatura 1826–1855 gg. Po podlinnym dyelam Tret'ego Otdeleniya Sobstv. Ye.I.V. Kantselyarii s 7 portryetami* (SPB, 1908).
—— *Ocherki po Istorii Russkoi Tsenzury i Zhurnalistiki XIX stolyetiya* (SPB, 1904).
—— 'Tainoye obshchestvo brat'yev Kritskikh', *Byloye*, no. 6 (SPB, 1906).
Léouzon, le Duc. L. *La Russie Contemporaine* (Paris, 1853).
Leroy-Beaulieu, A. *The Empire of the Tsar and the Russians* (London, 1894).

Letters from the Continent; describing the manners and customs of Russia (London, 1812).

Liprandi, I. P. 'Zapiski', *R. Star.* (1872), vol. 6.

Lomachevsky, A. I. 'Zapiski Zhandarma', *Vyestnik Yevropy* (1872), Mar., Apr., May.

Luchinsky, G. 'Fiskaly', *Br. Efr. Enc.* vol. 36.

—— 'Sheshkovskii (Stepan Ivanovich)', *Br. Efr. Enc.* vol. 39.

Lyall, Robert, M.D. *The Character of the Russians and a Detailed History of Moscow* (London, 1823).

Markyevich, A. I. *Grigorii Karpovich Kotoshikhin: ego Sochinenie o Moskovskom Gosudarstve v polovine XVII vyeka* (Odessa, 1895).

Marnitz, L. von. *Memoiren von Ya. I. de Sanglen* (Stuttgart, 1894). *See* Sanglen.

Maxwell, John S. *The Czar, His Court and People* (New York and London, 1848).

May, J.-B. *Saint-Pétersbourg et la Russie en 1829.* 2 vols. (Paris, 1830).

Mazour, A. G. *The First Russian Revolution, 1825: the Decembrist movement* (California, 1937).

—— *Russia Past and Present.* 3rd printing (New York–London, 1953).

Merezhkovsky, Dmitri S. *December the Fourteenth.* Trans. by Nathalie A. Duddington (London, 1930).

Mérimée, Henri. *Une Année en Russie. Lettres à M. Saint-Marc Girardin* (Paris, 1847).

Metternich, Prince. *The Memoirs of Prince Metternich, 1773–1835.* Trans. in 5 vols. (London, 1880–2).

Mikhailovsky-Danilevsky, A. I. 'Iz vospominanii Mikhailovskago-Danilevskago', *R. Star.* (1899), vol. 100; (1900), vols. 103, 104.

Milyukov, A. N. 'Fyodor Mikhailovich Dostoyevskii', *R. Star.* (1881), vol. 30.

Milyukov, P., Seignobos, C., Eisenmann, L. *Histoire de Russie.* 3 vols. (Paris 1932–3), vol. 2.

Modzalyevsky, B. L. *Pushkin. Pis'ma. See* Pushkin.

—— *Pushkin pod Tainym Nadzorom* (Petrograd, 1922).

Monas, S. *The Third Section. Police and Society in Russia under Nicholas I* (Harvard University Press, 1961).

Montgomery Hyde, H. *Princess Lieven* (London 1938).

Morokhovyets, Ye. A. (pod red.). *Krest'yanskoe Dvizhenie 1827–1869* (Moscow, 1931).

Nesselrode, Count. *Lettres et Papiers du Chancelier Comte de Nesselrode, 1760–1856.* 2 vols. (Paris, 1908–12).

Nesselrode, Countess. '14 dek. 1825 g. v pis'makh gr. M. D. Nessel'rode', *Kr. Arkh.* (1925), no. 10.

Nicolas Mikhailovich (Le Grand Duc). *Le Comte Paul Stroganov*, trad. française de F. Billecocq. 3 vols. (Paris, 1905).

—— *Le Tsar Alexandre Ier*, trad. du russe par la Baronne Wrangel (Paris, 1931).

Nifontov, A. S. *Rossiya v 1848 godu* (Moscow, 1949).

Nikitenko, A. V. *Zapiski i Dnevnik*, izd. 2-oe. 2 vols. (SPB, 1904, 1905).

Okun', S. B. *Istoriya SSSR 1796–1825* (Leningrad, 1948).

—— *Ocherki Istorii SSSR. Konyets XVIII–Pervaya Chetvert' XIX vyeka* (Leningrad, 1956).

—— *Ocherki Istorii SSSR, vtoraya chetvert' XIX vyeka* (Leningrad, 1957).

'O Perlyustratsii Pisem v nachale XIX vyeka', *Kr. Arkh.* (1927), no. 25.

Panteleyev, L. F. 'Zamyetki L. V. Dubel'ta', with introd. foreword by S. Mel'gunov, *Golos Minuvshago* (Moscow, 1913), Kn. III.

Parry, Albert. *Whistler's Father* (New York, 1939).

Pelchinsky, V. S. *La Russie en 1844. Système de Législation, d'Administration et de Politique de la Russie par un homme d'état russe* (Paris, 1845).
'Perepiska velikago Knyazya Konstantina Pavlovicha s Grafom A. Kh. Benkendorfom, 1826–28', *R. Arkh.* (1884), 6.
Petrov, A. A. 'Orlov, Aleksei Fyodorovich', *RBS*.
Piksanov, N. 'Dvoryanskaya Reaktsiya na Dekabrizm (1825–7)', *Zven'ya* (Moscow–Leningrad, 1933), vol. 2.
'Pis'ma M. M. Foka k A. Kh. Benkendorfu (perevod s frantsuzskago)', *R. Star.* (1881), vol. 32.
'Pis'ma velikago Knyazya Konstantina Pavlovicha k Grafu A. Kh. Benkendorfu, 1829–31', *R. Arkh.* (1885), 1.
Platonov, S. F. *Lektsii po Russkoi Istorii*. 7-oe izd. (SPB, 1910).
Podzhio, A. V. 'Zapiski Dekabrista', *Golos Minuvshago* (1913), Kn. 1.
Pokrovsky, M. N. *Russkaya istoriya s drevnyeishikh vremyon*. 4 vols. 3-e izd. (Moscow, 1920), vol. 4.
Polievktov, M. A. *Nikolai I. Biografiya i Obzor Tsarstvovaniya* (Moscow, 1918).
Polnoe Sobranie Zakonov Rossiiskoi Imperii. 1-oe Sobr. 1649–1825; 2-oe Sobr. 1825–81 (SPB).
Popov, M. M. 'K kharakteristike imperatora Nikolaya I', *R. Star.* (1896), vol. 86.
'Po povodu Instruktsii Grafa Benkendorfa', *R. Arkh.* (1889), 7.
Pososhkov, I. T. *Kniga o Skudosti i Bogatstve* (izd. Akad. Nauk, Moscow, 1951).
Predtechensky, A. V. *Ocherki obshchestvenno-politicheskoi istorii Rossii v 1-oi chetverti XIX veka* (Moscow, 1957).
'Preobrazhenskii Prikaz i Kantselyariya', *Br. Efr. Enc.* vol. 25.
Presnyakov, A. Ye. *Apogei samoderzhaviya. Nikolai I* (Leningrad, 1925).
—— 'Samoderzhavie Nikolaya I', *Russkoe Proshloe* (Petrograd–Moscow, 1923), no. 2.
'Priglasheniya v Tret'e Otdelenie V. G. Belinskago v 1848', *R. Star.* (1882), vol. 36.
'Proyekt o Ustroistve Voyennoi Politsii pri Gvardyeiskom Korpuse', *R. Star.* (1882), vol. 33.
Przecławski, Józef. 'Vospominaniya O. A. Przhetslavskago', *R. Star.* (1874), vol. 11.
Public Record Office, Series *F.O. 65, 181*.
Pushkaryov, S. G. *Rossiya v XIX vyeke (1801–1914)* (New York, 1956).
Pushkin, A. S. *Polnoe Sobranie Sochinenii*. 9 vols. (izd. Academia, Moscow, 1937).
—— *Pushkin. Pis'ma.* Ed. by B. L. Modzalyevsky. 3 vols. (Moscow–Leningrad, 1926–35).
Pypin, A. N. *Obshchestvennoe Dvizhenie v Rossii pri Aleksandre I*. 3-oe izd. (SPB, 1900).
Quennell, P. *The Private Letters of Princess Lieven to Prince Metternich 1820–1826* (London, 1937).
Raikes, Thomas. *A Visit to St Petersburg in the winter of 1829–1830* (London, 1838).
Recollections of Russia during Thirty-Three Years' Residence by a German Nobleman. Revised and trans. with the author's sanction by Lascelles Wraxall (London, 1855).
Riasanovsky, N. V. *Nicholas I and Official Nationality in Russia, 1825–1855* (California, 1959).
Robinson, L. G. *Letters of Dorothea, Princess Lieven, during her Residence in London, 1812–1834* (London, 1902).
Rowan, R. W. *The Story of Secret Service* (London, 1938).
Rudakov, V. Ye. 'Rozysknaya Ekspeditsiya', *Br. Efr. Enc.* vol. 27.
—— 'Sobstvennaya Yego Imperatorskago Velichestva Kantselyariya', *Br. Efr. Enc.* vol. 30.

'Russkaya Kul'tura i Frantsiya', *Literaturnoe Naslyedstvo* (Moscow, 1937), vol. 2.
Russkii Biograficheskii Slovar' (1896–1918).
'Russkii Dobrovolets v ryadakh ispanskikh Vosstantsev v 1830', *Kr. Arkh.* (1937), no. 83.
Sablukov, N. A. 'Reminiscences of the Court and Times of the Emperor Paul the 1st of Russia up to the period of his death', *Fraser's Magazine for Town and Country* (1865), vol. LXXII.
Sadikov, P. A. *Ocherki po Istorii Oprichniny* (izd. Akad. Nauk, Moscow–Leningrad, 1950).
Saint-Edmé, B. 'La Biographie du Général-en-Chef-de-Cavalerie Comte de Benckendorff.' *See* Sarrut.
Sanglen, Ya. I. de. 'Zapiski Ya. I. de Sanglena', *R. Star.* (1882), vol. 36; (1883), vol. 37.
Sarrut, Germain. *La Biographie des Hommes du Jour* (Paris, 1839).
Sbornik imperatorskago russkago istoricheskago obshchestva. 148 vols. (SPB 1867–1916).
Schiemann, Theodor. *Geschichte Russlands unter Kaiser Nikolaus I.* 4 vols. (Berlin, 1904–19).
Schnitzler, J. H. *Secret History of the Court and Government of Russia under the Emperors Alexander and Nicholas.* 2 vols. (London, 1847).
Selivanov, I. V. 'Zapiski Dvoryanina-Pomyeshchika', *R. Star.* (1880), vol. 28.
Semyevsky, M. I. 'Erazm Ivanovich Stogov. Yego posmertnye zapiski', *R. Star.* (1886), vol. 52.
—— *Slovo i Dyelo 1700–1725. Ocherki i Razskazy iz Russkoi Istorii 18-go vyeka* (SPB, 1884).
Semyevsky, V. I. 'Doneseniya L. F. Dubel'ta kn. A. I. Chernyshovu', *Golos Minuvshago* (1941), kn. IV.
—— *Obshchestvennye Dvizheniya v Rossii v I-uyu polovinu XIX vyeka* (SPB, 1905).
Sergeyev, A. 'Graf A. Kh. Benkendorf o Rossii v 1827–30gg. (Yezhegodnyye Otchety Tret'ego Otdeleniya i Korpusa Zhandarmov)', *Kr. Arkh.* (1929), no. 37; (1930), no. 38.
—— 'Graf A. Kh. Benkendorf o Rossii v 1831–32gg.', *Kr. Arkh.* (1931), no. 46.
Seton-Watson, Hugh. *The Russian Empire 1801–1917* (Oxford, 1967).
Shchegolev, P. Ye. *Alekseyevskii Ravelin* (Moscow, 1929).
Shil'der, N. K. *Imperator Aleksandr Pervyi. Yego Zhizn' i Tsarstvovanie.* 4 vols. (SPB, 1897).
—— *Imperator Nikolai Pervyi. Yego Zhizn' i Tsarstvovanie.* 2 vols. (SPB, 1903).
—— *Imperator Pavel Pervyi. Istoriko-biograficheskii Ocherk* (SPB, 1910).
—— *Tsesarevich Konstantin Pavlovich* (SPB, 1899).
Shompulev, V. A. 'Iz dnevnika Zhandarma 30-kh godov', *R. Star.* (1897), vol. 90.
Shtraikh, S. Ya. *Roman Medoks, russkii avantyurist XIX v.* (Moscow, 1929).
'Slovo i Dyelo Gosudarevo', *Br. Efr. Enc.* vol. 30.
Smirnova, A. O. *Zapiski* (SPB, 1897).
Solov'yov, S. M. *Istoriya Rossii s drevnyeishikh vremyon.* 6 kn., 2-e izd. (SPB, 1894–7).
Squire, P. S. 'Metternich and Benckendorff, 1807–1834', *The Slavonic and East European Review*, vol. XLV, no. 104 (Jan. 1967).
—— 'The Metternich–Benckendorff Letters, 1835–1842', *ibid.* no. 105 (Jul. 1967).
—— 'Nicholas I and the Problem of Internal Security in Russia in 1826', *ibid.* vol. XXXVIII, no. 91 (Jun. 1960).
Stählin, Karl. 'Aus den Berichten der III. Abteilung S.M. Höchsteigener Kanzlei am Kaiser Nikolaus I.', *Zeitschrift für Osteuropäische Geschichte*, vols. 6 (1932); 7 (1933).

Stead, Philip John. *Vidocq. A Biography* (London, 1953).
Stogov, E. I. 'Ocherki, Razskazy i Vospominaniya E. I. Stogova', *R. Star.* (1878), vols. 22, 23.
—— 'Zapiski E. I. Stogova', *R. Star.* (1903), vols. 113, 114, 115.
Strakhovsky, Leonid I. *Alexander I of Russia* (London, 1949).
Sumner, B. H. *Survey of Russian History.* 2nd revised ed. (London, 1947).
'Tainaya Kantselyariya v Tsarstvovanie Petra I. Ocherki i Razskazy po podlinnym dyelam', *R. Arkh.* (1885), 2, 3.
Tatishchev, S. S. *Imperator Nikolai I i inostrannye dvory* (SPB, 1888).
Temperley, H. *The Unpublished Diary and Political Sketches of Princess Lieven* (London, 1925).
Tolstoi, Count A. K. 'Son Popova', *R. Star.* (1882), vol. 36.
Tolstoi, P. M. 'Iz pamyatnikh zamyetok P. M. Golenishcheva-Kutuzova-Tolstago', *R. Arkh.* (1883), 1.
Tourguéneff, N. *La Russie et les Russes.* 3 vols. (Paris, 1847).
'Tret'e otdelenie i Krymskaya Voina (iz zapisnoi knizhki arkhivista)', *Kr. Arkh.* (1923), no. 3.
'Tret'e Otdelenie Sobstvennoi Ye.I.V. Kantselyarii o Sebye Samom', *see* Bogucharsky.
Trotsky, I. M. *Tret'e Otdelenie pri Nikolae I* (izd. Vsesoyuznym Obshchestvom Politkatorzhan i Ssyl'nykh-poselentsev, Moscow, 1930).
Trubetskoi, S. P. *Zapiski Knyazya S. P. Trubetskago* (SPB, 1906).
Un des crimes du gouvernement russe. Episode de la vie d'une femme écrite par elle-même (Genève, 1876).
Ustryalov, N. *Istoricheskoe Obozrevanie Tsarstvovaniya Nikolaya I* (SPB, 1847).
Varadinov, N. *Istoriya Ministerstva Vnutrennikh Dyel* (SPB, 1858–63).
Vasilenko, N. 'Prikaz Tainykh Dyel', *Br. Efr. Enc.* vol. 25.
Vassilyev, A. T. *The Ochrana, the Russian Secret Police,* ed. and introd. by René Fülöp-Miller (London, 1930).
Vasyutinsky, A. 'Tainaya Politsiya vo Frantsii i Avstrii v epokhu restavratsii', *Golos Minuvshago* (1913), Kn. III.
Veretennikov, V. I. *Istoriya Tainoi Kantselyarii Petrovskago Vremeni* (Khar'kov, 1910).
Vernadsky, George. *History of Russia.* New revised ed. (Yale, 1949).
Vigée-Lebrun, Madame. *The Memoirs of Madame Vigée-Lebrun.* Trans. by Lionel Strachey (London, 1904).
Vigel', F. F. *Zapiski.* izd. S. Ya. Shtraikha. 2 vols. (Moscow, 1928).
'Vnutrennyaya Strazha', *Br. Efr. Enc.* vol. 6.
Volkonsky, Kn. M. S. *Zapiski Sergiya Grigor'evicha Volkonskago* (SPB, 1901).
'Volneniya chuvashskogo krest'yanstva v 1842g.', *Kr. Arkh.* (1938), no. 87.
Vorontsov, Kn. *Arkhiv Knyazya Vorontsova,* ed. by P. Bartyenev, 40 vols. (Moscow, 1870–95).
Waliszewski, K. *Le Règne d'Alexandre Ier.* 3 vols. (Paris, 1923–5).
White, R. J. *Waterloo to Peterloo* (London, 1957).
Yakovlef, J. [Tolstoi, Ya. N.]. *La Russie en 1839 rêvée par M. de Custine ou Lettres écrites de Francfort* (Paris, 1844).
Yanovsky, A. Ye. 'Zhandarmy', *Br. Efr. Enc.* vol. 11.
Yastrebtsev, Ye. 'Sheshkovskii, Stepan Ivanovich', *RBS.*
Yatsevich, A. *Pushkinskii Peterburg* (Leningrad, 1931).
—— *Pushkinskii Peterburg.* 2-e izd. (Leningrad, 1933).
Yefremov, P. A. 'S. I. Sheshkovskii', *R. Star.* (1870), vol. 2.

Yengalychev, Kn. N. N. 'Vissarion Grigor'evich Belinskii', *R. Star.* (1876), vol. 15.

'Yezhegodnye Otchety Tret'ego Otdeleniya i Korpusa Zhandarmov.' *See* Sergeyev.

Zhedyonov, N. N. 'Sluchai v Peterburge v 1848 g. Razskaz byvshago gvard.ofitsera', *R. Star.* (1890), vol. 67.

Zherve, V. 'Dubel't, Leontii Vasil'evich', *RBS.*

Zhikharyov, M. 'P. Ya. Chaadayev', *Vyestnik Yevropy* (1871), Sept.

Zhirkyevich, I. S. 'Zapiski I. S. Zhirkyevicha', *R. Star.* (1878), vols. 22, 23; (1890), vol. 67.

BIBLIOGRAPHY

Index[1]

[1] Names of source writers are recorded only if they are contemporary writers, i.e. covering the
period approximately 1790–1855 (with occasional exceptions, e.g. Kotoshikhin and Pososhkov).